FIGHTER GROUP

FIGHTER GROUP

The 352nd "Blue-Nosed Bastards" in World War II

LtCol (Ret) Jay A. Stout

STACKPOLE
BOOKS

Published by
STACKPOLE BOOKS
5067 Ritter Road
Mechanicsburg, PA 17055
www.stackpolebooks.com

Printed in the United States of America

10 9 8 7 6 5 4 3 2 1

Library of Congress Cataloging-in-Publication Data

Stout, Jay A., 1959–
    Fighter group : the 352nd "Blue-Nosed Bastards" in World War II / Jay A. Stout.
        p. cm.
    Includes bibliographical references and index.
    ISBN 978-0-8117-0577-6
    1. United States. Army Air Forces. Fighter Group, 352nd—History.   2. United States. Army Air Forces. Fighter Group, 352nd—Biography.   3. World War, 1939–1945—Aerial operations, American.   4. World War, 1939–1945—Regimental histories—United States.   I. Title.   II. Title: 352nd "Blue-Nosed Bastards" in World War II.
    D790.252352nd .S76 2012
    940.54'4973—dc23

                            2012019815

Especially for Betty Powell.
Because she deserves it.

CONTENTS

INTRODUCTION

It wasn't quite a stagger, but it was something less than a walk. Weighed down with their parachute packs, jackets, Mae Wests, helmets, and other flight gear, the pilots moved slowly toward their assigned aircraft. Enlisted maintenance men, performing last-minute checks, crawled over, under, and around the P-51s. Unseen aircraft thrummed above the clouds as other elements of the day's mission headed toward their rendezvous points. After being on combat operations for more than a year, the noise was a regular part of their lives, and the men paid it scant attention.

Even parked, the 352nd's blue-nosed P-51 Mustangs looked ready for combat. Whereas other aircraft—the British Spitfire, for instance—might be described as beautiful, the P-51 offered a handsome, muscular, and perfectly proportioned appearance. Rather than projecting a fierce image, it had the confident, easy, all-American good looks that automatically reassured men.

Many of the P-51s scattered around the airfield at Bodney were newer, with bubble canopies. These wore no paint, their aluminum skins shining bright in the cloud-silvered light. Others were veterans of earlier battles and had traditional birdcage canopies; they were finished in worn, olive-drab paint that was chipped and rubbed with grease and oil. All of them were deadly, and the men who flew them believed themselves to be the most fortunate combat pilots in the world.

Don Bryan sighed with relief and looked up from where he was pissing on the tailwheel of his P-51. It was a ritual he practiced before each mission. A full and painful bladder was a distraction he didn't need while escorting the seemingly endless bomber streams for five hours or more. Such missions were challenging enough already. They required concentrated attention not only to flying the aircraft and maintaining proper formation, but also to rubber-necking the surrounding skies for enemy aircraft. Moreover, it was difficult not to feel trapped inside the cramped cockpit while sucking air from a rubber oxygen mask clamped too tightly to his face. And then there was the matter of German pilots and antiaircraft gun crews who were eager to kill him. In light of all that, draining his bladder at the last possible minute seemed to make good common sense.

As time had passed, the act also assumed the characteristics of a good luck sacrament. Bryan had survived more than a year of combat and saw no reason to change his routine.

Not far away, he spotted George Preddy climbing into his fighter. Preddy was one of the highest scoring aces in the Eighth Air Force and commanded Bryan's squadron, the 328th. It was just one of the 352nd Fighter Group's three fighter squadrons, the other two being the 486th and the 487th. All around the airfield, other pilots clambered into their aircraft or were already snugly strapped in. Bryan checked his watch. The group was scheduled to start its engines in two minutes. He gave his John Henry a quick shake, tucked it away, and fastened his trousers. Kirk Noyes, his crew chief, waited for him on the left wing of his fighter, *Little One III*.

Noyes had been Bryan's crew chief since the 352nd arrived at Bodney during July 1943. He was a serious man and wasn't amused by Bryan's bladder emptying, but neither did he bother him about it. The two men had a good arrangement. Noyes always made certain that their assigned aircraft was in tip-top shape, and Bryan always brought it back. And sometimes he shot down Germans with it.

After he finished snapping into his parachute, Bryan climbed onto the aircraft's left wing, slid past Noyes, stepped down into the cockpit, and strapped himself to the seat. Noyes pulled a rag from his pocket and wiped down the windscreen a final time; it couldn't be clean enough. Finished, he wished Bryan happy hunting and returned to the ground, where he waited with his assistant crew chief and armorer.

The weather at Bodney was gray but fresh on November 2, 1944. A cold breeze laced the bare-branched trees that lined much of the airfield's periphery and sunlight pierced the clouds in bright, striated columns. Bryan saw a puff of smoke from an aircraft across the field an instant before he heard the bark. Immediately, there was more smoke and a rising growl as the Packard-built Merlin engines of fifty-four blue-nosed P-51s spun to life. Bryan finished his pre-start checklist and nodded at Noyes, who stood in front of the aircraft with a fire extinguisher. His eyes swept the cockpit once more before he primed the engine, and then he threw the start switch.

The starter, whined and the four-bladed propeller in front of Bryan ticked in circles for a few seconds. There was a sharp chuff, a clot of smoke and flame from the exhaust stacks, and then a low roar as the engine caught and the propeller blades whirled into a translucent gray disk. Bryan set the fuel mixture and throttle, glanced at his engine instruments, then nodded at Noyes. The crew chief ducked under the wing of the aircraft—staying well clear of the propeller—and tugged the wheel chocks free. Bryan's armorer stood nearby, smiled, and raised a thumb. Earlier, he had loaded the aircraft's six machine guns with nearly 2,000 rounds of .50-caliber API—or Armor Piercing Incendiary—ammunition. The guns, their muzzles plugged with pressed cardboard discs that kept out dirt, water and small critters, were ready for action.

Already, the group's fighters were moving toward the takeoff end of the field. Because they couldn't see directly to the front over the long noses of their aircraft, the pilots taxied in a series of small S-turns. The P-51s, so graceful in the air, resembled great waddling, blue-nosed aluminum ducks on the ground. Bryan eased off the brakes, advanced the throttle, and let *Little One III* roll forward. He returned Noyes's thumbs-up as he turned to join the rest of the group.

Dirt, leaves, and bits of dry grass lifted from the ground by dozens of whirling propellers whipped past the fighters as they snaked their way into takeoff position. Bryan heard a small tick as a pebble bounced off the right side of his fuselage. He mentally checked off the other three members of his flight—Yellow Flight—as they fell into position behind him. He checked his watch again as the 352nd's first four-ship of P-51s raced down the grass field and lifted into the sky, exactly on time. The radio was silent as it always was when the group went on a mission.

Less than a minute later, Bryan readjusted the silk scarf around his neck, completed his takeoff checklist, cranked his canopy forward, and locked it shut. The roar of engines was muffled to a dull thrum. When the flight in front of him started its takeoff roll, he felt the propwash gently jostle his own aircraft. Immediately after, he edged forward, checked his instruments one more time, and then looked to his right as his wingman, element leader, and number-four man lined up in a close echelon slightly behind him.

With his flight in position, Bryan pushed his throttle smoothly forward and released his brakes. At the same time, he instinctively stepped hard on the right rudder to counteract the tremendous torque generated by *Little One III*'s powerful engine. The V-1650, a Packard-built derivative of the excellent Rolls-Royce Merlin, could quickly snap an aircraft out of control if not handled properly. The other three pilots of Yellow Flight rolled with him.

Little One III bumped along the grass, but the bumping grew less sharp as the trim little fighter accelerated toward flying speed. Bryan's feet danced automatically on the rudders as he kept the aircraft tracking straight. A quick look over his right shoulder confirmed that the other three aircraft in the flight were maintaining their positions. A few seconds later, he nudged the control stick forward and felt the aircraft's tail lift clear of the ground. Immediately after, he lifted the fighter airborne and pulled the landing gear handle up.

Bryan quickly trimmed the flight controls as the aircraft picked up speed. In the distance, he saw the rest of the group's formation in an easy turn back toward the airfield. His peripheral vision caught his wingman sliding underneath him to the left side, balancing the flight into a more maneuverable fingertip formation. Bryan took up a rendezvous heading to join the rest of the fighters. Behind him he could see the last of the group's P-51s lifting off from Bodney.

After joining and making a low, high-speed pass over the airfield, the blue-nosed P-51s of the 352nd Fighter Group punched up through the clouds and climbed on a course for the North Sea. As did every other pilot in the group, Bryan checked his engine instruments and made certain that fuel was transferring normally from all tanks. It was important that the fuselage tank behind him be at least partially emptied before he did any heavy maneuvering. Full, it pushed the aircraft's center of gravity nearly out of balance.

Approaching the continent, Bryan checked his new K-14 gunsight. At the same time, his flight's pilots loosened the formation and put a few hundred feet between themselves. This allowed Bryan to maneuver as required to maintain position with the rest of the escorting fighters once they joined the bombers. It was also the best formation for aggressive positioning in the event that enemy fighters made an appearance. The last thing a pilot needed to worry about was colliding with members of his own flight. Most of all, the added space allowed each pilot to pay less attention to maintaining his place in the formation, and to concentrate more on searching the sky in all directions, especially the critical arc that extended from either side and directly behind to the six-o'clock position.

The mission that day was a massive one. The Eighth Air Force put up more than 1,000 bombers and 900 fighters for a strike against Merseburg's petroleum infrastructure.

The straight and heavy white contrails the bombers created—and the wavy smaller marks left by their escorting fighters—were visible from more than fifty miles. The 352nd joined the bomber stream on schedule, and the three squadrons took up their assigned positions.

Bryan, at the head of Yellow Flight, followed Preddy's weaving flight path at 28,000 feet while watching for enemy fighters. Flak bursts dotted the sky as the enormous formation neared Merseburg. The radio crackled with clipped reports as the group's pilots called out contrails coming from the east that they suspected were being created by enemy aircraft.

Their suspicions proved well-founded. "Shortly after that," Bryan recalled, "I saw the contrails and was able to identify them as Me-109s. There seemed to be about 50 of them; approx 40 in a box with several more above them as top cover. By the time I could get in a position for my bounce, about 10–15 of them had started down on the bombers; the others were preparing to start down."

Don Bryan checked his gun switches on, rolled over on a wing, and led his flight down into one of the biggest aerial battles of World War II.

CHAPTER 1

They Were Boys First

"I begged my daddy to take me to a field near town where a barnstormer was giving rides in an old biplane," remembered Robert Powell. "I was only seven years old." Powell had been born on November 21, 1920, at his home in Wilcoe, West Virginia, a coal-mining town owned by the United States Steel Company.

"We drove out to the field and I waited my turn," remembered Powell. "The price was two dollars, which was a pretty fair sum of money at the time. I think the rent for our house was only about seventeen dollars."

Powell's father gave him five dollars to pay the pilot. "Well, I handed him that five dollar bill and he took me up for just one real quick trip around the field. It was enjoyable enough but it wasn't particularly memorable." After he was back on the ground, Powell and his father watched the flyer take a few more customers aloft before they climbed into the family automobile and headed for home.

"We were most of the way back to the house," Powell recalled, "when my daddy asked, 'Where's my change?' It wasn't until then that I realized that the pilot hadn't given me any change." He had been cheated. "Boy, oh boy," remembered Powell, "Daddy was good and mad. I didn't hear the last of that for a while!"

Robert Powell was not one of those boys who grew up dreaming of becoming a pilot. "Airplanes were interesting to me, and I built models and things of that sort but flying airplanes wasn't something I thought I'd ever do. In fact, we seldom ever saw an airplane in that part of West Virginia."

The family was hit hard by the Great Depression, as was all of Wilcoe. While his father went back into the mines and his mother took a job at J. C. Penney, Powell did his part by selling eggs and magazine subscriptions. At the same time, he did his chores, studied hard, and played baseball.

He also became an excellent boxer. "One day in high school in between classes, the fullback of our football team knocked my books out of my grip and onto the floor," Powell recollected. "I jumped up and started punching him. He grabbed my hands, laughed at me and said, 'You're a feisty little bastard. Why don't you come out for the boxing team? We need a flyweight.'" Powell weighed 110 pounds.

The boxing coach was serious not only about boxing, but about discipline and conditioning. Because there was no bus service after the boys finished practice, he made them run home—backward. "He told us that boxing required as much backward movement as forward and he wanted us to learn balance," Powell said. "He often got in his car after practice and drove the roads to check on us. If he caught us walking or not running backward, he'd make us do a lot of extra pushups at practice the next day."

The training and conditioning—in combination with Powell's native talent and tenacity—paid off. Although he broke both his thumbs in the final round of his final fight, he won the West Virginia Golden Gloves championship in 1938. Moreover, he earned a new nickname: "Punchy."

Despite his success at boxing, baseball was his first love, and his skill at the game earned him a college scholarship at West Virginia University. Nevertheless, the Japanese attack on Pearl Harbor changed his life just as it did the lives of millions of young men like him. He was in his third semester when his best friend talked him into taking the examinations required to qualify as a cadet in the U.S. Army Air Forces. "Anyway, we skipped a couple of days of school and hitchhiked down to Pikeville, Kentucky, to take the exams," Powell recollected. "They were quite difficult but I managed to pass them. However, they weren't ready to send me to training so I went home and worked at the local newspaper. After a few months, they sent orders for me to report to Santa Ana, California, for preflight training."

More than halfway across the country Fremont Miller lived a life that was very different from Punchy Powell's. He was born at home on December 29, 1918, on an irrigated homestead near Crowheart, Wyoming.[1]

"There was no doctor for any of our births, not even a midwife," he remembered. The squared-log house was small and Miller and his brother slept in the pantry. "We had a mattress made of ticking which was filled with oat straw. Every year when the oats were threshed, we got a new filling which smelled nice and clean. But every time it was filled, it came out round instead of flat and we would have to jump up and down to flatten it out so we wouldn't roll off."

Mifler's recollections make it quite clear that rural life in Wyoming was not a sanitized, pastoral existence. The family took advantage of every resource the land offered, including its wildlife. "I caught coyotes by digging the pups out of their dens in the spring," he recalled. "We would keep them in a pen during the summer and feed them on the prairie dogs we trapped and killed. In the fall we would sell the [coyote] skins." Mail-order giant Montgomery Ward paid much-needed money for animal pelts.

Miller remembered an elk calf that he found in the wild and brought home. It grew to be a full-size cow and wandered the property—essentially as a pet—until it ravaged a neighbor's garden. "So we had to butcher and eat her," he recalled.

Life on a Wyoming homestead during this period demanded that a boy master many skills. Virtually everything on the ranch needed maintenance or repair on a regular basis, and Miller grew adept with hammer and saw, wire and rope, and leather and steel. Motor vehicles were just becoming established as a part of ranch life, but at the same time, horses were still invaluable. At the time, most cattle were still herded by hands on horseback. As he came of age during this transitional period, Miller became expert with both engines and horseflesh.

He graduated from high school, where he excelled at football, in 1937 and subsequently attended Colorado A&M University for three semesters before returning home while his brother finished college. The two of them were growing a promising beekeeping business, and they planned to alternate stints at school until they both graduated. "I thought about little but my bee business in 1938, 1939, and 1940," Miller said. His brother graduated according to plan in 1941, and Miller returned to school that fall. But just as it did everywhere else in the United States, the attack on Pearl Harbor overshadowed school, football, beekeeping, and almost everything else in Wyoming.

Miller recounted the surge of outrage and patriotism following the Japanese attack: "Everybody and his skinny brother wanted to fight for his country. I was one of those. The day after Pearl Harbor, I went from Fort Collins to Denver to enlist in the Air Corps. There were so many boys enlisted at that time that they didn't have enough camps to put all of us in."

Like nearly everyone who enlisted in the early days of the war, Miller was sent home until there was somewhere to train him.

Theodore Fahrenwald was born in Cleveland, Ohio, on December 26, 1919, and moved with his family to Chicago in 1925.[2] His father, a successful inventor and mining engineer, had been born in a sod house in South Dakota. The elder Fahrenwald shared his love of the outdoors, especially hunting and fishing, with his son. Ted was a precocious boy, intelligent and charming, and aside from his interest in the open spaces, he grew fond of practical jokes, even at a young age. His sister Caroline recalled one of his stunts: "During a particularly rough Chicago winter, he found a poor cat that had frozen to death in a horrible position; its teeth were bared and its claws were spread. Ted left it by our front door where my very proper mother and I had to step over it on returning from our shopping trip."

Young Fahrenwald liked speed and excitement, too. "Our house was on a hill," Caroline recalled, "and when I was pretty small, he talked me into riding with him down the sidewalk on an old wooden desk chair. The only way to stop was to fall over onto the grass at the bottom. Once was enough!"

"When he was about sixteen," Caroline continued, "our father took him on a business trip to Florida, where he left him for a few days on his own so that he could visit with family friends and then return by himself. Dad received a telegram that read, 'Need money, bringing home an Indian.' Dad wired some extra money and Ted roared up our driveway a few days later on an Indian motorcycle. Being Ted, he was allowed to keep it."

Fahrenwald was sent to a local military academy for high school; it was thought that he might benefit from exposure to a more disciplined school environment. The rigor of the military school did nothing to stifle Fahrenwald's magnetic personality. His sense of humor and gift for story-telling made him popular wherever he went. Following graduation, he attended Carleton College in Northfield, Minnesota, where he focused on flying and poker and shortly earned a private pilot's license. Academics were a lower priority.

Automobiles were deadly machines prior to the war, and accidents were common. Fahrenwald met trouble late in 1941. His sister recalled: "A car accident required a body cast, which he wore for several weeks, until the news of Pearl Harbor came. He soaked off the cast so that he could pass the physical and enlist." Despite his unilateral and medically uninformed decision to rush the healing of his own body, Fahrenwald was found fit for flight training, and he left Carleton early in 1942.

There was a young man in Greensboro, North Carolina, who knew he wanted to be a fighter pilot. George Earl Preddy Jr. was born on February 5, 1919, and grew to be a small, wiry boy with dark hair and big ears.[3] His nickname was Mouse. But there was nothing mousey about George Preddy. Although he was too small—120 pounds—to be competitive on most of his high school's athletic teams, he taught himself gymnastics, tennis, and basketball. He was keenly competitive. One friend remembered, "He was a great little scrapper and he would never give up."

He was also hardworking and intelligent. During the summers, he set up a concession stand, which he called The Mouse Hole, at nearby Memorial Stadium and made a little cash. Preddy finished high school at age sixteen and went to work at a local cotton mill for fifteen dollars a week while he saved for college.

George Preddy was also compassionate beyond what might have been expected of a boy his age. One of his dear friends lost his mother and had nowhere to live but the Greensboro YMCA. Preddy couldn't stand the notion of the boy being alone and convinced his mother to let him join the family. The boy shared a bedroom with Preddy and his younger brother Bill for five years until reaching adulthood.

Preddy's sensitivity showed in the face of tragedy as well. His older sister Jonnice died giving birth in 1939. The heartbreak left him stoic. On that day, without any outward emotion, he penned a poem and left it for his parents on the coffee table in their living room.

What is this thing?
This trance I'm in?
I know not what death brings.
I know she's gone,
Her soul has fled,
But to me her sweet voice rings.
She lingers in this very room,
She directs me in my role.
I know she dwells not with the dead,
She lives within my soul.

Aside from paying for school, Preddy's job at the cotton mill also paid for flying lessons. His interest in flying was sparked during high school by stories he read about various flyers and their exploits. World War I combat flying figured prominently in those stories and Preddy was intrigued by the notion of aerial combat and chivalry in the skies. Ultimately, during 1938, his interest turned to keen passion when he took his first airplane ride in a 1933 Aeronca. Badly bitten by the flying bug, he earned his private pilot's license in early 1939 and spent that summer and the next flying throughout the region giving airplane rides for money. It was easy and exciting but what he made in cash only barely covered his fuel expenses and little more.

At the same time he was spreading his wings, World War II started in Europe. Preddy was anxious as he felt that the United States was sure to be pulled into the conflict. If it came to that, he wanted to do his part from the cockpit of a fighter rather than from the muddy misery of the battlefield. Consequently, he caught a train from Greensboro to Pensacola, Florida, where he took the physical examination for U.S. Navy flight training.

He failed. He was told he was too small, his spine had too much curve, and his blood pressure was too high.

Undaunted, Preddy returned home and trained hard to overcome the deficiencies the Navy's doctors had noted. Once he felt fit enough, he went back to Pensacola for another physical. He failed that one as well. And later, he missed the mark again on his third attempt. Preddy was stubborn and persistent, but he wasn't dimwitted. Rather than giving the Navy a fourth opportunity to turn him down, he went to an Army Air Corps base, where he passed the physical with no difficulty whatsoever.

While he waited to be called to flight school, Preddy joined a National Guard coast artillery outfit where he underwent training similar to what he would receive in basic training as a cadet in the Army Air Corps. It was good experience and he received a small amount of pay as well. However, the plan almost backfired when his unit, the 252nd Coast Artillery, received orders to Puerto Rico. Preddy was in danger of getting lost in the shuffle. Aware of his plight, one of the unit's officers issued orders that held Preddy back in garrison while he waited for orders to flight school. They finally arrived in April 1941.

Donald McKibben was born in Hornell, New York, just north of the Pennsylvania border, on September 23, 1921. His father was a weaver in a hosiery factory. "I was the fourth of eight children," McKibben remembered. "As such, and since I grew up during the Great Depression, I learned a lot about survival skills." He was forced to refine those skills even further beginning in 1933 when his father died and his family was separated.

Disaster struck the town in 1935 in the form of a massive flood. The great inundation proved to be a windfall for young McKibben. "I spent that summer cleaning mud from houses that had been flooded," he recalled. "And I was allowed to keep a few musty books that I salvaged from one house. One was *Bartlett's [Familiar] Quotations* and another was the 1928 *Aircraft Year Book*."

But steady employment was scarce, and McKibben felt fortunate when he landed jobs at a hardware store and, later, behind the counter of a soda fountain. "My first major purchase with money from my jobs," McKibben recalled, "was a camera. My goal was to become a big-time journalist and photographer. I tried unsuccessfully to emulate the style of Damon Runyon in a column I wrote for the weekly high-school newspaper." Although he might have failed to match Runyon's inimitable style, McKibben nevertheless held the column for three years when it had traditionally been awarded on a yearly basis to distinguished senior classmen.

McKibben's talent rose above high-school doings. "The *Hornell Evening Tribune* offered me a job as a full-time reporter and photographer after I graduated." As McKibben had no money for college, he accepted the position. "It was an enriching experience. Not only did I get to write the story, take the photographs, and process the film, but I also learned to convert the photographs, to halftone engravings for the letterpress printing operation."

Starting in 1938, tens of thousands of young men and women took advantage of the Civilian Pilot Training Program, which the government funded to create a pool of pilots with an eye toward enhancing the nation's military preparedness. The idea of flying appealed to McKibben, and he enrolled in 1940 when the program became available in his area. "The evening ground school courses were essentially free, but flight instruction cost more than I could handle," he recalled. "However, I scored very high in the final written examinations and was awarded free flight instruction, which led to a private pilot license in February 1941."

The more McKibben flew, the more he fell in love with flying. "I began to have second thoughts about becoming a famous journalist." Nevertheless, he didn't have the prerequisite college hours to enter the Army Air Corps, and he was doing well at his work. "I was offered and accepted the position of news editor of the weekly *Genesee Country Express* in nearby Dansville. That was quite an ego booster for a nineteen-year-old.

As it turned out, I was merely a placeholder for the previous news editor while she was on extended leave. She returned in the spring of 1941 and I was out, but one of my news contacts helped me arrange an interview with Eastman Kodak in Rochester and I was hired as a sales trainee."

Kodak sent McKibben to Milwaukee, Wisconsin, but he was still enamored with the idea of flying in the military. "As I could not qualify as an aviation cadet because of my age and lack of college, I applied to fly with the Royal Canadian Air Force through the Clayton Knight Committee." The Clayton Knight Committee was an organization that was technically illegal although it operated with the complicit disinterest of the Roosevelt administration. It recruited American flyers to fly for the Canadians. As part of the Royal Canadian Air Force, they often saw action against Germany's Luftwaffe alongside Britain's RAF. It is estimated that the committee arranged for 10,000 American volunteers to fly for the Canadians.

"During the fall of 1941, I received word that my paperwork was in order for my enrollment into the Royal Canadian Air Force," McKibben remembered. "All I needed to do was complete a physical examination in Toronto." He hesitated since he didn't have the money for travel expenses and was additionally reluctant to take time off from the job he had just started.

And then the Japanese attacked Pearl Harbor. "Within a few weeks, the Army loosened their qualifications for aviation cadet training," McKibben recounted. "I applied, passed all their tests, and was formally enlisted and promptly placed on leave." A month later, McKibben was on his way to flight training.

While young men across America were growing from boyhood into manhood, Gen. Henry "Hap" Arnold, the head of the United States Army Air Corps, was trying to build a world-class air force out of an air arm that was not. Considering the deteriorating global situation, it was only just in time, on November 14, 1938, when President Roosevelt announced dramatic expansion plans for the Army Air Corps. As things grew worse abroad, the already outsized expansion plans grew even more so.

For instance, in 1938 the service numbered only 20,000 men and operated a mere 1,600 aircraft. Roosevelt's initial announcement called for expanding the aircraft inventory more than fivefold to 10,000 new aircraft. Less than two years later, during May 1940, he called for American industry to be expanded to deliver 50,000 aircraft *per year*. Ultimately, that seemingly outlandish figure would be overshadowed by the numbers actually produced.

The notion of an Army Air Corps equipped with tens of thousands of aircraft was fine—so long as there were pilots to fly them. But in 1940, there weren't. That Arnold and his staff were scrambling to get a grasp on what the nation's requirements would be is indicated by the ostensibly absurd annual pilot training goals that were established at 7,000 per year during May 1940. That number was raised to 12,000 per year in August and subsequently to 30,000 by the end of the year. To put these numbers in context, it must be considered that there were still only 3,640 trained pilots on hand during July of that year.

Nevertheless, the United States gave Arnold and the Army Air Corps what was essentially a blank check. Although the nation was not yet at war, it was scrambling to get on a war footing. The pilot-training spigot was turned on, contracts were let, new airfields were built, and raw aviation cadets were inducted into service. The results were immediate. On the eve of the nation's entry into the war in 1941, the U.S. Army Air Corps was renamed the U.S. Army Air Forces and trained 27,000 new pilots. By the end of following year, 1942, the service had the capacity to start 10,000 new aviation cadets per month, and it maintained a candidate pool of 50,000 qualified young men through most of the war.

Although the specifics of pilot training varied somewhat through the war, the basic construct remained consistent. Candidates were first sent to classification centers where they were screened and designated for training as pilots, navigators, or bombardiers. Those young men who successfully passed the screening were designated aviation cadets and sent to preflight training where they began physical conditioning and academic studies related to aviation. This was performed within the construct of an intensive military indoctrination.

After successfully completing preflight, pilot trainees were sent to primary flight training at one of approximately sixty airfields where they received about sixty hours of flight training. This training was provided by civilian instructors in one of several different primary trainer types. The next stop was one of thirty basic training bases where pilot trainees received roughly seventy-five hours of flight instruction provided by military flight instructors. The final phase was Advanced Flight Training, where the cadets flew the AT-6 Texan for approximately seventy-five hours.

On successfully completing all three phases, the trainees were designated as pilots and commissioned as officers. They typically received orders for further training in combat aircraft before being sent overseas. In the case of those pilots who had been selected for fighters, particularly early in the war, some were sent to fighter groups slated to be sent overseas, while others were sent to fighter groups formed specifically to prepare replacement pilots. Often, the training they received was on one fighter type, whereas the aircraft they ultimately flew in combat was a different type.

Although each pilot in the 352nd Fighter Group obviously had a unique training experience, Punchy Powell's was fairly typical. After completing preflight training at Santa Ana, California, he was sent to the Mira Loma Flight Academy in Oxnard, California, for primary flight training. He recalled the hazing he experienced: "We had upperclassmen from West Point, and they treated us like we were plebes. Among everything else, we had to eat 'square meals.' We had to lift the food from our plates vertically until it was even with our faces and then move it horizontally into our mouths. And of course, we had to keep one hand under the table at all times."

Another seemingly absurd practice had the cadets "clearing the airspace" when they walked from one point to another. Upon reaching a turn, on a sidewalk for instance, they were required to look up, down, and side to side. If the way was clear, they stretched their arms—their "wings"—and banked into a turn toward where they wanted to go. Perhaps it was intended to instill discipline or attention to detail, but mostly, it was simple persecution intended to put the trainees under stress.

The harassment was practically unbounded, and the cadets were fair game at virtually any time. "They'd come into our rooms and wipe their feet on our floor," Powell remembered, "and then yell at us because our floor was dirty. And they'd make us stand so rigid at attention that we'd have fourteen chins."

"They'd put their noses almost against ours," Powell recalled, "and shout at us and we'd have to answer all their questions without making any mistakes. I remember one question in particular: 'Cadet, why did you join the Air Corps?' And we'd have to give the answer almost like a chant: 'Sir! Pa beat Ma, Ma beat me, the food at home was pee-poor, and my girl and the bank note were both thirty days overdue, sir! That's why I joined the Air Corps, sir!"

The students at Mira Loma flew the PT-13B Kaydet. It was a relatively docile but rugged biplane that could stand up to the considerable abuse that was visited upon it when the Army introduced legions of hamhanded students to the wonder of flight. "Quite a few cadets were washed out," Powell recounted. "Some of them didn't make it because they couldn't hold their breakfasts down, others couldn't do the aerobatics, and others found out that they just didn't like flying."

Powell did fairly well. "I soloed after eight hours. They required that you solo sometime between six and twelve hours of dual instruction. If you couldn't do it, you were eliminated. Of course, there were guys who were washed out who could have been good pilots, but they just couldn't keep up with the pace that the Army set."

Following primary training at Mira Loma, Powell was ordered to Gardner Army Air Field, near Taft, California, for the basic phase, in which students were instructed for the first time by military pilots. There the students flew the BT-13 Vultee Valiant, which was a radial-engine monoplane with fixed landing gear and an enclosed cockpit. "Basic was no lark," he recalled. "My first instructor was a grizzly bear. He was most unhappy about being an instructor, and I think he took it out on us. I never liked being shouted at and didn't take to that sort of instruction too well."

The instructor liked to make his points in a fashion that had a lasting effect on his students. On one sortie, he noticed that Powell forgot to put on his lap belt. "He told me to fasten it, but every time I got the two sections within inches of connecting, he hit the control stick and bounced my head off the canopy. It hurt. After three or four times, I finally got it fastened. It was a good lesson."

The instructor was transferred when Powell was halfway through the basic syllabus. "I was assigned to a Chinese-American instructor," Powell remembered. "His teaching method was much more suited to my personality; he spoke softly and explained things well. He did not shout or beat me on the head. And he took time to carefully review my performance after each flight and suggest ways for me to improve."

By the time the students reached advanced training, there was little emphasis on screening out the weak players; most of them had been washed out during the earlier phases. Rather, the emphasis was on exposing the students to flying that was more relevant to combat operations. The aircraft they flew was the North American AT-6 Texan. Like the BT-13, it was a low-wing monoplane with a radial engine and enclosed cockpit. However, it was faster and had retractable landing gear. Powell's experience at Luke Army Air Field was typical. "I loved aerobatics and formation flying and did quite well, with no major goofs."

Among the young men eventually assigned to the 352nd, George Preddy was one of the first to see combat. After leaving Greensboro for flight training in April 1941, he earned his wings on December 12, less than a week after Pearl Harbor. He received orders to the 49th Pursuit Group, and the following month, he was aboard the former luxury liner *Mariposa* en route to the South Pacific as part of the first tranche of reinforcements the United States sent to shore up its defenses there.

The *Mariposa* took its cargo of ammunition, guns, P-40 fighters, and 4,000 men to Melbourne, Australia. Preddy had continued to develop during his short time in the Army. Aside from his love of reading and sports, he liked cards, dice, women, and liquor. He found them all in Australia. When the ship docked on February 2, 1942, Preddy had a good night. He wrote in his diary: "Went into a little town called Bacchus Marsh tonight and picked up a girl. Went to bed on the floor about midnight." One of his squadron mates recalled Preddy's personality: "To me, he was a happy-go-lucky type, maybe on occasion even a hell-raiser, who made certain he got the maximum out of life."

The American pilots in Australia at that time were mostly neophytes. They stayed that way for some time because there were very few aircraft available for them to fly. Accordingly, the men of the 49th got very little practice. When they finally received their first few P-40s, a type that most of them had never flown, they wrecked them with dizzying alacrity.

Their poor flying skills were amplified by spotty maintenance. Further, Australia's vast size and punishing weather, together with the remoteness of the fields from which the 49th and other units operated, greatly hampered the ability of the Americans to put meaningful numbers of aircraft into the sky.

After traversing the continent from the very south to the farthest point north, the 49th Pursuit Group started flying from airfields near Darwin during March 1942. Clashes with the enemy varied in intensity. The Japanese mounted raids for several days at a time and then disappeared for weeks or more. Preddy, who was assigned to the 49th's 9th Fighter Squadron, saw little action although he did damage a Mitsubishi Zero and a bomber on April 27. This lack of action, combined with his competitive nature, caused him some amount of disquietude.

It also exacerbated the less-than-loveable demeanor he sometimes assumed when he drank. He was handled during these episodes by his good friend I. B. "Jack" Donalson. Donalson was a tough Texan who had been sent to the Philippines just before the Japanese attack on Pearl Harbor. While there, he downed three Japanese aircraft before joining an infantry unit and later escaping to Australia. He subsequently scored two more aerial victories against the Japanese. Although he had earned his wings and commission only a few months before Preddy, he was already an experienced old hand. He remembered Preddy:

George liked to gamble. He'd get loaded and join a game of craps. He liked craps especially. And that's when George used the expression, 'Cripes a'mighty.' He'd roll the dice and holler 'Cripes a mighty!' He lived like tonight was going to be his last night, and that's just the way he lived. He was wild; when he got drunk, he would get mean. But I could always handle George. So when George would get belligerent, I would say, 'Now George, you've had enough'; he'd want to fight but I'd get him off to bed. The next morning he was raring to go and sorry he had caused any trouble. You know, he was kind of a little guy, but tougher than a boot.[4]

Despite his off-duty shenanigans, Preddy was serious about flying and took every chance he could to get airborne, even if it was only for training. In fact, training sorties made up most of his flying through the early part of June 1942. Japanese raids intensified during the middle of the month, but Preddy found the enemy only once and received three bullet holes in his aircraft for his trouble.

The following month proved worse. On July 12, while on a training mission, Preddy and his squadron mate, John Sauber, collided. Sauber was killed, but Preddy was able to bail out. As his parachute settled him through the scrub trees and brush, he was badly gouged and sliced in the thigh, hip, and shoulder.

Preddy's combat flying in Australia was over, and he was evacuated to Melbourne, where he stayed bedridden until July 28. He had time to reflect and made an entry in the back of his diary that illustrated, in part, the type of man he was. Always intensely interested in bettering himself, he composed a list of thirteen rules to help guide the way he lived. They were a window to Preddy's own assessment of his shortcomings as well as what was important to him. Through his career, he excelled at holding to some of them while his adherence to one or two others sometimes went wanting.[5]

1. No smoking at any time or under any circumstances.
2. Drink intelligently and sparingly.
3. Eat sensibly.
4. Exercise regularly and diligently.
5. Learn all possible about flying or any other job at hand.
6. Always be willing to go out of the way to learn something new.
7. Always try to give the other man a boost.
8. Fight hardest when down and never give up.
9. Don't make excuses but make up with deeds of action.

10. Learn by experience.
11. Listen to others and profit by criticism.
12. Live a clean life.
13. Trust in God and never lose faith in Him.

During his recuperation, Preddy met and fell in love with a local girl, Joan Jackson. During their courtship, they took in all the social life that Melbourne could offer. Joan was not a drinker and was no doubt a stabilizing influence on Preddy during this period. His diary entry of September 9, 1942, notes his fondness for her: "Had dinner at Joan's house this evening. It was a very enjoyable evening. Her Dad is a famous golfer and a very nice fellow. Also her sister is a clever girl and very attractive. I think I could love Joan."

Preddy might have loved Joan, but he received orders back to the States. He left Australia on October 23, 1942, with a promise to continue his relationship with her via mail. It had been less than nine months since he set foot in Australia. Only half of that period was spent on combat operations, and although he gained valuable experience, Preddy scored no aerial victories.

CHAPTER 2

Birth of the 352nd Fighter Group

The enormous expansion of the U.S. Army Air Forces was well underway by late 1942. As the service grew from its prewar strength of approximately 20,000 men to its eventual size of 2.4 million men, it was compelled to create entirely new air forces—sixteen of them—and the wings, groups, and squadrons to populate them. Consequently, the 352nd Fighter Group—one of an eventual seventy-five fighter groups created during the war—was officially ordered into existence by the 1st Fighter Command on September 29, 1942, at Mitchel Field, New York. At the same time, it was ordered to Bradley Field at Windsor Locks, Connecticut.

The new group and one of its three assigned squadrons, the 328th, were staffed by personnel from the 326th Fighter Group, a training unit already established at Bradley Field. The other two squadrons, the 21st and 34th, then based at Selfridge Field, Michigan, were administratively transferred without men and equipment to the 352nd on the following day.

During the few weeks following its formation, the 352nd did little other than collect personnel and get its administrative house in order. A month later, on October 28, 1942, it was ordered in its entirety to Westover Field at Chicopee Falls, Massachusetts. It was during this time that the 352nd's first commanding officer arrived on November 23. Lieutenant Colonel Edwin Ramage was twenty-nine years old and had climbed the ranks from first lieutenant to lieutenant colonel in less than three years. Immediately prior to assuming command, he had served in Iceland for more than a year.

After less than three months at Westover, the group was ordered to
Trumbull Field at Groton, Connecticut, on January 14, 1943. It was a wet
and muddy place and the men immediately started calling it "Grumble"
Field. It was there that the 352nd received its first aircraft, P-47Cs, on
January 18.

At the same time that the 352nd was standing up, the strategies that
dictated its later employment were still being debated. That argument had
been ongoing for years and centered on the concept of the self-defending
bomber and whether such an aircraft could penetrate—unescorted—deep
into enemy territory during daylight without sustaining prohibitive losses.
Even on the eve of World War II, there was uncertainty about the value of
fighter escorts or the possibility of building a fighter capable of escorting
bombers to far-flung targets.

Various Air Corps studies dissected the problem and came to conclusions that were neither convincing nor consistent. For instance, Air Corps
Study Number 35, *Employment of Aircraft in Defense of the Continental
United States*, dated May 1939, was doubtful not only that fighter escorts
were needed, but that they could be built if they were: "The high operating
speed of modern bombers increases the difficulty of interception by hostile
pursuit and thereby lessens the need of support by friendly pursuit. . . .
There appears to be little, if any, possibility of ever building an accompa-
nying fighter with an operating range comparable to that of bombardment
and also fighting characteristics, which would enable it to cope with the
enemy pursuit in the vicinity of the bombardment objectives." In other
words, not only was a fighter escort not needed for the bombers, but it
would be impossible to build a good one if the need did exist.

However, Air Corps Study Number 53, *Fire Power of Bombardment
Formations*, dated January 3, 1940, presented conclusions that were in
direct conflict. To be fair, the study's authors knew that Arnold did not
agree with the earlier report. Moreover, they were able to consider the first
few months of the air war in Europe. The study's authors declared:
"Whenever air opposition is likely, they [bombers] will require pursuit
[fighter] support if losses are to be kept within reasonable limits." It additionally declared that "Pursuit protection for long-range bombers during
daylight operations against objectives known to be defended by pursuit is
of great tactical importance and the pertinent technical problems incident
to the provision of such protection merit thorough investigation."

In particular, three notions that the board recommended for consideration included the development of long-range fighters, the refueling of fighters from bomber aircraft, and parasitic fighters that might be deployed and recovered from bombers as they flew their missions.[1]

Of those three options, the concept of aerial refueling was ahead of its time and would have been of limited value regardless. Quite simply, industry was incapable of developing an aircraft that could carry an effective load of bombs as well as enough fuel not only for itself but also for its escorts. Moreover, there were the technical issues associated with developing an aerial refueling capability in both the fighters and bombers. Too, even if the development and technical issues could have been resolved, aerial refueling operations en route to and over enemy territory would have been extremely challenging.

Technical challenges and operational considerations were even more germane to the other idea of parasitic fighters. This notion of fighters carried by bombers was, quite frankly, stupid. It betrayed an embarrassing lack of critical thought on the part of the study's authors. For one, it would have required the design, development, and production of an entirely new bomber big and powerful enough to lift both a fighter and a useful load of bombs. Even were it accomplished before the war ended, the concept was unproven. It is very likely that successfully employing such fighters operationally would have been impossible.

The first recommendation, the development of long-range fighters, was the most practical yet was not immediately pursued with any vigor. Neither the British nor the Germans had been successful in producing such an aircraft, and the Royal Air Force, totally committed to night bombing, showed little interest in pursuing the idea.

Although the scheme of extending the range of existing fighter types by stuffing them with fuel seemed obvious, it presented complex problems. For one, there was limited volume available into which fuel could be put. To begin with, fighters were typically already overburdened with guns and ammunition, radios, all manner of fuel and exhaust plumbing, oxygen bottles, armor plate, and various flight-control components. Further, fuel was heavy. Adding more often stressed aircraft structures to a point beyond which they were designed to endure.

Moreover, the weight of additional fuel made aircraft sluggish and less maneuverable. Consequently, engines of increased power were needed to counter the penalties incurred by the added weight. However, more powerful engines consumed more fuel and thus negated the value of the added fuel to a significant degree. Also, aircraft that were heavily loaded were more difficult to handle and prone to accidents. Finally, even if a reasonably effective long-range fighter could be fielded, it was widely believed that it couldn't compete with defending fighters that were optimized for speed and maneuverability. For all these reasons, it was a widely held tenet that an effective long-range escort fighter was not feasible.

It logically followed, then, that heavy bombers had to defend themselves. To varying degrees, many believed that the newest designs—particularly the B-17—were capable of doing so. However, as heavily armed as the most modern bombers were, virtually everyone agreed that more defensive firepower would be welcome. This being the case, there was considerable interest in the concept of a convoy defender—that is, a very heavily armed bomber, without bombs, intended to fly with the bomber formations to augment their firepower.

This concept eventually reached fruition in a variant of the B-17, the YB-40, that proved too heavy, slow, and ill-equipped for the mission and was withdrawn from service after flying just more than a dozen missions over a three-month period that ended in July 1943, more than a month before the 352nd even began combat operations.

Regardless, early in the war, there was still much to be learned on all sides. Mistakes would be made but progress would be made as well. And rather than ridiculous concepts such as parasitic fighters, or less bizarre ideas such as the convoy defender, the ultimate success was achieved through incremental range improvements to already existing fighters, including the P-38, P-47, and P-51.

Of these, the standard American fighter escort aircraft in England early in the war was the P-47 Thunderbolt. It was a monster unlike anything flown to that point. Built by Republic Aircraft Company in Farmingdale, New York, it was designed by Alexander de Seversky and Alexander Kartveli and traced its heritage back to Seversky's P-35 and the later P-43 Lancer. Both were indifferent designs that saw limited operational service. The P-47A was a proposal that failed to impress the Air Corps, but the significantly different and much larger P-47B showed promise and a prototype was ordered in September 1940.

The aircraft was designed to take advantage of the new Pratt & Whitney R-2800, air-cooled, eighteen-cylinder radial engine that produced more than 2,000 horsepower. For high-altitude operations, a turbosupercharger was installed in the fuselage behind the pilot. The complex ductwork associated with the device pushed out the aircraft's belly, which subsequently required the wings to be installed relatively high on the fuselage. It was this arrangement, together with the massive engine, that gave the aircraft its distinctly "tubby" lines. Few people ever described the P-47 as beautiful.

Beautiful or not, the P-47's performance made it competitive with its contemporaries—both Allied and Axis. The prototype first flew on May 6, 1941, and eventually turned in a top speed in excess of 410 miles per hour. And although its climb rate and maneuverability at low altitude were not particularly outstanding, they were not unsatisfactory. Moreover, its performance improved dramatically at high altitude, especially as improvements were added. Further, its power and weight made it much faster in a dive than both the Me-109 and FW-190.

Its range was not as great as Lockheed's P-38, but it was better than that of the Spitfire and the German fighters; they were not designed with long range as a high priority. And importantly, later iterations of the P-47 carried more fuel that increased its reach even more. Its armament of eight .50-caliber machine guns—four in each wing—was absolutely devastating; a short burst could literally shred an opponent.

And it was massive. In fact, it was the largest single-engine fighter produced during World War II. Although its thirty-six-foot length and forty-foot wingspan were greater than average, its weight was truly extraordinary. Empty, the P-47 weighed nearly 10,000 pounds. In comparison, its chief opponent, the Me-109G, had an empty weight of just less than 6,000 pounds. The structure underlying its weight, together with armor, self-sealing fuel tanks, and the extraordinarily rugged R-2800 engine, made the P-47 an extremely tough aircraft to knock down.

Like all aircraft, the early P-47s experienced growing pains. There were structural issues as well as problems with the engine and the canopy. The controls were excessively heavy in various flight regimes, and the big, four-bladed propeller swung precariously close to the ground during takeoff and landing. Too, fuel and exhaust leaks combined to cause a few aircraft to explode in flight. Nevertheless, most of these issues were resolved in the P-47C that began to equip the 352nd during January 1943.

The 352nd's pilots adapted well enough to the fighter. It was likely easier for some of the old hands who had flown the P-40 and the P-39. But the largest aircraft that most of the youngsters had flown was the AT-6 advanced trainer, which weighed much less than half of what the P-47 weighed. Furthermore, the 600-horsepower engine of the AT-6 was little more than a noisemaker compared to the P-47's massive Pratt & Whitney. Consequently, the P-47 made an intimidating first impression.

On the other hand, it was not a difficult aircraft to fly. It flew honestly, and its controls, if heavy, were well-harmonized, honest, and responsive. Its wide-tracked landing gear made taxiing, as well as takeoffs and landings, easier than they otherwise would have been. The engine was very smooth, reliable, and powerful. And later, the pilots would be awed by the tremendous firepower of the eight machine guns.

Mostly, it was the P-47's physical size that impressed the pilots. Whereas the larger flyers described the cockpit as roomy, the smaller ones remarked that it was cavernous. Indeed, some of the more diminutive among them could barely see out of the cockpit. Don McKibben of the 352nd's 21st Fighter Squadron recorded his thoughts on being introduced to the big fighter:

> The sheer size of the Thunderbolt was intimidating to a kid who had just stepped out of AT-6s. That fact encouraged me, before my first flight, to spend as much time as possible in the cockpit of a parked ship, mentally practicing every step from buckling into the seat to engine shutdown, and memorizing the location of every instrument, switch, and control. I didn't want to waste time looking for them should this seven-ton monster decide to test me. That first flight was actually somewhat anti-climatic, and over time I began to think of the Thunderbolt as less of a monster, and more like a big, cuddly bear. But with claws.

Still, McKibben never got over the P-47's size. "Being one of the smallest guys in the group, I somehow always felt like I was a passenger, rattling around in that huge cockpit like a pea in a barrel."

Don Bryan had more than two hundred flight hours in the P-40 when he was assigned to the 328th Fighter Squadron to fly P-47s. "I didn't like the P-47 at first," he recalled. "The main reason was that I nearly crashed one on takeoff. The spring on the rudder lock was broken and the lock flipped back and locked my rudder. I had to use the right brake to stay on the runway until I got airborne."

Bryan's experience was due to a maintenance issue rather than anything inherent in the P-47's design. In fact, maintaining the big brute was especially problematic for the 352nd's maintainers during this early period. First, there wasn't a lot of hangar space available and much of the work had to be done in the cold and wet and mud. What is more, the P-47 was new and both the manufacturer and the USAAF were constantly uncovering new issues. As a consequence, maintenance and operational procedures underwent continuous modifications. Further, the mechanics were also newly trained and were doing much of their learning on the job. Finally, parts and equipment were in short supply and aircraft often stayed grounded for want of one or more critical items.

The official history of the 352nd's communications sections recalled the difficulties that were typical across the entire group during the early days:

> Immediately the problem arose which has caused these sections more trouble than anything else from that day to this [late 1944]—lack of supplies and equipment. Lack of major controlled items of equipment hampered training in their use. Lack of sufficient supplies of expendable items hampered maintenance. It was soon discovered that only by worshipping the principle of GRAB could an organization function efficiently: grab replacement parts, grab radio tubes, grab spare sets, grab men. We grabbed.

More basic clerical tasks were also difficult. For whatever reason, the 34th Fighter Squadron couldn't get its officers paid for nearly two months. The system was so broken that the men had to rely on the Red Cross for hardship payments of twenty-five dollars each. They drank and ate at a local bar on credit. It was an absurdity indicative of the sorts of administrative pains the nation's servicemen endured as the military expanded many times over.

Exacerbating everything from flying and maintenance to simply getting around was the fact that the weather in New England was miserable during the early months of 1943. Many of the buildings the men worked and lived in were tarpaper shacks that did little to keep out the cold. Too, the airfields from which the group operated were under continuous construction, and if the ripped up ground wasn't frozen, it was a sodden, muddy mess. Inside, the clerks huddled around ineffective little potbellied stoves to hold off the cold. They were the fortunate ones. Virtually all the aircraft maintenance was performed outside and it was too often an exercise in frigid frustration marked by smashed fingers and torn and bloody knuckles.

Ultimately, although the 352nd's early difficulties were confounding, they were not overwhelming.

One of the pilots who reported for duty as the 352nd was forming was George Preddy. After returning from Australia, Preddy went home on leave before receiving orders to complete a couple of short assignments. His good friend from Australia, Jack Donalson, was already with the 352nd and he politicked successfully to get Preddy into the unit. John C.

Meyer, the commanding officer of the 34th Fighter Squadron, recalled Preddy's arrival on January 15, 1943.

> If ever anyone looked like a nonfighter, it was George. He was small and slight, and physically unimposing. And his voice, words, and demeanor did nothing to modify the impression given by his appearance. He spoke softly, without even a hint of brag-gadocio in word or tone. I later asked Jack [Donalson] if he was sure we had the right Preddy.[2]

Preddy remembered that first meeting and described Meyer as "darn nice." During the period following Preddy's arrival, Meyer assessed his flying abilities and leadership qualities. He liked what he saw and made him a flight commander. As Preddy was one of the more experienced pilots in the 34th, Meyer relied on him to help mentor the youngsters dur-ing the months leading up to the 352nd's deployment overseas.

Of all the officers that made up the 352nd, John C. Meyer was arguably the most capable. And although he never commanded the group, he was widely acknowledged among those who were there as the domi-nant officer during virtually the whole of the 352nd's existence—an excel-lent flyer and a hard, but fair leader.

Following high school, Meyer attended Dartmouth University for two years, where one of his professors remembered, "Johnny Meyer had the brightest mind" of any student he had ever taught. Despite his academic promise, Meyer left Dartmouth to join the Army Air Corps in 1939 and was commissioned a second lieutenant in July 1940. After a stint as a flight instructor, he went to Iceland and flew with the 33rd Fighter Squadron from July 1941 to September 1942. After returning to the States and joining the 352nd, he took command of the 34th Fighter Squadron on December 5, 1942.

George Arnold, one of the men that Meyer later led in combat, recalled: "He was one hell of a leader. I don't think there was anybody in the squadron who wouldn't follow him anyplace he wanted to go; he wouldn't ask anyone to go anyplace or do anything that he wouldn't go or do first. That included everything from bars to dangerous strafing missions."[3]

Fremont Miller graduated from training as part of class 43-B and was assigned to the 328th Fighter Squadron at Westover Field during February

1943. "That was one of the highlights of my life when I was assigned to fly fighter planes. All during training I was told that I would be too large to fit into a fighter plane." Compared to most of his comrades, Miller was a monster at six feet, two inches tall and more than two hundred pounds. "But the P-47 was very roomy and I had no problem at all."

At the time, the 352nd was racing to get itself ready for combat. Miller was part of that race and was sent flying as often as possible in order to pad the hours in his logbook. "I had to fly day and night," he remembered, "because I had to get in the number of hours I needed to catch up with the rest of the pilots who already had the required hours to go overseas." Miller recollected that winter in New England presented some interesting flying: "It was still winter there and snow was piled up on the sides of the runways ten feet high. It was almost like landing in a canal."

The USAAF's dramatic expansion posed all manner of logistical and operational challenges. Consequently, units were split and relocated so often as to confound their coherency and training. Such was the case with the 352nd. On February 17, 1943, the group was temporarily split when the 328th Fighter Squadron was sent to Mitchel Field, near New York City. Only three weeks later, 352nd's headquarters and the 21st and 34th Fighter Squadrons were transferred to Republic Field, Farmingdale, New York.

Training accidents and fatalities occurred almost as soon as the 352nd received its first P-47s during January 1943. In fact, mishaps throughout the USAAF were endemic. It was to be expected when so many young, inexperienced men—trained by other young men only marginally more experienced—were put at the controls of high-performance aircraft.

The 352nd's first losses were especially painful. On February 11, 1943, four lieutenants from the 21st Fighter Squadron—Charles Meyer, Raymond Burke, John Pavlovic, and Eugene Drake—were sent to Providence, Rhode Island, to bring back new P-47s. Visibility dropped to zero following their takeoff and all four men were killed trying to find somewhere to land. It was the first of many times that the weather demonstrated it was just as deadly as the Luftwaffe.

But it wasn't always the youngsters who were killed. The 21st's commanding officer, William J. Hennon, was also an early casualty. He disappeared on March 31, 1943, while flying a BT-14 from Farmington to Groton, Connecticut, to pick up Frank Greene, who had just been released from the hospital.[4] Ted Fahrenwald, a young pilot with the 21st Fighter Squadron, recalled the incident in a letter home on March 31, 1943: "Our squadron CO, Bill Hennon, disappeared the other day. Took off on a routine cross-the-Sound [Long Island] flight and ain't been heard from since. Right after he got off, one of these infamous Long Island pea-soup fogs socked in tight. A great guy he was, with 22 Jap planes to his credit. One of the 10 top fighter aces in the Air Corps."

Actually, Hennon had not been credited with twenty-two aerial victories against the Japanese. He had been in the Philippines with the 21st Fighter Squadron when the war started. He retreated with remnants of that unit and downed seven enemy aircraft while flying the P-40 from Australia and Java during the early months of the war. Nevertheless, he was one of the USAAF's few aces at that point and his loss was sorely felt.

Fahrenwald's recollection of a typical stateside training flight illustrates how ad hoc and unstructured the USAAF's pilot training was during the early part of the war. He described how he and three other 352nd pilots took off on a flight, "for a little instrument practice, but instead we checked each other out on various reckless acrobatics." On that same flight, they also "caught a torpedo boat out on the [Long Island] Sound and gave him a good buzzing."[5]

Not long after, on April 22, 1943, Fahrenwald recalled how similar stunting cost a life. Tom Colby, Edwin Heller, Ray Barnes, and Fahrenwald climbed to 33,000 feet in their P-47s whereupon the leader, Tom Colby, rolled his ship over and dove for the ground at a very steep angle. The other three pilots followed and their speed built quickly. It wasn't long until the heavy fighters were caught hard in the grasp of compressibility.

Fahrenwald forgot all else except what he needed to do to survive. He pushed the throttle full forward and "put both feet on the instrument panel and pulled back on the stick as hard as I could."[6] He might as well have saved his energy. His controls "were solid as though set in concrete, except for sudden violent tail flutter which battered the rudders back and forth." It was only as the big fighter dropped into denser air that it began to respond to Fahrenwald's desperate heaves on the control stick. "The nose came up a fraction and I regained control and was very happy as very few pilots came out of such a dive."

Fahrenwald, Colby, and Heller returned safely. Barnes was missing. It wasn't long before the telephone rang. Fahrenwald recalled that "some character wanted to report a meteor hitting the ground." He, Colby, and Heller took off again and found the crater that Barnes's ship had punched into the sandy Long Island soil. Barnes had not escaped. "That made number eight [non-combat fatalities] for the squadron," Fahrenwald remembered. "Five others quit. That left eleven of the original twenty-four pilots."

These encounters with compressibility were increasingly common not only within the USAAF, but across military aviation in general. The most modern fighters could climb much higher—up to 30,000 feet or more—than previous models. Steep, high-powered dives from those heights quickly took aircraft to speeds they were not intended to handle.

For instance, although the P-47 had a redline—that is, never-exceed—speed of .72 Mach, about 550 miles per hour, it could reach dive velocities that exceeded .85 Mach, nearly 600 miles per hour. At these airspeeds, approaching the speed of sound, the flow of air over the fighter was interrupted or separated and a shock wave was created. This manifested itself in airframe buffeting, decreased elevator authority, and a nose-down pitching moment. Likewise, the rudder became unresponsive. On the wings, the distribution of forces around the ailerons was very dynamic and caused shuddering so violent that the control stick was often snatched out of the pilot's hands. Quite frequently, the stick slammed repeatedly from side to side and bruised the pilot's legs.

It was only after the aircraft slowed as it entered denser air at lower altitudes that a pilot had any chance of recovering. Still, the danger was not over. The massive control inputs that had no effect earlier suddenly became very effective and many pilots blacked out as the controls suddenly "bit" into the air and snatched the fighter out of its dive. Some of those pilots did not regain consciousness before their aircraft fell out of control and crashed. There were even instances of fuselages breaking or wings snapping off under the enormous stresses brought on by high-speed dive recoveries.

Compressibility was poorly understood, even by the pilots. Many of them didn't believe such a phenomenon existed, or were unprepared to acknowledge it until they had experienced it themselves, sometimes with disastrous results. Official training was often sketchy and incomplete; word-of-mouth procedures made the rounds. These included such obvious actions as reducing power (although some pilots insisted on increasing power to full throttle), rolling nose-up trim on the elevators, and fish-tailing to generate drag and slow the aircraft. Some aircraft, including the P-38 and P-47, were eventually equipped with dive brakes that created drag and prevented the aircraft from flying into compressibility. And training improved over time. Although accidents caused by compressibility never went away, they became fewer than they might otherwise have been.

Aside from compressibility, the 352nd's fledgling pilots found many other ways to have accidents. Hayes Button forgot his guns were armed and fired a burst at Don Bryan during a mock dogfight. Another pilot made practice strafing runs against oil storage tanks near Brooklyn and accidentally opened fire. Earl Hayward was killed when he crashed into Hofstra College's Barnard Hall on March 23, 1943, while taking off out of Mitchel Field. Fortunately, no one on the ground was hurt. Another pilot killed himself when he flew into the ground doing aerobatics.

If not infinite, the number of ways that the new flyers found to wreak havoc on themselves and others was certainly considerable. Ted Fahrenwald recalled how Joe Gerst visited mayhem on the Republic factory adjacent to Farmingdale Army Airfield.[7] "The other day, Joe, after towing the target sleeve for our aerial gunnery, buzzed the field and pulled the lever which is supposed to release the long cable and target. Then he peeled up, dumped his gear, and came in to land." Unbeknownst to Gerst, the cable and target sleeve did not separate from his aircraft. Unawares, he continued his turning approach to land. Fahrenwald remembered: "Joe dragged the cable, plus a fifty-pound lead weight down through Republic's parking lot and beat in about fifty shiny automobile tops, hoods, windshields, and such, and then through a sentry box." The sentry was found unhurt, albeit speechless.

In fact, mishaps seemed to be a near-regular feature of Fahrenwald's stateside flying. He nearly lost another comrade on May 23, 1943, while on a training sortie: "Old pal [Donald] McKibben and I took off in tight formation and climbed up to . . . ten feet. Off we went, whooping up and down the beaches, scaring tourists, aircraft spotters, etcetera. Then we really let down, flying abreast, across Peconic Bay out towards the end of Long Island."[8]

Farhrenwald watched McKibben's P-47 settle lower and lower until the thin margin between it and the water disappeared. McKibben remembered that the water of the bay was incredibly smooth and unmarked by even the "faintest ripple." With no waves—that is, no surface definition—the water was like a mirror and blended almost perfectly into the sky. "I thought I was high enough," he recalled, "but suddenly my altitude was two or three feet below sea level. I didn't learn this from the altimeter but rather from the sudden and noisy deceleration as my propeller dug into the water."

McKibben heaved back on the control stick even as the sudden slowing of the aircraft slammed him forward against his harness. Still, he managed to haul the ship free of the water. "I had enough momentum to pull up a few hundred feet. The engine was running, but I wasn't feeling any thrust." It was likely that the propeller, striking the water at a rate of more than a thousand times per minute, was damaged and unable to bite enough air to keep the big fighter airborne. With little in the way of good choices, McKibben decided to put the aircraft down in the sound.

He set up a controlled descent and landed his aircraft on the water. Although his head slammed against something hard inside the cockpit, he was relatively unhurt. "All things considered," he said, "it wasn't a bad ditching. The fuselage was bent right behind the cockpit, so that when the plane finally settled down, the cockpit was near the apex of an inverted V, sticking out of the water." In fact, although he had just flown his aircraft into the water for the second time, McKibben was still dry. "The water did not fill the cockpit right away and I loosened my parachute straps and started to exit."

His egress was complicated by the canopy. "I had tried to slide it back just prior to impact and it was stuck only partially open." Something caught the inflation lanyard on his Mae West life preserver as he struggled to clear the aircraft through the tiny opening. It inflated and made his exit that much more difficult. "I managed to make myself small enough to get out and step onto the right wing," he recounted. "That was when I finally got wet, but only below the knees."

Finally clear of his sinking aircraft, McKibben reached back into the cockpit, wrenched the rubber dinghy free, and inflated it. "I climbed in, waved to Ted, who was circling overhead, and started paddling toward shore. Meanwhile, a concerned citizen rowed a boat out from shore to meet me and escorted me to his home." From there, McKibben was picked up by an amphibious aircraft and, with his head bandaged, was eventually delivered back to Republic Field.

"I was directed to report to the Officer of the Day, Lieutenant Colonel Eugene 'Pop' Clark, who also happened to be the deputy group commander," McKibben remembered. The young lieutenant strode into the room and locked himself at attention in front of Clark's desk. "I gave him the smartest salute I could muster, and reported as ordered. As Officer of the Day, he had his sidearm at his hip. He studied me a long time without saying a word."

Bruised and sore, and with his head swathed in a bandage, McKibben presented a pitiable picture. Finally, Clark reached to his side and pulled the .45-caliber pistol out of its holster. He put it on the desk, pushed it toward McKibben, and asked in a sardonic tone, "Well, do you want to finish the job?"

That evening marked the last time the incident was officially mentioned.

Ted Fahrenwald experienced his fair share of mishaps and managed to damage a number of P-47s long before the 352nd ever got to England. He recounted an incident that took place on April 6, 1943, when he had a newly joined pilot flying on his wing:

So when we land, I am number three, and set down on the old runway neatly. Then I take a look into my rear-vision mirror and wot [sic] do I see but a large radial engine and twelve-foot prop that is increasing in size very rapidly. A P-47 bearing down upon me from the rear. Here's this guy and he's landed much too close behind me and too fast. So I give my ship full throttle and kick her off the runway and he scoots past my tail with an inch to spare. So there I am doing 80 or 90 mph across field and stream and I see a revetment looming up in front of me. I put on brakes and nose over, and in this awkward position I slide into said revetment. Bust up a propeller and various odds and ends. . . . This is the fourth Thunderbolt I've busted up, and this is the second time it ain't been my own fault. The colonel congratulates me, this time for quick thinking, and the other guy has been discarded from the squadron.[9]

Only four days later, on April 10, William Hendrian was nearly killed during a mock dogfight. "One of the other fellows ran into me and chopped off parts of one of my wings and my fuselage right behind the cockpit. I didn't make it back to the base but I was able to belly it into an athletic field without hurting myself or anyone else, so I felt pretty good about that."[10]

Excerpts from George Preddy's diary outline other accidents during this period.[11] On February 22, 1943, he noted: "Hamilton hit a truck on takeoff and made a crash landing minus one wheel. Luckily, he wasn't scratched." On April 27 he recorded, "[Jerry] Powell went up on a hop at 1615 hours and as yet has not been heard from." Powell was killed, likely by a mechanical malfunction. On May 10, Preddy wrote, "Jamison [Robert] spun in landing yesterday afternoon while I was at Islip. Believe his engine cut out on the approach. A nice kid he was." On June 2, he described another accident. "Returning to the field, Strickland fell out of formation at 22,000 feet and went straight into the ground. Almost certainly due to lack of oxygen. He was surely a swell kid."

These incidents are only a sampling of the mishaps, serious and trivial, that marked the 352nd's preparations for combat. They are quite representative of USAAF operations during the war; accidents, rather than combat, accounted for two-thirds of all losses. In fact, whereas the USAAF lost approximately 4,500 aircraft in combat against the Japanese, it crashed or otherwise destroyed more than 7,100 aircraft in the States.[12] The 352nd's experience was consistent with these statistics; it lost more aircraft during its first few months of training than it did during its first several months of combat.

The pilots passed the time they weren't training in myriad ways. Don McKibben remembered that he and his good friend Harold Riley fancied themselves jazz musicians.

> I did not play an instrument, but had convinced myself that I could handle drums. Riles had some experience on drums. Lacking the real thing, we discovered that with a couple of fly swatters and a newspaper, one could do a pretty good imitation of drumming with brushes, which we did, accompanying radio and recording artists such as Benny Goodman, Artie Shaw, etc. Riles and I developed a theory: Fighter pilots who are also jazz musicians, or have a deep appreciation of jazz, are likely to be good teammates in the air. . . . Each senses what others in the ensemble are trying to do, and supports them in the effort, without being asked.[13]

At the same time that the USAAF was forming new fighter groups, it was also training pilots to replace the inevitable losses those new fighter groups would experience. Punchy Powell was one of those replacement pilots. He earned his wings and was commissioned a second lieutenant on January 4, 1943. While the 352nd was training in the frigid northeast, Powell was sent to Florida to train with the 305th Fighter Squadron.

"We were sent to a tiny town southeast of Tallahassee, called Cross City," he remembered.[14] Cross City was little more than a gas station and a few houses. "On my first trip to the post office," Powell recalled, "I opened the door and a pig ran out before I could step in. We were quartered in single-story tarpaper barracks that were about sixty feet long and mounted on stilts so they wouldn't flood during heavy rains. We showered in a separate building and the ground was so sandy you had to shake off your slippers to keep from sanding the floors."

Powell recalled his first day with the 305th: "When we arrived they were flying P-39s and we were all pretty disappointed after having heard what we had about that fighter." The diminutive Bell P-39 Airacobra was not a particularly easy aircraft to fly and had a not wholly-deserved reputation for being of little use except as an easy target for enemy fliers.

"However," Powell continued, "the next day several P-47s were flown in. The ferry pilots flew the P-39s away and left us with the Jugs. These were the early model P-47s with the Curtiss Electric propellers which we found would occasionally run away. This happened to one of our guys during takeoff; he extended a clearing into the woods from the end of the runway. He wasn't hurt and there was little damage to the P-47 except for the big dents in the leading edges of the wings."

"Anyway," recalled Powell, "we had to study the P-47 manual pretty carefully before we got our first flight. It was quite a big jump from the AT-6 to the Thunderbolt but we were so young, stupid, and naïve that we just did it. I don't remember much of a discussion on the subject."

Powell flew the P-47 for the first time on January 30, 1943. "What a hoot! After checking the magnetos at the end of the runway and setting the trim for takeoff, and still a little nervous, I pushed hard on the brakes as I went forward with the throttle." When Powell turned the big fighter loose, it leapt for the far end of the airfield and pushed him hard back into his seat. "The tail came up quickly as I hurtled down the runway," he recalled. "About halfway to the end, I felt the plane getting lighter, and with a little back pressure on the stick, I was airborne and climbing out over the pine tree jungles of Florida."

"After one takeoff and one landing with that big wide landing gear," remembered Powell, "we thought we were in the world's greatest fighter plane. There were about fifty of us and we got about an hour of flight time each day. We also had a BT-14 [North American trainer aircraft] which we used for instrument flying practice."

Just as their counterparts in the 352nd engaged in high-speed, low-altitude tomfoolery with their aircraft in the Northeast, Powell and his comrades did the same in Florida. "We would sometimes fly out over the Gulf of Mexico just barely above the water at the fishing boats. The crews would dive from the decks—they must have just loved to swim!"

Powell's recollections support the fact that most of the units training in the States had very little idea about where they would eventually be sent. "We were issued jungle kits—including a machete—that made us think we were going to the Pacific, or perhaps Africa." This was not unusual; in fact, it wasn't uncommon for units to be shipped to one theater while equipped for operations in another.

"We all flew about fifty hours in the Jugs before we were given orders to Camp Kilmer, New Jersey, for processing overseas. We still had no idea where we were going." It wasn't until they were shipped to Nova Scotia during late March 1943 that it became clear to Powell and his fellow replacement pilots that their final destination was England. A short time later, they embarked aboard the converted French liner *Avant Pasteur* and started across the Atlantic. Powell recalled a night of reflection while en route.

> I found my way one moonlit night to the very bow of the ship and stretched out on my stomach looking forward into the ocean as the ship plowed through the waves. The phosphorescence of the water separating at the bow of the ship was fascinating. It was a moment of lonely reflection. This was too much of a great adventure for me to be truly homesick, but I found myself thinking about the past year of my life and wondering what might lie ahead. I was not a pessimist by any means, but I wondered if I would ever see my folks again and if I would measure up in combat.

Meanwhile, the 352nd was still training.

On April 29, 1943, the 352nd's 21st Fighter Squadron was redesignated as the 486th Fighter Squadron and the 34th Fighter Squadron was redesignated as the 487th Fighter Squadron. These redesignations were unpopular with the pilots of the affected squadrons. In particular, the 21st had a heritage, albeit undistinguished, dating back to World War I of which the men were quite proud. It seemed to them that the new designations served no purpose other than to suit the sensibilities of some unknown bureaucrat. John C. Meyer was particularly displeased as he had been vigorously committed to building unit pride in his 34th Fighter Squadron. In fact, he required his pilots to wear blue ascots and carry riding crops with handles fashioned from spent .50-caliber machine-gun cartridges.

Lieutenant Colonel Joe L. Mason took command of the 352nd on May 17, 1943. A native of Columbus, Ohio, he entered the Army Air Corps only five years earlier and was commissioned a second lieutenant in October 1938. During his brief career, he had served as a bomber pilot and a flight instructor. He transitioned to fighters and served briefly as the commander of the 315th Fighter Squadron. Immediately prior to taking command of the 352nd, he was the operations officer of the Philadelphia Air Defense Wing.

Mason was a good example of the risks the USAAF was forced to assume as it expanded. He had been commissioned less than five years when he was made commander of the 352nd. It was almost bizarre that he was promoted from second lieutenant to lieutenant colonel during that time. Yet it was not atypical during this period: there simply weren't more experienced officers available. As a point of reference to what had been more traditional, Haywood Hansell, one of the USAAF's great thinkers and one of the Eighth Air Force's early combatant commanders, was commissioned as a second lieutenant in 1929. During the succeeding ten years, he was promoted only once and was still a first lieutenant in 1939.

Regardless, Mason would shortly lead three squadrons of aircraft—and all their men and equipment—into combat an ocean away.

The 352nd neared full strength as personnel continued to arrive through the spring of 1943. Rather than a collection of individuals that didn't know each other, as had been the case only a few months earlier, the group operated more and more as a cohesive, fully trained team. Still, men occasionally arrived and left as assignments were changed for a variety of reasons—or as was seemingly quite often the case, for reasons that no one could fathom. One of the reasons that made sense was the selection and transfer of enlisted men for officer training.

John C. Meyer, the commanding officer of the 487th, didn't like it regardless of whether or not it made sense. He gathered his men and informed them that requests for officer training—regardless of whether they were qualified or not—would be disapproved. The time was fast approaching when the group would be ordered into combat and he needed a complete and unified team. Although any number of his enlisted men might have made excellent officers, their departure would do the 487th no good. He needed good mechanics, armorers, radiomen, and such. As they were already trained and part of the squadron, Meyer saw no benefit to the squadron in allowing them to leave.

There is little doubt that Meyer's declaration did not sit well with some of the men. Certainly a few of them had aspirations of becoming airmen themselves and Meyer stood in the way. Nevertheless, his logic was arguably sound and the 487th proved to be a very effective unit up and down the rank structure largely because of his leadership.

Meyer gave George Preddy more and more responsibility as the 487th upped its flying tempo in preparation for deploying overseas. Nevertheless, as the squadron commander, he also played no favorites. When Preddy ditched an equipment inspection before it was over Meyer put him "under arrest of quarters" and restricted him to the base for the remainder of the 352nd's time in the United States. It was a typical example of Meyer's approach to discipline; he expected his men to adhere to regulations, and when they didn't—regardless of who they were—he held them accountable. Ultimately, though, as the exact date of the unit's departure was unknown, Meyer lifted Preddy's restriction on May 31.

The 352nd's three different squadrons converged on Westover Field in Massachusetts, during late May 1943. There were more pilots than aircraft and the 486th's Ted Fahrenwald made the trip from Farmingdale by car. His letter home recounted not only the difficulty of wartime travel when tires were rationed, but also the rash exuberance of the young men the nation was readying for war:

> I drove my V-8 up, and a hilarious trip it was. Rocky [Lloyd Rauk] and Frank Cutler and me. After the fourth [tire] blowout we got angry—and being full of beer, too—we beat great dents and holes in the car with crowbars, threw the hood away, wrenched off the headlights, and I wanted to roll it down a cliff up in Connecticut somewhere. But Cutler pleaded for the old car and we finally got her up here. No windows, tho, and with an axe we cut a navigator's hatch in the roof.[15]

During the final weeks of spring 1943, the men of the 352nd still had no clear idea of where they would be ordered. This point is made clear by the letter that Ted Fahrenwald wrote on June 3, 1943: "Time in the States grows short," he recalled. Will soon be lookin' down on a bunch of furriners. Can't tell you when we're leaving because I don't know . . . twenty-four hours or days, since all incoming and outgoing mail, phone calls, telegrams, etc. are now censored. Please no telegram wishing me bon voyage on my summer cruise to England (?), India (?), Kiska (?), Greenland (?), Australia (?) All I can chat about is last month's weather and other similar excitin' topics."[16]

Although they were only a short time away from deploying overseas—and despite the fact that they had been training together for

months—the men of the 352nd were still green. Farhenwald's letter of
June 4 recounts just how inexperienced the group was:

> Another thriller-diller today. The three squadrons of our group
> flew together. Thirty-six P-47s in tight formation. At takeoff, the
> weather was lousy . . . very dense haze, almost a fog. Anyway,
> down the runway we go, one at a time and into the air. We form
> up in short order, and when we get upstairs the weather closes in
> solid. So we sit on top of the clouds at 10,000 feet, thirty-six of us
> careening around together like sheep. Then down we dive looking
> for the ground thru the now-heavy fog. We hit some real soup, and
> the squadrons (twelve ships each) get separated and lost. My gang
> feels its way down to 1,000 feet and we kin barely see the ground
> and can see nothing out to the sides—hardly one another. . . .
> Finally, we spot an American [Airlines] airliner and tell him we're
> lost and low on gas, and to lead us somewhere, hey?[17]

With the airliner's help, Fahrenwald and the rest of the 486th made it
back to Westover. Likewise, the 487th and the 328th also returned without
losing any aircraft although Fahrenwald noted that all the pilots were
"wringing wet from honest sweat and very low on fuel." The three
squadrons had done little more than take off, climb through several thousand feet of clouds, and get lost. It was an ignominious performance. The
352nd was expected to levy a beating upon the vaunted Luftwaffe over
Europe, not lose its way on a training mission while flying out of its home
base in the States.

During early June 1943, while still at Westover, the unit gave up its
aircraft and much of its equipment preparatory to going overseas. Consequently, the pilots had too much time on their hands. They often partied in
the evenings and the festivities occasionally got out of hand. On one night
in particular, someone in the 486th Fighter Squadron's barracks unwound
the fire hose and turned the water on full. "It was a big, fat, canvas fire
hose that sent water cascading down the stairs in a miniature Niagara
Falls," recalled Don McKibben.[18] "And I remember that Frank Greene had
an urge to converse with someone in the next room. As the partitions
between the rooms were nothing more than a single sheet of gypsum board,
he simply butted a hole in the wall with his head and started talking."

The 486th's commander, Luther Richmond, woke up when the shooting started. He looked out his window and noted the lights and clamor coming from the adjacent barracks. Richmond crawled out of bed, put his uniform on, and strode toward the sounds of the party. Aside from the gunplay, an additional clue that things were seriously out of control was the water gushing down the stairwell from the second floor and out onto the ground. Richmond's shoes and trousers were soaked by the time he reached the top of the stairs.

He was mad. But he was given a start when he turned down the long corridor that ran the length of the second floor. There, Frank Cutler, one of the 486th's young pilots, stood in the stream of water that rushed down the middle of the hall. He was very drunk. And naked. And he was holding a .45-caliber pistol.

Richmond took only a second to recover his wits before ordering Cutler to hand over the gun. Cutler had a wild look on his face and didn't seem at all inclined to obey his commanding officer. Richmond shouted the order again. Cutler finally dropped his eyes, shuffled over to Richmond, and gave him the pistol.

A bill for $1,500 in damage caught up with the 486th in England several months later.

After he arrived in England and passed through a week or so of administrative processing, Punchy Powell was sent to the airbase at Atcham, near Shrewsbury, on the border with Wales. It was where the USAAF's P-47 RTU (Replacement Training Unit) was located. Although fully trained fighter groups like the 352nd were sent to England in their entirety, the USAAF used Atcham to keep replacement pilots like Powell trained and ready.

Because there were not enough P-47s to go around, the replacement pilots were allowed to fly whatever was parked around the airfield, including some war-weary Spitfires. "I flew about twenty hours in the Spitfire," recalled Powell. "It was a good flying airplane but it lacked range."

"Johnny Woods was one of the guys in our bunch I was quite fond of," Powell recollected. "He had an Alabama drawl you couldn't cut with a knife. We used to get flight time by taking turns flying the little L-4 Piper Cub together. We were cruising one day at a couple of hundred feet when we spotted two girls on horseback on a winding lane. They looked pretty good to us so we circled them while we followed them to their village,

Eaton Constantine." When they arrived at the largest house in the village, the two young women dismounted and handed their horses to a pair of groomsmen.

Powell and Woods were not ready to simply wing away. "Johnny pulled a piece of paper and a pencil out of his flight suit pocket and wrote a note which said, 'We'll be over to see you soon.' He wrapped the note around the pencil with a rubber band and I flew down between the Dutch barn and the big house where everyone in the small village was watching."

Woods dropped the note. "We watched them pick it up and read it," Powell remembered. When the girls waved, Powell wagged the little aircraft's wings and headed for Atcham.

They rode bikes to the village a few days later. "Standing near the gate was a tall English woman," Powell recalled. "I greeted her in my best southern manner and swung my finger in a circle and explained that we were the pilots who were flying overhead a few days earlier. She smiled and said, 'Yes, I suppose you came to meet our daughters?'" Powell and Woods allowed that they indeed were eager to meet the girls.

Their home was Eaton House and the girls were Mary and Kay Brookes, daughters of a successful farmer and horseman. The groomsmen that Powell and Woods had noted from their aircraft were actually Italian POWs who had been sent to work on the farm.

The Brookes family was very gracious to the two Americans; Powell and Woods continued to visit through the rest of that spring and into the summer. Powell remembered being amused by the Italian POWs. "We were usually in uniform and when we entered the yard, they'd throw us a fascist salute."

But the friendly dynamic was dealt a sorrowful blow after a few weeks. "Johnny and I were out flying Spitfires one day," remembered Powell. "We were buzzing and he got too low and clipped a tree and went in and was killed."

"Soon after Johnny was killed, I took Charlie Reed on a visit with me." Powell said. "As cocky as I was, I figured I couldn't handle two English girls. Charlie had been in the cavalry and knew and loved horses. Mr. Brookes and Charlie immediately hit it off because of their mutual love for horses—he even let Charlie ride one of his horses in a race."

Powell recalled the bucolic character of the relationship: "The girls sometimes packed sandwiches and we rode up on the Wrekin, a heavily wooded mound of earth which stood up from the surrounding countryside. They were nice company and we were invited to join them for a couple village dances and they occasionally joined us at the officers club."

And although the two Americans spent quite a bit of time with Kay and Mary, their friendships grew at a measured pace that never became physical. Before their affections evolved into anything more, the demands of the war ended it all. Powell and Reed both received orders to operational units.

On May 23, 1943, Powell was in Atcham building flight time. At the same time, the 352nd's men were still in the States putting the finishing touches on their training. Back across the Atlantic, the Eighth Air Force was steadily evolving; the raids it was putting over Europe were increasing in size and sophistication. Meanwhile, in Germany, Messerschmitt's engineers were frantically developing the Me-262 twin-engine jet fighter to counter the growing strength of the American raids.

On that day, *General der Jagdflieger* Adolf Galland, the commander of the Luftwaffe's fighter forces, traveled to Messerschmitt's flight test airfield at Lechfeld to fly the Me-262 for the first time. The flight made him an ardent believer in jet propulsion. The aircraft had a top speed that was nearly a hundred miles per hour faster than the latest propeller-driven types. Galland recognized that such performance would render American bomber escorts impotent. Barely able to contain his enthusiasm, he wrote an animated note to Field Marshal Erhard Milch, the Luftwaffe's Air Inspector General, who was responsible for aircraft development and production. Galland closed the missive with a gross understatement: "This aircraft opens up completely new possibilities."

And yet, with the Germans on the cusp of being able to introduce a radically new capability, the 352nd had yet to deploy to England and was months away from flying its first combat sorties in the P-47.

Only a couple of days before the 352nd was due to ship overseas, Luther Richmond, the commander of the 486th Fighter Squadron, called his pilots together. He talked of the seriousness of the 352nd's mission; he wanted them to be sure of what they were going to be asked to do, and to be equally sure they were prepared to do it. He closed the meeting by directing any of them who were not committed to making war to see him afterwards.

Three men approached him after the meeting. They were immediately sent out of the unit with no time or opportunity to gather their belongings. Richmond did not want them or their misgivings to affect the remainder of the squadron. It was time for war and he wanted only those who were ready for it.

CHAPTER 3

To England

The 352nd, aboard the RMS *Queen Elizabeth*, sailed out of New York on July 1, 1943. The ship was a new one, having been put into service only three years earlier in 1940. Originally built as a passenger liner, wartime exigencies required the ship to operate as a troop transport. The 352nd's men, along with thousands of men from other units, were crammed into stinking cabins strung with rope hammocks stacked in columns of six. It was nearly impossible to turn around without bumping into someone else, yet the men passed the time peaceably enough reading or talking, but especially gambling. By the end of the passage, a small number of savvy gamblers possessed most of the cash aboard the ship.

The *Queen Elizabeth* was fast and required no escorts. The trip passed quickly and the men disembarked at Gourock, Scotland, on July 6 and subsequently traveled through Scotland and northern England by train. After a short time in transient quarters at RAF Watton, the 352nd took possession of the airfield at Bodney on July 8, 1943.

Bodney was located in a region of East Anglia in Norfolk County characterized by gently rolling terrain. It was approximately twenty miles south of King's Lynn, thirty-five miles northeast of Cambridge, eighty miles north of London, and forty-five miles west of the North Sea. It was a grass airfield bounded by a hard-surfaced road and had only been in existence since 1940. The RAF used it for a couple of years as an auxiliary bomber base for nearby Watton but it had seen only sporadic use for several months prior to the 352nd's arrival. The living facilities were Spartan, consisting mainly of Nissen huts for billeting. They were perennially cold and damp, and the men often complained that they were little more than

"glorified sewer pipes." Many of the main buildings were more permanent, being built of brick or cinder block. It was officially designated Army
Air Forces F-141.

By the time the 352nd arrived at Bodney on July 8, 1943, the Eighth
Air Force had been flying combat operations for almost a year. It flew its
first mission, a tiny raid of a dozen B-17s, on August 17, 1942. The effort
was little more than a proof of concept and there is no indication that the
Germans were impressed.

The genesis of the USAAF in Europe began in February 1942 when
Brig. Gen. Ira Eaker, the head of VIII Bomber Command, arrived in England with a staff of six. Carl Spaatz, Eaker's superior officer, was made
head of the Eighth Air Force and joined him during July that same year.

Both were close confidants of Arnold and the careers of all three had
crossed continuously during the decades following World War I. Spaatz
was the only one of them to have seen combat and he shot down two German aircraft during a very brief stint at the front. Although they had different styles, both Eaker and Spaatz were men who got things done. Whereas
Eaker, despite his poor, rural upbringing, was a polished man of letters,
Spaatz was shrewd, brusque, and forceful. Each was the perfect comple-
ment to the other.

As the USAAF's effort against the Germans expanded during late
1942, Spaatz was promoted to command of all the American air forces in
Europe and the Eighth was given to Eaker in December. By the time the
352nd arrived in England during the summer of 1943, Eaker—by now a
major general—was guiding the Eighth through a metamorphosis that
would ultimately turn it into the most powerful air force in history. Nevertheless, at that point, it was not. Rather, it was fighting a desperate air war
while simultaneously laying the administrative, logistical, and operational
groundwork necessary to assimilate the huge wave of men and material
coming from the United States.

The 352nd was among the units at the fore of that wave.

A great deal of tumult marked the history of the Luftwaffe during the
time leading up to the 352nd's arrival at Bodney. This upheaval was pri-

marily due to personalities. The largest of all belonged to *Reichsmarschall* Hermann W. Göring, the Commander in Chief of the Luftwaffe. Born in Bavaria in 1893, the son of a diplomat and judge, Göring was a precocious and strong-minded child who was indulged at every turn by family and friends. From an early age, he was enamoured with the notion of adventure and chivalry, but was an indifferent student at best.

He received a regular commission in the Prussian army in 1912. After the outbreak of World War I, he was sent to the Vosges region but the posting didn't offer him enough action. After his application for duty as a pilot was rejected by his commander, he simply detached himself without orders and made his way to a flying unit in Darmstadt. There, again without orders, he flew several missions as an aerial observer and gradually assimilated himself into the unit; such was the power of his personality. In his capacity as an aerial observer, he subsequently won the Iron Cross, Second and First Classes.

After taking leave and paying for his own flying lessons, he started flying combat operations as a pilot at the start of 1917. He was subsequently posted to a series of different fighter squadrons, or *Jastas*, where he tallied a number of aerial victories early on. He was later wounded and his scoring record stagnated although he received a number of awards, including the coveted *Pour le Mérite*, the Blue Max. During the summer of 1918, he was made the commander of *Jagdgeschwader* 1 (1st Fighter Wing), better known as Manfred von Richthofen's Flying Circus, and held that post until the end of the war. He finished the war credited with twenty-two aerial victories.

Despite his successes, Göring's arrogance made him unpopular with his peers. Feeling betrayed and embittered by Germany's surrender, he tried his hand at a number of flying jobs without achieving any real successes. He fell in love with and married the Swedish Baroness Carin von Kantzow, the estranged wife of Baron Nils von Kantzow. He also joined the Nazi party and gained the confidence of Adolf Hitler, who put him in charge of the *Sturmabteilung*. These were Hitler's feared Storm Troopers, or Brown Shirts. Göring was badly injured during the Beer Hall Putsch of 1923 and during his recovery became addicted to morphine; it was a dependency from which he never really recovered.

There followed a period of sickness and mental instability during which he lived an itinerant lifestyle in various countries and relied a great deal on the generosity of friends. He finally returned to Germany, re-established contact with Hitler, and won a seat to the Reichstag in 1928. When Hitler was appointed Chancellor on January 30, 1933, Göring was named to a number of posts, among which was Reich Minister for Aviation. On

Hitler's renouncement of the Versailles Treaty in 1935, the Luftwaffe was publicly revealed and Göring was confirmed as its commander. By 1940, he had been named *Reichsmarschall*, second in power only to Hitler.

Göring achieved these successes mainly through his force of character and loyalty to Hitler. Although he was extremely bright, his was an innate intelligence rather than one that was built on study and academics. He was cunning, with an enormous capacity for magnanimity, which he exhibited regularly on the behalf of friends, subordinates, and even persecuted Jews. He was an extremely dedicated family man with a great love for children. On the other hand, he had a coarse, bombastic, even ruthless side and did not brook challenges to his authority. He sometimes went on tirades during which he threatened to have people shot. He carried himself with an air of self-confidence—or arrogance—that was so natural as to be forgiven by most. In all of Germany, perhaps all of the world, he saw Hitler as his only superior.

But Göring was also weak. He had a fondness for soft living and fine things, and he loved to dress in outlandish uniforms that crossed the line into costumery. He grew obese over time and was caricatured and lampooned because of it. Although he had been an ardent advocate of a first-class air force during the first few years at its head, he gradually lost interest and devoted much of his time to collecting stolen art from across occupied Europe. He became peevish and tended to isolate himself following the Luftwaffe's defeat in the Battle of Britain. His interest in commanding the Luftwaffe diminished further even as increasingly powerful bomber raids began to turn Germany into rubble, both day and night.

Because Göring did very little real work, he needed someone to do it for him. Erhard Milch was that man. Milch, who served as an artilleryman during World War I, and later as an aerial observer, was the son of a navy pharmacist. By the end of the war, he had risen to the rank of captain and was made commander of *Jagdgruppe* 6 (6th Fighter Group). After the war, he resigned his commission and played a leading role in the evolution of Germany's civil aviation system that culminated in his assignment as director of the nation's flag carrier, Deutsche Lufthansa AG.

Milch was recognized as a brilliant technician and an organizational wizard. Too, he knew Göring and had helped him when he was looking for employment during the 1920s. He had additionally made Deutsche Lufthansa aircraft available to the Nazis during Hitler's 1932 political campaign. The Nazis didn't forget, and when they came to power, Milch was made State Secretary of Aviation on February 22, 1933. He was one of those seemingly tireless individuals and this characteristic—combined with his great personal ambition—covered nicely for Göring's antipathy to anything that resembled real work. Promotions and responsibilities continued until Milch, who was also named Göring's deputy, was made *Generalfeldmarschall* in 1940.

Milch's position of power was somewhat awkward because his father was a Jew. Because Göring could be practical where his personal interests were concerned, and additionally because he didn't particularly share Hitler's hatred of the Jews, he papered over Milch's inconvenient parentage. He secured a completely fabricated affidavit from Milch's mother declaring that she had committed adultery with a lesser German aristocrat, Hermann von Bier, and that Erhard Milch had been born from that illicit affair. Göring bragged in this instance and in others, "I will say who is a Jew and who is not!"[1]

Milch was a chief driving factor in the meteoric rise of the Luftwaffe. Nevertheless, he still encountered difficulties caused in part by his ego and ambition and in part by typical pettiness, jealousy, and ignorance. He was often stymied by the Luftwaffe General Staff, which reported directly to Göring. As Göring's deputy, Milch believed, logically, that the staff also worked for him. The staff didn't agree and further resented Milch's power because he had not been a military careerist. Perhaps what irked the staffers most was the fact that he immersed himself in their business so deeply that he knew as much or more about it than they. And he was stubborn.

Göring did little or nothing to mitigate this friction and it persisted throughout Milch's career. Another source of problems that dogged the Luftwaffe's ability to perform was Göring's indifference to the mundane but necessary work required to build and operate an air force. Although Göring understood combat aviation at a tactical level, he had no experience or interest in the vast administrative effort necessary to develop and manufacture aircraft, and to train the men required to supply, maintain, and operate them—among the myriad other necessary tasks.

Hitler's meddling was additionally bothersome. The Führer consistently mandated poorly considered regulations or decisions on aircraft types and armament. Even Göring lamented Hitler's obtuseness about combat aviation and the Luftwaffe: "The Führer does not ask me *what kind* of bombers I have, he only wants to know *how many*!"

The cases of Ernst Udet and Hans Jeschonnek provide additional perspective on just how dysfunctional the Luftwaffe's leadership was under Göring. Udet, having scored sixty-two aerial victories, was Germany's second-highest scoring ace during World War I. He was a superb pilot and an excellent tactician. He was also a flamboyant and well-loved character who had a taste for good liquor and beautiful women. In this, he was not so different from his wartime acquaintance, Hermann Göring.

What he was not was an organizer or an administrator in the sense that Milch was. Notwithstanding that fact, he joined the Luftwaffe soon after it was formed and played a role in its evolution and growth, especially its development of the dive bomber. He eventually rose in rank and importance to become the Luftwaffe's Director of Air Armaments.

Udet, however, was wholly unsuited for the job and when the Luftwaffe was staggered by the RAF during the Battle of Britain, and later during the invasion of the Soviet Union, Göring blamed Udet. Near the end of 1941, the pressure became too much and Udet, an alcoholic, killed himself with a gunshot to the head on November 17.

Hans Jeschonnek was also a World War I fighter pilot, although he enjoyed much less success than Udet, having been credited with only two aerial victories. On the other hand, he was brilliant at all the things Udet was not. He was a superb staff officer and strategist, and he understood politics. Jeschonnek rose to become Chief of the General Staff of the Luftwaffe before the war; however, like Udet, Jeschonnek became a whipping boy for Göring as the Luftwaffe began to falter. And like Udet again, he could not stand the pressure and committed suicide on August 18, 1943.

During its operational life, the pilots of the 352nd were primarily concerned about Germany's fighters. The man in charge of the Luftwaffe's fighter arm was Adolf Galland. Galland joined the Luftwaffe soon after its inception and flew ground-attack missions during the Spanish Civil War as part of Germany's Condor Legion. At the start of World War II, the charismatic Galland flew ground-attack missions again before convincing his superiors to let him transition to fighters.

It was an excellent decision. Galland flew Me-109s during the fall of France in 1940 and subsequently during the Battle of Britain. He proved to be not only an excellent pilot, but a superb and immensely-liked leader. By late 1941, he had scored nearly 100 aerial victories when the commander of Germany's fighter forces (*General der Jagdflieger*), Werner Mölders, was killed in a flying accident. Galland, who was commanding JG 26 (*Jagdgeschwader* 26) in France, was subsequently leapfrogged over many senior officers to replace Mölders. He was twenty-nine years old.

Whereas Göring was lazy and bombastic, and Milch was ambitious, Galland was forthright, compelling, and not easily intimidated by his superiors. Moreover, he knew his job and was eager to get it done right. Thrust into his new position straight from combat, no one in the Luftwaffe knew better than he what was needed to keep Germany secure from the Allied air offensives that were soon to come. Galland's personality and forcefulness would clash dramatically against the arrogant ignorance of his superiors through the end of the war.

In the end, the Luftwaffe fighter force that contested the 352nd, the USAAF, and the rest of the Allies was one built largely by Milch, led by Galland, and hamstrung by Göring and Hitler. Of course, virtually none of the 352nd's pilots knew or even cared. For the most part, they just wanted to fight.

Other than a couple of training hacks, there were no aircraft at Bodney when the 352nd arrived. However, it was only a few days before the first P-47s began to trickle in. George Preddy, always eager to be in the air, hadn't changed. Ralph Hamilton remembered that the first available aircraft was wrecked almost immediately and that Preddy wasted no time climbing into the next one as soon as it arrived. "He gave us a great buzz job; as he went across the field, he pulled up into a barrel roll. There was no problem, but he soon discovered that his landing gear was still extended. I don't think he ever lived that one down!"[2]

As more and more P-47s arrived, the group's pilots picked up where they left off in the States. Training began anew but it was tailored to the tactics that the preceding groups from VIII Fighter Command had developed. As was typical for a newly arrived unit, seasoned pilots from other groups as well as VIII Fighter Command headquarters were temporarily assigned to help acclimate the 352nd.

Besides the pilots, the maintenance and support personnel readied for the coming operations. Although much of their equipment didn't arrive for nearly a month, there was still plenty to do. John C. Meyer remembered this work: "As we accepted and modified airplanes, stacked bombs, and stored pile upon pile of ammunition, a bond of excitement encompassed our polyglot group and drew us into closer camaraderie. This strange community, particularly in an aura of danger, dropped its cosmopolitan values and substituted valor, life, and discretion."[3]

While the 352nd was readying for combat during July 1943, the Eighth Air Force's bomber groups flew ten missions over the continent and sustained a 6.6 percent loss rate.[4] Although seemingly small at first blush, such losses meant that the average bomber crew could not expect to survive the required mission count of twenty-five. As most losses during that part of the war were caused by Luftwaffe fighters, the Eighth's bomber crews were desperate for more and longer-ranged escorts. To their way of thinking, the 352nd couldn't get into combat soon enough.

The situation was worse the following month, August 1943. The Eighth flew only seven missions, two of which penetrated into Germany. The first was sent on August 12 to Bochum and Bonn. The loss rate was 10 percent.[5] Less than a week later, the Eighth mounted its infamous raids against Regensburg and Schweinfurt. The carnage was even more horrific; a total of sixty aircraft were lost and many more were badly damaged. The loss rate was nearly 20 percent. Almost all the bombers that were lost were shot down when they flew beyond the range of the P-47 groups that were assigned to escort them.

Although the Eighth Air Force's fighter component, VIII Fighter Command, hadn't yet rated them prepared for combat, the 352nd's men were ready to get into the fight. George Preddy's diary entry for July 28, 1943, reflects this: "Flew down to Debden today where the old Eagle outfit is stationed. They sure have a good setup. The squadron I visited this afternoon was on a Ramrod [bomber escort] mission this morning and accounted for five FW 190s to a loss of two. Another group of P-47s shot down sixteen. This sure makes a guy want to get some action." Preddy's entry for the following day reflected his continuing boredom: "Still having quite a few recognition classes. Otherwise little else of value."[6]

Things only got worse. It was three weeks later, on August 18, when he remarked in his diary: "Getting rather fed up with sitting around when the other outfits are getting all the action." On August 28, he noted: "Diary discontinued until something interesting happens."[7]

Punchy Powell made it to the 352nd during August 1943. "My good friend Fred 'Pappy' Yochim and I had gone through all of training together and we both ended up at Atcham. For whatever reason, he was sent to the 352nd as a replacement pilot ahead of me. After a couple of weeks he approached the commanding officer of the 328th, Major Everett Stewart, and told him about me. And that's how I ended up in the 352nd."

Punchy Powell remembered his first exposure to Bodney and the 352nd. "When I arrived in August 1943 I was picked up at the train station [Watton] by a sergeant driving a jeep. We drove through the night for a short while until arriving at a mansion. It was Clermont Hall. The night was pitch black. I managed to get out of the jeep with my B4 bag and trench coat and open the first of the blackout doors at the entrance without falling down."

Powell dragged his bag into the small space and let the outside door close behind him before he opened the interior door. The bright lights inside nearly blinded him. "The first thing I saw as my eyes adjusted was a pilot climbing the grand stairwell with a drunk girl over his shoulder. She waved at me. I put my bag down, dropped my coat on top of it, and thought to myself that I'd found a home!"

Although the group was housed in Nissen huts on the airfield when it first arrived at Bodney, Clermont Hall was loaned to the USAAF through a Lend-Lease Act arrangement and the 352nd's officers were relocated there a month or so later. "It was pretty much stripped of the portraits and other nice furnishings," Powell remembered, "but there was a snooker table that we used quite a bit." The men were billeted two or more to a room depending on its size.

Outside of motion pictures, most of the men had never seen such a place. To live so grandly was almost otherworldly; most of them grew up in much more modest circumstances. As might be expected, they adapted readily. Gordon Cartee remembered that he looked forward to flying a mission and returning to dress in his battle jacket as it enhanced the enjoyment of a fine martini before dinner.

The English women also appreciated the estate and the men who were temporarily living there. "While we were still living in Clermont Hall," Powell recalled, "someone made a photo of me on my cot next to the wall. Up above me on the wall were a couple swastikas. I sent the photo home to my folks and my mother wrote back asking if those swastikas indicated victories. I wrote back to her and answered that yes, they were victories in a manner of speaking, but not the flying kind."

The 352nd's flyers stayed at Clermont Hall until mid-October 1943 at which time they returned to their Nissen huts at Bodney.

CHAPTER 4

Combat

The 352nd Fighter Group flew its first mission on September 9, 1943; it was little more than a patrol that didn't take the group too far afield. Regardless, the men prepared as seriously as if they were flying all the way to Berlin. Indeed, these early missions were designed as much to ease the pilots into combat flying as they were to have an operational impact. The group's intelligence section recalled how months of training and preparation on its part ensured the pilots went to their aircraft as well-prepared as possible.

> There before them on the large briefing map they could see their route, represented by a brilliant red ribbon, running from Bodney out from England over the North Sea, into enemy territory and back home. The courses of other fighter groups and bombers, U.S. and Allied, were also shown, flak information, everything to give the pilot an accurate picture of the mission. It was a dramatic portrayal—the pilots seated in the darkened room, the map and group leader in the flood lights, blackboards showing runway in use, wind direction, squadron order of take off, course to be flown by magnectic [*sic*] heading and distance, check points, time of take off, etc. . . . Colonel Mason glanced at the operational clock, called for synchronization [of] watches, announced take off time and the first briefing was at an end.[1]

Nothing noteworthy happened on the first mission. The group's second mission was launched later that same day. The mission summary report notes that it was recalled by higher headquarters although Fred Allison's diary declared that the group did make it over the continent: "Big news. Became operational last night 10 pm. First escort mission for me this afternoon over Ostend, Belgium. No activity, no enemy sighted."[2]

The third effort, five days later on September 14, was just more than an hour-and-a-half run across the North Sea to Holland. It was unremarkable except that the 328th Fighter Squadron's William Alm inexplicably disappeared and was never heard from again. The group's first loss on a combat mission was one that couldn't even be explained. It was sad and frustrating. It came on top of the death of Arthur Eaker (no relation to Ira), also of the 328th Fighter Squadron. He was killed a day earlier while landing after a local flight.

No enemy aircraft were sighted on the group's fourth mission on September 14; however, a few were spotted a day later but were too far away to engage. Nothing was seen a week later on September 22 when the sixth and seventh missions were flown. On the seventh mission, eight of the group's forty-eight aircraft—more than 15 percent—aborted. It was an indication that the unit's maintenance effort was still somewhat green. Predictably, no enemy aircraft were encountered on the eighth and ninth missions flown on September 23 and September 24. The ninth mission was noteworthy as the three squadrons put a total of fifty-five aircraft aloft; it was a fine answer to the poor showing of a couple of days earlier.

The group's run of bad luck continued on September 26, 1943. An excerpt from the mission summary report for September 27th almost sounded like wishful thinking: "Bogies believed sighted vicinity Knocke [Holland] headed up coast." It was more than ten days before the 352nd flew again. On October 8, no enemy aircraft were encountered, nor did the Germans show on the following day.

The mission summary reports during this period read like a laundry list of non-events. Admittedly, the group's initial assignments had them operating close to England where they were expected to build experience rather than find action, but even later, the group's encounters with the enemy were fleeting at best. Indeed, the Luftwaffe was never sighted on most missions.

So, through no fault of its own, after a month of operations that included thirteen missions, the 352nd had nothing to show for everything that had been invested in it. And that investment had been considerable. Notwithstanding the sixty or so aircraft the group had on hand, it had trained for half a year on an equal number of aircraft back in the States. All that flying required scarce fuel, oil, and other material.

But those costs were only part of the equation. Not to be discounted was the tremendous expense to train not just the 100 or so pilots, but also the much more numerous enlisted men who maintained the aircraft, performed the administrative tasks, cooked the food, did the laundry, and manned the control towers amongst many, many other duties. Too, there were ground officers—roughly 100—who led the enlisted men and performed other specialized tasks. Further, there were the costs associated with building the tremendous infrastructure—airfields, barracks, and such—that was necessary to wage a war. Finally, just getting the men and material to where they needed to be to fight was very expensive; the United States built thousands of ships for just this purpose.

This brief compilation describes only a portion of the considerable investment the nation had put into the 352nd. And it doesn't count the lives that had been lost to that point—many in training—including William Alm during the third mission. They represented a human cost that was simply not quantifiable.

The men were as dissatisfied as anyone. In fact, they wanted nothing more than to fly and fight. Ted Fahrenwald wrote: "The only hard feelings ever stirred up amongst the pilots are created when the schedule for these [*sic*] flying a mission is juggled, and certain pilots are replaced by others. Then the air is filled with sad cries: 'Goddam it, Joe flew the last two while I sat here on my tail and now he's goin' on this 'un! And I ain't, goddam it.'"[3] The desire for real combat burned hot in the young pilots.

Don McKibben recalled his feelings during that time: "The tension, at least in my 'C' Flight, built to the point where guys were becoming pretty irritable." That irritability was evident one evening during the period when a pilot in McKibben's hut was being kept awake by a raucous card came. His entreaties for them to end their game were unsuccessful and he resolved the impasse to his favor when he grabbed his .45-caliber pistol and shot the lights out with three quick shots.

The 352nd's fourteenth mission on October 10, 1943, marked a slight change in its fortunes. Although the pilots never got a chance to fire their guns, they saw many more enemy aircraft than they had encountered during all their previous sorties combined. An excerpt from the mission summary report listed the various encounters:

Enemy A/C seen immediately after R/V with bombers. They followed along penetration track, keeping out of fighter range, and made feints at top cover squadron. In vicinity of Hortogenbusch ['s-Hertogenbosch], flight of three (3) led by Captain Jackson, 486th Fighter Squadron, turned in on attack at approximately 12 enemy aircraft which broke formation and scattered. Upon leaving bombers at point 10 miles north-west Wessel, 12 ME-109's sighted making contrails at approximately 32,000 feet. On withdrawal, 3 or 4 ME 109's followed flight of 486th Squadron out of Dutch Coast but made no attack.

Still, seeing enemy aircraft was not the same as shooting them down. There were two significant issues that kept the 352nd's pilots from scoring. First, there was no compelling reason for the Luftwaffe fighter pilots to attack the bombers while the American fighters were in close escort. They could simply look for gaps in the escort coverage or wait until the escorts ran short of fuel and were compelled to return to England.

The second most important factor was misguided direction from VIII Fighter Command that forbad the American escorts from chasing after the German fighters. Rather, once the enemy attackers turned away and were no longer a threat to the bombers, the escort pilots were required to return to the bomber stream. This was likely the reason that Jackson's three ships gave up their chase after scattering the flight of German of aircraft.

It was a flawed concept and directly counter to the old meme that "the best defense is a good offense." Forced by poor policy to surrender the initiative to the Germans, the American fighter pilots could only hope to be in a good position to protect the bombers when the Germans finally attacked. It was a misguided rule that served no real purpose other than to give the bomber crews some sense of comfort at seeing their own fighters close by.

There was actually a third factor that worked against the 352nd's pilots: luck. Simply put, there was no way to accurately predict when and where the Luftwaffe pilots might show. Depending on when and where a particular fighter group was scheduled to fly, it might or might not encounter the enemy. That the 352nd was short on good fortune in this regard is validated by the fact that other groups did score during this period. For instance, on September 27, the 4th, 56th, 353rd, and 78th Fighter Groups claimed a total of twenty-two enemy fighters shot down while the best the 352nd mustered for the day was a possible sighting of German aircraft along the coast of Holland. Likewise, other groups knocked down eighteen enemy aircraft on October 4, when the 352nd didn't even fly. And twelve enemy aircraft were claimed by other units on October 8, a day during which the 352nd never saw a German aircraft.

After sighting so many aircraft on October 10, 1943, the 352nd suffered through another long dry spell. Nothing was seen on October 14. This date came to be known as Black Thursday or, alternatively, Second

Schweinfurt. The Eighth's bomber groups went back to Schweinfurt and were absolutely savaged. Although real damage was done to the ball-bearing factories that were so crucial to Germany's war effort, sixty bombers were lost—an attrition rate that not even the United States could sustain. Although other fighter groups accounted for the destruction of an estimated thirteen Luftwaffe fighters, the 352nd escorted a diversionary raid and encountered no enemy aircraft.

Still, this second mission to Schweinfurt—together with other raids that were brutally battered during the same timeframe—provoked a foundational change in the Eighth Air Force. The Eighth's bomber groups were rarely ever again sent beyond the range of their fighter escorts. From that point, if the Luftwaffe wanted to hit the American bombers, it had to fight through their escorts or find gaps in the protection.

Although it was never publically acknowledged or stated, this decision obviously ended the debate about the self-defending bomber. Notwithstanding the fact that it had to withdraw units from the Mediterranean and the Eastern Front to do it, the Luftwaffe proved with finality that such a notion was bankrupt.

And in doing so, it seemed that the Germans had made irrelevant the enormous air force that the USAAF was building in England. Without longer-legged fighter escorts, the bombers were essentially limited to targets in occupied France and along the northern and western peripheries of Germany. To get deeper into Germany—in fact, to win the war—the range of the escorts had to be extended.

The problem had not been unanticipated. In fact, increasing the range of aircraft of all types had been of paramount importance since the beginning of flight. Nevertheless, during the 1930s, the notion of fighters escorting heavy bombers over long ranges was something that was never settled on as an absolute requirement among American air strategists. It was only after defensive fighters started downing bombers over Europe prior to the U.S. entry into the war that Henry Arnold, the chief of the Army Air Corps, ordered his experts to investigate ways to stretch the reach of his fighters.

The most obvious way to achieve that goal was to increase the amount of fuel the fighters carried. There were two basic ways the aircraft could be modified to carry more fuel. The first, as noted by Air Corps Study Number 35, *Employment of Aircraft in Defense of the Continental United States*, was by increasing the internal capacity. This approach had some promise, but was constrained by a number of factors that included the available volume, the strength of the aircraft's structure, and the effects of extra fuel on the aircraft's handling characteristics and performance.

The second concept focused on external fuel—that is, fuel carried in tanks suspended below the fuselage or wings. During combat, the notion was that the tanks would be dropped so that the fighting performance of the aircraft was not degraded. These "drop tanks" weren't a new idea; the Luftwaffe used them in combat during the Spanish Civil War and they had been tried years earlier by other air arms, including the Air Corps. Nevertheless, the development of truly useful modern drop tanks offered challenges. These included extra weight and drag, as well as the incorporation of new fuel feed systems and the means to control them. Also problematic was the equipment necessary to routinely hang and jettison the tanks. Finally came the design and construction of the tanks themselves. They had to be pressurized for operations at high altitude, aerodynamic, light, durable, easily produced, simple to use, and inexpensive enough to be discarded during operations.

Arnold's technical officers pursued both approaches—increased internal fuel volume and drop tanks—with vigor. In fact, experiments had been ongoing with external tanks since before the U.S. entered the war, although most of those efforts were focused on ferry tanks, rather than tanks suitable for combat operations. The chief difference between the two types was that the ferry tanks were generally larger and unpressurized. Without pressurization they were unable to feed enough fuel to the engine at high altitude. But work by the USAAF's Materiel Command resulted in combat tanks of 75- and 150-gallon capacity that were tested and proved by the summer of 1943.

At the same time that work was being performed back in the States, the Eighth Air Force was casting for solutions in England. Eaker was keen to get drop tanks for the fighters and had made it his fourth-highest priority by June 1943. He underscored the issue by declaring that the lack of drop tanks "constitute[s] the only reason why our P-47s are not going with our bombers as far as the Ruhr at least." The following month, Maj. Gen. Frank "Monk" Hunter, the commander of VIII Fighter Command, told Eaker—likely for the record—that his fighters could not get the job done without drop tanks and that it was not his responsibility to find them.[4]

To be sure, there were some fledgling efforts to use the tanks that were on hand. For instance, the 4th, 56th, and 78th Fighter Groups hung partially filled 200-gallon ferry tanks from the fuselages of their P-47s with some success on a penetration to Kassel and Oschersleben on July 28, 1943. The defending Luftwaffe fighters were surprised by the presence of American fighters so deep over the continent. The P-47 pilots claimed twenty-five aerial victories against seven losses. Nevertheless, the big, balky, unpressurized tanks were little more than a stopgap measure.

In the meantime the British were contracted to produce a 125-gallon American design made of steel. It was to have been delivered in quantity beginning in April 1943, but for a variety of reasons, the schedule was not held. Instead, the British offered a 108-gallon paper design. It was sound and producible, if not quite structurally strong enough. American engineers made improvements and the plastic-impregnated paper tanks were tested and approved for use on July 1, 1943. A British firm, Bowater, was put on contract to ready the P-47s for the new tanks, which began to arrive at the fighter groups in real numbers during September 1943.

Punchy Powell remembered the first mission the 352nd flew with the new drop tanks on September 27, 1943. On that day, the bombers were flying to Emden, Germany, and the 352nd was flying escort. The tanks were hung from the fuselage. "Evidently, the brackets under the belly did not fit many of the tanks properly," recalled Powell. "During takeoff from the rough sod airfield, the tanks shook loose from some of the planes and the guys in the trailing flights had to do quite a bit of swerving to miss them. Afterward, the brackets were adjusted and the problem was eliminated."

In truth, fitting the P-47s with the unfamiliar drop tanks wasn't a simple matter for the 352nd's ground crews. Aside from tweaking the fit between the racks, the wings, and the tanks, there was the matter of the actual fuel line—the conduit that delivered the fuel from the drop tank into the aircraft itself. It was made of glass so that it would fracture easily under the weight of the tank when it was jettisoned. Early on, however, it often broke too easily, especially on takeoff, as Punchy Powell recalled: "For safety we took off using our main internal tank and then switched to the drop tank shortly after getting airborne. But if the glass line on the drop tank was broken, the engine would get no fuel and would start to cut out. Then we had to switch back to the main tank. Of course, without the fuel from the drop tank, we'd have to abort the mission." It wasn't long before this problem was mitigated by fitting sections of rubber tube to the ends of the glass line to make it more resistant to the jostling and bouncing of taxiing and takeoff.

The ideal mission profile had the P-47s over the continent as the drop tanks were emptied, at which point they were released. Rid of the aerodynamic drag of the tank, and already at altitude and range with nearly full internal tanks—a main and an auxiliary—the P-47s were ready for combat. Powell recalled the standard practice in the 352nd: "After takeoff—for which we always used full throttle—we joined in formation, switched to our drop tanks, and climbed on course for the continent. As we gained altitude, we pulled the mixture control back to put less fuel into the engine, until it started to cough. Then we pushed it up just a little bit to smooth out the engine and ensure it had enough fuel to keep running. Using this technique, called 'leaning the engine,' we could get the fuel consumption down to about 85 or 90 gallons per hour." The early models of the P-47D that the 352nd operated carried a total of only 305 gallons internally.

There was no fuel indicator for the drop tank. A pilot knew the drop tank was nearly empty and that it was time to switch to the main tank when the engine started to surge and sputter. Once the switch was made—using the fuel valve selector just below the throttle quadrant on the left side of the cockpit—the drop tank was released using a switch on the right side of the cockpit next to the pilot's thigh. In the event that contact with enemy fighters was imminent, the fuel supply was switched from the drop tank to the main tank and the drop tank was jettisoned regardless of how much fuel it had. "If we got into a fight," Powell said, "we'd push our mixture control and throttle full forward. Then, aside from fighting, we really had to watch our fuel because at full throttle we'd burn about 150 gallons per hour. If we started fighting at the limits of our range, the pucker factor really went up as we started back home across the North Sea with very little fuel."

Nevertheless, as useful as the expendable fuel tanks were, they still had to be operated correctly, and virtually everyone who flew combat operations for any length of time had a story to tell. Bill Reese of the 486th Fighter Squadron had an incident that was fairly typical. While on an escort mission, Reese was mesmerized by the hellish maelstrom created by the bombers. Smoke from the target—a railroad intersection—reached up to 18,000 feet. "I was thinking how I would hate to bail out in the vicinity of all this when my engine quit."[5]

A rush of adrenaline jolted his hands automatically around the cockpit. "Calm, cool and collected one minute and [by the] next few seconds I had pulled, twisted, shoved, and flipped every switch, control, and valve that was movable." Whatever he did worked, and the engine caught and "was running nice and smooth. About ten minutes later, I figured out that I had let my drop tanks run dry and, of course, that was one of the valves I had turned."

Another common mistake was neglecting to switch the fuel valves to an internal source before dropping the external tanks. More than one pilot, before jumping an enemy fighter or in response to being attacked, jettisoned his drop tanks without switching to internal fuel tanks. The subsequent sound of the engine sputtering to a stop was heart-stopping. Karl Dittmer of the 487th Fighter Squadron did just such a thing when bandits were sighted: "I punched off my tanks only to have the good sounds abruptly quit."[6] Fortunately, his engine started again following a hasty switch to an internal tank. Dittmer's happy ending notwithstanding, it is quite likely that some pilots jumped out of perfectly good aircraft because in the heat and confusion of combat, they failed to realize that their engine was starved for fuel even though there was plenty aboard the aircraft.

The 108-gallon tanks from the early period of the 352nd's career developed into a mainstay for the USAAF and were used through the end of the war. Other sizes were less commonly used. Later, when the group transitioned to the P-51 Mustang, they most often used 75-gallon tanks—one suspended from each wing.

And although the manufacture of drop tanks had gotten off to a halting start in both the United States and England, once production began in earnest, they were seldom in short supply. In fact, by the end of 1943, every fighter base in England had two or three thousand tanks on hand.[7] From that point they became an integral part of fighter operations.

Still, the extra range from the new drop tanks—together with the fact that the bombers no longer went anywhere without fighter escort—didn't make an immediate difference to the 352nd. The Luftwaffe wasn't spotted on the mission of October 16, 1943, although some unidentified aircraft were seen on October 18. And on October 20, approximately twenty Me-109s made halfhearted head-on feints against the bombers the 352nd was escorting, but dove away when the 352nd's pilots tried to engage. The mission on October 22 was aborted because poor weather precluded the group from finding the bombers.

The group didn't fly a single mission during the next twelve days. When it flew again on November 3, the twelve or so enemy fighters that were spotted refused to fight. Another group of ten German fighters spotted two days later north of Amsterdam exhibited the same reluctance. Adding salt to the wound on this day was the fact that the 56th Fighter Group, which went operational in April, scored its hundredth aerial victory. On the mission of November 7, the 352nd saw another group of ten aircraft, also north of Amsterdam. It fled when a flight was sent after it.

Morale among the group's pilots ebbed. The fact that their mere presence around the bombers provided a certain measure of protection and fulfilled their mission to some degree was unsatisfying to most of them.

Although virtually none of the 352nd's men knew or cared during the frustrating months of late 1943, the overarching mission of their parent command, the Eighth Air Force, was to destroy Nazi Germany. More specifically, it was "The progressive destruction and dislocation of the German military, industrial and economic systems and the undermining of the morale of the German people to a point where their capacity for armed resistance is fatally weakened." This was the opening sentence from the statement describing the objective of the joint Anglo-American Combined Bomber Offensive (CBO).

A concept born out of the Casablanca Conference of January 1943, the CBO was a political palliative that allowed the British and Americans to pursue their separate air wars against Germany while cooperating in detail during those situations where it was in their best mutual interests. Much energy was spent by the various American and British staffs to ensure that they pursued—at least to some extent—strategies that worked toward the common goal of the destruction of Germany.

Although the emphasis of the CBO changed several times during the course of the war, its chief goal from June 1943—three months before the 352nd flew its first combat sortie—until April 1944 was the destruction of the Luftwaffe's fighter strength. This effort was named POINTBLANK. During the fall of 1943, the 352nd's pilots, as yet untested, were eager to do their part. The problem was that the Luftwaffe failed to cooperate.

The German response to the escalation in the numbers and sizes of the American bombing raids through 1943 was to increase the number of fighters deployed to the Western Front at the expense of the Mediterranean and Eastern Fronts. Whereas there were 670 fighters in place on January 1, 1943, that number had increased to 1,660 by November 1, 1943. During the same period, the number of Luftwaffe fighters on the other two fronts decreased by a combined total of nearly 200.[8]

Still, notwithstanding the fact that the 352nd had yet to score a single aerial victory, and considering the additional fact that VIII Fighter Command was still a pale shadow of what it would become, the average German fighter pilot was under ever-increasing pressure. Some of them were losing confidence in their leadership.

Heinz Knoke remembered a cordial exchange with Göring on November 17, 1943, when the *Reichsmarschall* presented him with the German Cross in Gold at Achmar for having scored fifteen aerial victories against the American heavy bombers. Knoke, a veteran squadron leader with JG 11, was struck by Göring's dress. His uniform was gray and heavily hung with gold braid and he wore scarlet doeskin boots. Knoke also observed that Göring appeared ill and that his face was swollen. "I am forced to the conclusion that he wears cosmetics," he recalled. "He has a pleasant voice, however, and is extremely cordial to me. I know that he takes a genuine interest in the welfare of his aircrews."

However, Knoke recounted his surprise when Göring addressed the assembled airmen. After citing the performance of the RAF's fighter pilots during the Battle of Britain as an example to emulate, he declared that Germany's own airmen were wanting. "It seems to me, however," wrote Knoke, "that the Commander-in-Chief of the German Air Force has only a vague idea of what happens when we engage in combat with the strong American formations." The German flyer wrote that the true reasons for their shortcomings were lackluster equipment and inferiority in numbers. "We need more aircraft, better engines—and fewer headquarters."[9]

The 352nd regularly received aircraft to replace those lost through accidents and enemy action. New fighters were typically sent to England by ship, only partially assembled. Once ashore, they were put together, given a cursory check, and then flown to their destination units. These new aircraft were thoroughly checked out by the 352nd's maintenance types before being allowed to fly operationally. Ted Fahrenwald received his personal aircraft on November 14, 1943:

She's the new Thunderbolt with the so-called secret engine which develops 2,000-plus HP [horsepower] when needed. Which makes me the proud possessor of [the] fastest ship anywhere. Should walk away from or catch anything that flies these days. And she's mine all mine. The boys are workin' on her down in the hangar, and after the acceptance check is finished and after I put a dozen hours on her to break in the engine, I'll be able to cut loose. . . . So today I arranged to have some of the boys taken off KP and put on a special detail which consists of them sanding the rough camouflage paint down to a smooth, fast surface. Dunno why those fatheads back in the States keep sending us ships with a built-in headwind.[10]

CHAPTER 5

On the Scoreboard

After the effort of November 7, the 352nd flew three more missions without so much as seeing an enemy aircraft. And then finally, on November 26, 1943, the group scored. Few were surprised that the first pilot from the 352nd to knock down an enemy fighter was John C. Meyer. A hard-nosed, intelligent, and hard-flying pilot, the commander of the 487th Fighter Squadron was generally recognized as the best leader in the group.

On the early afternoon of that day, the 352nd escorted formations of B-24s and B-17s on their withdrawal route east of Groningen, in the Netherlands. A gaggle of four Me-109s was spotted harassing a pair of B-24s that had fallen out of formation and were cruising at about 18,000 feet. The 352nd's P-47s were nearly a mile higher at 23,000 feet. Meyer recalled: "I and my [Yellow] flight closely supported by Blue Flight [led by John Bennett] went into a dive to intercept them when two of them separated as they were breaking away from their attacks on the bombers."[1]

Meyer pushed the nose of his aircraft into a steeper dive and went after the second of the two enemy fighters, which made a right turn and started up into a chandelle. A chandelle was a maneuver used to quickly reverse directions. It was performed by pulling the aircraft into a climb to slow it and then using coordinated rudder and aileron inputs to execute a quick, 180-degree heading reversal. Done correctly—and assuming it wasn't started too late—it allowed the pilot to meet attacks from the rear, with a head-on counterattack.

In this instance, it didn't work. Meyer followed the German through the maneuver and closed to 300 yards—almost directly behind him. He opened fire with a short burst from his eight .50-caliber machine guns. "The E/A [enemy aircraft]," Meyer continued, "which I identified as a Me-109 'F' or 'G' with rocket guns slung under each wing, exploded with a large burst of flame and disintegrated in the air. Fragments from him flew past me in my turn and struck and damaged Yellow Four flown by Major Therriault."

Another enemy fighter appeared immediately in front of Meyer. The German pilot turned but Meyer was able to pull inside him. "I took a wide two-ring shot at him using about 45 degrees deflection, which placed him out of my sight below the fuselage of my ship, so [I] saw nothing that followed." Robert Ross, Meyer's wingman, reported that the enemy fighter was badly hit and that a great amount of white smoke issued from the right side of the engine cowling.

"At this moment," Meyer continued, "I was attacked from above and the right by a third E/A so I continued my turn very steeply and found myself right head on to him." Meyer loosed a short burst at the enemy fighter from point-blank range but noted no hits. The two aircraft passed head-to-head and away from each other.

Below and behind Meyer, Donald Dilling was hot after the aggressive German. He sent two short bursts of machine-gun fire after the fleeing Me-109. "Then I turned left sharply and got into position dead astern of him and about 200 yards away. I opened fire and saw many bursts in both of his wings and in his fuselage."[2] Badly hit, the enemy fighter executed a slow roll and dove earthward.

Dilling continued hard after him. "I followed him closely and fired another long burst. He stopped rolling and I approached to within about 75 yards firing all the time, observing strikes in the wing roots and fuselage." Under the fusillade of heavy machine-gun fire, the stricken Me-109 stopped maneuvering and simply fell toward the ground trailing heavy black smoke.

While Meyer and Dilling scored the group's first aerial victories, Blue Flight, led by John Bennett, was also in the middle of the fray. Bennett's encounter report described the action: "Yellow leader [Meyer] blew up the second of these [Me-109s] as they broke away from the bombers while the other one had chandelled to port and appeared to be in the process of getting himself into position to attack Yellow leader."[3] Bennett dove down on the German fighter.

"The enemy must have sighted me," Bennett reported, "because he started to dive away but I followed and opened fire at about 300 yards, closing to about 150 yards firing intermittently. I saw many strikes in the forward part of his fuselage." The Me-109 made a slow, listless pull out of its dive and arced over to the right. "At this time," Bennett recalled, "I was less than 100 yards away and fired at him again using about ten degrees deflection and saw a heavy stream of mixed black and white smoke envelope him."

Bennett nearly ran over the German aircraft before he broke off his chase. "I could not see him from that position because of the smoke and was afraid of ramming him. He was taking no evasive action of any kind." Robert Berkshire took over as Bennett pulled away from the badly hit Me-109. "He [Berkshire] fired four short bursts into him hitting him in the wing roots and fuselage." Flames erupted from behind the enemy aircraft's cowling and Blue Flight watched as it fell burning and out of control toward the ground.

The 352nd was awarded three aerial victories for the encounter. Meyer and Dilling were credited with one Me-109 each, while Bennett and Berkshire shared credit for the other. The pilots noted in their encounter reports that they were able to maneuver their P-47s at least as well as the Luftwaffe fliers were able to turn their Me-109s. Although technically a more agile machine than the P-47 at the altitude at which the fighting occurred, the Me-109Gs the 352nd knocked down that day were hampered by the considerable weight and drag of the "rocket guns" that Meyer noted in his encounter report.

What Meyer actually saw were Werfer-Granate 21 (WGr 21), antiaircraft rocket tubes mounted under the wings. The rockets were large; they were more than eight inches in diameter and the explosive warhead alone weighed ninety pounds. The rocket body and warhead together with the launch tube weighed approximately 250 pounds. Aside from the weight, the entire assembly created a great amount of drag that considerably degraded the carrying aircraft's performance. Consequently, the Me-109 carried only two, one under each wing.

The WGr 21 was a derivative of the Nebelwerfer 42 artillery rocket. It was modified into an antiaircraft weapon as an expedient response to the increasingly large American bomber formations. Although the defensive armament of the bombers was by no means perfect, it was nonetheless effective to some extent and certainly dangerous—and frightening—to anyone attacking German fighter pilots. The rockets had a range of about 1,300 yards that allowed them to be launched from outside the range of the .50-caliber machine guns that the bombers carried.

The WGr 21 had a huge warhead that was devastating against the bombers, literally blowing them out of the sky and sometimes knocking down more than one at a time. On the other hand, it was slow and difficult to aim properly; it had to be launched from a precise range at a specific elevation and airspeed. And of course, the aim had to be true. It also had a timing fuze rather than a proximity fuze, which made accurate launching that much more critical. Still, it was not an overly intractable problem assuming that the pilot had ample time to make his attack.

However, as the American fighter forces grew in size and capability, it became increasingly difficult for the German fliers to get into a position from which they could accurately launch their rockets. Even if they were able to lug the cumbersome weapons through the screen of escort fighters, they often had little time to get into position. Indeed, many of the rockets were launched from well outside the proper parameters because the pilots were attacked by American fighters.

On the day that the 352nd scored its first aerial victories, George Preddy was forced back early by mechanical problems and missed the fight. He was genuinely upset and wrote in his diary: "I know that my day is coming and I am going to do everything possible to be ready when I do meet that [*sic*] Luftwaffe. Starting right now I am going to get in top physical and flying condition."[4]

The mission of November 26, 1943, also included a curious incident. The mission summary report noted: "As group withdrew from bombers, vicinity Tessel at 1322 hours, Group leader notified by Bomber intercom that a German B-24 was in formation with one of the B-24 boxes." Unfortunately, no other details are provided except that Col. Joe Mason, "orbited with flight to encounter [the supposed German bomber] but could not locate enemy aircraft." What motivated the bomber crews to make this call, and whether or not it was valid, is unknown.

The Eighth Air Force's decision to limit bombing missions to targets within the range of protective fighter escorts paid off during November 1943. Although six of the eight large missions sent out that month hit targets in Germany, the loss rate was only 4 percent. This was a marked improvement over the previous several months. On the other hand, targets in the interior of Germany went unmolested. Until it could hit those, the Eighth could hardly claim to be fighting an effective strategic air war.

Just as the Americans were struggling to modify their fighter aircraft to meet long-range escort requirements, the Luftwaffe was also working to create a specific sort of fighter. It needed to carry armament stout enough to knock down heavy bombers, yet it also had to perform well enough to fight on at least even terms with the American escort fighters. Achieving just such a balance was a difficulty with which the Germans struggled through the entire war.

Aside from the WGr 21 rockets, the Luftwaffe experimented with a variety of armament combinations for both the FW-190 and Me-109 that, if not endless, was certainly varied. For example, depending on the variant, the Me-109 carried one, two, or three 20-millimeter or 30-millimeter cannon in its nose and wings, sometimes with a pair of 13-millimeter machine guns, one on each side of its nose. Whereas the lighter machine guns were fairly ineffective against the bombers, the larger and heavier 20-millimeter cannon could bring a ship down with approximately twenty rounds, on average.

The 30-millimeter cannon, heavier still, could knock down a bomber with only about three rounds. Of course, there were disadvantages associated with the cannons. They were heavier, had a slower rate of fire, and were less accurate and more expensive than the machine guns. Too, because the ammunition was larger and bulkier, the fighters carried less of it.

The FW-190 had wings that were better suited for internally carried cannons than the wings of the Me-109. The different sub-variants of the FW-190A could carry two 20-millimeter cannon in each wing, while the later, but larger and lighter FW-190D carried one 20-millimeter cannon in each wing. All variants carried at least two machine guns in addition to cannon.

Although they generally didn't know the specifics about various upgrades to the different enemy fighters, the pilots in the 352nd knew that the Germans—just like the Americans—were constantly seeking ways to squeeze more performance from their aircraft. Still, regardless of what the Germans did with the Me-109 and the FW-190, it didn't make much of a difference to the 352nd's pilots in a practical sense; their job was still to shoot the enemy fighters down. Don McKibben made the following observation: "Enemy aircraft were enemy aircraft and all were entitled to the same treatment as the occasion demanded." And in the heat of air combat, it was virtually impossible to tell one variant of a particular type from another anyway. Don Bryan confirmed this: "To us, an '09 [Me-109] was an '09 and an FW [FW-190] was an FW."

The Germans also experimented with variously armed twin-engine fighters. It stood to reason that larger aircraft could carry heavier armament. And indeed, the Luftwaffe flew a number of different twin-engine types against the American bombers, especially early in the fighting. Although the Me-110 proved vulnerable to fighters during the Battle of Britain, when properly armed, it proved effective against unescorted bombers. Equipped as a night fighter, it also downed considerable numbers of British bombers. The same was true of the Ju-88, which was normally used as a fast bomber. However, both types were little more than helpless when set upon by American fighters.

The Germans responded with faster and more sophisticated twin-engine aircraft such as the Me-210 and Me-410. Still, even these newer types—although they could have been effective against the big, lumbering B-17s and B-24s—never really had a chance at penetrating the screen of protective fighters. In fact, the Luftwaffe eventually gave up on these types. As the war continued, the 352nd encountered them much less frequently than they did the more numerous Me-109s and FW-190s.

One of the group's earliest aerial victories was a twin-engine fighter knocked down by Virgil Meroney on December 1, 1943, while leading the 487th Fighter Squadron's Green Flight. After shooting down an Me-109 approximately ten miles south of Rheydt, in northern Germany, Meroney spotted another aircraft he identified as an Me-210 or Me-410. "I positioned myself up sun and dove in to attack," Meroney recalled. "The enemy aircraft was flying on top of a solid overcast."[5] The German pilot, perhaps knowing there were American fighters in the area, may have been staying close to the clouds in order to make a quick, diving escape. As it developed, he never had the opportunity.

"I was following him at 700 yards, altitude 12,000 feet, and as he was getting closer to the clouds, I began firing and closed to 300 yards." Meroney noted hits on the aircraft's cockpit and left engine before breaking off his attack and setting up for another. He scored more hits and closed to 250 yards before breaking off. "I made a third attack and ran out of ammo, and observed a crew member fall out of E/A. I pulled away and watched him disappear through clouds, but he did not open his parachute." The number-four man in Meroney's flight, Richard Grow, finished the already riddled German fighter. It was last seen afire as it fell into the clouds.

The Luftwaffe occasionally used single-engine fighters to protect the heavier twin-engine fighters. This was evident from an encounter report filed by John Bennett. While escorting bombers in the vicinity of Zwolle in the Netherlands on December 22, 1943, he tangled with both an Me-109 and an FW-190. Using the eight guns of his P-47 to good effect, he and his wingman, Ernest McMahan, blew a wing from the Me-109 while the FW-190 escaped only lightly damaged. Bennett remembered that "Both the Me-109, and the FW-190, were painted black and yellow with a checkered effect, and they certainly acted like experienced and seasoned pilots. They were aggressive and tough in their tactics . . ."[6]

Bennett latched onto George Preddy and his wingman, Richard Grow, and rejoined the bomber stream; McMahan was separated from Bennett. "Our three-man flight continued at 27,000 feet at seven o'clock to a box of bombers when we saw six Me-210s at 22,000 feet making passes at one of the bombers." Preddy and Grow dove on the Me-210s while Bennett remained high as protective cover. "Captain Preddy," Bennett recalled, "failed to catch his Me-210, which evaded into the clouds. Glancing over my shoulder, I saw eight Me-109s attacking me, all firing at me, but the deflection was too great. I chopped my throttle and turned into them, and they overshot me."

Bennett subsequently dove into the clouds and escaped. Of his attackers, he wrote: "These eight Me-109s were a light blue color, and in good formation when I saw them. And they did not carry rocket guns or belly tanks. They obviously were furnishing top cover for the twin-engine A/C attacking the B-24s."

George Preddy scored his first aerial victory on December 1, 1943, more than a year and a half since he flew his first combat sortie out of Darwin. He was leading the 487th's Red Flight on an escort mission to Solingen, Germany, when he spotted a single Me-109 approximately 3,000 feet below him. The enemy aircraft was trailing a box of bombers. Preddy attacked immediately and the German went into a diving left-hand spiral. It didn't work; the P-47 was faster in a dive. "As I closed from 400 to 200 yards, I fired and saw strikes on the wing roots and cockpit.[7] The airplane began smoking and fell out of control at about 7,000 feet. I fired another burst closing to about 100 yards. After I broke off the attack, the enemy aircraft disintegrated."

December 12, 1943, was a good day for the 352nd. The group's mission summary report duly listed the destruction of six Luftwaffe aircraft for the loss of none of its own. It also noted times, locations, weather conditions, and various observations that might have been of interest to higher headquarters. For instance, it described that a formation of Me-109s that the group encountered was "painted brown and gray with red markings on tail and nose," while a formation of FW-190s was "silver with light blue camouflaging."

Detailed it was, but the group summary report hardly matched the color and narrative power of Ted Farhenwald's letter home.[8] In it, he noted the twin evils of bad weather and limited fuel that were a constant plague on the initial operators of the P-47. Early in the mission, the group encountered a towering mass of cumulus clouds: "We meet this job about forty or fifty miles out to sea, and the whole outfit had to quit flying our beeline course and orbit around and around, climbing for altitude, to get over it . . . which used up quite a bit of my precious fuel." Still, the escort portion of the mission was fairly uneventful, as Fahrenwald described: "There isn't much flak and while we are with the Forts [B-17s] they are not much bothered by any snooping Hun fighters, and finally, when we're all low on gas, Colonel Joe Mason hollers on the RT: 'OK gang, everybody out!'"

Fahrenwald's flight, led by Frank Greene, lagged the rest of the group and made a couple more sweeps across the top of the bomber stream before turning for England. "But then we spot twelve disorganized contrails hiding in the sun, and by the very fact of their sloppy formation, we see 'em and know they are Jerries waiting for us to leave our bombers. So Greene and Marshall and McKibben and I turn away from home and go lickety-split towards these bandits."

Although Fahrenwald's tone was devil-may-care, it must be considered that the fliers were toeing a very fine line. If they delayed too much longer—or got caught up in a hard fight—they wouldn't have enough fuel to get home. They would then be forced to choose between bailing out over enemy territory or taking a chance on ditching in the North Sea and hoping for rescue. Such a hope in late December, when the waters were especially frigid, was very optimistic.

"They have a little altitude on us," Fahrenwald remembered, "and as we draw near them one Hun turns chicken and peels straight downward for home. Next thing I see are two Me-109s whizzing by me, a little to the right and a hundred feet straight over my cockpit and their guns are winking and blinking." The two elements making up Greene's four-ship flight came apart as they met with the Germans. "Mac [McKibben] and I lose the other two of our flight so we stay upstairs and fence around with a half-dozen Jerry fighters," Fahrenwald recalled. "We can't afford to mix it with them as we are right at the point of no return. Low on fuel, but finally we turn our tails to 'em and drive for England."

Meanwhile, Greene and Al Marshall went after another group of Me-109s that dove for the deck. Fahrenwald recounted their combat: "But another 109 dives on Marshall, gets on his tail, and begins to do a little fancy shooting. Marshall sees 20-mm shells busting and tracers going past his canopy and he hollers to Greene that he's being massacred. So Greene does a stunt or two and ends up on this Jerry's tail, lets him have a couple of good bursts in the cockpit and down goes Jerry, smoke and flames."

After clearing the fight, Fahrenwald and McKibben eased back their throttles to save every ounce of fuel possible. "We get over Amsterdam finally and then Mac sez to me, 'Hey they're shootin' at us, Faro.' And I look ahead and there parked some short distance off my nose are fourteen gobs of flak. We change course a bit and then there appears eight or ten jagged black gobs of smoke right between us, and we are not flying far apart." Finally, the two pilots reached the North Sea and started a gentle descent toward England as they simultaneously tried to will the needles on their fuel gauges to stop falling.

The pair were skimming only feet above the angry-looking gray waves of the North Sea when Fahrenwald's low-fuel light illuminated, indicating that he had only about fifteen minutes of fuel remaining. "So now I really begin to sweat but at the right time we make landfall and the two of us set down at a big coastal bomber base. Mac runs outta gas while taxiing and mine is coughing. So we gas up, have a bite to eat, and then rat-race all the way home."

Most of the enemy aircraft the 352nd's flyers encountered were camouflaged on top with combinations of dark gray, green, and brown. The undersides were generally painted light gray or blue. But there were exceptions. The group mission summary reports and individual encounter reports occasionally described color schemes that varied from standard. These included aircraft that were painted entirely light blue, aircraft that weren't painted at all, aircraft with red and white striped noses, aircraft with yellow noses, aircraft painted in black and yellow checks, and so on.

Several interesting FW-190 paint schemes were encountered in a single engagement near Furstenau on December 22, 1943. David Zimms described the unusual arrangement of one of the enemy aircraft in his encounter report: "The E/A was painted yellow on the underside of the fuselage and the wing roots with a red stripe on each wing root."[9] Quentin Quinn described another oddly painted fighter: "The FW-190 was silver except for yellow wingtips and the black crosses on both wings."[10] And James Laing recorded another: "E/A was a very light tan with even lighter [wing] tips and huge black crosses on the wings."[11]

It is likely that some of the more unusually painted German aircraft were unit leaders. The Luftwaffe, especially later in the war, was keen to mass as many aircraft as possible against the American bomber formations. Once they made contact with the Americans, their formations were often blown apart. Getting them back together was easier if the leader was more readily identifiable from a distance.

Still, most of the 352nd's pilots found little that was remarkable about how the Germans camouflaged their aircraft. This was in part due to the fact that lighting conditions could change or mute colors. Moreover, air combat was literally a life-and-death activity; registering color schemes for later recollection was low on the list of priorities. Finally, there was the fact that most of the Luftwaffe's camouflage arrangements simply weren't noteworthy.

Although the 352nd's pilots had scored a few victories by mid-December 1943, encounters with the enemy were still few and far between. This particularly chafed the most eager pilots. Ted Fahrenwald recounted their frustrations in a letter home:

> We had a small party in the Club last night for no special occasion. Ed Heller, the mighty Irishman, is so mad that he's not had a decent shot at anything so far in this war that he hollers, 'I gotta hit somebody I just gotta!' He trudges around the Club asking people if they mind if he hits 'em, just a small blow. He finds no takers. (Ed stands six-one or two or so and weighs a couple of hundred pounds . . .) Finally he tops off his drink and hauls off on a brick wall. A mighty blow, and he busts a little finger. Ho ho ho! A lot of sympathy from us he got too. . . .[12]

Fahrenwald wrote most of his letters home on Don McKibben's personal typewriter. It was dear to McKibben as he had acquired it at a precious price with hard-earned cash prior to joining the service. It was too bulky and weighty for him to take to England as personal property but he refused to be easily separated from it and devised a scheme to get it overseas. "I donated it to the Army Air Corps, specifically, our squadron clerk, for use on official business while the outfit cruised to the U.K. aboard RMS *Queen Elizabeth*. When I finally got it back, the cover had been painted with a very official-looking, much-hyphenated number. Our squadron clerk was a very resourceful guy."[13]

On December 20, 1943, George Arnold of the 487th Fighter Squadron was part of Winfield McIntyre's Yellow Flight. The P-47s escorted the bombers partway to Bremen that morning and made their way back across France to England. "It was a beautiful day," Arnold remembered. "We were flying at about 23,000 feet and could see for miles."[14] Through that clear sky, they spotted a lone B-17 far below them.

"It was all shot up," Arnold recalled. "Part of its tail was gone and it was running on just a couple of engines. And all around it were a bunch of German fighters making attacks." The enemy aircraft had cornered the cripple and were chopping it out of the sky. Powerful though the bomber's defensive armament was, it was still not a good enough match for a pack of German fighters.

"That was the only time I really got mad," Arnold said. "That poor old thing was barely flying and the Germans wouldn't leave it alone. It reminded me of a bunch of schoolyard bullies." The P-47 pilots immediately powered over into a high-speed dive.

"The bomber was down around 15,000 feet and I got going really fast," Arnold said. "I pulled in behind one of them, but I was going so fast I didn't even have time to shoot." He tried desperately to slow his aircraft but still ended up coasting past the enemy fighter, an Me-109. "I looked at him and he looked at me, and then quicker than a jackrabbit, he flicked over and away. McIntyre came down in a dive and followed him."

McIntyre nearly committed the same error as Arnold. "I closed rapidly on the E/A, so I chopped my throttle, pulled off to the right, and then fell in line astern." The enemy pilot, apparently intent on knocking down the stricken bomber, did not maneuver. McIntyre opened fire with his eight .50-caliber machine guns and "saw many strikes on the wings and fuselage." He noted that the Me-109—light blue in color—"rolled over to the left, on its back, and went down."[15]

Don Dilling had already knocked down one of the German fighters and was chasing the same Me-109 as McIntyre when he pulled up and out of the way to watch McIntyre shoot it down: "About this time, the EA rolled, was apparently out of control, and went straight down into the deck, where it exploded, sending up a huge cloud of black smoke. I corroborate the claim of one Me-109 destroyed, made by Yellow leader [McIntyre]."[16] Altogether, the flight claimed five enemy fighters that day.

A couple of days later on December 22, 1943, the 352nd formed part of the fighter escort for a force of nearly 600 bombers as they withdrew from Germany across Holland following their raid against the marshalling yards at Osnabrück. George Preddy led the 487th's Blue Flight on that afternoon. He gave cover to Meyer's Yellow Flight as Meyer took on a single Me-109. Preddy then led his formation of P-47s against a flight of three Me-109s that evaded him by diving into the clouds. Blue Flight was scattered and Preddy managed to collect only his wingman, Richard Grow. The two of them pushed their aircraft hard to climb back to altitude and join the bombers.

"When we reached 15,000 feet, I noticed another Me-109 above us positioning for an attack," Preddy recorded. "He made an attack on the two of us and we turned into him."[17] The enemy pilot must have been exceptionally skilled as Preddy noted that he and Grow fought the lone Me-109 for nearly fifteen minutes. The engagement ended only when the German chose to dive away into the clouds.

With no Germans left to fight, Preddy and Grow chased after the bomber formation and picked up the flight's element lead, John Bennett, along the way. "We sighted the bomber formation about 25 miles west of and above us," Preddy recalled. "We continued climbing towards the bombers and leveled off at 26,000 feet on the down-sun side still quite a few miles out. I saw a B-24 straggling to the left and below the formation. He was being attacked by six Me-210s, but they saw me coming and immediately dispersed."

The B-24 was *Lizzie*, a ship from the 445th Bomb Group based out of Tibenham, England. Captained by Glenn Jorgenson, the crew had battled engine problems since getting over the continent but managed to stay with the formation and made the bomb run over Osnabrück. Once clear of the target, however, the bomb group left *Lizzie* and two other bombers behind.

Allan Matthews, the copilot, recalled what happened as the rest of the 445th disappeared toward the west: "We began to dive for the overcast but upon nosing down, we saw ten or fifteen Me-109s attacking one of our straggling ships; not desiring to dive through the mass of fighters, we held our altitude. A few seconds later, the bomber burst into flames and spun into the overcast. The fighters then swarmed over on the other straggling bomber and upon making eight or ten passes succeeded in knocking it down."[18]

Jorgenson's crew was next. "As we saw the bomber spin into the overcast, our gunners warned us of an attack from the rear. We proceeded to dive, climb, swerve and everything possible to throw the fighters off. The gunners reported eight Me-210s coming in at five and seven o'clock. On their first pass, number one engine began to run away. It evidently was hit as it ran up to 5300 R.P.M. until it melted. On the same pass, a 20-mm exploded in number 3 gas tank leaving a four-inch hole, but no fire."

The fighters came back around for another pass. Matthews recalled how *Lizzie* was savaged: "Two or three shells exploded in the bomb bay throwing parts of the bomb racks into the radio compartment breaking the gas gauges and damaging the radio. The hydraulic system was also knocked out, leaving the tail turret inoperative. The gunner was unable to rotate the turret as the cable was broken, however, he continued firing. Another 20-mm went into the nose compartment exploding in the stomach of the navigator, killing him instantly." The bombardier was also hit and the cockpit caught fire.

Matthews continued the story: "Two or three more shells exploded in the waist, slightly injuring both waist gunners, but they also continued firing. A Ju-88 fired a rocket that went through both rudders leaving two holes about the size of a basketball in them. Meanwhile, the engineer in the top turret scored a direct hit and the fighter burst into flames and spun down. The right waist gunner got off a few good bursts into another fighter leaving him smoking."

Then the German fighters disappeared. They fled as Preddy, Grow, and Bennett dove on them. Preddy fired at one of the twin-engine fighters from outside maximum range and drove it away from *Lizzie*. He picked out another and opened fire from directly astern at a range of 200 yards. "The enemy aircraft began to disintegrate with large pieces flying off and he went down into the clouds in flames."

As the Me-210 went down, Grow warned Preddy that an Me-109 was closing on him from behind. "I threw the stick in [the] left corner and saw the enemy aircraft behind me and out of range. I continued down skidding and slipping. Grow then called that an enemy aircraft was on his tail but I was unable to locate him." Preddy's wingman was never seen again.

Although Grow was lost, Preddy shook off the remaining enemy fighters, dove into the clouds, and raced for home. Jorgenson and Matthews wrestled their badly damaged B-24 back to England on two engines and landed at Manston only minutes before running out of fuel. Jorgenson and three of his crewmen were wounded. Their navigator was dead.

For his actions that day, Preddy received credit not only for his second aerial victory, but was additionally awarded the Silver Star for driving off the enemy fighters. His citation noted how, even though outnumbered, Preddy "unhesitatingly led his flight in an attack on the enemy and pressed it home with such viciousness that the enemy planes were scattered and forced to cease their attacks . . ."

The Eighth Air Force mounted its largest mission to date on Christmas Eve, 1943, when it sent 722 bombers and 541 fighters against targets in northern France. It was a less than happy day for Daniel Britt of the 487th Fighter Squadron, who broke both his legs in a crash landing after running out of fuel.

There was no mission on Christmas Day. The terse notes Fred Allison recorded in his diary described a day that was probably typical for most of the men: "Very quiet day. Nice turkey dinner. No missions today. First Christmas in E.T.O. [European theater of operations]. Hope to be home long before next Xmas."[19]

John C. Meyer, the 487th's commanding officer, understood and appreciated the long hours his maintenance men worked. In his Christmas letter to the squadron, he opened with an acknowledgement of their work: "It's about 2:00 A.M. Christmas morning, and as I am writing this, a large number of you men are lying on your backs beneath airplanes. With cold bodies and frozen hands, you are working outside my office. You are working yourselves on Christmas Eve so that in case our Squadron is called upon to perform its mission tomorrow, on Christmas Day, we will be ready. To you men especially I extend my Christmas Greetings."

He also extended his respect and gratitude to the support troops beyond the aircraft mechanics: "I know that at times it must irk you—those of you who do not fly—to learn about your comrades in arms, who are engaged in more spectacular fields of glory, and that you are impatient to join them. I also know that at times you long to be with your loved ones at home. But I also know, because you have shown me, that yours is the courage and stout-heartedness that can meet any demands cheerfully and willingly, without hope of reward other than that which comes with a job well done . . ."[20]

As a pilot, Meyer was extremely competitive. And although George Preddy was not considered to have the same leadership skills as Meyer, his flying skills were comparable. Punchy Powell recalled that Meyer and Preddy occasionally went on training sorties together which were really little more than airborne arm-wrestling matches. "Meyer described himself and Preddy as evenly matched," Powell recalled. "Sometimes he would win and other times Preddy would get the best of him. They were two outstanding pilots."

While he was generally not considered a warm and gregarious sort, Meyer did understand that others were. Don Bryan remembered an incident that occurred soon after the group arrived in England: "I had a book I was reading and one of the guys in the squadron was bugging me to hurry and read it so that he could borrow it. I finally finished and came up behind him and swatted him on the rump as hard as I could with the book. Except that it was J. C. Meyer and not my buddy. I think he was as surprised as I was. I asked for his pardon and explained what happened and he didn't kick the hell out of me."

The group's public-relations office wrote a release that assessed Meyer's character from the perspective of the men he led: "The pilots, crew chiefs, armorers and others refer to him as 'the best CO [commanding officer] in the business.' They also are aware of his sharp tongue, and say, both ruefully and joyfully, 'When he chews you out, you stay chewed out. Funny thing is, he's always right, too.'"[21]

Crew chiefs were justifiably quite particular about the aircraft they were assigned to maintain. This was understandable as, for all practical purposes, the reason they were overseas was to maintain that aircraft. They also were particular about who flew it. Certain pilots—usually new ones—were sometimes hard on machines; this consequently created more work for the ground crews. On the other hand, the regular pilot of an aircraft and its designated crew chief generally got along fairly well as they had a shared interest in the aircraft's wellbeing.

Still, for various reasons, pilots were often assigned to fly aircraft other than their own. Or new pilots who had no regular aircraft were scheduled to fly missions in whatever was available. For instance, they might fly the aircraft of a pilot who was sick or away on a pass. As a consequence, crew chiefs sometimes practiced backhanded methods to regulate who flew their machines. One pilot recalled that "the crew chiefs could sneak a peek at the board in our ready room which listed who was flying what plane, and if they didn't like the pilot, they would find some excuse to pull their plane from the ready list."

Another reason the ground crews were fussy about who flew their aircraft was the fact that they received awards and incentives for maintaining their machines in top condition. For instance, if their ship flew a certain number of sorties without an abort, they might receive a pass to London or some other hotspot. Their best efforts could be derailed by a less-than-aggressive pilot who heard engine noises—real or imagined—and aborted the mission.

Punchy Powell recalled one pilot who had a reputation for imagining rough engines whenever the scheduled mission was particularly long or dangerous: "He borrowed my aircraft but aborted the mission because he said the engine was running rough. Well, as soon as he got back, I jumped in and flew it and there wasn't a thing wrong with it. He cost my crew a Bronze Star Medal because he turned back with an imaginary engine problem. I really chewed his ass and would have beat it too, if he hadn't outranked me."

Ted Fahrenwald and his ground crew had a scheme that kept other pilots from flying his aircraft:

Nacherly, I hate to have any other pilot fly my ship, as there are some knuckleheads in the outfit—guys who habitually substitute brawn for brains, and are mighty rough on a precision machine like this ship. So whenever I land and taxi back to my revetment, I announce officially that something's haywire with the ship, whereupon Sgt. German rips a couple of panels off'n the cowling to make it look good. So far, no one but me has flown 'er, and she's the best ship on the line.[22]

Pilots often received brand-new mounts because of bad flying or bad luck. For instance, if a pilot's normally assigned aircraft was shot down or badly damaged while it was being flown by a squadron mate, it was usually replaced with a new one. This was a particular windfall to those pilots who were flying worn hand-me-downs. That was the case for Jack Diamond of the 487th Fighter Squadron. Squadronmate Rollin "Red" Frum was flying Diamond's aircraft when he was hit by ground fire while strafing an airfield. "The hydraulic system was knocked out and the landing gear could not be lowered. As a result he bellied in on the grass field and the plane was taken out of service." Diamond's stricken aircraft was replaced by a factory-fresh aircraft, which pleased him very much.[23]

Crew chiefs sometimes took liberties with their aircraft that were occasionally at odds with the technical manuals. Don Bryan remembered that during the 352nd's first winter at Bodney, he was still flying an early model of the P-47D. "Other P-47s were getting water injection which provided an additional two hundred horsepower for short periods of time in the event of an emergency," he remembered. "But my aircraft didn't have it and was one of the slowest in the group."

Bryan approached his crew chief, Kirk Noyes, and asked when his aircraft would be modified with water injection. Noyes told him that his aircraft was too old; the conversion kit would not fit. The only way for him to get a faster aircraft was to get a new one. "That was fine with me," Bryan said, "until he reminded me that he was assigned to the aircraft and not to me."

"I thought about that for a while," Bryan recounted, "and decided that I'd stick with Noyes and the old aircraft. When I told him that I was sticking with him, he sort of smiled and let me in on his plan." Noyes told Bryan that he could get extra power—a lot of extra power—if he removed the governor from the turbosupercharger. Once that was done, the engine's manifold pressure could be pushed to prodigious levels. Of course, if pushed too hard, the engine would destroy itself.

Bryan came out to his aircraft early one morning a few days later after Noyes made the modifications. It was very cold and the aircraft was shiny-slick with clear ice. "I got started and we taxied out. We started our takeoff and got airborne, but because of the ice on the wings the aircraft wasn't climbing like it should have. It became very clear that I wasn't going to clear the trees at the far side of the airfield." Panicked, Bryan shoved the throttle full forward. The engine responded with a roar and lifted the aircraft clear of the trees. "Our manifold pressure limitation for takeoff was 62 inches of mercury," he recalled. "When I finally had enough altitude and pulled the throttle back, I looked down real quick and saw the manifold pressure dropping below 70 inches." Noyes's modification saved Bryan's life.

Many pilots were very generous, as they should have been, with the praise they gave their mechanics. The maintainers worked long hours, often in the cold and wet and dark, and without any chance at fame or glory. That they did so well was remarkable considering the fact that most of them had no real prior mechanical experience yet were responsible for keeping the highly complex engines and airframes in good repair.

Still, their record was not always stellar. Nearly every mission saw aircraft abort for various reasons. Depending on where they were when they turned back, the malfunctioning aircraft often required an escort. For instance, it was prudent to escort an aircraft with a bad engine that had to traverse half of Europe and the North Sea in order to get back to base. The loss of these perfectly good escort aircraft degraded the group's effectiveness on any given mission just as much as the loss of the malfunctioning aircraft.

The 487th Fighter Squadron's Standard Operating Procedures (April 1, 1944), authored by George Preddy, outlined the procedures for aborting aircraft:

> Aircraft or engine troubles will not be discussed by radio. Any troubles developing should be studied by the individual pilot and the decision is his. If the pilot aborts, he says, "Going Home," plus his call sign and nothing else. Well over the channel, if the trouble is anything which might become serious, he should request the escort of his wing-man or element leader. Over enemy territory, at least one flight will accompany the aborting ship. It is your ship, your neck, and your decision.

Donald Dilling's experience while flying the mission of December 30, 1943, offers a good example of how circumstances could box the pilots into low-fuel situations from which they could not recover. On that day, the 352nd was tasked with covering the bombers as they withdrew across Belgium and France. The weather was filthy and the pilots were forced to navigate via dead reckoning, without reference to landmarks. Compounding the poor flying conditions was the fact that the 487th's pilots jettisoned their external fuel tanks early during the mission when an enemy fighter was spotted. And the situation was further exacerbated when the escort leg of the mission lasted ten fuel-sucking minutes longer than scheduled.

Finally, the 487th left the bombers and headed for home. "We were letting down gradually from 30,000 feet to twelve or fourteen thousand over Calais when three 190s bounced us," recalled Dilling.[24] He had been credited with three aerial victories since the 352nd had started combat operations, but on this day Dilling wasn't sure he had enough fuel to reach England. He certainly didn't have enough fuel to win a dogfight and also make it home. "As I looked at my gauges one of the 190s made a pass at me and missed. As he went by at little more than wing's length, I could see the pilot wearing a white silk scarf with his goggles pulled down over his eyes." With no other good options, Dilling rolled his aircraft over and dove for the clouds.

Dilling escaped the German pilot but in the process his compass failed and began to spin. Inside the clouds he had no idea which direction he was headed. "After a few minutes flying in the soup, I spotted land off to my right and thought, I've got to get this thing down before I run out of gas." Dilling believed he was over the Thames delta but in reality he was still over northwestern France. Even when he was hit by a heavy antiaircraft barrage, he still failed to understand that he wasn't over friendly territory. "I took a couple of hits in the tail section and headed back in over the land cursing those crazy sons of bitches—thinking I was over England."

With no airfield in sight, Dilling let his aircraft down and prepared to belly it into a field. He aborted his first attempt when a farmer suddenly appeared in his immediate path. A moment later, he successfully dropped the big fighter into a turnip patch. Safe and uninjured, Dilling took his time getting out of his parachute harness and climbing out of the P-47. "Still thinking I was in England, I began walking towards a well near the top of the hillside, but stopped abruptly when some children started yelling at me in French to leave because the Germans were looking for me."

Dilling was stunned. It took him only an instant to recover his wits before he sprinted back to his aircraft. There, he pulled out an incendiary grenade which was intended to destroy the aircraft in just such a situation. The grenade sputtered and failed. With no other good options, he fled his barely dented fighter and reached the cover of a blackberry thicket just moments before two truckloads of German soldiers arrived.

While one party of soldiers guarded his aircraft, another searched unsuccessfully for him. Ultimately, the search party gave up and Dilling was left shivering and unmolested in the brush. "Since it was still daylight, I could not leave my hiding place so I spent the rest of the afternoon studying a French-English dictionary I had with me." At nightfall, Dilling left his hiding place and started a journey that took him across France, over the Pyrenees into Spain, and back to England. From there, he was returned to the States. Aside from Dilling, Hayes Button and Winfield McIntyre also ran out of fuel and came down on the wrong side of the Channel. Both were quickly captured and spent the rest of the war as POWs.

Thousands of American aircraft went down over Europe during the war and it is well documented that the Germans salvaged many of them.

Most of the material was scrapped and recycled. Indeed, especially late in the war, some of the aircraft the Luftwaffe flew were made of metal that had earlier been winging over Europe as American bombers or fighters. Even fuel from downed USAAF machines was recovered and used.

The Germans actually made some of the lesser-damaged aircraft airworthy again. Many of these were used to familiarize Luftwaffe fliers with the characteristics of the aircraft they were fighting. No doubt it was useful to closely examine or fly the American equipment to get some idea of its strengths, as well as any weaknesses that might be exploited. In fact, beginning in 1943, the Luftwaffe formed many of these aircraft—painted with German markings—into a special unit. It was known informally as Zirkus Rosarius after Theodor Rosarius, its commander.

Rosarius's stable of Allied aircraft included an example from the 352nd. When Donald Dilling of the 487th Fighter Squadron bellied his P-47, *Queen City Mama*, into a field in northern France on December 30, 1943, the aircraft was scarcely damaged. It was recovered, repaired, painted with German markings, and flown again.

It has been debated for some time whether or not captured American aircraft were ever used by the Germans against their original owners. Anecdotal accounts are not unusual, but firm, irrefutable proof is elusive. Nevertheless, a contemporaneous VIII Fighter Command document listed several incidents:

> The first instance of a German-flown P-47 was when it accompanied an Me-109 on June 25, 1944, and made six or seven approaches to one of our bomber formations, but without attacking! The captured B-17's were used to shadow our formations and to act as decoys, possibly as practice targets for fighters to learn the proper approach against the real thing. November 30, 1943, marked the date when the first P-38's were used by the enemy, for it came out of one of our bomber formations on a mission for which no Allied Lightnings were booked for escort. It had no Allied markings, and when the P-47 pilot pulled alongside, the Nazi "dove for the deck." Another enemy piloted P-38 was shot down on the same mission by an American pilot.[25]

This P-38 was probably the same P-38 that Hayes Button of the 487th engaged on November 29, 1943. Button spotted a P-38 with outdated USAAF markings attack a group of P-47s. Button attacked it and set an engine afire.

An example from a 352nd mission summary report from much later in the war is also interesting. It was filed by the 487th Fighter Squadron on April 10, 1945, and summarizes the day's bomber-escort effort. Line six of that standardized document was headed "Anything Unusual." In this instance, it directed the reader to the reverse side, where the following account was entered: "5 camouflaged shiny olive colored P-51's with white spinners, no identification on tails; only white star insignia; vicinity of Havelberg and Wittenberge—1515 hrs. at 22,000'—one plane joined with four others and came in from the rear and side into the bombers knocking one B-17 down." The report makes no other mention of the incident.

Whether the report is a mistake or not is unknowable. Certainly, the Germans salvaged American aircraft they could have used in the manner described, but such actions would have been little more than stunts that could not have produced substantial results. On the other hand, it is possible that the 352nd pilot or pilots who made the report simply misidentified German aircraft as American, although the details described suggest otherwise. It is quite possible, considering the timeframe and location, that the aircraft were Soviet Yak-9s, which bore a marked resemblance to the P-51. It is unfortunate that a better account does not exist; certainly such an incident generated a good deal more discussion among the pilots than what the official document records.

These accounts also conflict with Göring, who, during postwar debriefings, said that captured Allied aircraft were flown only for training and evaluation. Arguably, Göring had nothing to gain by lying, but on the other hand, it is certain that he was not aware of everything that went on in the Luftwaffe. He did acknowledge that the Gestapo used captured Allied bombers to drop agents in the Balkans.

The P-47 marked the men who flew it with a telltale brand. Punchy Powell explained: "If we had to wear our Class A uniforms, we naturally wore our spit-and-polish dress shoes but we didn't wear them when we flew not only because we didn't want to tear them up, but also because they were cut below the ankle like a dress shoe and they would quite likely come off if we bailed out."

"Most of the time," he continued, "we wore our G.I. shoes, which came up to the ankles a bit. They also had a rough finish that wasn't intended to be kept polished." Powell recalled the mark the P-47 put on the shoes. "There was a little slot in the left side of the P-47's fuselage with a spring door that folded inward. To mount the plane you stuck your right toe through this door and into the slot and grabbed a pullout handle up higher on the fuselage to pull yourself up to where you could put your left foot on the trailing edge of the wing. From there you climbed up the wing to the cockpit."

The engine on the P-47, even when well maintained, always leaked a small amount of oil that was swept back along the fuselage. Some of it was invariably caught in the foot slot. "The toes of our right shoes—with that rough leather—soaked that oil up," Powell remembered, "so that it took on a brownish-gray sheen. Whenever you saw a guy with a shoe like that, it was a dead giveaway that he flew P-47s."

However, not all of the men wore this type of shoe. Many of them were impressed with the higher, sheepskin-lined boots that the RAF fliers wore. They were romantically good-looking and warm and many of the 352nd's pilots paid to have them specially made. "But we found out later that it wasn't such a good idea," Powell said. "Don Dilling went down over France and made his way back to England through Spain. The people who helped him over the Pyrenees Mountains told him that there had been RAF pilots who were left behind because of their feet; they'd sweat during the day in those boots and freeze at night." Subsequently, many of the 352nd's pilots who had bought the expensive boots returned to wearing the workmanlike government-issue boots.

Only about one in twenty men at Bodney was a pilot. The rest performed necessary but unheralded tasks. On average, the station burned nine tons of coal per day. USAAF

Used less often than their 75-gallon counterparts, the 108-gallon, plastic-impregnated paper fuel tanks could be easily handled by one ground crewman. USAAF

The 75-gallon expendable fuel tanks were hung from the P-51's wings and were made of steel. USAAF

When the 352nd finally scored its first aerial victories on November 26, 1943, John Bennett shared credit for downing an Me-109. Later, his P-51 was the only 352nd aircraft to be painted with a shark's mouth. USAAF

Chaplain George Cameron played "Taps" every Sunday. He was tireless in raising college funds for the children of fallen 352nd airmen. USAAF

The 352nd's chaplain, Capt. George Cameron, led a sunrise service on Easter Sunday, April 9, 1944. USAAF

Aside from Virgil Meroney, who scored nine aerial victories in the P-47, Don Bryan was the next most successful Jug pilot in the 352nd, with four kills. His final total was 13.3. USAAF

Robert Frascotti, in a tragic takeoff accident, flew his P-51B, *Umbriago*, into the 352nd's still uncompleted control tower during the early-morning darkness of D-Day. USAAF

This Me-262, chasing a P-47, was captured on William Gerbe's gun camera film on November 1, 1944, before he and a 56th Fighter Group P-47 pilot shot it down. USAAF

Good formations were important to survival. Those who didn't stay with the rest of the group often didn't make it. USAAF

Colonel Joe Mason commanded the 352nd for most of its combat career. Despite the fact that he wasn't respected by all, the group performed well under his stewardship. USAAF

Major Steve Andrew shot up an FW-190 on April 30, 1944. The pilot bailed out but fell directly into Andrew's propeller. USAAF

After more than three days in the frigid North Sea, Fremont Miller's legs were nearly amputated. To help him get around during his recovery, enlisted men at Bodney built him a hand-powered bike. USAAF

William Whisner wasn't happy when his aircraft was named to honor England's Princess Elizabeth. One of the 352nd's stalwarts, he was an ace during both World War II and the Korea War. USAAF

William Schwenke went down off the French coast during the 352nd's armed reconnaissance mission to the Calais area on March 11, 1944, and was never recovered. USAAF

Glennon Moran was not one of the 352nd's original pilots, but with thirteen aerial victories scored from the end of February to the first of August 1944, he was one of its most successful. USAAF

Edward Gignac was one of the 352nd's most able leaders. He was badly injured while flying a P-39 in the Southwest Pacific prior to joining the 352nd and was killed by ground fire on June 7, 1944, at the controls of Willie O. Jackson's P-51, *Hot Stuff.* USAAF

John C. Meyer in the cockpit of his first P-51, *Lambie II.* Meyer, the commanding officer of the 487th Fighter Squadron, was the 352nd's dominant leader. USAAF

Flying with a massive hangover, George Preddy made history on August 6, 1944, when he shot down six German aircraft. USAAF

While Germany was reeling from air and ground assaults, the 352nd's Mustang Blues football team went 4-2-1 during their 1944 season. USAAF

Cyril Reap was not a pilot, but as the 352nd's chief engineering officer, he was in charge of the maintenance of the group's aircraft. Accordingly, he was responsible to a considerable degree for the unit's successes. USAAF

Willie O. Jackson, the 486th's commanding officer, was well respected and was with the 352nd from the beginning to the end of its operational career. He finished the war with seven aerial victories. USAAF

A staged publicity photo. The guns could be cleaned and reloaded while still in the aircraft and were actually removed from the aircraft only very infrequently. USAAF

The transition from the P-47 to the P-51 during the spring of 1944 required the group's maintenance men to be retrained on the P-51's Packard-built Merlin engine. USAAF

Karl Waldron was credited with downing three German fighters during the wild melee of November 21, 1944. USAAF

Don McKibben of the 486th Fighter Squadron survived the midair collision of March 8, 1944, when the group lost four P-47s. USAAF

Carl Luksic, on May 8, 1944, was the first American fighter pilot flying out of England to down five German aircraft during a single sortie. USAAF

The massive size of the P-47's Pratt & Whitney R-2800 radial engine is apparent. USAAF

The men at Bodney constructed a coffee cart that the Red Cross staffed. USAAF

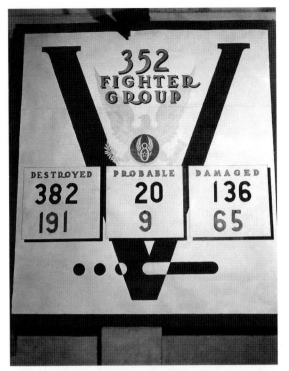

The 352nd maintained a Victory Board that tallied the group's successes. The upper numbers indicate the claims made while the lower numbers indicate the claims approved to that point by higher headquarters. This photo likely dates from the late summer of 1944. USAAF

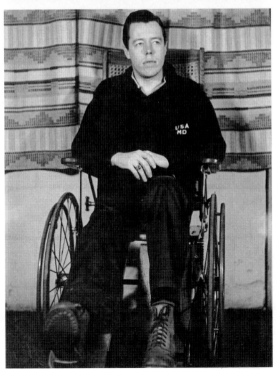

Meyer was taken out of combat by an automobile accident in Belgium while en route to a public-relations radio interview. Here he is recovering in England. USAAF

The 352nd's training activities at Trumbull Field, Groton, Connecticut, during the early months of 1943 were hampered by cold and snow. 352ND FIGHTER GROUP ASSOCIATION

George Preddy with his crew chief, Lewis Lunn. USAAF

German fighter pilots braved dangers besides those presented by their American counterparts and the gunners aboard the bombers. Here an FW-190 pilot has a close call with falling bombs. USAAF

Early members of the 487th Fighter Squadron on December 20, 1943. From the left: Harold Riley was shot down and killed by ground fire on March 11, 1944; Winfield McIntyre ran out of gas over France and was made a POW on December 30, 1943; Clay Davis was forced down over Europe on August 14, 1944, and successfully evaded; Don Dilling ran out of gas over France on the same day as McIntyre and successfully evaded; Daniel Britt broke both his legs in a landing accident on December 24, 1943. USAAF

Frank Cutler was a mercurial figure who was variously loved and loathed. He scored seven aerial victories, including one in the midair collision that killed him on May 13, 1944. USAAF

James Bleidner, on the right, was John C. Meyer's armorer during the entire period Meyer was in combat. Sanford Moats is the pilot talking to the other armorer, Jack Rider. USAAF

Leo Northrop watches Don McKibben fly his silverware through an exacting set of maneuvers. USAAF

Eight-victory ace Ray Littge knocked down two Me-109s with this aircraft on November 27, 1944. He named it *E Pluribus Unum*. It was later assigned to Flight Officer Charles Cole, who renamed it *Joanie* after his wife. 352ND FIGHTER GROUP ASSOCIATION

Chet Harker is pictured with his P-47, *Cile—Luck of the Irish*. It was destroyed when Don McKibben bailed out of it during a midair collision on March 8, 1944. 352ND FIGHTER GROUP ASSOCIATION

Don Bryan with his P-51, *Little One III*. Bryan was credited with 13.3 aerial victories. USAAF

Glennon Moran's P-51 *Little Ann* shows obvious wear and tear. 352ND FIGHTER GROUP ASSOCIATION

Karl Dittmer's *Dopie Okie*. Dittmer flew with the 352nd after completing a tour flying B-24s. 352ND FIGHTER GROUP ASSOCIATION

CHAPTER 6

A New Year

Keeping secrets about operational plans, equipment, and unit disposi-
tions was important to the war effort. Accordingly, all personnel
received briefings about the sorts of information they could share in their
letters and other communications. For instance, it was forbidden to reveal
their specific location but it was permissible to "mention names of towns,
cities, or places visited provided such towns, cities or places are located
more than twenty-five miles from the place where the writer's station or
unit is located at the time the correspondence is originated and the distance, direction, or time of travel from their stations to the cities mentioned
are not stated or implied."[1]

But aside from counting on individuals to adhere to official directives,
the military required that every letter and telegram be reviewed by a cen-
sor. Although there was a censorship officer assigned to the unit, it was
impossible for one man to police the outgoing mail from nearly a thousand
other men. Accordingly, the pilots were often assigned ancillary duties as
censors with specific instructions outlining exactly how those duties were
supposed to be carried out.

Still, in practice, the actual censorship of letters mostly fell somewhere between bored neglect and what was officially mandated. It was difficult to get enthusiastic about the task when the odds were so tiny that a
member of the unit would try to send sensitive information to the enemy
through a letter. Too, the physical act of censoring was time consuming.
Each letter had to be opened, read, sealed, signed, and stamped. Few letters actually needed censoring, although the always chatty Fahrenwald had
half a page of his letter from December 4, 1943, simply torn away.

There was also the fact that it was often difficult to decide what might be interesting or useful to the enemy in the extremely unlikely event that mail reached enemy agents or sympathizers. In other words, there was plenty of gray area. Taken to extremes, virtually everything might be considered sensitive. For instance, the following note home was likely harmless: "Thanksgiving dinner was swell! The entire unit stood down for the day and enjoyed turkey with canned cranberries and sausage stuffing." Yet the most ardent secret keepers could argue that such information might be valuable to the Germans in determining the morale of the Americans, their operational tempo, and their shipping capacity.

Fahrenwald recalled that censorship duty was a "pretty big chore. They [enlisted men] write an awful lot of letters, and lately more and more to English lassies. The boys get around some."[2] Don McKibben recalled the task as "a pain in the butt." Punchy Powell also remembered censoring as a mind-numbing assignment. "I don't think any of us liked doing it. We scanned the letters very loosely if at all. I felt like it was an invasion of privacy and don't really remember actually reading any letters; I just approved them and let them fly."

McKibben remembered shaking his head after reading a letter written by a corporal who misrepresented himself as a pilot:

He must have convinced his female correspondent that it was only a matter of time before Ike stepped down to make room for her hero. This guy flew tough missions with breezy disdain for the enemy. Flak? Like popcorn, only darker. He was obviously confident that the addressee of his letter had no interest in checking facts, so he did not burden his story with them. His war was a hell of a lot more interesting than ours. And we, as censors, did not need to get in the way. We simply signed off, and turned to the next letter in the pile.

Still, there were instances when the mail was actively censored. "I sent a few photos home with some of my letters," remembered Powell, "and one of the photos of myself wearing my A-2 jacket got censored. When it arrived at my home, a tiny section had been cut out of the picture. It was the painting of a P-47 just below the wings on my jacket. It was kind of stupid—as though the Jerries didn't know what we were flying and from where."

The young men of the 352nd knew to some degree that the war would prove to be a—if not, *the*—watershed mark in their lives. For the pilots, the war created circumstances of life and death, of sadness and exuberance, and especially of camaraderie that would never exist again. It was the same for their enemies. Although his language and tone are different, Heinz Knoke, the German fighter pilot, wrote of the same sorts of feelings that are apparent in Ted Fahrenwald's letters home:

> . . . the wonderful fact of flying and the spirit of chivalry which still exists in battle far above the clouds resulted in a sense of unrestricted happiness and peace of mind. The ever-present prospect of sudden death adds a zest to life while it lasts. Dedicated as we are to the serious business of fighting for our country, we are able to enjoy the mere fact of existence with a superb exhilaration simply because it is so uncertain and precious. We regard life as a jug of delicious Rhine wine . . . draining it to the dregs in an atmosphere of companionship and gaiety.[3]

Knoke, unwittingly, further underscored the similarities between the fliers of the opposing sides when he recalled the morning of January 1, 1944: "My men are sleepy and suffering from hang-overs when they report at the dispersal point," he wrote. "I heard them return singing from town in the small hours of the morning. My own head is splitting also." Knoke's weariness of the American raids was obvious in his next sentence: "All day long we can only hope that just for this one day the Yanks will not come over."[4]

Actually, the Yanks did come over although nothing about the mission marked it as memorable for the 352nd. An FW-190 that was harassing a straggling bomber was bounced south of Callac, France, but escaped by diving into the clouds. Earl Abbott's aircraft was hit by flak but remained flyable. Finally, upon arriving back over England, the 352nd's fuel-starved P-47s were forced by lowering weather to recover at several different airfields. It wasn't until the next day that they were all accounted for. Although they are rarely featured in popular histories for obvious reasons, these sorts of mostly uneventful missions where weather was the primary danger made up a significant part of every fighter group's experience over that part of Europe.

The start of 1944 saw an important change at the top of the Eighth Air Force. Command was passed from Ira Eaker to James "Jimmy" Doolittle. Although Eaker had done herculean work to get the Eighth Air Force in place, trained, and into combat, Henry Arnold, the overall commander of the USAAF, was not convinced that Eaker was aggressive enough in prosecuting the air war. Arnold's dissatisfaction, together with political considerations relating to the coming invasion of Europe, combined to send Eaker to command the Mediterranean Allied Air Forces, while Doolittle took his place at the head of the Eighth.

Eaker was a consummate organizer, politician, and professional military man. Doolittle embodied many of those same qualities but was more sensational. He was a famous air racer during the 1930s and was technically brilliant, having pioneered the science of instrument flight and having also done important work with high-octane aircraft fuels. Moreover, flying USAAF B-25s from Navy aircraft carriers—previously an unthinkable notion—he led a famous and daring raid against Japan earlier in the war. His name was famous in households across America and Arnold expected him to put more initiative into the Eighth's operations.

Spaatz, meanwhile, was moved to England, where he was given a new post. As the overall commander of the U.S. Strategic Air Forces (USSTAF) in Europe, he directed the operations of the Eighth Air Force in England and the Fifteenth Air Force in Italy. The changes were seen as critical to the final neutralization of the Luftwaffe.

Observations and reactions to the changes from average airmen were scarce. Ted Fahrenwald remarked on it: "Jimmy Doolittle is our new boss over here now, and that guy ought to be able to dream up something wild for us to do in our spare time. Looks like the Big Wheels are getting squared away for a colossal fight pretty soon."[5]

The primary mission of the Eighth's escort fighters up until Doolittle's assumption of command was to protect the bombers. Although it was a fine distinction, Doolittle directed that although the bombers were still to be protected, the fighters were to go after the Luftwaffe wherever and whenever it could. Indeed, Doolittle ordered William Kepner, the commander of VIII Fighter Command, to tear down a sign that read, "THE FIRST DUTY OF THE EIGHTH AIR FORCE FIGHTERS IS TO BRING THE BOMBERS BACK ALIVE." He ordered Kepner to replace it with one that declared, "THE FIRST DUTY OF THE EIGHTH AIR FORCE FIGHTERS IS TO DESTROY GERMAN FIGHTERS."

According to Doolittle, Kepner was overjoyed; he had advocated such a philosophy for several months. "Tears came to Bill's eyes," Doolittle recalled. He made it clear to Kepner that he wanted the fighters to take the offensive. "I told him he would still assign fighters for escort duty, but the bulk of them would go hunting for Jerries."[6] Kepner's fighters were—from that day forward—directed to pursue German fighters in the air and on the ground.

However, the change might not have been as dramatic or marked as Doolittle made out. The history of VIII Fighter Command that was published prematurely in October 1944—more than half a year before the end of the war—recalled the situation somewhat differently. In fact, it conflicts almost completely with Doolittle's recollection:

> There was little change of policy in the long-range escort work of the command, but General Kepner, *even more* [emphasis added] than his predecessor [Hunter], emphasized it as the first duty of the fighters to bring the bombers home. "Chasing the Hun from the Sky" gave way to "nursing the bombers home," until such time when our astounding air victories could permit more fighters to be detached for the job they loved best—"Bashing the Boche." General Kepner's first motto to the pilots was printed and posted in every group's briefing room. It read as follows: "We have two scores we are aiming at—first, the number of bombers we bring back safely, and second, the number of German fighters we destroy.[7]

The document also included a statement that was at extreme odds with Doolittle's recollections: "Under General Hunter [Kepner's predecessor], the fighters had the idea that their primary objective was to shoot the Hun out of the sky."[8]

Regardless of who said what and when, VIII Fighter Command grew considerably stronger during early 1944 and there were soon enough fighters to not only protect the bombers but to search out and kill the Luftwaffe. The fighter command's pilots, including those of the 352nd, embraced this notion with vigor. Punchy Powell remembered: "We weren't so closely tied to the bombers. We flew looser and wider and could chase after the Germans when they showed." Moreover, after completing their escort duties on any given mission, the fighter groups were encouraged to go hunting for the Luftwaffe wherever it might be, but especially on its airfields.

The 352nd's pilots were horrified, just like every other flyer in the USAAF, at the gut-wrenching sight of heavy bombers knocked down by enemy fighters or flak. Each one of the big ships took down the equivalent of a baseball team; the lucky ones among the crews parachuted clear of their stricken ships. The unlucky ones rode them down to a fiery impact with the earth. "It hurt my stomach every time I saw a bomber get shot down," remembered Punchy Powell.

But sometimes the bomber crews were their own worst enemies. The best defense against Luftwaffe fighters was a good, tight formation. Dense formations put up more concentrated defensive fire, which of course was more effective not only at shooting down attacking fighters, but also in dissuading attacks in the first place. However, flying close formation took both skill and muscle. After several hours of flying, both deteriorated and accidents were more likely.

The 352nd's mission summary report for January 4, 1944, described such an incident: "Two B-17s from second box had mid-air collission [sic] approximately six miles south of Nordhorn 1016 hours at 24,000 feet. The wing of one plane and the tail of the other seen to break off and both bombers tumbled toward the ground completely out of control. Approximately six parachutes seen immediately after collission [sic]."

On that same day, one of their Luftwaffe counterparts was nearly killed while bailing out. When the 352nd's pilots noted in their encounter reports that enemy pilots bailed out of their aircraft, it was typically noted as little more than a punctuation point to an aerial victory. Yet jumping clear of a stricken aircraft was fraught with hazard, as was emphasized by Heinz Knoke's experience when his Me-109 unit was sent to intercept bombers over Münster. His engine was knocked out by friendly flak and he was subsequently set upon by a Thunderbolt that set his ship afire. He had little time to appreciate the fact that his attacker was in turn shot down.

Making ready to abandon his Me-109, Knoke jettisoned his canopy and released his lap belt. "Before I am ready, however, I am jerked out of the seat by the slipstream." With his parachute caught up in the baggage compartment, aerodynamic forces twisted and pinned Knoke against the fuselage of the plummeting Me-109. "It whips at my left leg scrabbling in the air and almost twists it off. I am screaming with pain . . . the flames are licking across my body."[9]

Exercising formidable strength, Knoke manipulated the aircraft's control stick with his foot so that its dive was momentarily arrested. He was thrown free and knocked unconscious by pieces of the disintegrating aircraft. Although he never pulled the ripcord, his parachute somehow came open while he fell unawares through the clouds. After slamming into the frozen ground, he was taken to the hospital, where he was diagnosed with a skull fracture, paralysis of his right side, fractured vertebrae, and a gash, among other injuries.

On crutches, Knoke was back in combat less than four weeks later on January 30, 1944.

Aside from crediting their flyers with aerial victories, the Luftwaffe maintained a point system that was intended to measure with more fidelity the success of an individual fighter pilot; these point totals were tallied towards awards. Very simply, a pilot was awarded four points for bringing down a four-engine bomber, two points for a twin-engine bomber, and a single point for a fighter. But because the big B-24s and B-17s were often brought down by more than a single fighter and the Luftwaffe didn't award shared credits, a further refinement to the point system was developed.

This fine-tuning related to the downing of heavy bombers. If a pilot shot up a B-24 or B-17 badly enough that it fell out of its protective formation, he was awarded two points. This was no small feat, as it required the attacking pilot to brave the concentrated defensive fire of many bombers. One bomber alone carried ten or more .50-caliber machine guns and a pilot that attacked a full formation came within the lethal range of several dozen of these guns. In fact, Don Bryan of the 328th Fighter Squadron maintained that had every second round loaded into the bomber guns been tracer ammunition, the resultant display would have dissuaded even the most aggressive German fighter pilots from attacking. This action of cutting a heavy bomber out of formation was called a *Herausschuss*.

Likewise, a pilot that finished off a heavy bomber was awarded two points. Depending on how badly damaged the bomber was when it dropped out of its formation, this could still be quite difficult. Aside from the considerable firepower that even a crippled bomber could muster, the big ships could often could absorb tremendous damage and were sometimes quite difficult—and dangerous—to knock down. This act was known as an *Endgültige*.

Punchy Powell was flying as the element lead—the third aircraft—as part of Maj. Everett Stewart's Yellow Flight on January 5, 1944. Everett was leading the 328th Fighter Squadron as the group retrograded back to England following a bomber-escort mission. "We were in the vicinity of Averdon, France, at about 20,000 feet," Powell recounted, "when we spotted a really big aircraft below us. There was concern that it might be a decoy or a setup; the Germans would occasionally put one or two aircraft down low and then have an entire squadron of fighters sitting high above, ready to ambush anyone who took the bait."

The aircraft they spotted was an He-177. Built by Heinkel, it was an ill-conceived brute of a bomber. It had exactly the same wing span as the B-17 and was only two feet shorter, but it was much faster. It could also carry a bigger bomb load but at the same time it was very maneuverable considering its size. Protection came in the form of two 20 millimeter cannon and six lighter machine guns. It was powered by four engines of the same DB 605 type that drove the Me-109; they were mechanically combined in pairs to create a single, bigger engine designated the DB 610. These melded-engine units were mounted in nacelles, one per wing. Each drove a single propeller. Technically, and in appearance, it was a twin-engine aircraft.

Despite its impressive specifications, the He-177 was an abject failure. Designed and built as a heavy bomber, it never really served with distinction in that role. Moreover, it was technically complex and quite prone to engine failures and fires. The engine arrangement was particularly problematic and difficult to maintain. Just more than 1,000 aircraft were produced but it failed to score any meaningful successes.

Just why a single He-177 was motoring over France unprotected was anyone's guess. Ted Fahrenwald recalled: "Well, this knucklehead barges right into the middle of our fifty-ship fighter formation and we are so amazed at his crust that for a moment nothing at all happens . . . We all pounce like a band of starving wolves, and it is a case of first come first served and this other outfit gets there first."[10]

The 328th Fighter Squadron was Fahrenwald's "other outfit."

"Major Stewart," Powell recalled, "called out over the radio that he was taking our four-ship flight down to attack this big German aircraft—at the time we had no idea that it was an He-177." Stewart ordered the rest of the squadron to remain overhead as top cover as the four big P-47s dropped down. They caught it at about 15,000 feet as it continued its dive. "It was painted with a mottled black and green camouflage," Powell remembered, "with big black crosses on top of the wings and a gray underside. Just as we got within firing range, the pilot pulled the power on his right engine and started a violent right turn." The unorthodox maneuver caught Stewart by surprise. He and his wingman, John Coleman, were moving too fast and could only spray a few rounds at the bomber before they skidded past.

Powell, farther back, had enough maneuvering room and racked his P-47 onto its right wing. Pulling hard he drew lead on the German aircraft. "The tail gunner was firing at me," he recalled. The enemy gunner was ineffective; Powell squeezed the trigger on his control stick and both felt and heard the muffled, juttering rumble of his fighter's eight guns. "I scored quite a few hits. He smoked and caught fire as he rolled off to the right and went down." Above him, Powell's squadron mates watched the bomber hit the ground in the vicinity of Charvigney. Fahrenwald described the crash: "a couple of thousand feet off the deck the bomber explodes and falls in two parts in the woods. He explodes again with a tremendous blossom of red flame, starting forest fires."

After landing, Powell had the good sense to share the aerial victory with Stewart (his commanding officer) and Coleman. As it turned out, it was the first downing of an He-177 by Eighth Air Force crews.

The weather during much of January 1944 was poor and the 352nd did not do much flying. George Preddy took time to write home to his parents. He rarely mentioned his flying and in his letter of January 18 he described how he was watching his roommate's dog while the other man was away on temporary duty. "She is one of the little Spaniels I was telling you about and she is growing up to be real pretty. Every night she pulls our shoes out in the middle of the floor. If there is any paper for her to get hold of, you can be sure of having it torn up and scattered all over the place. I'm thankful she is pretty well house broken. That was the big headache for a long time."[11]

The nature of the air war was such that the 352nd's pilots generally did not know there was a mission scheduled until the actual day arrived. For the most part, because its primary mission was bomber escort, the 352nd's operations were tied to the bombers; if the bombers flew, the 352nd flew. Perhaps the most important factor around which bomber operations revolved was the weather. Good weather was especially desirable over the target to ensure the best bombing results. It did no good to put together the massive effort that was a bombing raid only to scatter bombs all over the countryside. Certainly, it was worth something to have the opportunity to shoot down defending German fighters, but if the weather was bad over Europe, the Luftwaffe often stayed on the ground.

However, weather conditions over the target aside, the weather also had to be good enough over England not only for the bombers to take off, but to form and proceed to the target en masse. Likewise, the bombers required somewhat clear skies en route in order to maintain their formations. Finally, once the mission was complete, the visibility and cloud ceiling over England had to be good enough for the pilots to safely recover back to their bases. The Eighth's leadership lived in constant fear of the fickle English fogs. They were petrified at the not unrealistic notion of hundreds of mission-weary crews trapped above the clouds, unable to land at airfields they could not see. Haywood Hansell, an Eighth Air Force bomb wing commander and a foundational USAAF strategist, articulated this terror:

> If the weather on return to base was "socked in," then disaster could ensue. As any visitor to England and all members of the Eighth Air Force will recall, England is occasionally hit by dense fog over large areas, and that fog can be so dense that it is difficult to walk from the mess to the operations office—to say nothing of finding hardstands and the airplanes. . . . It is quite possible that the entire Eighth Air Force could be lost on a single afternoon by returning to England and finding all bases "socked in." The weather was actually a greater hazard and obstacle than the German Air Force.[12]

Those fears notwithstanding, Spaatz believed that the risks were necessary in order to keep pressure on the Luftwaffe. Soon after Doolittle took command in January 1944, he recalled two massive raids because he believed the weather was about to deteriorate and trap the bombers and fighters above the clouds. As it happened, the bases remained clear. Spaatz was furious with Doolittle and took him to task. Doolittle recalled Spaatz's comments: "I wonder if you've got the guts to lead a big air force. If you haven't, I'll get someone else who has."[13]

Considering the confounding nature of the English weather, it was remarkable that such a tragedy never occurred.

The bugaboo that was compressibility still plagued the pilots in combat, much as it had during training. The excitement of the chase—or the primal urge to escape—often had the 352nd's P-47 pilots hurtling toward the ground at airspeeds well beyond what the aircraft was designed to endure. On January 29, 1944, Clayton Davis of the 487th was one of those who nearly lost his life to the phenomenon.

On that day the group was covering the bombers as they withdrew when Davis spotted an FW-190 as it made a diving attack on a B-17 near Malmedy, Belgium. The enemy pilot was aggressive; following his attack on the bomber, he turned and flew through the 487th's formation, firing all the way. Davis watched the German pilot finish his attack, pull up, stall, and nose downward. "I started after him in a vertical dive from 20,000 feet," Davis recorded. "He recovered and kept going down. At about 300 yards I gave him a burst and pieces started coming off of the FW-190."[14]

The enemy aircraft was finished but Davis had let his ship's airspeed rocket out of control. Almost two miles above the earth and still hurtling downward, the young pilot struggled with all his might to recover the plummeting ship. "I went past him [the FW-190] at about 10,000 feet in a compressibility dive and was just able to pull out on the deck." Shaken by his encounter with the high-speed phenomenon—and near certain death—Davis didn't even bother to rejoin his squadron. Instead, he stayed low to the ground, pointed his Thunderbolt west, and raced home to Bodney alone.

George Preddy had been credited with two aerial victories as January 1944 drew to a close and he flew the same mission as Clayton Davis on January 29. The skies over England were overcast but the clouds were high enough that the group was able to take off, form, and climb to altitude without incident. Following the completion of its escort duties, the group left the bombers and turned toward home, low on fuel. "The Group Leader called for everybody out and I started to join him," Preddy recalled, "when my number two man, [William] Whisner, called that the bombers were being attacked."[15]

Preddy dove on an FW-190 that was trailing a box of bombers. Whisner attacked another. Preddy never lost his advantage as he fired at the German through a series of climbing and diving turns. "I got a good long burst at 300 yards and saw hits all over the ship. The engine was evidently knocked out as I closed very rapidly after that. The last I saw of

him, he was at 1,500 feet going down at an increasing angle to the left."
Finished with the enemy aircraft and dangerously low on fuel, Preddy
turned toward Bodney with one eye on his fuel gauge and the other on the
hostile sky.

In the meantime, Whisner's opponent was doing his best to escape.
"He took violent evasive action—skidding, turning, and throwing everything into one corner. At 3 or 4,000 ft. I was able to get a good shot, and
observed strikes on wing and engine." Whisner pressed his P-47 hard after
the German as the two aircraft dove through a layer of clouds. "When I
came out below," he remembered, "I was beside him at 100 yards, and he
was in a dive smoking badly at 800 ft. above the ground. I was certain that
he couldn't recover before crashing, and being all alone, I pulled up hard
with everything on the fire wall."

As it happened, Whisner spotted Preddy and joined him. The two of
them descended below the clouds and headed west toward England.
"George never talked much on the radio—nor did he talk much ever," recollected Whisner. "I called him on the radio and asked his intentions, as we
were approximately 100 miles inside the continent. No answer." Preddy
continued to drone west over the enemy-held territory at an airspeed that
was appropriate for saving fuel, but not so much for staying alive in the
event that they were attacked by German fighters. Of course, depending on
where it happened, running out of gas could get a pilot just as dead as an
encounter with the Luftwaffe. Whisner made a couple more radio calls
suggesting that they increase their airspeed. Preddy never responded.

Finally, Whisner couldn't stand it anymore. Nearing the French coast
north of Calais, he reefed his aircraft into a hard diving turn to the right,
firewalled his throttle, and increased his airspeed before hauling the P-47
around into a hard left turn and back on course. A belt of antiaircraft guns
wrapped the coast and he was anxious to make himself as difficult a target
as possible. Racing just above the ground, he looked ahead and to his left to
where Preddy's aircraft loped along as if it were on a training flight. A
cluster of antiaircraft rounds burst nearby. "He received four 88 mm
rounds which missed," Whisner recounted, "and then four more which
bracketed him. He was still flying slow at 500 to 1,000 feet altitude."

Preddy's aircraft was hit. "She began smoking but didn't lose power
so I climbed 5,000 feet and gave a Mayday," Preddy recalled. "It was my
own fault really. While I didn't have too much gas, I could have done a lot
more twisting, and made it a lot more difficult for them to get a bead on
me. But I didn't do nearly enough squirming."[16]

Whisner dipped his left wing and climbed toward Preddy's smoking
P-47. "As I closed on him, I observed that he opened the canopy and

heavy smoke was coming from the cockpit as well as from the engine. I called him and suggested he should bail out as the aircraft could explode. No reply." Whisner called again and Preddy responded by calling Air/Sea Rescue, who gave him a steer toward landfall.

Preddy's engine finally quit and the heading from Air/Sea Rescue immediately became irrelevant. Powerless, the P-47 dropped toward the frigid sea. Low clouds obscured the surface and Whisner pulled up and circled once rather than try to fly formation with Preddy's doomed aircraft in the dark murk. A moment later, he dropped the nose of his fighter and slipped into the clouds at a shallow angle. "At just above 100 feet, I observed waves/foam/water below and suddenly—to my right—I saw a P-47 strike the water. Then, there was a parachute opening and even before I could start a turn, George swung once in the chute and was in the water."

"I hit the water and went six feet under but came right up again," Preddy said. "I had undone the leg straps of my chute before I landed, so I was able to move around pretty freely, though a gust of wind caught the chute when I came to the surface and carried me a little ways." It took Preddy ten exhausting minutes to get his rubber dinghy inflated and crawl out of the water.

Whisner called the Air/Sea Rescue station at Marston and worked with them to get a fix on Preddy's position. Then, low on fuel, he was relieved by another 352nd P-47 flown by Fred "Pappy" Yochim. Yochim had drawn spotter duty that day and it was his job to assist fliers that went down in the sea. It didn't take long before he guided a Walrus, an RAF amphibious biplane, to where Preddy bobbed in his dinghy. That Whisner and then Yochim and the British rescue crew were able to find him in the miserable weather was little short of miraculous.

Yet finding Preddy and getting the rescue aircraft down on the water and in position to pull him out wasn't the end of the story. Preddy later recalled: "The Walrus ran over me three times before they could get me inside. They damned near killed me! They felt so badly about it they gave me a bottle of brandy to drink on the way to shore."

He had time to drink it. As it turned out, the left wingtip pontoon of the Walrus tore off when the pilots tried to haul it airborne out of the rough water. To keep the left wing out of the water, one of the pilots, an Australian flying officer named E. "Tug" Wilson, scrabbled out onto the right wing as a counterbalance. By the time a torpedo boat arrived to tow them to Ramsgate, Wilson's arm had to be forcibly unwrapped from the wing strut. As it turned out, Wilson and Preddy learned they had Australian friends in common.[17]

Back at Bodney, there was concern about Preddy's well-being. "But George was tough," Whisner recounted, "and as I recall, two days later we

were drinking in the bar at the officers club, speculating on George's rescue and health, when he walked in wearing an RAF uniform. He shrugged
off any hardship and advised us that he had laid the gal whom we all knew
from her voice on the Marston Control Radio. She had a lovely sexy voice
and we had all speculated on how great it would be to meet her."[18]

Preddy's rescue happened because of the British. Their rescue organization was the product of extensive work started before America's entry
into the war. Although the British had a patchwork of procedures and
equipment in place earlier, it was only during 1941, when crew losses at
sea approached 200 per month, that a concerted effort was made to form
an organization—the Air/Sea Rescue Directorate—dedicated exclusively
to rescuing airmen downed at sea.

After starting with a hodgepodge of temporarily loaned aircraft and a
few boats, the value of Air/Sea Rescue soon became apparent, and it was
allocated permanent aircraft, specialized boats, and personnel. Moreover, to
increase the chances of aircrew survival, it provided training to combat personnel, and additionally developed or improved purpose-made equipment
such as life vests, inflatable dinghies, signaling equipment, and rations.

Perhaps most valuable was a system of "fixer" stations that were net-
worked to the actual rescue units. When an aircraft transmitted a distress
signal or requested a location "fix," the bearings of its signal from three
separate stations were forwarded to a central chart room where they were
plotted. The intersection of the bearings gave a quite accurate location
that—when combined with the aircraft's speed and course—dramatically
enhanced the chances of rescue. This information was used to get aircraft
and boats on the way even before anyone got wet.

The results were immediate and encouraging. Whereas before the formation of Air/Sea Rescue a crew that went into the water had virtually no
chance of survival, those odds improved to 36 percent by the end of 1942,
when the Americans began arriving in strength. At that time the Eighth Air
Force's leadership initially failed to appreciate or support the importance
of Air/Sea Rescue but its perspective quickly changed as it began to lose
aircrews at sea. Thereafter, it became an eager partner with the British and
their already established rescue organization.

When new units arrived, their pilots were sent to classes that familiar-
ized them with their equipment and taught them techniques to increase
their odds of surviving in the unhappy event that they went down in the
water. Punchy Powell recalled this training: "They sent us to a nearby
indoor swimming pool that had a high diving board. We had to jump into
the water with our Mae West and dinghy attached and they timed us to see
how fast we could get into the dinghy." Thankfully, the men did not have

to inflate the dinghy themselves. It was deployed and filled by a CO_2 cartridge that fired when a cord was pulled.

"We were told that we needed to get out of the water and into the dinghy in less than thirty seconds," Powell said. "The North Sea was so cold that if we didn't get out of the water quickly, our muscles would seize." There is little doubt that men perished because they simply couldn't get into their rafts.

By the summer of 1943, the USAAF had formed its first system of fixer stations and later that year instituted its version of the RAF spotter plane concept. Operational units scheduled aircraft to patrol specific areas through which its aircraft were planned to return following a mission. These aircraft, in radio contact with Air/Sea Rescue, marked the positions of downed aircraft and helped guide rescue planes and boats.

In fact, Punchy Powell's first mission with the 352nd was a spotter sortie. "I flew on Bill Hendrian's wing for nearly two-and-a-half hours. These didn't count as combat missions. Instead, you were assigned to cover the approximate return route of the group to watch for aircraft that might be in trouble. But of course," he recalled, "we'd help anyone that needed it—fighters and bombers. We coordinated with Air/Sea Rescue and relayed the approximate positions of any aircraft that were in trouble."

That the USAAF was able to afford the men and aircraft and fuel for these missions is telling. Where the Luftwaffe was growing increasingly desperate for aircraft and crews at that point in the war, the Americans and British had resources to spare that in turn were available to rescue their most valuable assets—their aircrews. They also served the other purpose, as noted by Powell, of easing new pilots into operations.

Air/Sea Rescue continued to evolve in complexity and capability. During early 1943, only 6 percent of USAAF crews that went into the sea were recovered.[19] At the end of 1943, that percentage rose to nearly 40 percent. By May 1944, the USAAF was operating a special unit of P-47 spotter aircraft, a detachment from the 65th Fighter Wing. The entire mission of this unit was to assist airborne aircraft in distress as well as downed aircrews.

Another concept that improved the rescue rate was the positioning of boats well out to sea so that, when cued, their transit time to the downed aircrew was significantly decreased. All of these factors and more combined to increase the chances of survival for the downed aircrew. An indicator is the fact that during the month of September 1944, 90 percent of the crews who went into the water were rescued.

CHAPTER 7

The Missions

The P-47, as big and ungainly as it was, bore some resemblance—when it was airborne—to the FW-190. This was especially true until about mid-1944 when the USAAF's P-47s were still being flown with an olive-drab paint scheme. An incident described by the 352nd's mission summary report for January 7, 1944, illustrates this point: "Major Richmond, 486th Squadron Leader, was bounced by P-38 immediately after r/v, vicinity Arlon 1233 hours, 25,000 feet. P-38 was below formation at offset, circled above flight and came in close on Major Richmond's tail in definite offensive maneuver. Squadron Leader immediately waggled wings to afford further identification and P-38 finally broke away." If nothing else, the lone P-38 pilot should be credited with having the guts to take on what he believed was a squadron of FW-190s.

A similar incident took place only two weeks later on January 21, 1944: "Early return Blue Flight of 328th Sqdn. Fired on by No. 4 pilot of a flight of P-47s with markings 'HV' [61st Fighter Squadron, 56th Fighter Group], south of Manston, 1500 hours at 8,000 feet." The aggressor in this instance was from the 56th Fighter Group, which was actually the first to deviate from the standard white cowl band prescribed by VIII Fighter Command for its P-47s. In order for its pilots to better identify other P-47s from within the group, the 56th switched to colored cowl bands for its three squadrons: red for the 61st, yellow for the 62nd, and blue for the 63rd. Evidently, word was passed about the new color scheme as the 352nd's mission report from February 8, 1944, noted: "New markings 56th Group did not interfere with proper identification."[1]

Proper identification of friend and foe was an issue that never went away. As the number of P-51s in theater continued to grow during early 1944, the type's resemblance to the Me-109—especially when painted olive drab—caused confusion. For a while after the P-51 was introduced, the bomber gunners were especially notorious for hammering away whenever the sleek little fighters approached too closely.

Edwin King, an RAF exchange pilot with the 352nd, recalled an incident later in the year following the group's transition to the P-51. He was flying on George Preddy's wing on a bomber-escort mission: "On the latter part of the return we had to give close support to a Fortress [B-17] which had a wing and the fuselage damaged and one engine feathered and it was straggling badly. The crew of the bomber fired on us whenever we got too close. However, we stayed with them until they reached the English coast and then we parted company."[2] No doubt, the bomber's crewmen reported that they had been persistently dogged by German fighters, but had held them off with concentrated gunfire until they were safely across the English Channel.

But as noted in the 352nd's mission summary report for February 10, 1944, it wasn't just the bomber gunners who had problems distinguishing the Me-109 from the P-51. After spotting a formation of Me-109s near Oldonzoh, the 352nd—still equipped with P-47s—gave chase. "Combat ensued until P-51s joined fight," the report stated. Evidently, there was quite a bit of confusion when the Mustangs joined the melee. "During heat of battle," the report continued, "R/T call identifying P-51s caused our group to cease firing resulting in Me-109s getting away with claims of only four damaged." It is easy to sense the group's irritation with the relatively new fighters in the sentence that followed: "Had P-51s remained away from combat, those engaged believed further victories would have resulted."

That same mission presented another interesting incident related to aircraft identification. The summary report noted: "12/15 Me-109s seen S/O Enschede, 30,000 ft, 1110, with British markings, repeat, British markings." No other mention is made of this strange encounter. It might be easy to suppose that the 352nd's pilots mistook RAF fighters for Me-109s, but this seems unlikely as the Me-109 was the chief German fighter type and by that time in the war it was certainly very familiar to the American fliers. On the other hand, there is no reliable record that the Luftwaffe ever operated its aircraft painted in RAF markings. There is a good chance that the British fighters were Mustang Mk IIIs. The 352nd's pilots wouldn't have been the first by far to mistake the Mustang for the Me-109.

Like the Me-109, the Spitfire was very familiar to the 352nd's pilots but it was also misidentified on occasion. Early in the war, Spitfires were used to escort bombers outbound from England and across the Channel until just past landfall over France or the Low Countries. Once the bombers had completed their mission, freshly fueled Spitfires picked them up as they started back across the Channel. Punchy Powell almost attacked one of these escorts late in 1943: "We had gotten badly separated during a mission and I was on my way back with one other pilot when we spotted a B-17 down low in the haze with fighters flitting around it." The two Americans dove on the fighters. "I came up behind one of them and was about to cut loose when my wingman called out—just barely in time—'Don't shoot, Punchy! They're Spits!'" Slightly higher and off to one side, Powell's wingman recognized the elliptical wings that were unique to the Spitfire.

To preclude incidents of this sort—and worse—the 352nd's pilots were repeatedly drilled on aircraft recognition. This was true of all the fighter groups. Punchy Powell remembered that it was an important part of squadron life: "Our S-2 [Intelligence] guys, Dave Lee and Otto Ziebell, really worked hard on this for the pilots. First, in our pilot room, hanging from the ceiling, were many, many, small aircraft models about six or eight inches long, some of metal, some of other material." Powell recalled that the enthusiastic intelligence men even had models of Russian and Italian aircraft. "They would sometimes challenge us to see how many we could identify correctly in a limited time. Ziebell and Lee also held frequent training sessions during which they flashed all types of aircraft on a screen for one or two seconds to test us on our aircraft identification skills. We used to sit around and challenge each other, often taking bets."

The Germans likely underwent similar training. Still, during the first several months following VIII Fighter Command's introduction of the P-51, they also had difficulty distinguishing it from the Me-109. This is illustrated in John Meyer's encounter report of April 15, 1944, during which he led his squadron against a couple of different airfields. Recalling his attack against the first, he reported: "Approaching the field, I observed several flak towers and gun emplacements; the field seemed to be well defended, however, as on other occasions I saw German troops who made no move to man their guns or take cover. I believe this is due to their difficulty in recognizing the P-51 from the Me-109."[3] His experience when he hit the second airfield was similar: "Again, the problem of recognition seemed to confound the Huns, for as I attacked the Ju-52, the crews turned and watched me, but made no move to seek cover until I started firing."

A great deal of planning happened behind the scenes before the 352nd's pilots were wakened for a bomber-escort mission. For the most part, the pilots had little idea or appreciation of the considerable work that went into the effort. For instance, the Eighth Air Force's fighter component, VIII Fighter Command, typically received a warning order at approximately 5:00 P.M. the day before a mission. With that warning order, the command's planners could do some rough work but nothing with any fidelity. Sometime around 9:00 P.M., details of the mission arrived and the planners assigned portions of the route to the various fighter groups based chiefly on the readiness and experience of the groups and the types of aircraft they operated. Additional fighter groups were assigned along portions of the route where enemy fighters were expected.

As the mission details were evaluated, the rendezvous times, specific checkpoints, target times, altitudes, and routes were defined and assigned. Based on that information, the planners worked a timeline backward to calculate takeoff times. Working further back, and allowing adequate time for breakfast, briefing, and preflight preparations, wakeup times were determined. The planning grew to be very complex, especially later in the war when enormous raids of a thousand aircraft or more hit multiple targets and were supported by feints and other diversions.

The plans were put together by experts from a variety of disciplines: meteorologists, intelligence experts, logisticians, and airmen, among others. That many of the airmen were experienced pilots who had finished their operational tours or were pulled from combat duty for other reasons was a tremendous boon. It was especially valuable that they understood not only the basic plan, but also the different vagaries associated with actually flying the complex missions.

It was often past midnight when the fighter plan was briefed to the commanding general and his staff. Barring dramatic changes, the scheme was finalized and transmitted to the fighter groups. However, weather and other developments could cause changes to the plan even after the groups got airborne.

The 352nd began preparations for a specific mission beginning with the arrival of the mission field order (FO). It came as a staccato, clattering directive over the unit's teletype (TWX) machine located in the intelligence (S-2) section. The noise immediately drew the attention of clerks who hovered over the machine as it banged out the mission's details. Coded sections were subsequently deciphered and disseminated to the other sections, particularly the operations, or S-3, shop. However, the briefing details—and the briefing room itself—were generally prepared by the S-2.

The 352nd's intelligence section recorded the activity that was typical upon receiving orders for a mission: "The S-2 and S-3 room, later known as the War Room, became the nerve center of the field. It was here where the duty intelligence officer received the field order and plotted the mission, the Group and Squadron leaders, pre-briefed and post briefed, maps made and distributed to Group and Squadron leaders, special mission tactics planned, escape and evasion equipment distributed to Headquarters flying personnel, and dozens of other detailed yet important tasks performed."

While the group briefing was readied, arrangements were made to wake the pilots. This was usually done by a clerk from either the S-2 or S-3 sections. The pilots might or might not have had an idea that there would be a mission when they went to sleep the previous evening. Weather was a key indicator; if flying conditions were miserable and expected to remain so, the pilots could be fairly certain that there would be no mission. On the other hand, fair weather produced a fair chance of a mission.

Another determining factor was the tempo of operations. "If the bombers flew a heavy mission one day," remembered Don Bryan of the 328th Fighter Squadron, "we could generally count on getting the next day or two off while they rested and got themselves put together again." This was especially true early in the 352nd's combat career, but less so as the Eighth grew in size and was able to sortie almost daily.

Reflecting back on operations from a pilot's perspective, George Arnold recalled that the day-to-day routine was not overly rigorous. "Our schedules were fairly flexible," he recalled. "We had to report down to the flight line by a certain time each day, unless we had a mission; on those days, of course, we'd be up early."[4]

Even then, "early" differed for the fighter crews when compared to their bomber comrades. The bomber crews were often out of bed at three or four in the morning in order to see to their ablutions, eat breakfast, receive their briefings, ready their aircraft, start, taxi, take off, and gather their formations before they winged east for the continent. On the other hand, although the fighter pilots also had to shave, eat, and brief, it took them relatively little time to collect their gear, climb into their aircraft, start, taxi, take off, and head for their rendezvous points. Consequently, they were often able to get at least two or three more hours of sleep than the bomber crews.

But even if there was a mission scheduled, there was a decent chance that a pilot would not fly it. By plan, there were more pilots than aircraft, and consequently, not everyone could fly every mission. Donald McKibben described how the decision was made as to which pilots would fly on any given day: "Our squadron operations officer had the job of assigning pilots and aircraft. In general, his decisions were based on each pilot's accumulated time, and his availability. He tried to keep everything as equal as was reasonably possible. He also tried to keep element leaders and wingmen together as much as possible. However, there were no iron-clad rules, and quite often we flew missions with a grab-bag cast of characters."

Punchy Powell remembered how assignments were posted: "Each pilot belonged to one of four administrative flights within a squadron: A, B, C, or D. The flights had a leader and a total of seven or eight pilots. Each pilot had a small plaque inscribed with his name. If he was flying that day, it would be hung from small nails on the mission board in our squadron ready room. Each squadron usually put up four flights—sixteen aircraft—on a mission. Those flights were delineated by color: Red, White, Blue, and Yellow." So then, under each color on the mission board were hung four names. The first name was the flight leader, the second was his wingman, the third was the element leader, and the fourth was the element leader's wingman, also known as Tail End Charlie.

Still, all the pilots were required to go to the briefs. There was no predicting when last-minute replacements or additions would be required and the information that was passed, particularly the intelligence brief, was generally useful for future missions. McKibben recalled that after the pilots finished breakfast the entire group was briefed together:

We wrote mission-specific data on our palms or wrists. This included the engine start time and the takeoff time, etc. We also synchronized our watches. The takeoff time wasn't really important for most of us as we simply followed the leader. On some missions, we carried a simple five-inch square map of western Europe in a plastic envelope on which there were grease-pencil lines and other notations that indicated the course out, the location and time that we were to rendezvous with the bombers, as well as the time and location that we were to head home. This was tucked into the pocket of our flight suits, just below the right knee.

The group and squadron commanders were given strip maps marked with more comprehensive data.

George Arnold recalled the now-iconic wall map of Europe that was part of virtually every briefing across the Eighth Air Force. "It was covered by a curtain until everyone arrived. When they pulled it back, we saw ribbons running from Bodney to another set of ribbons that marked the bomber routes. Our rendezvous points were marked as was the point where we had to turn back so that we had enough fuel to get home."[5] The pilots were also briefed on which bomber units they were expected to escort and what their markings looked like.

The pilots were showed locations where antiaircraft fire was expected to be especially heavy. Further, they were told where they could anticipate encountering German fighters as well as information on what types they might be and how many. "We also received a briefing on the weather conditions," Arnold recalled. "It was never right." At the conclusion of the briefing, the group commander usually stood to summarize the effort and his expectations and to give a bit of a pep talk.

The drone of bombers overhead often greeted the pilots as they exited the group briefing. They were the same bombers the group would escort. Don McKibben described the subsequent flow: "The three squadrons were based at different points around the perimeter of the field, so after the general briefing, we dispersed to our respective areas and gathered our gear—our parachutes and escape kits—from a building that adjoined the squadron ready room. I never carried anything with me that wasn't needed for the mission; that meant my sidearm stayed behind. It was burdensome, and I did not intend to take on the Wehrmacht with it in the event I was shot down and cornered." Back at their own areas, the squadron pilots usually did not conduct their own separate briefings but occasionally the squadron commanders or flight leaders took a moment or two to emphasize certain points.

When the time for starting engines drew near, the pilots walked to their planes with their parachutes slung over their shoulders and their escape kits tucked into their jackets. Many of the men had their flight jackets modified with inside pockets specifically designed for the escape kits. The ground crews waited at the aircraft, having already readied it for the mission. Often, the crew chief or his assistant was wiping the canopy and windscreen one last time. It was impossible to have them too clean; spotting the enemy first could quite literally make the difference between life and death.

Some pilots inspected their aircraft carefully before climbing in but others went straight to the cockpit after a quick chat with the crew chief. "I had no pretensions about my qualifications as an aircraft mechanic," McKibben said, "and never tried to test or second guess my ground crew. The airplane would not have been waiting for me if it were not okay to go. And it always was." Such was the expertise of his ground crew that McKibben never aborted a sortie due to mechanical problems.

Whereas some men said a prayer or rubbed a special talisman or lucky charm, McKibben had no particular rituals that he performed prior to flying a mission. On the other hand, Don Bryan ceremoniously kicked both of his aircraft's tires before walking back to the empennage and urinating on the tailwheel.

At the appointed time, the pilots cranked and warmed their engines and performed their cockpit checks. "All of the squadrons' ships were parked in the same area," said McKibben, "and we knew who was in our flight and who we were supposed to follow so it was no problem to taxi out to the runway in the proper order. Bodney was a grass field, so we were able to take off four abreast and get airborne in short order." The 352nd wasn't cued to take off by a flare or signal of any sort; as soon as the leader had the group organized behind him, he ran his engine up to takeoff power, released his brakes, and led the first flight of four airborne.

The four-ship flights were arranged in an almost line-abreast formation with the lead just slightly ahead, his wingman set back on his left, his element leader set back on his right, and the element leader's wingman set just a bit back on the element leader's right. The aircraft were separated one from another by about a single wingspan.

"Once the tails of the aircraft in front of him lifted off the ground," said Punchy Powell, "the next flight leader added power at the same time that he released his brakes and put in a boot full of right rudder." Rather than going to full throttle, the flight leader stopped just short so that his wingmen had enough power to stay in position. This was part of being a good flight leader. None of the aircraft performed exactly alike and a flight leader with a strong aircraft who kept his throttle firewalled could quickly leave the rest of his flight behind.

Powell recalled that the 352nd was able to get all three squadrons, sixteen aircraft each—plus spares—airborne in less than four minutes. "We had that wide grass airstrip which let us get a lot of aircraft grouped together at the end of the field and then off the ground really quickly." The squadrons took off in order and flew generally straight away from the field for a couple of miles before making a turn back toward Bodney during which the last few pilots were able to join. "By the time we got back over the airfield," recalled Punchy Powell, "we were in nice, tight, good-looking formations that were a great boost for the morale of everyone on the ground." From that point, the group climbed on course in a stair-step arrangement of four-ship flights.

The group leader had a packet prepared for him by the S-3 which he used to navigate to the rendezvous point with the bombers and thence along the rest of the assigned route. "These worked quite well," remembered Powell, "although sometimes the winds aloft were not as predicted; this could cause problems with the rendezvous." Fighter-control squadrons—

one per each of VIII Fighter Command's three wings—rendered assistance as required. "It was infrequent that we missed a rendezvous with our assigned bombers," Powell said. "And most of those occurred early in our operational career. As the raids got bigger, it got easier to see the huge black masses of bombers. And it got much easier as the controllers got more experience. We really never had any problems after about April of 1944."

Radio communications were essential to the execution of the raids. However, both the communications plans and equipment were fairly simple. The SCR-522 radios that the fighters carried had only four VHF channels—A through D—that were preset on the ground. Don Bryan remembered that the radio was fairly reliable and Edwin King, an RAF exchange pilot, also noted that it was "very satisfactory."

Only one frequency could be monitored at one time. Considering how many aircraft were involved in a mission, it was essential that good discipline was exercised and that the radio was used only when required. Depending on a variety of factors that included the weather, the aircraft's altitude, and the physical condition of the aircraft's radio, they could reach out to 150 miles or more. Typically, a single radio technician was responsible for maintaining the radios of five or six different aircraft.

The group's operational frequency was tuned to "A" channel. On this frequency, the group received updates on such matters as the position and altitude of particular bomber groups, weather conditions, delays, and changes to the plan. This was also the channel which the pilots used for communicating with each other during the missions. Additionally, the fighter-control squadron used it to pass information from various radar stations as appropriate. The channel was also used administratively for the pilots to communicate with the control tower at their own base.

The 352nd's intelligence section recounted how the ranking officers not flying a mission monitored "A" channel as they waited for their comrades to return. "While the mission was in progress, the 'wheels' of the inner circle, who were not flying that day, could sweat out the show in the War Room and follow its progress by listening to the radio tuned to the fighter R/T [radio transmitter]. They could, and usually would, sprawl their frames across the large plotting table and await the return of the aircraft."

"B" channel was reserved exclusively for use by Air/Sea Rescue. Pilots in distress contacted Air/Sea Rescue stations on this frequency when it became likely they would have to bail out or ditch their aircraft. The Air/Sea Rescue stations fixed the locations of these distressed crews and dispatched boats or aircraft to recover them. Additionally, the stations provided recovery headings for aircraft that were lost or low on fuel.

Communications between the bombers and fighters were established on "C" channel. Usually, one pilot per squadron was assigned responsibility for monitoring this frequency to ensure that, if needed, information was passed from the bomber formation leader to his escorting fighters and vice versa. It was also monitored by control towers so that aircraft forced to land at airfields other than their own could establish contact.

"D" channel was somewhat of a catch-all or backup frequency that was common to the fighter groups within a fighter wing, of which there were three in VIII Fighter Command. Primarily, it was used by aircraft needing a location "fix" or heading to home base. It additionally served as a backup frequency for Air/Sea Rescue. On occasion, fighter controllers used it to warn of enemy aircraft or to assist fighter groups as they rendezvoused with their assigned bomber groups.

The pilots also communicated with each other via hand signals. For example, climbs and descents, turns, fuel quantities, and other commands or information were readily exchanged so long as the pilots were close enough to see each other. Ted Fahrenwald described some of these in a letter home: "A jerk of the head means throttle back. A fist run forward inside the canopy means more throttle. A raised hand with fingers clawed means to change gas-tanks. A whirling forefinger followed by outstretched five-fingers means a peel-off with five-second interval between ships." And if the pilots were not within hand signaling range of each other, they could still transmit their intentions to a limited extent by wagging their wings to signal turns. If all else failed, the wingmen generally couldn't go wrong so long as they followed their formation leaders.

After reaching the enemy coast, the four-ship flights within each squadron—which were generally arranged in a line-astern, or stair-step, formation from each other—spread out and maintained about a hundred yards between individual aircraft. This was close enough so that the flight leader could maneuver without losing anyone but far enough away so that the pilots could scan the skies without being fearful of running into each other. Too, it provided enough maneuvering room in the event that the flight was jumped by enemy fighters.

Air combat operations by their nature were hectic and confusing. Keeping everyone sorted out—one from another—was difficult to do. Nevertheless, each pilot had a specific radio callsign on each mission that distinguished him from everyone else. The naming convention started at the group level. The 352nd's radio callsign was Hatfield. It was used only to identify the group rather than individuals. Each squadron also had its own specific radio callsign. In the 352nd, the 328th Fighter Squadron was Turndown, the 486th was Handspun, and the 487th was Crown Prince.

Each squadron was subsequently divided into separate four-ship flights distinguished by color. These colors were usually white, yellow, blue, and red although other colors such as green, purple, and black were sometimes used. White Flight was usually led by the squadron commander or his designee. The leader of a particular flight was identified by the word "leader"—for example, Yellow Leader. Subsequent members of the flight were designated numerically. Yellow Leader's wingman was Yellow Two, Yellow Leader's element leader was Yellow Three, and the number-four aircraft in Yellow Leader's flight was Yellow Four. Accordingly, the number-two pilot in the 486th's Yellow Flight would have been Handspun Yellow Two. These callsigns applied only to given missions on a particular day. For instance, a pilot might fly as Blue Three on one day and White Four the next. These callsigns also had nothing to do with colors or markings on the aircraft.

The system evolved as units grew in size. The squadrons were eventually assigned more than thirty aircraft each and during late April 1944 the decision was taken to divide the group into three separate mission groups with distinct callsigns. Group A was Topsy, Group B was Bearskin, and Group C was Cloister. The squadrons were also split into three distinct groups, A, B, and C. The A and B groups were subsequently given new callsigns, whereas the C groups were used so infrequently that they went unnamed. The A and B groups in the 328th were known as Ditto and Tarmac, respectively. In the 486th, they were known as Angus and Rocket, whereas in the 487th they were called Transport and Vicar.

In practice, the radio callsign system worked well enough except during occasions when the fighting grew especially intense. During those times it was difficult to remember who was who. As much as the system made sense, the callsigns were a mouthful and not particularly easy to spit out in the heat of combat. It must also be considered that when formations became separated in particularly wild fighting, it was virtually impossible to distinguish one aircraft from another anyway.

The 352nd's aircraft markings followed VIII Fighter Command convention. Both sides of the fuselage behind the cockpit were painted with the national insignia. A two-letter squadron identifier was painted in front of it. The 487th Fighter Squadron's designator was "HO," whereas the 328th's was "PE" and the 486th's was "PZ". Behind the national insignia was a single letter that was normally the first letter of the last name of the pilot. For instance Preddy was assigned to the 487th and his aircraft, *Cripes A'Mighty*, was marked with an "HO" in front of the national insignia and a "P" behind.

A few months after the group transitioned to the P-51, the single letter behind the national insignia was moved to the tail, where there was more room. It was often the case that there were several pilots in the squadron whose last names started with the same letter. In those instances, the single letter was underlined or marked with a dot, or a pilot was simply assigned a different letter.

During escort operations one fighter group was generally assigned to rendezvous with a specific bomber unit and take it to a particular point before passing it to another fighter group. The practice applied during the penetration to the target as well as the withdrawal back to England. It was known as the relay system and it maximized the range performance of the fighters and allowed the bombers to penetrate deeper with escorts than they otherwise would have been able.

This was because the fighters had to weave to keep pace with the slower bombers. Essentially, the fighters were covering much more distance—albeit in turning flight—than the bombers. And in so doing, they consumed a good deal more fuel than they would have were they flying a steady course. The relay system allowed a fighter group to take off and fly directly to the rendezvous point.

Early in 1944, the Eighth's planners tailored the escort plans for each mission by fighter type. Short-legged RAF Spitfires took the bombers to landfall over the continent before turning for home. At that point, P-47s penetrated with the bombers before passing them to longer-legged P-38s and P-51s. Escort planning was somewhat simplified later in the war as VIII Fighter Command transitioned almost entirely to the longer-legged P-51.

Once the rendezvous was made, the fighters typically stacked themselves at least a thousand feet above the bombers, with one squadron to each side and one to the front. John C. Meyer wrote contemporaneous notes on the subject while the 352nd was still flying the P-47. "Upon rendezvous with the bombers," he recalled, "the group generally breaks down into eight-ship sections of two flights, each operating independently and at various ranges from the main bomber force. One flight of this section remains in close support of the other on bounces. This method has been the most successful one tried by this organization."[6]

The fighters typically weaved not only to see better in all directions, but also so that they could maintain a fighting speed without overrunning the bombers. This was necessary because the bombers usually flew at about 160 miles per hour indicated airspeed while the fighters maintained an indicated airspeed of about 250 miles per hour. This higher airspeed made them better able to intercept Luftwaffe fighters and better able to defend themselves if bounced.

This basic arrangement varied quite often depending on the particular situation. For instance, the front squadron, especially later in the war, often pushed ahead to disrupt German fighter formations. Sometimes, particularly when there were a great many bombers to protect, the squadrons set up an oval track that covered a geographical area rather than a specific bomber unit. And in those instances when the squadrons were broken up in combat with German fighters, they often returned to the bombers and set up their coverage in an ad hoc fashion as best they could.

Virgil Meroney wrote a contemporary account that recorded the 352nd's procedures upon encountering the enemy: "Each flight can make a bounce; the others covering. We try to keep a section of two flights [four aircraft each] together at all times. In the flight, the element leader can make the attack while calling it in and the flight leader and his wingman will follow him. In so far as the wingmen [numbers two and four in a four-ship flight] are concerned, they can lead the attack only if the flight or element leader cannot see the enemy aircraft." Meroney also noted that it was a bad idea for a wingman to chase after enemy aircraft on his own. "He may get one or two e/a, but the chances are he won't get back to get his name in the *Stars and Stripes*—air discipline."[7]

As Meroney recorded, once a fight began, the flight leader and the element leader—numbers one and three in a four-ship flight—did the shooting while numbers two and four, the wingmen, provided protection, or cover. This arrangement worked well, but sometimes wasn't possible to maintain when the flight came under attack. In these instances the wingmen were oftentimes forced to split off in order to keep from being shot down. And occasionally, the leader's maneuvering was so violent and unpredictable that the wingmen just couldn't keep up. Moreover, the wingmen were sometimes presented shooting opportunities that they just could not resist and went off on the chase.

John C. Meyer commented on the role of the wingman: "The wingman's primary duty is protection of his element leader. . . . The wingman flies directly in trail on the attack. This provides maneuverability and he is there to follow up the attack if his leader misses. Once, however, the wingman has cleared himself and is certain his element is not under attack, he may move out and take one or the other e/a under attack [if] more than one target is available. Good wingmen, smart wingmen, are an answer to a leader's prayers."

Upon completing a mission, if the 352nd hadn't blown itself apart in a fight, it usually returned to Bodney en masse. The three squadrons typically split themselves into four flights of four aircraft each and descended toward the field at close interval. "We came across the field in fingertip formation at about a hundred feet," recollected Punchy Powell. "Then, as the flight lead pulled up, the other three pilots followed him into a climbing, nearly vertical turn to the left. Everyone in the flight separated slightly as they chopped their throttles back to idle. At the top of the climb—at about a thousand feet—we were slow enough to lower the wheels before dropping our noses on the turn toward final approach."

As the pilots descended in a turn toward the field, they eyeballed their touchdown points while making sure they left room for other ships to land. At the same time, they glanced over the right side to make sure that—in their turn—they weren't on a collision course with an unseen aircraft. "As we turned onto final, still in a turn," Powell continued, "we dropped about twenty degrees of flaps. The three wingmen and the lead aircraft were spaced out about fifty or sixty feet from each other on touchdown. It was a point of pride among us to not touch our throttles from the time we pulled them back to idle until we landed. We got pretty good at it." Once they were safely on the ground, the pilots threw a quick look behind them to make sure that no one was landing long—potentially on top of them—and then ran up their throttles to clear the landing area.

However, there were times when pilots were separated during a fight and not able to return with their squadrons. Meyer's writings covered these instances: "Usually, if the combat is of any size or duration," he recalled, "flights become separated. The element of two becoming separated, however, is a cardinal and costly sin. We find it almost impossible for elements to rejoin their squadrons or flights after any prolonged combat." In those cases, Meyer was of the opinion that his pilots should know no strangers—so long as they were on the right side. "However, there are generally friendly fighters in the vicinity all with the same intention and we join any of them. A friendly fighter is a friend indeed, no matter what outfit he's from."

Robert Powell's recollections were consistent with what Meyer wrote: "When planes got separated in a melee, they came back in smaller groups or even ones and twos unless they found another formation to join. If we were low on fuel when we crossed the coast, we often landed at other bases where we could get enough gas to get back to Bodney. Usually, these were American bases because most of the RAF airfields were toward southern England whereas we were concentrated in East Anglia."

After taxiing back to his parking spot, the pilot shut down the engine and completed the aircraft's Form 1. He recorded the flight time of the mission as well as any maintenance issues. "Once I climbed out, I'd usually talk with the crew chief about the airplane and anything interesting that happened during the mission," remembered Don McKibben. "A trip to the latrine was really important, too."

From their aircraft, the pilots walked back to their squadron, where they dropped off their parachutes, Mae Wests, and escape kits. If they had scored, or had another reason to file an encounter report, they usually debriefed with the S-2, or intelligence, officers, who took notes and compiled the reports. "That usually happened after Doc Lemon gave those of us who wanted it a shot or two of booze," remembered Punchy Powell. "It tended to loosen tongues a bit."

CHAPTER 8

Fuel and Nerves

Fremont Miller was proclaimed the group's most beloved pilot by more than one of his peers. Physically, he towered over the other men and was so massively strong that he was in a class by himself. "On the few sunny days we enjoyed when we weren't flying," Punchy Powell recalled, "we often sprawled out on the grass to soak up the sun. When we got bored, we'd challenge Fremont to a wrestling match which would start with four of us—one each on his arms and legs—against just him. Within seconds it was over; he'd have tossed each of us several feet through the air. We'd give it up and just be content massaging whatever part of our bodies we had landed on."

As big and brawny as he was, Miller was equally gentle. "He was a big honey bear, as nice and kind and soft-spoken as you could imagine," Powell recalled. "But he had a bothersome habit of shaking hands like a lady. It was a little off-putting." When challenged about his dead-fish handshake, Miller explained. "When I was in high school, I lost my temper and hit a boy so hard that he was unconscious for three days. I prayed to God that if he let that boy live, I'd never again use my strength in a way that was wrong." The boy lived. "So," Miller said, "I'm careful with my handshake."

He scored his first aerial victory on February 4, 1944, near Brussels. Flying as Don Bryan's element leader, Yellow Three, Miller spotted a flight of four FW-190s diving on a box of B-17s. He called Bryan and dove down after them. "I took after the fourth one and stayed with him. After he made his pass, he fired a short burst at the bombers and pulled up and started turning to the right."[1]

Miller closed the distance and fired a short burst at the enemy fighter, which rolled over on its back and spiraled earthward. "I gave him several short bursts, observing strikes all along his left wing and on the fuselage." The German aircraft stopped spiraling and Miller put several more bursts into it. The canopy flew off and Miller kept firing and scored more strikes in the cockpit area. The enemy pilot never jumped clear and the burning aircraft fell straight down into a cloud deck.

The Luftwaffe's pilots were still aggressive during this period and Miller was attacked from behind by another FW-190 as he climbed back to join the rest of his flight. "I rolled over and started down and left him very soon," Miller remembered. Once he shook the enemy pilot, he started another climb and was once again attacked. This time, Miller simply hid: "I went into a big cloud and lost him." Finally free of the persistent enemy pilots, Miller joined with a flight of 352nd aircraft and made it back to Bodney unscathed.

The pilots of the 352nd liked the P-47 well enough. If it wasn't pretty, it was at least tough and fast. Up high, it turned as well as anything else and nothing was as fast in a dive. Indeed, Ted Fahrenwald devoted part of nearly every letter home to his love of the Thunderbolt. He derided the P-38 in comparison to his beloved mount: "One man in the crew, one engine, and one fan is all I want. A P-38 doing a barrel roll looks to me like a bunch of kindling wood flopping around the sky. But what a slick, lovely clean aircraft are our Thunderbolts! Queen of the skies, no less. Clean bullet-shaped fuselage and clipped wings with a pleasing parabolic curve to 'em. A powerful radial in the nose, and the fastest job airborne."[2]

The chief complaint about the P-47 was that it didn't have enough range. George Arnold of the 487th Fighter Squadron had an extremely close call on February 3, 1944, that illustrates the point: "We were sent on a fighter sweep over France and there was a lot of weather, a lot of clouds. We climbed up to altitude and flew over to France and made our way around via dead reckoning and kept looking for the ground to try and figure out where we were." The weather didn't open and the 352nd never really rendezvoused with the bomber stream. Nevertheless, the Germans did make a small showing and the group had a series of small scraps during which an FW-190 was bagged, but the Luftwaffe fliers evened the score by downing Ray Cornick of the 328th Fighter Squadron. Arnold wasn't able to get into the shooting. "After a while," he recalled, "it was decided that the mission was not going to be successful and we turned for home."[3]

There was a problem in that no one knew for certain where home was. Above the clouds with no visible landmarks, it was impossible to update the formation's position. Further, without being able to reference the ground, there was no way to tell if winds had pushed the formation from its preplanned course. It was a danger inherent to dead reckoning above the clouds and it birthed a common joke of the day: "With dead reckoning, if you reckon wrong, you're dead."

"We turned west for home," Arnold said, "and after a while a hole opened up in the clouds and we saw land with a big body of water on the east side. So we figured that the land was England and the water was the North Sea." The P-47s circled down through the opening until they were only a thousand feet or so above the water. "And as we got low," recounted Arnold, "I saw a lot of strange-looking snubbed-nosed sailboats that I had never seen before and so I wondered what part of England it was. Anyway, once we got below the cloud cover, we turned west toward Bodney."

Once the formation crossed over land, Arnold noted that things didn't seem quite right. "I saw windmills and canals and thought that it was a part of England that was new to me. " In fact, Arnold started to second-guess their navigation and thought that the flight might have overshot England and reached Ireland. "Then I spotted some large radio towers and wondered what they were for, and then I noticed some tracers and flak—they were shooting at me!" Still, Arnold wasn't quick on the uptake: "I thought that those dumb Englishmen would shoot at anything."

The formation of P-47s had slowly disintegrated since the time it dropped through the break in the clouds. At this point Arnold's wingman, Joseph Sweeney, was his only company. "A short time later," Arnold said, "I came to another big body of water and it was only then that I realized where I was. The first big body of water I had seen was the Zuider Zee and the land we were flying over was occupied Holland!" The water he had just reached was the North Sea.

Arnold was in big trouble. "I only had about forty gallons of gas." It was a pitiably small quantity of fuel. Arnold doubted that it was enough to get him across the North Sea to England. This new reality abruptly turned the water below him into an impossibly frigid expanse of storm-whipped waves that threatened to claw him out of the sky.

"I didn't have enough gas to get back," Arnold declared. "But then I remembered something I had heard that could increase range in a situation like this. It had come from Charles Lindbergh—some of the work that he had done." The concept directed the reduction of the propeller's pitch so that it turned at a much lower RPM. Simultaneously, the fuel mixture—or amount of fuel the engine consumed—was leaned back to a point where the cylinder head temperature pushed against allowable limits. The combination supposedly yielded dramatically increased range. Arnold could lose nothing by trying.

"I reduced the RPM from 2,000 to 1,200 and leaned the mixture to about 218 degrees," Arnold said. He also worked to keep himself from fixating on his fuel gauge. "I called Air/Sea Rescue to get a heading. They came in very clear and were very helpful and encouraging. At the same time I could see B-17s making their way back to England. I wished that I could fly under one so that they could drop me a line and pull me up through their bomb bay."

Of course, Arnold knew that such a thing was pure fantasy, but he was anxious and frightened. Unless immediately rescued, he would almost certainly perish if he went into the water. He knew that the odds of a speedy rescue were not especially good. "I wanted a cigarette but I didn't have any matches so I broke into my escape kit and got one." Arnold lit his cigarette and puffed nervously while he received encouragement and range and heading updates from Air/Sea Rescue.

"There wasn't any radio talking amongst us," he recounted. "We were all fighting for our own survival by this time." It was during this period that Arnold's wingman, Sweeney, disappeared. It was axiomatic that the wingman always had less fuel than his leader. Staying in position required constant corrections using both the engine and the flight controls. Those corrections consumed fuel; if Arnold was low on fuel, his wingman was even lower.

"Finally, I spotted the coast," remembered Arnold, "and thanked the Air/Sea Rescue people with the promise of a box of cigars." Serendipity put an airstrip directly on his nose. Without wasting a drop of fuel, he lowered his landing gear and flaps and settled the big fighter onto the single strip. "It was under construction," he said. "There was no one there." After he shut his engine down, he found a few members of the construction party. They took him to their shack, where they warmed and fed him while he waited for fuel to be trucked in from a nearby RAF base.

"They got over there pretty quick and filled one of my tanks; it was enough to get back to Bodney," Arnold said. "Anyway, when I finally got back to base, they were really surprised, as I was more than two hours late. They thought I was lost. My wingman [Sweeney] never made it back. We never did find out what happened to him although he certainly went down in the channel."

George Preddy wrote a letter to Sweeney's brother not long after Sweeney was lost:

> On that particular day, we had a long, rough mission. Returning across the North Sea, everybody was running low on gas, but Joe was lower than anybody else. He was last seen still out over the water by one of the boys who was flying with him. I feel sure he ran out of gas and sat down in the water. Shortly after our planes were refueled, eight of us went back over that particular area searching and could find no trace. I know that rather than have suspense of his fate hanging with you, you would rather hear the truth, even though it be bad.[4]

A day later, on February 4, 1944, the 352nd nearly lost another of its original pilots. Wendell "Wendy" Parlee, a member of the 328th Fighter Squadron, was almost bagged by FW-190s near Brussels. He was part of Yellow Flight, led by Don Bryan. After chasing and losing a four-ship of FW-190s, Bryan led the flight after another.

They were bounced from out of the sun. "I didn't see him until he had hit me," remembered Parlee. "I broke right and down while Lieutenant Bryan turned into the E/A. I caught a glimpse of him then. He was painted with black and yellow wings and a red nose."[5]

Parlee's aircraft was hit hard: "I received considerable damage in both wings from exploding 20-mm cannon shells; there were hits in the fuselage and hydraulic system. There was a hole in the left side of the cockpit which jammed the prop control and small holes in the canopy. I took a bit of shell fragmentation in my leg."

With his hydraulics and trim tabs shot out, Parlee was barely able to wrestle the badly vibrating P-47 toward home. Compounding his difficulties, aside from his wounds, was the fact that his airspeed indicator was inoperative. Further, a haze of hydraulic fluid blanketed his canopy and windscreen, dramatically reducing his visibility. "After leaving the enemy coast," he recounted, "I called Air/Sea Rescue and got very good reception. They vectored me to Manston, where I decided to crash-land due to the small degree of control I had of the plane and the fact that the hydraulic system was out."

Parlee horsed the barely flyable ship onto the ground without sustaining any further injuries. The aircraft was a wreck and was removed from service. His performance was near-heroic yet the episode badly affected the veteran flier. "Wendell continued to fly," remembered Punchy Powell, "but he had problems that weren't apparent to the rest of us. He felt he had lost his nerve. Making himself get into his aircraft before each mission became more and more difficult; he finally went to the brass and turned in his wings—he didn't believe he could fly combat anymore."

After evaluating his case, the leadership of the 352nd convinced Parlee to go to a rest home to shake whatever demons plagued him. Parlee agreed and left Bodney for a short period of recovery. After returning to operations following his brief respite, he performed well and no one noted any issues with his performance. In fact, Parlee scored an aerial victory on March 16, 1944, when the 328th Fighter Squadron raced to attack an Me-109 that was harrying a B-24. The enemy pilot showed steel when, rather than fleeing, he tore into the P-47s.

"When I first saw him, he was firing at another P-47 at about 18 to 20 thousand feet," Parlee remembered.[6] "When I got on his tail, two other P-47s were ahead of me making their attack." The other two pilots misjudged their closure and flew past the Me-109, leaving Parlee alone and in perfect firing position. "After they over-ran him, I got on his tail and fired at him, taking the best aim I could with him using violent evasive action." The German's gyrations were for naught and Parlee's rounds tore pieces from his aircraft; soon after, the Luftwaffe flier jettisoned his canopy and bailed out. "After I pulled up," recalled Parlee, "I looked back and saw his parachute open."

Despite his success, Parlee continued to fight the anxieties that had bedeviled him since his crash at Manston. Still, he flew missions whenever he was scheduled. "But finally, he just couldn't do it anymore," remembered Powell. "He went to the command and told them 'no more.' When they pressed him for his reasons, he told them that during a recent mission he had held back—that he didn't pitch into the fight like he knew he should have. And in so doing, he knew that he put his comrades, his friends, in danger. He knew that he was a liability rather than an asset."

Parlee was taken off of combat status. He was one of approximately 110 Eighth Air Force fighter pilots so removed. "It was one of the bravest and most generous things he could have done," Powell recounted. "He could have continued to fly and hang back and no one would have known the difference. But he knew that doing such a thing would put the lives of his friends at risk. Instead, he was man enough to stand up and highlight the fact that he was scared and unable to do what he was supposed to do. Some guys wouldn't have had the guts to do that. None of us thought any less of Wendell for what he did."[7]

There were no recriminations against Parlee. He had performed well previously and the fact that he had been so badly shot up earlier was considered a mitigating factor. He was sent back to the States, where he provided valuable service as an instructor.

The 352nd's loss of Parlee to stress was not unprecedented. He was one of approximately 5,000 airmen of all types that the Eighth Air Force removed from flight duty due to "operational fatigue" or the more severe "operational exhaustion." Powell remembered the pilots in the 352nd called it "battle fatigue." In fact, releases from service because of psychiatric issues were a consistent and significant drain on the American military through much of the war; at one time, such discharges approached 10,000 per month.[8]

The rest home to which Parlee was sent was one of an eventual fifteen such facilities. They were part of a formalized plan that the Eighth's medical experts designed to get disturbed men back into service as soon as possible. The effort dated from 1942 and was operated from English estates, manor homes, and hotels. The men, who generally stayed about a week, mocked them with a variety of derisive names, such as "flak houses" and "looney bins."

Nevertheless, the homes actually did provide a good measure of respite from the rigors of combat. In fact, the men were encouraged to wear civilian clothing and it was intended that rank be left at the door. Staffed in large part by the "right sort of women" considered to possess high moral ideals, the homes offered a broad variety of indoor and outdoor diversions. Indeed, some of the larger estates offered horseback riding, canoeing, and archery.[9] There were libraries, board games, and cards for those who preferred less physical sorts of relaxation.

The homes were often used not just for hard cases but as an outlet for men when they reached the middles of their tours or when they started to exhibit the first signs of weariness or anxiety. It was easier and better to treat such issues early before they developed into something more critical. In fact, Ted Fahrenwald had such concerns about his own mental state one evening:

Had a few beers tonight at the Club and walked from there into A-Flight's hut. Had only been there a short while when I saw a duck waddle across the floor. From under one bunk, across the floor, and under another bunk. I looked around, careful-like, but nobody else seemed to notice this phenomenon. So I kept my mouth shut and shrugged it off as just another symptom of flak-happiness.

Just before I left, however, I poked my head back thru the door-
way and casually asked if they kept a duck in their hut. They said
yes, Thank God.[10]

Although they were part of what was still described as the "vaunted"
Luftwaffe, the German fighter pilots defending against the American
bomber raids knew that their situation was desperate and growing more so.
On February 24, 1944, Heinz Knoke wrote: "The Squadron loses another
six killed at noon today in a dogfight with Thunderbolts, Lightnings, and
Mustangs covering another heavy bombing attack. Our little band grows
smaller and smaller. Every man can work out for himself on the fingers of
one hand when his own turn is due to come."[11] Less than two weeks later,
on March 4, Knoke wrote: "Out of all the 'old-timers,' I now have only
Wenneckers and Fest left with me. The other pilots are all young and inexperienced and have been with us only since January."[12]

Within a few months, Wenneckers and Fest were also gone.

The young and inexperienced pilots that came to JG 11 out of training
were not as well prepared as those that had come before. For example, on
March 4, Knoke took a recently joined pilot on a low-level training flight.
The youngster simply flew into the ground and was killed. The air combat-
fueled exuberance and excitement that Knoke had shared with his fellow
pilots through much of the war was nearly gone by that time; nearly all of
his early comrades were dead. Having himself been shot down four times
already, it was a small wonder that Knoke had not also been killed.

Published accounts of air combat generally conclude with the destruction of one or more aircraft. This makes sense since shooting down aircraft
is the entire point. However, the reality was that most of the combat sorties
the American fighter pilots flew were cold, boring, and uneventful. And
when aerial encounters did happen, they very often did not end conclu-
sively, no matter how accomplished or skilled the participants. Indeed, the
USAAF flew more than 527,000 effective fighter sorties over Europe during the war but only 7,422 enemy aircraft were destroyed by fighters in air
combat.[13] This meant that aerial victories were scored on less than 2 percent of the USAAFs fighter sorties against the Luftwaffe.

This is underscored by George Preddy's account from the 352nd's mission of February 13, 1944, during which he was leading the 487th Fighter Squadron's Red Flight. A formation of unidentified aircraft was spotted below to the right. Preddy wheeled the flight around to investigate: "As we approached them, they made a 180 and passed under us. I recognized them as about twelve FW-190s. They all dived for the deck and I dived on the last enemy aircraft. I was closing slowly and opened fire at 500 yards. The enemy aircraft took evasive action as we passed right over Lille. I broke off the attack as I could not get close enough for a kill. I attacked another FW-190 on my left but could not close on him either."[14]

This account also illustrates the fact that the frontline aircraft of both sides were very evenly matched. Preddy was unable to coax enough speed out of his P-47 to close the range on the first FW-190. But neither was the German aircraft able to leave Preddy behind. Likewise, Preddy, an excellent pilot, had no success in his tangle with the second FW-190.

The fact that the German pilots did not turn to fight with the 352nd's fliers also bears consideration. Most likely, it was due to direction from the Luftwaffe's leadership that they focus their attacks on the bombers while avoiding more dangerous—and less profitable—combat with American fighters. Or perhaps the German formation leader did not believe his pilots were ready for combat with the P-47s. There is also the possibility that the FW-190s did not have enough fuel for a protracted engagement. Or they possibly fled out of a sense of self-preservation.

For a variety of reasons, it is true that the victors have the advantage when writing the history of a particular conflict. For instance, the conquerors sometimes forbid the vanquished to write about their wartime experiences. And often the records of the defeated are destroyed and not available to support the perspectives of the losing side. Further, publishers and audiences are not always ready for accounts from the losers. Additionally, it is not uncommon that the men defeated in war distance themselves from the past; they have no wish to relive or preserve their wartime pain and trauma.

These factors certainly applied in varying degrees to World War II. Where the air war is concerned, American accounts of shooting down Luftwaffe aircraft far outnumber German narratives describing aerial victories over USAAF fliers. There are a number of reasons for this. First, the Americans actually did score more aerial victories over the Germans than the other way around. And nearly every USAAF score was documented in an official encounter report that survived the war. On the other hand, there was little official firsthand documentation from USAAF flyers who were shot down as they were almost always captured or killed.

Nevertheless, the Luftwaffe did shoot down significant numbers of American aircraft. There were many skilled German fighter pilots still flying into mid-1944, and although the war ground their numbers down, there still remained, even at the end of the war, a small core of pilots who really had no equals in terms of experience and aerial victories. Indeed, the pilots of the 352nd occasionally came under the guns of very competent German fliers. Some of them survived while others did not.

An example of those who did not is described in the group's mission summary report for February 8, 1944. After making a rendezvous with its assigned formations of B-17s near Mariembourg, Belgium, the 328th Fighter Squadron lost three P-47s with their pilots in short order: "Immediately after R/V [rendezvous], Red Flight, 328th Squadron, bounced by 4 FW-190s from out of sun as they went to assistance of straggled bomber being attacked by FW-190." The three lost pilots were Harold Nussman, James Meagher, and John Walker.

Raymond Phillips, Nussman's wingman, was the sole surviving member of Red Flight. "We were making a turn away from the sun when we were bounced," remembered Phillips.[15] "The first I knew of the bounce was when Lt. Nussman, Red Leader, pulled up with an Me-109 on his tail." Because Phillips was assigned to monitor "C" Channel so that the squadron could maintain contact with the bombers, he couldn't hear the flight's radio calls on "A" Channel. "He [Nussman] was still wiggling his wings to warn me even though the E/A had perfect deflection. At that time my ship was hit by enemy fire which turned me away from Lt. Nussman." Phillips only barely managed to escape his pursuer before joining with the 328th's Yellow Flight and nursing his damaged aircraft back to an emergency landing at Lympne.

CHAPTER 9

Moral Dilemma

That there was a certain sort of chivalry in the skies over Europe during World War II is undeniable. There are verified accounts of German fighter pilots stopping their attacks to allow bomber crews to parachute from mortally stricken ships. And it wasn't uncommon for a victorious pilot to wag his wings in salute as his vanquished foe hung below a parachute. Nevertheless, the air war was bloody business and the objective of both sides was to wipe out the other.

One way to do so was to destroy as many opposing pilots as possible. Consequently, the logic, if not the morality, of killing a helpless pilot or one who bailed out of his aircraft made perfect sense. Even so, a few fliers, both German and American, ruthlessly killed their counterparts whenever and wherever they could. Some of these men were cold-blooded, sometimes even shooting pilots and crewmen in their parachutes.

Virgil Meroney of the 487th Fighter Squadron never shot a German pilot in his parachute. On the other hand, he understood the mean realities of warfare and had no qualms about killing an enemy pilot, regardless of whether or not he was helpless. His encounter of March 8, 1944, is indicative. Meroney and his Blue Flight were at the rear of the 352nd's formation as it reached the end of its escort leg. The group turned to leave the bombers as they crossed the Dutch border into Germany near Meppen. "Three Me-109s came out of the sun with a lot of speed and made a ninety-degree attack on the rear bombers, breaking away in rolls," Meroney recalled. "I called them in and went after the lead two as they stayed together, the third having broken in a different direction."[1]

When the Germans attacked the bombers, Meroney's Blue Flight was loping at a leisurely cruise speed in order to pace the bombers and it consequently took precious time for Meroney's P-47 to catch the diving Me-109s. While he was still a thousand yards in trail, two other P-47s dove between his flight and the two enemy aircraft. At that point the lead enemy fighter broke up and away in a hard chandelle. Meroney followed and took a ninety-degree deflection shot from about four hundred yards as the German pilot tried to get into a firing position on the other two P-47s. Meroney's fire drove the enemy pilot down toward the deck. He closed the range as they both leveled off at very low altitude.

"I fired several bursts at him at tree top level," Meroney continued. "When I got some hits, he pulled straight up, and by cutting my throttle, I stayed with him and fired another burst at one hundred yards, getting many hits. Big pieces fell off the E/A, and it was covered with flames." Meroney overtook the enemy aircraft as its pilot jettisoned his canopy. The American eased into position just off the right side of the flaming aircraft. "I was sitting right on his wing and got a good look at him."

"The pilot was trying to get out of the burning plane," Meroney said. "As he was still alive, I skidded underneath to give him another burst but before I got my sights on him he bailed out and immediately opened his chute. The burning plane spun down and crashed."

Although he had deliberately tried to kill the enemy pilot while he was still with his ship, Meroney did not try to fire on him as he descended in his parachute, or after he reached the ground. This might have been because he and his flight were low on fuel and there was no knowing if there were other enemy aircraft in the area. Indeed, that more pilots and crewmen were not shot in their parachutes was probably due at least in part to the nature of aerial combat. The fights were a confusing whirl and a pilot who concentrated too long and hard on killing a man in a parachute could easily fall prey himself and end up, ironically, in the position of being shot up while in his own parachute. Not molesting enemy pilots in their parachutes was a practical matter as well as a chivalrous one.

Still, both the Germans and the Americans did shoot men in their parachutes, albeit infrequently. Richard "Bud" Peterson, a P-51 pilot with the 357th Fighter Group based out of Leiston, recounted a mission during which he saw an Me-109 pilot shooting bomber crewmen as they descended in their parachutes. "Normally," he said, "*no one*, including the Germans, would shoot anyone that was in the parachute. It just wasn't done.[2] There was no challenge to shooting anyone in a parachute for God's sake." All the same, on one mission, Peterson remembered that "the sky was full of bomber chutes," and flying among those parachuting bomber crewmen was an Me-109.

"The son-of-a-bitch was going from parachute to parachute," recollected Peterson, "shooting up guys in parachutes! Oh, this was too much as far as I was concerned." Peterson tore after the German fighter. "I didn't want to blow him up," he said. "I wanted him to bail." Peterson was furious. "So I was pecking away at him." Peterson fired short bursts at the German fighter. Finally, he scored enough strikes on the Me-109 to force its pilot to jump. Peterson described his immediate reaction at seeing the German pilot leaving his aircraft: "You've met your maker, Buster."

"And I damned near emptied my guns on this guy," he recalled. "He was mincemeat by the time I got through with him." Peterson, who finished the war credited with fifteen-and-a-half aerial victories, remembered that there was some nervousness when other members of his unit heard of the killing. It was the sort of thing that might start a retaliatory response from the Luftwaffe. "But they had to be there to know what I was seeing," Peterson said. "Those [parachuting bomber] guys were helpless."

Thaen Kwock Lee was a B-17 waist gunner with the 483rd Bomb Group, a Fifteenth Air Force unit. His aircraft was shot down by Me-262s late in the war on March 22, 1945. He recalled being taken under fire by German fighters as he descended:

> Three fighters came after me. The first one missed and the second also missed. When the third one came by I was too low for him to shoot at me. When I hit the ground a burst of machine gun was fired at me. I hit the dirt fast. Then German soldiers came and drove me on a motorcycle to a building. On the way we passed a row of dead American airmen, about twelve of them covered with blood soaked parachutes. I knew they were shot dead on the way down.[3]

Nevertheless, some American pilots also went after their vanquished German counterparts without any provocation whatsoever. This is indicated by the encounter report of Edmond Zellner of the 328th Fighter Squadron. On May 19, 1944, while escorting bombers in the vicinity of Wittenberge, Germany, Zellner dove on an Me-109 and shot it down. Alone, he scanned the nearby sky. "I then spotted a green-nosed P-51 [from the 359th Fighter Group] on the tail of another Me-109 at about 15,000 feet. As I was alone, I joined him for mutual protection," recalled Zellner.[4]

"The e/a took evasive action and got in my line of flt so I fired upon him. There were a good many hits around the wing roots and fuselage and as my guns stopped, the enemy pilot bailed out. The Green-nose P-51 flew through the parachute, and the enemy pilot was last seen tumbling to the ground."

It wasn't commonly known or talked about, but there were instances when pilots in the 352nd went after German airmen who had bailed out. Chet Harker and his crew chief Rebel Harris became angry with Frank Cutler after Cutler brought Harker's ship back from a mission with evenly spaced dents in the leading edges of its wings. The dents had been caused by parachute shroud lines.

Bill Reese intended to kill the pilot of an Me-109 he shot down on December 27, 1944. "His chute opened and I swung around and started a long straight run for him. I had my sight on him and he knew what I was thinking about. He started kicking and waving his hands, and I kept my nose aimed right on him, making little corrections as he lost altitude. At the last second I couldn't do it." Instead, Reese flew close by the enemy pilot's parachute and watched it collapse then inflate again. He subsequently left the enemy pilot unmolested. "I had some strange feelings about all this. I thought sure I would pull the trigger in such a situation."[5]

And the group mission summary report for November 1, 1944, stated unambiguously that a German pilot was shot in his parachute. The report goes into much more detail than usual in a discussion about the downing of an Me-262 that was seen to have shot down an unidentified P-51. The German jet was finally bagged by the 486th Fighter Squadron's Red Flight after an extended chase. The report noted: "Pilot baled [sic] out from the flat spin and shot while in parachute." The report, unusually, does not list the pilot or pilots to whom the aerial victory was credited.

Shooting jet pilots in their parachutes was justified by some as a necessary evil. It was believed that these pilots were a special elite and that training them to fly such aircraft was a protracted and expensive effort. This logic held that killing such men whenever possible could help shorten the war. For their part, many German pilots were so concerned about being attacked in their parachutes that they waited until they were at low altitude before pulling their ripcords.

But for the most part the vast majority of the men of the 352nd—like the vast majority of the pilots among all the belligerents—could not reconcile themselves to the notion of killing helpless enemy airmen even if it made sense in the context of the hard reality that was war. "I recall a philosophical conversation with Ted Fahrenwald on this subject," said Don McKibben. "We decided that cold logic argued for killing a parachuting enemy pilot if he stood a good chance of surviving to fly again. We also decided we would not do it."

Many pilots shared the same view as Don Bryan who remembered: "I didn't kill pilots. I shot down aircraft." Certainly, Bryan and the others knew there were men at the controls of the aircraft they blasted out of the sky, but for the most part it was the machine they were trying to destroy rather than the pilot. If the opposing airman perished with his aircraft, it was simply the brutal nature of war. But shooting him while he was in his parachute was quite another matter that few of them could stomach.

That was the case with Stanley Miles on May 13, 1944, when the 352nd encountered a massive formation of enemy fighters. At the start of the engagement his horizontal stabilizer was damaged by a drop tank released by an enemy pilot. "It jammed something, so that I couldn't climb, no matter how hard I pulled the stick back. I could do anything else, but not climb."[6] Despite the injury to his aircraft Miles chased down an Me-109. He shot the aircraft up and the enemy pilot bailed out.

"I had my gun camera running," he recalled, "so I got some good shots of the tracers hitting the plane and the pilot jumping out. My wing-man was still with me, so I eased around, came back and got some nice film footage of the German pilot in his chute." Miles considered shooting the enemy pilot as he drifted helplessly toward the earth. It was a topic that he and his squadron mates had considered in earnest. "One school of thought was that if you didn't shoot the guy, he'd land and be right back up fighting you the next day. I couldn't do it, however, and just took the film footage of him."

This wasn't the only time that a German flyer was convinced he was about to be riddled by gunfire as he floated to earth. Many American fighter pilots used their gun cameras to ensure they had adequate proof of their victories. Robert O'Nan of the 487th Fighter Squadron did this on April 10, 1944, after forcing an FW-190 pilot to abandon his aircraft: "I followed the plane down where it crashed, exploded and burned up, in the middle of a plowed field. I took pictures of this. I also got pictures of the pilot dangling in his chute."[7]

Still, the fact that Americans shot Germans in their parachutes is buttressed by the fact that Eisenhower, the Supreme Allied Commander in Europe, felt compelled to specifically forbid the practice. The directive he issued to both Spaatz and British Air Chief Marshal Arthur Tedder, dated June 2, 1944, was focused mainly on directing the two air commanders to take special care not to kill French civilians inasmuch as was possible during the upcoming invasion. However, the last sentences left no doubt that the issue of shooting German crews in their parachutes had reached the very highest level of Allied command and that it was from that point forward expressly forbidden by Eisenhower himself: "I would add that similar considerations apply to enemy airmen compelled to escape by parachute. Such personnel are not legitimate military targets, and may not be deliberately attacked."[8]

Up to that point, there was no rule or law of war forbidding the practice although it would be outlawed following the war. In fact, a parachuting airman was technically considered to be fleeing rather than surrendering. Regardless, Eisenhower's letter made the practice unlawful for Allied airmen in Europe.

By early 1944, the Eighth Air Force was growing at a rate that far outpaced the Luftwaffe's ability to match it. And there were Germans who realized they were caught in a dilemma that defied easy resolution. If the Luftwaffe did not rise to meet the American bombers, the Americans would pummel Germany's industry into dust. On the other hand, if the Luftwaffe did choose to fight, the Americans would destroy it, and Germany's industry would be rubbled anyway.

The German leadership knew of the obvious need for more aircraft and more pilots to fly them. They also argued amongst themselves about how to best use the fighter forces they did have. It was in March 1944 that Göring realized his mandate directing the fighter pilots to concentrate solely on the American bombers and to ignore their escorts was counterproductive. It was also getting good men killed. It put them in an awkward situation akin to being in a gunfight with two men, but being allowed to shoot at only one.

Still, Göring didn't execute a complete about face. Instead, the fighter *Geschwadern* (wings) facing the American bombers were each organized into two more heavily armed antibomber *Gruppen* (groups) that were to be protected from the American fighters by a single *Gruppe* of *leichte* (light) fighters. In theory, the concept had some merit; however, it was difficult to coordinate the movements of three *Gruppen* that were unwieldy enough individually, and were even more so when brought together. Too, once the fighting started, the organization of the three different *Gruppen* typically disintegrated very quickly so that there was really very little distinction in the actions of the aircraft and the pilots that made up the two different *Gruppe* types.

During most of 1943 the Luftwaffe's fighter pilots had the luxury of attacking the bombers without being harassed; they only had to wait for the American fighter escorts—low on fuel—to turn for home. That was no longer the case by early 1944. First, the bombers were no longer sent to targets beyond the range of their fighter protection. But more important, longer-range P-51s, P-47s, and P-38s, equipped with expendable fuel tanks, were increasingly able to escort the Eighth's bombers virtually anywhere they needed to go.

There was debate among the German leaders over the notion of hitting the American bombers early as they penetrated over the continent. This would force the escort fighters to release their drop tanks before they were empty. Short on fuel, they would be unable to fly their entire escort route. The problem was that the Luftwaffe fighter pilots would still have to fight the USAAF fighter pilots. And that was exactly what the Americans wanted. A German pilot shot down and killed over northern France or the Netherlands was just as dead as one shot down and killed over Germany.

Moreover, if the Luftwaffe based its fighters close enough to interdict the bombers as they made landfall over Europe, those bases would have been within the range of virtually every combat aircraft not only in the USAAF's arsenal, but also the RAF's. Simply maintaining and operating from such bases might have taxed the Luftwaffe to a point that the results would not have been worth the investment. Certainly, the Germans did operate from bases in France and the Netherlands until later in the war, and they were bombed, but the main effort against the USAAF bomber streams was mounted from bases in Germany. But again, the American leadership didn't care where the Luftwaffe fighters were based, so long as they showed up and could be killed.

This was also partly why the Americans stopped camouflaging their aircraft after the first few months of 1944. Aside from the expense and hassle of painting, aircraft left in a bare metal finish were easier for German pilots to see. And a German pilot who spotted an American aircraft and showed up to fight was a German pilot who might be shot down. So, not camouflaging their aircraft made simple good sense to the Americans.

One means by which the Luftwaffe leadership tried to overcome American numerical superiority was through the application of mass. From late 1943 and through the rest of the war they tried to aggregate large numbers of fighters against a single point in the bomber stream to overwhelm both the bombers and their escorts. But bringing many aircraft together, often from separate airfields, was complex enough during good conditions. When friction was introduced in the form of poor communications, bad weather, roving American fighters and inadequately trained pilots, the difficulty grew many times over. And even when the Luftwaffe fighter pilots did manage to get together in formations of fifty, or one hundred, or more, they were so unwieldy as to be ineffective. It was rare indeed when such formations reached the American bombers intact.

Aside from hitting the bombers while they were airborne, the Luftwaffe leadership discussed striking Allied bases in England. Although the Germans might have succeeded in mounting a large one-time effort during the daytime, they likely would not have been able to mount a continuous campaign, and never tried. The Germans did enjoy some episodic successes such as when they attacked American bombers returning to their fields after nightfall on April 22, 1943. On that evening, they destroyed fourteen aircraft.[9] Nevertheless, they failed to initiate a comprehensive campaign.

CHAPTER 10

March Madness

As the time for the invasion approached, the requirement for intelligence on the disposition of German forces in northwest France grew greater. Eisenhower's staff was desperate for whatever information it could get, and it relied to a great degree on information brought back by Allied flyers. One way to kill two birds with one stone was to send fighters on armed reconnaissance missions. Groups were sometimes given targets in an area of interest and tasked not only with shooting up their target and everything they found on the way out and back, but also with noting the locations, sizes and types of any enemy forces they saw.

The 352nd was assigned one of these missions on March 11, 1944. Each of the three squadrons was tasked with shooting up a separate enemy airfield; this was also consistent with Doolittle's goal of neutralizing the Luftwaffe prior to the invasion. Ted Fahrenwald wrote a letter that recalled the briefing: "About 6:30 A.M. today, there was a Group Pilot's Briefing, which was surprising since the field was buried in fog and the clouds were on the ground. So Colonel Joe L. Mason asks for thirty-six volunteers for a risky trip. We all wanted to go along, so the squadron commanders picked out twelve pilots apiece and the others are asked to leave." Once the briefing was complete, despite low ceilings and visibility over England and northwest France, the three squadrons took off into the gray mist at 0810.[1]

The weather was horrible for an effort of this sort. The visibility was only a quarter mile in places and never better than a mile. The three squadrons started across the English Channel near the Straits of Dover. "So I damn soon find myself skimming the choppy waters of the Channel," Fahrenwald recounted, "getting salt spray on my windshield, for the waves are just a few feet beneath us and the ragged clouds are just a few feet above my canopy. I'm at one end of a long line-abreast string of thirty-six ships, and they look mighty mean. All bobbing and jerking up and down slightly, for it's difficult flying in that little slot between waves and clouds. We dump our belly tanks at a signal and I see them bounce and splash behind the other ships.".

The group made landfall at Le Treport, whereupon the squadrons headed toward their separate targets. The dismal visibility made it difficult not only to make out anything on the ground but also to maintain a coherent formation. It wasn't long before the squadrons started fragmenting into individual flights and elements and even single aircraft.

Aside from causing the 352nd's formations to come apart, the weather made precise navigation impossible. But it wasn't the weather alone that made the mission so difficult; the Germans were an even bigger factor. The mission summary report described how the effort disintegrated: "None of the three designeated [sic] A/Ds [airdromes] strafed [on] account of heavy accurate small-arms fire coupled with medium accurate flak, beginning while Group was three miles off shore and continuing uninterrupted during entiere [sic] time P-47s over Pas-De-Calais Area. . . . Necessary evasive action precluded all attempts at compass navigation. Also responsible for inability to hold squadron flights together. . . . Hundreds of machine gun positions over entire area, emplaced for crossfire of all R.R. [railroad] intersections and highways."

Realizing that there was little chance that any of his squadrons would make it to their targets, Mason authorized them to freelance against targets of opportunity. John Bennett's encounter report typified the experiences of many of the 352nd's fliers that day:

> Gun emplacements seemed to be everywhere imaginable, hay stacks, church steeples, and in open fields. I noticed tracers coming in at me from eleven o'clock, so I gave a burst at what appeared to be a gun emplacement. Immediately thereafter my ship was hit by a 20-mm shell, which knocked out my radio, guns, fuel gauges, prop pitch control, in fact every electrical gadget in the cockpit. However, I continued on in with the squadron. A few minutes later I took a reciprocal heading and ended up coming out alone still on the deck . . .[2]

Ralph Hamilton's ship was also hit on the route in. Although he suffered a cut on his face, his aircraft was still flyable and he pressed on with his flight leader who was fired on by a gun emplacement located in a wooded area. "I opened fire at it," Hamilton recalled, "and just a little later at a flak tower under construction. Some hits were scored but my fire was not too accurate as my plane was right wing heavy after being hit and rather hard to coordinate."[3]

Ted Fahrenwald's narrative lent color to the terror:

> The country is hilly and the tops of the hills are in the low-hanging clouds. It's a case of jerking the ship up a hillside into the soup, counting 'one, two, three' and pushing the stick forward and hoping you're over the hill. Off to my right I see a Thunderbolt explode and hit the ground. But we try to bore inland, individually. The Jerries cut loose at me with rifles, bricks, shotguns, water pistols, bofor-guns, 88mm guns, rocks, light and heavy machine guns, old shoes, etc.

Very little of value was destroyed or even damaged. The poor weather simply made it too difficult to see, and if something worthwhile was spotted it was often too late to fly into a good position to attack it. What was hit reads like an assorted list of scraps: The 352nd's commander, Joe Mason, blasted away at a flak tower and a gun emplacement on the beach; John Thornell shot up a radio tower, some troops and a B-17 that had belly-landed in a field sometime before; Jack Donalson worked over a number of gun emplacements and shot up a rifle range where German soldiers were practicing their marksmanship; Lothar Fieg fired at a flak tower; after shooting at another tower of some sort, William Halton fired his guns "purely at random"; John Coleman shot his guns at "some suspicious looking buildings"; and John Meyer "observed strikes on the rear portion of an army truck."

What was left of the 352nd's formations continued to break up. "In another left turn I lost my element leader because of the visibility," remembered Punchy Powell, "and took up the briefed course, looking for targets. I was alone." Powell was caught in a fusillade of ground fire that he escaped only through aggressive maneuvering. Immediately after, he fired a short burst at a flak tower, "observing the usual strikes all around the apertures at the top." Still alone, Powell continued toward the coast. "On the way out I spotted two planes, turned to attack them, but found them friendly, so I joined them and returned with them."[4]

Other pilots weren't so fortunate. The 328th Fighter Squadron's John Thornell and William Schwenke—Red Flight numbers two and three, respectively—strafed a B-17 that had belly-landed into a field sometime during the previous few days. After finishing with the bomber, the two of them started after a set of gun emplacements dug into a hill. "It was at these positions," Thornell recalled, "that Lieutenant Schwenke, Red 3, was hit. I saw strikes on his engine, but we crossed out together with his ship smoking."[5]

Schwenke's rationale for pressing for home with a damaged aircraft is impossible to determine for certain. Perhaps he knew his ship wouldn't make it back to Bodney but was willing to take his chances in the channel rather than going down over France and spending the remainder of the war as a POW. Or, there is the possibility that when he crossed the French coast with Thornell he was fully confident that the aircraft would take him the rest of the way home.

Thornell remembered that Schwenke's engine failed immediately after crossing the coast. "He [Schwenke] called me and said, 'I am bailing out; stay and get a fix for me.'" Schwenke climbed to a thousand feet and jumped clear of his aircraft. "His chute opened immediately," recounted Thornell, "and he hit the water OK. I made a sixty-degree turn and came back slow just as his ship sunk [sic] and observed his chute go down but did not see any dinghy."

William Halton, Red Flight's leader, had gotten separated from the rest of the flight and only became aware of Schwenke's plight when he heard calls over the radio. "After crossing out," he recalled, "I heard my Red 2 [Thornell] calling in a Mayday for Red 3 [Schwenke].[6] I flew north along the coast until I found Red 2 and Yellow Leader and Yellow 3 circling the spot where he had gone in. We four stayed and circled until two more P-47s arrived to take over and direct the Air-Sea Rescue service."

Halton's next observation conflicted with the group's mission summary report which declared that a dinghy was seen where Schwenke went down. "I did not see any evidence of Red 3 except an oil slick where his ship had gone in." John Coleman, Yellow Three, also reported, "No evidence of the survival of the pilot was noticed."[7]

Thornell and the other three pilots looked for their comrade as long as their fuel allowed but finally had to give up. "We stayed out over the oil slick for forty-five minutes, then came back home," Thornell remembered. "A Walrus was over the spot when we left." No evidence of William Schwenke was ever found. It is possible that he struck the aircraft when he bailed out and was knocked unconscious and drowned, or that he became entangled in his parachute after falling into the sea and was pulled underwater when it sank.

Besides Schwenke, Harold Riley of the 487th was also shot down and killed. Riley had been Don McKibben's jazz musician friend and was likely the pilot of the P-47 that Fahrenwald saw shot down. Another aircraft, flown by Robert Berkshire of the 487th, made it back to England before crashing at the airfield at Manston. Berkshire survived uninjured. Fahrenwald himself scooted back to the channel as fast and as low as he could: "Flew down a narrow gulch and I spotted the 20-mm shells exploding on the back beside me. So, I cruised thru a city to get away from the fancy shooting. I think it was Amien or Abbeville," he recalled. "Flew right down the main street at the first-story level. Shops and houses and stuff going by lickey-split [*sic*], to say the least. People dashing madly about . . . wonder I didn't lop off a few heads with my prop."

Like Fahrenwald, the rest of the group's pilots straggled back from the mission as best they could. Ray Phillips was part of the 328th's White Flight. He remembered that the four aircraft weren't safe even after they returned to friendly territory. "When we got back to England someone on the ground opened fire at us with a great many tracers, which came very close to us."[8]

The mission was a disaster. The 352nd destroyed little of value at a cost of two pilots and three aircraft and another pilot wounded. To be sure it reconfirmed what Allied planners already knew, northwest France was infested through and through with German ground units. The 487th's intelligence officer, Seymour Joseph, detailed that fact in a comprehensive report delivered up the chain of command. An excerpt illustrates how overrun the French countryside was with German defenders:

> In general, the defensive installations consisted in the main of small arms, .30- and .50-caliber machine-gun nests, of the type to be used against ground personnel rather than anti-aircraft. They were of various kinds. There were pits dug into the ground with the tops both flush and raised, sometimes covered with a camouflage net. Some were well sandbagged and others had concrete breastwork[s]. Some were circular, others angular and some just a straight line. They were situated in open fields both with and without camouflage and around the edges of fields on the outskirts of small towns, in haystacks, silos, church steeples, in wooded areas, on military crests of hills covering avenues of approach from the west . . .[9]

Each aircraft's ground crew included an armorer. The ground crew for John C. Meyer's aircraft was headed by the crew chief, Bill Conkey. Bill Kohlas was his assistant. Jim Bleidner was the crew's armorer. A radio technician, responsible for the equipment on several aircraft, also worked with the crew when required.

Bleidner's primary duties centered on the .50-caliber machine guns that armed all the aircraft Meyer flew during his time with the 352nd. The guns were typically cleaned and reloaded immediately after every mission. Normally, the armorers of aircraft that hadn't fired their guns on a given mission pitched in to help those whose aircraft had. The guns were not normally removed from the aircraft for cleaning but rather the armorers checked them for general integrity, punched the barrels with a bore brush, patch and cleaning solvent, and checked and oiled the receivers and other components.

After cleaning the guns the armorer removed and inspected the ammunition that the supply group brought to each individual aircraft hardstand in wooden boxes. Bleidner was fastidious about the ammunition he loaded into Meyer's aircraft: "I inspected each round, looking particularly for any evidence of corrosion around the primer that might make that round fail to fire."[10] If even a single round did malfunction, the ammunition belt could not advance and that particular gun would be useless for the remainder of the sortie; from the cockpit there was no way for the pilot to eject the faulty round.

The type and ratio of the ammunition that was loaded in each aircraft varied depending on the unit, the period of the war and even sometimes from pilot-to-pilot. However, most units settled on a simple load of armor-piercing incendiary (API) rounds. They were distinguished by blue-painted tips. Tracer rounds had red-painted tips and were abandoned by many fighter groups as they had slightly different trajectories and additionally alerted unaware enemy pilots that they were under attack. The pilots of the 352nd had little use for the tracers. Bleidner noted that he and his fellow armorers used them for a single purpose only: "We loaded five tracers near the end of the belt to warn the pilot that he was getting low on ammunition."

The armorers additionally checked the guns for wear and tear. After regular usage the rifling inside the barrels—the lands and grooves—were worn smooth. Without these twists there was little gyroscopically-stabilizing spin imparted to the rounds as they left the barrel. They consequently sprayed from the aircraft with very little accuracy. "We used a tiny periscope," Bleidner recalled, "to look down the barrel. A worn barrel would look smooth like a shotgun."

Gun barrels were also worn out by long bursts of fire. Pilots were trained to fire in short bursts of one or two seconds. But in the excitement of combat some held the trigger for much too long. A burst of five seconds could wear the barrels smooth or even melt and twist them. "J. C. Meyer," noted Bleidner of his experienced commander, "would never do that."

Changing a barrel was not a particularly difficult task. "There was a spring-lock that was released to unscrew the barrel from the receiver," recalled Bleidner. "Once the barrel was removed it was pulled out through the leading edge of the wing and a new one was slid into place and screwed into the receiver."

A less frequent but more demanding task was harmonizing, or aiming, the guns so that the rounds converged at a particular point. This convergence point varied depending on the unit and the pilot, but it was generally about three hundred yards in front of the firing aircraft. This was within the heart of the effective range of the M2 .50-caliber machine gun that was the standard armament for U.S. aircraft.

Bleidner described how a hoist was used, "to raise the empennage of the aircraft to the right level. There was a lug or tab on the left side of the cockpit, aft of the trim wheel, where a level was attached to check that the nose of the aircraft was at the correct attitude. A similar tab was used to check the level of the wings."

Once the aircraft's attitude was set and checked, the armorers aligned the individual guns. Bleidner recounted the procedure: "We set a stand a thousand inches from the leading edge of the wing with small targets set for each element of guns. Then we aligned the gunsight and the gun camera on the target. Then we put tiny periscopes in the gun so that we could see through the barrel to the target. There were four screws in the gun mount that were turned to move the barrel to match the target." Once the barrel was precisely aligned a wire was threaded through holes in the screw heads to lock them—and the barrel—in place. This process was repeated for each gun until they were all harmonized to fire their rounds through the same point in space.

It was obviously important that the guns fired their rounds where the pilot aimed them. Sanford Moats's had an experience with poorly boresighted guns when he was caught up in a fight with an Me-109 near Merseburg, Germany. "I dropped twenty degrees flaps and after two more turns I was closing on the tail of the E/A. He leveled off and nosed into a dive."[11]

Moats dropped down after the German. "I soon closed to 300 yds, set my manifold pressure to his and taking careful aim fired." The Me-109 continued his dive undamaged. "I observed no hits and checked my procedure several times. Finally I drove up to point blank range and firing, observed damaging strikes on the E/A which caused a large leak in his left wing tank." The German pilot dived into a cloud in an attempt to escape Moats. It didn't work; Moats caught him as he came out the bottom. "I closed to 300 yds and again taking careful aim I fired, observing no strikes. In desperation I sprayed bullets all over and knocked his engine out."

The enemy aircraft hit the ground and slid through a clump of trees, shedding parts along the way. "The jar threw him into the air sideways and he bellied in through two fences and a plowed field, sliding sideways to rest in a wheat field." After he spotted the enemy pilot clearing the wreck, Moats decided to strafe it. "My strikes were so far out of line with my sights I realized what had been wrong and pulled my strikes through the E/A which was smoking badly."

Fortunately, Moats's experience was not a common one. Almost to a man, the armorers took intense pride in their work. After all, when considered logically, the aircraft that the mechanics worked so hard to maintain were nothing more than vehicles used to carry the armorer's guns. In the end, it was the guns that dealt the killing blows in air combat.

Once an armorer's gun-related tasks were complete, he typically assisted the other two men in the crew, just as they sometimes helped him; it was normal for the men to cross-train each other. Again, Bleidner's recollections are instructive: "We taught the mechanics to service the guns, and they taught us how to maintain the spark plugs."

Of course, all members of the ground crew were at the ready on the day of a mission. Bleidner recalled that, "When a mission was on, almost all of the pilots reported to their planes about fifteen minutes before the mandated time for starting engines." Bleidner remembered that Meyer was more casual. "Our squadron commander, J. C. Meyer, usually strolled out of the ready room with less than five minutes to go as he pulled on his long leather gloves and let his white scarf fly in the breeze. Underneath his flight suit he had on long winter underwear, which was probably never washed for superstitious reasons. He also wore a sweater with a big 'D' from his time at Dartmouth College."

Bleidner described Meyer's startup ritual:

Bill Conkey, Bill Kohlhas, and I would be anxiously waiting at the plane and would offer a salute as he approached. J. C. [Meyer] would climb into the cockpit and settle himself in as Conkey and Kohlhas fastened his seat belt. Then Conkey would start up the engine. Meyer always refused to start the engine because he felt that Conkey knew all its idiosyncrasies better than he did. J. C. would hand me a small piece of onionskin paper that had the details of the radio calls, rendezvous times, and headings to be put into a cellophane envelope attached to the control panel. Of course, I would be trying to do this as the engine started and the prop wash threatened to take it away. One day that happened and he flew without the memo. When he returned, he gave orders to the intelligence section to give me that piece of paper early so I could get it in place before engine start.[12]

For all his quirks Meyer appreciated the work of his ground crew; there is little doubt that he understood the value of the men to his own success. This is evidenced by the loyalty and admiration he evinced from his men, officer and enlisted alike. "He understood the proper relationship between officers and enlisted men," said Bleidner. "He knew how important it was to build and maintain the esprit de corps of a military unit and he required himself and his officers to be responsible for the training, discipline and welfare of the troops under their command."

Generally, but not always, fighter pilots tended toward smaller-than-average size. George Preddy was a good example as were Don Bryan and Don McKibben. There were at least a couple of reasons for this. First, the cockpits of many of the fighters were small—the P-47 being an exception—and better suited for short-statured pilots. Too, the bombers, especially the B-24, required a lot of big muscle to fly well. Bigger men were often assigned to bombers for this reason alone.

Among the small pilots in the 352nd, one of the most interesting and beloved was Edward "Pappy" Gignac of the 486th Fighter Squadron. Diminutive at only five feet and a couple of inches, Gignac made up for his short stature through grit, talent, and force of will. He was quiet, but intelligently fierce. As a young man he regularly won money in boxing challenges, captained his baseball and football teams, and was a champion ski jumper at the national level for Middlebury College in Vermont where he studied on a scholarship.

Eager for more challenge and excitement, Gignac left school to fly for the Army in 1941. Like Preddy, Gignac completed flight training immediately after Pearl Harbor and was shipped to the South Pacific. But whereas Preddy flew P-40s out of Australia, Gignac was assigned to a unit that flew P-39s and a Lend-Lease variant, the P-400, out of Port Moresby, New Guinea. Although the aircraft was hopelessly outclassed by the Japanese Zero, Gignac nevertheless won the Silver Star when he broke up a heavily-protected bomber formation on June 18, 1942. Again, like Preddy, Gignac

was badly injured in a flying accident and after several months of recuperation was ordered back to the United States.

Assigned to a P-47 training unit, Gignac grew restive for combat and
secured orders to the 352nd in early 1943. He was put to work immediately; as one of the unit's few combat-experienced aviators he was heavily
relied on to help get the unit trained. Despite his small stature the rest of
the 352nd's pilots readily accepted and respected him and by the time the
group shipped for England he was a cornerstone of the 486th's leadership.

Ted Fahrenwald was quite fond of Gignac. "One of my good friends
of the squadron, Capt. Eddie Gignac, is really a character. Had quite a
writeup in last month's Esquire as regards his sports and war record. . . .
He's a little guy built like a keg. Face all scarred up from various crashes,
including shot down twice in New Guinea by the Nips. Anyway, Gig is a
natural born clown, and is full of the wildest lying stories I've heard in a
long time."[13]

Al Wallace, a fellow 486th pilot, was a good friend. "We used to kid
him a lot because he was so short. In fact, his crew chief made up remov-
able wooden blocks to put on his rudder pedals so he could steer the plane
on the ground. Before that, he had to drop his seat so he could reach the
rudder pedals and, if you were taxiing beside him, all you could see was
the top of his head."[14] Gignac received his nickname, "Pappy" because his
prominent cleft chin bore a resemblance to that of Pappy Yokum, a character from the Li'l Abner comic strip.

Gignac first scored in the air on January 10, 1944, when he shared
credit for an Me-110. He scored again on March 8, 1944. Wallace also
recalled a "victory," for which Gignac received no credit. The two of them
were part of a detachment sent to an aerial gunnery school in Scotland.
Gignac was the high scorer on the first day but his hits on the towed target
registered as long streaks which belied the fact that he was shooting from
very nearly astern the aircraft towing the target. It was obviously very dangerous. "They warned him about it," recounted Wallace, "but the next day
he did the same thing and shot down the tow plane." Fortunately, the pilot
was not injured and landed the damaged plane on a nearby beach. Gignac
smoothed things over with a heartfelt apology and a conciliatory drink at
the officer's club.

"Another peculiarity he had," recounted Wallace," was that he loved
to have a cigar on the last part of the flight home. We'd be flying formation
with him and he'd start bouncing around as he tried to light up his cigar.
Then, when he landed, he'd throw the canopy back and a cloud of smoke
would billow out. The first time I saw it, I thought he was on fire."

CHAPTER 11

Mustangs

The 352nd Fighter Group received its first P-51B Mustangs, seven of them, on March 1, 1944. Although many of the pilots had seen the trim little fighter while flying missions, this was the first time that most of them had seen it up close. "We knew about the transition to P-51s a few weeks before it happened," recalled Don McKibben. "The 4th Fighter Group, the senior fighter group in the Eighth Air Force, had traded in their P-47s a short time earlier." The 352nd was fourth on the list of groups to receive the new fighter.

Arguably the best fighter of World War II, the P-51 almost didn't happen. By the time that officials from the British Purchasing Commission visited North American Aviation in early 1940, the company's engineers had been tinkering with various concepts for a new fighter for at least a couple of years. The British were interested in contracting the company to build the competent, if not outstanding, Curtiss P-40 under license. At the time, the British were buying every decent fighter they could get their hands on and Curtiss was already producing as many as it could.

The head of North American, James "Dutch" Kindelberger, believed his engineers could build a better aircraft, earlier, that would not only meet British requirements but also broaden the company's own business interests. A presentation was made to the purchasing commission for a design, ultimately named the NA-73X—the project was contracted as Work Order NA-73—which cost roughly the same as the P-40, but offered more advanced features and better performance. The concept was compelling and the British ordered 320 examples before metal for the first prototype was cut.

North American's staff went to work immediately and put in sixteen-hour days, seven days per week. Although the design was fairly mature when work was begun, changes were inevitable and final blueprints stayed only barely ahead of the actual manufacture of the prototype. This was due in part to the sophisticated elements that were incorporated into the airframe. It had a laminar flow wing that was thinner than conventional wings and was characterized by a sharper leading edge, nearly symmetrical upper and lower halves, and a maximum thickness halfway back from the leading edge rather than closer as was traditional.

The design of the wing promised excellent efficiency but it also demanded fine manufacturing tolerances. Moreover, its thinness left little internal volume for the arrangement of guns, wiring, cabling and other necessary fittings. The radiator placement—at the bottom of the fuselage and behind the pilot—was also unusual and was designed so that exhausted airflow actually augmented the thrust produced by the propeller. Further, the design of the engine cowling met ambitiously tight tolerances, yet was still practical and robust enough for everyday maintenance.

With so much sophisticated work incorporated into the design it is a wonder that North American's staff kept to schedule. In fact, they blew the schedule away in a spectacular fashion. Although the goal was to have a flying aircraft by January 1941, the NA-73X first flew on October 26, 1940. Its performance exceeded expectations, and although the prototype was crashed due to pilot error less than a month later on November 20, 1940, the aircraft was recognized as a winner and the British remained committed to its development and production. It was the following month, on December 9, that the British Purchasing Commission drafted a letter to North American which gave the design its legendary moniker: Mustang.

The difficult detail work required to make the new aircraft suitable for operations occupied much of 1941. Nevertheless the British were so confident in North American's design that they upped their order to 620 aircraft before they received their first operational example. The last of this initial variant, designated Mustang Mk I, was delivered during the summer of 1942. The type first saw combat with the RAF on May 10, 1942, and was well liked as a fast, long-range, low-altitude fighter.

The USAAF was slow to appreciate the Mustang's potential. As a British project, it had no advocate in the American service. While the P-38, P-40 and P-47 were developed to satisfy Army Air Corps requirements, the same was not true of the Mustang; it was the bastard child of a foreign relative. It had no sugar daddy. Although the USAAF received a pair of Mustangs from the original production batch, they generated little official interest. Too, patrons of other aircraft manufacturers such as Bell and Curtiss exerted influence that favored their own designs.

The USAAF only moved when it became apparent that its wartime requirements for aircraft would be massive. This coincided with the successful maturation of the RAF's Mustang design. Accordingly, a USAAF order for 1,200 P-51As—very similar to the Mustang Mk I—was placed during June 1942. At the same time the USAAF had no good candidate for a dive bomber and North American was approached to build a dive bombing variant of the Mustang, ultimately dubbed the A-36 Invader. The A-36, of which 500 examples were produced, performed quite successfully in the Mediterranean where it went operational during June 1943.

Of the 1,200 P-51As ordered in June 1942, and an additional 1,050 ordered soon after, only 310 were built before production of that particular model was halted. The problem was that the Allison V-1710 engine that powered the P-51A and the RAF's Mustang Mk I had only a single-stage supercharger rather than a two-stage supercharger, as did the Spitfire's Merlin engine. Although the Allison gave superb low altitude performance, range and reliability—superior in fact to the Rolls-Royce Merlin-derived engine which ultimately replaced it—its performance at high altitude was seriously wanting. And since the USAAF required a long-range, high-performance fighter to escort its bombers at high altitude, the P-51 needed an engine change if it was going to be relevant to the strategic air campaign that was being planned against Germany.

It got one. From the spring through the fall of 1942, the engineers at Rolls-Royce in England, and their counterparts at North American, worked to configure the P-51 for versions of the heavier, more powerful Rolls-Royce Merlin. The British used the Merlin 65 while the Americans used a heavily modified Packard-built variant of the Merlin, the V-1650-3. The British were first in the air on October 13, 1942.

The results were startling. Colonel Cass Hough was the senior technical pilot with VIII Fighter Command and he recorded his astonishment at the modified Mustang's performance. "I just assumed it would be a conventional airplane because nobody told me anything," he later wrote. Its performance was anything but conventional. "I got up to about 33,000 feet with it and it was so maneuverable; and I could tell without making any speed runs, assuming the airspeed indicator was calibrated reasonably carefully, that it was performing wonderfully. I just could not believe some of the things I saw after doing a couple of speed runs with it."

The Americans got their modified aircraft airborne on November 18, 1942 and the results were just as promising. Even before it flew, the USAAF ordered production changed from the P-51A to the P-51B powered by the Packard engine. More than two thousand were on order by November 1942 and orders for many thousands more followed. Models built at North American's Inglewood plant were designated P-51B, while those built at the company's new plant in Dallas were designated P-51C. There was essentially no difference between the two models.

The performance of the new aircraft equaled or bettered the best of any fighter anywhere. It had a maximum ceiling of 41,500 feet, a maximum speed of 439 miles per hour, and most important of all, a combat range without external fuel tanks of more than 750 miles. In the P-51B, the USAAF had a perfect bomber escort aircraft.

Most of the 352nd's flyers were enthusiastic about the new machine. "I fell in love with the Mustang on my first flight," Don McKibben said. Whereas it had taken McKibben time to get used to the enormous size of the P-47, he found the P-51's dimensions more to his liking. "The P-51 fit me just fine—when you strapped your body into that cockpit, the airplane became an extension of yourself."

Like most of his comrades, McKibben only missed the P-47 during dangerous strafing missions. "While I was not reluctant to give up the P-47, there were occasions when I would have liked to borrow one to replace the Mustang. When strafing at low altitude and subjected to heavy ground fire, I felt a bit naked; the plumbing for the Mustang's liquid cooled engine was very vulnerable."

Punchy Powell recalled that he and his squadron mates in the 328th Fighter Squadron had very little time to make the switch from their P-47s to the P-51. "We came back from a mission and found new P-51s parked on our hardstands. My crew chief told me that the colonel had ordered us to get straight into the Mustangs and get some flying time. I had to get our engineering officer, Gus Gustafson, to show me how to start the engine."

Powell got airborne and was immediately impressed not only by the new aircraft's performance, but also by its docility. "I did a quick set of aerobatics and some stalls before I took it back to Bodney and landed. It really flew nicely." This one flight, thirty minutes in duration, was the only sortie Powell flew in the P-51 before taking it into combat.

At this point the P-51 was still relatively new to operations and the 352nd's pilots learned to deal with early teething problems. "One was the tendency of the engine to foul spark plugs when idling and taxiing," recalled McKibben. "This caused a couple of engine failures and ungraceful landings in the weeds. We soon learned to clear the engine with a really robust run-up before taking off and that took care of the problem."

Not everyone was impressed with the change from the P-47 to the P-51. Don Bryan remembered the early P-51s with some derision. "The seat in that thing was terrible," he recalled. "It sat nearly vertical and after a few hours my back really started to hurt. And the heater was horrible. At the altitudes we flew we really froze."

But Bryan's primary criticism was with the new fighter's guns. "You have to remember that we came from the P-47 which had eight .50 caliber machine guns. When you pulled the trigger you heard a roar. On the other hand, the P-51B only had four guns and when you pulled the trigger it sounded like a toy: POP-POP-POP." Bryan had a point; the Mustang's rate and weight of fire was half that of the Thunderbolt.

However, the biggest failing with the guns was the fact that they jammed so easily. "You really had to be careful when you maneuvered that airplane," Bryan recalled. "If you turned very hard at all, the guns would quit." It was frustrating and dangerous and more than a few enemy aircraft escaped because of this fault.

The reason for these jams was that the internal configuration of various components and substructures within the wing was such that the guns had to be installed at an angle. Thusly affixed, the feed paths from the ammunition trays to the guns were somewhat convoluted. James Bleidner, John C. Meyer's armorer, remembered that under heavy maneuvering the suboptimal feed path and the angled gun mounting made it difficult for the two spring-loaded pawls on each gun to operate properly. These pawls were mounted on the receiver and held and fed the ammunition belt "The centrifugal force pulled the belt right out of the feed pawl. It was a major malfunction." Once this happened there was nothing a pilot could do from inside the cockpit.

It was maddening. John Coleman of the 328th Fighter Squadron had gun problems on May 13, 1944, when he led Blue Flight down into a whirling fight near Demmen, Germany. He closed on an Me-109 and fired three short bursts that failed to find their mark. "I finally closed to about twenty-five yards and scored hits on the fuselage and wings, blowing off his tail. He went straight into the grd from there, exploding. Three of my guns jammed on this firing."[1]

With only one operating gun, Coleman crept up on another Me-109. "He finally saw me, or was warned, and broke up for a cloud. I closed rapidly and as we both neared stalling speed I opened fire. I got good hits on the right wing and fuselage and he spun out. When I last saw him, he was spinning straight down at 500–1,000 feet."

John Galliga of the 328th Fighter Squadron had trouble on June 21, 1944 when breaking up a formation of Me-410s. "I singled out one 410 and closed to about 250 yards giving him a short burst."[2] The enemy fighter dove hard with Galliga fast on his tail. "I followed him down to

10,000 ft and fired again. His right engine began to smoke and I observed hits on his right wing and fuselage. Three of my guns were then jammed and Lieutenant Smith, Blue 2, moved in." With only one gun operable, Galliga watched as Smith finished what he would have liked to have done himself. "I pulled off to the right and saw many hits on the left engine and fuselage as a result of Lieutenant Smith's fire. The Me 410 attempted to crash land in a field with both engines flaming. However, he hit a rail road track and exploded."

Different fixes were tried across VIII Fighter Command. The 354th Fighter Group addressed the problem with some success by installing ammunition feed motors from B-26 gun systems. Bleidner and the other armorers of the 352nd did not want to degrade the performance of their aircraft by adding the extra weight of the motors. And there was the additional issue of modifying the aircraft in a way not specified by the technical manuals.

Instead, Bleidner and his fellow armorers fine-tuned the tolerances of every relevant component, on every gun, on every aircraft, so that the installation angle and feed path were slightly eased. "Each of the springs, clearances, head spaces and other elements had a distinct measurement within tolerances. We pulled the guns and brought each of those tolerances to an absolute minimum, replacing the parts if required in order to make the guns as efficient and jam-free as possible." The aggregate of the small adjustments was enough to ease the problems to a great degree.

The issue was significantly eased with the P-51D that arrived some months later. The guns were mounted vertically not because the wing was made thicker or deeper as is commonly supposed, but because North American's engineers did redesign work that made more volume available inside the wing.

Still, guns jammed for various reasons—albeit infrequently—until the end of the war. All of William Montgomery's guns failed to fire on September 27, 1944, when the 328th Fighter Squadron encountered a massive formation of enemy fighters near Frankfurt, Germany. Montgomery was Don Bryan's wingman as part of Yellow Flight and covered Bryan as he knocked down two German fighters. "At this point, I lost Capt Bryan (Yellow Leader) as I had tried to open fire at an E/A but my guns would not fire. After checking my gun switch I made several more attempts to open fire, but guns would not fire."[3]

Montgomery turned hard to the left to get out of the fight. As he did so he fell in behind an Me-109 that was also in a hard left turn. "The E/A saw me and tried to steepen his turn but as he did so, he stalled and snapped over on his back and then went into a spin, beginning at approx 21,000."

The enemy aircraft continued its spin through a layer of clouds and the enemy pilot ultimately jumped clear before it smashed into the ground.

Another issue with the P-51 was that the aircraft was difficult to handle when fully loaded with internal fuel. Although the aircraft initially carried 184 gallons when it was first produced, it wasn't long before—under urging from Arnold—an additional eighty-five-gallon fuel tank was installed behind the cockpit. When it was full this tank dramatically extended the aircraft's range, but caused changes in the aircraft's center of gravity. This change could cause the aircraft to depart controlled flight during hard maneuvering. Because of this, the pilots were careful to use part of the fuel from the new tank soon after getting airborne.

"There was a gauge for that tank," Powell remembered, "but it required a real neck twist to the left to get your eyes on it and focused. So our ground crews modified it for us with colored bands. If the needle was on red it was full. If it was on yellow it was about half full, and if it was on white it was about empty."

Engine problems, especially early on, were also somewhat problematic. The twelve-cylinder, Packard V-1650 engine that powered the aircraft was complex and made up of many critical components. The failure of any of them could cause the engine to deliver less power or even to cease operating altogether. And faulty maintenance was at least as big a contributor to engine issues as component or material failure; the engines were maintained by young men not long removed from high school.

Spark plug fouling from the lead of high-octane fuels was by far the biggest engine problem. Lead tended to build on the plugs when the engine was run for long periods at low power settings such as during a delayed takeoff or when cruising at lower airspeeds. The fouled plugs failed to properly detonate fuel which caused the engine to run rough, or even fail. However, if the pilot caught it early enough the fouling could be cleared by running the engine at high power settings for brief periods.

When the 352nd started operations in September 1943 the standard USAAF aircraft fuel was 100/130 octane. That is, at lean mixture settings the engine produced power as if it were burning 100-octane fuel, while at rich mixture settings the engine produced power as if it were burning 130-octane fuel. The use of this fuel required the spark plugs to be replaced or thoroughly cleaned after approximately five missions.

Higher-octane 100/150 fuel was introduced during the late spring of 1944, roughly coincident with the 352nd's transition to the P-51. The new fuel required that the engines undergo minor modifications, but it permitted them to be run at higher power settings which produced more power and greater airspeeds.

However, the higher-octane fuel came at the cost of increased spark plug fouling. Rather than cleaning or replacing the plugs at five-mission intervals, the new fuel required the same actions at two-mission intervals which of course demanded more work from the maintenance crews. During early 1945 a new formulation of 100/150 with increased levels of ethylene dibromide was introduced in an attempt to reduce plug fouling. However, the new blend proved too corrosive and it was discontinued within a few months. The men used the fuel for purposes other than what it was intended. Just as they might at home, they sometimes cleaned their tools, or hands with it. It was also used to dry clean clothing. Doing so was dangerous. The 352nd's daily bulletin for August 1, 1944, carried a warning to the men:

> The High Octane Aviation gasoline now in use is POISON. It contains Aniline Dyes and is heavily leaded. When this fuel comes into contact with the skin it causes, in some cases, a severe dermatitis; the lead is slowly absorbed and may cause lead poisoning. DO NOT LET AVIATION GASOLINE GET ON YOUR SKIN. If this gasoline comes into contact with the body, immediately wash it off with soap and water. CAUTION: DO NOT USE THIS GASOLINE FOR CLEANING CLOTHES.

In the end, a combination of good maintenance and material—and proper operating procedures—kept the vast majority of engines running smoothly. Nevertheless, that fact was little comfort to those whose engines did fail. A good example was Martin "Corky" Corcoran of the 486th Fighter Squadron. On March 4, 1944, he was part of a detachment of pilots ordered to ferry a handful of P-51s to Bodney. It was a type he had never flown before.

Still, in a letter to his wife after the incident he wrote that he was excited about the new fighter: "I was very much sold on the plane all during the flight. Then I came in to land and I was just a little long. I probably could have gotten it in but I was playing smart; I was going around to make a good approach."[4]

"Well," Corcoran continued, "I got partway around in nice shape, but then the engine and I began to have differences. It decided that was a heck of a good time to take a rest, and I—thinking entirely differently—started to pull and push everything in that cockpit that would push or pull." Corcoran reefed the aircraft around in a hard turn and tried to make the field, but the aircraft simply didn't have enough airspeed or altitude to make it.

Corcoran had no good options and precious little time. He raised the Mustang's landing gear and pointed it toward a freshly plowed field. "I headed for it and just as I was about to settle into it, the engine started to turn over in great style; I thought I had won my argument." But the engine's sputtering was nothing but a tease. "Within three or four seconds," recounted Corcoran, "the engine began to cough and spit. It had caught only just long enough to drag me out of a nice field and into a no-good, rutted, holey, hilly, junk patch."

Having failed to lower his aircraft's flaps—and with a tailwind—Corcoran hit the ground at more than 120 miles per hour. "Honey," the letter continued, "if you ever meet anyone in doubt about it, you tell them you have some firsthand information that coming in contact with old mother earth at that speed provided quite a jolt." In fact, the fuselage cracked and separated at a point halfway between the cockpit and the empennage. At the same time, Corcoran's head smashed into the gunsight. His forehead was badly gashed and blood poured from the wound.

"When the cockpit—about the only part left with me—came to a stop," recounted Corcoran, "I crawled out and took a look at the multitude of pieces of airplane lying about." It occurred to him that he had just crashed a brand new, quite expensive, taxpayer-owned aircraft but the torrent of blood streaming down his face distracted him from giving the matter much thought.

Bodney's "meat wagon" was quickly on the scene and Corcoran was taken to the station dispensary. "The doctors appeared to look upon my wound much more lightly than I. I was still afraid to move my head for fear it would fall off. I swear that much blood could not come out unless my throat was slit clear back to the vertebrae." Corcoran's wound was stitched and his head closely examined. "As you might expect," he wrote to his wife, "the X-rays of my head came back blank." Ultimately, after a few days of bed rest, Corcoran was returned to duty.

The P-47 had been a reliable if pudgy mount, and it was the fighter with which the men had first fallen in love. However, following the arrival of the pretty new Mustangs the pilots of the 352nd dumped their loyal Thunderbolts as if they were girlfriends that had gone fat and smelly. Indeed, Fahrenwald, who had unabashedly championed the virtues of the P-47 in dozens of letters, seemed almost embarrassed when he wrote home in mid-April soon after he began flying missions in the P-51: "I swore by the old Thunderbolt, but doggoned if this Mustang doesn't put her to shame. I kin do anything my bloodthirsty little heart desires with this baby."[5]

Still, Fahrenwald's "baby," showed that it had an irascible side. It was two weeks later when his engine quit over Germany. He managed to get it started again, and with Don McKibben as his escort, made it to the English coast before it failed completely. He was fortunate as there was an airfield almost immediately below; he dropped his nose and landing gear, turned for the field, and touched down just as he realized that the runway was still under construction.

Nevertheless, he came to a neat stop without striking any equipment or any of the "dark-complected folks" that were putting finishing touches on the surface. "So, I sit on the wing," he remembered, "wiping sweat from my brow and taking a long hard swig from my flask, and this ground-Colonel roars up on a motorcycle. 'Gawdammit!' he cries, 'whatcha mean landing on a new runway. Who give ya permission to land here?'" After offering the irate colonel a drink, Fahrenwald explained that the "laws of gravity gave me permission to land here."[6]

The paint scheme for the 352nd's aircraft was derived from a directive put out by VIII Fighter Command on March 23, 1944, as part of an effort to put order into the desires of different fighter groups, particularly the 56th, to mark their aircraft uniquely. This was motivated in part by identification issues during operations as well as by unit pride. Of the VIII Fighter Command's three wings, the 65th and the 67th—to which the 352nd belonged—were assigned solid colors, while the 66th was assigned checkerboard patterns.

For a short time after the first few P-51s were received, the noses went unpainted, or were painted with a blue spinner and matching nose band that extended from immediately behind the spinner approximately twelve inches toward the cockpit. It was about a month or so before the paint scheme that helped to immortalize the 352nd began to appear. The blue paint started at the spinner, wrapped itself under the front of the nose, and then swept up and back to the front of the windscreen. It was a viscerally appealing arrangement that experienced few variations through the remainder of the war.

Those variations were primarily related to color. The early olive drab–painted Mustangs wore a blue on the nose that was lighter than that of the later bare-metal aircraft. Still later in the war, the shade of blue was darker for reasons that are unclear now, but probably had to do with what shade was most available.

There was grousing from fliers in the other theaters of war that their counterparts in England received the best of everything. To some extent, this was true. The Allies had agreed that Germany had to be defeated first, and doing so required a strategic air campaign that demanded the finest equipment in the greatest numbers. And it was axiomatic that England was the best base for it. Further, of course, England offered luxuries and amenities beyond what was available in the jungles of New Guinea, or in the icy Aleutians or even Italy. Too, the most well-known media personalities considered England a plum assignment. Partly because of this the USAAF units based there received a great deal of publicity.

The 352nd's fliers knew and appreciated their good fortune. Ted Fahrenwald reveled in it in a letter home: "I was lucky to be stationed in England, for here we live the gay life in our spare time. Just hop into the cockpit, careen around uncivilized skies for a while, and then land back home again, stepping out back into luxury, comfort, and within range of queens and good whisky. I reiterate: Wot a way to run a war."[7]

Still, as much as England offered in the way of familiar comforts, it was not what many of the Americans were used to. A chief complaint was the seeming lack of hygiene and cleanliness. Fahrenwald shared a typical American perspective.

> In the famous Liverpool St. Station . . . there is a bar. . . . This one has a distinctive odor and within you will see three old and garrulous barmaids of a type one might find swamping out an office building [in the States] at five a.m. They run the joint. Fat, greasy hands, black fingernails, and sweat-soaked dresses. They peddle the bitters: a swish of a dirty glass thru a pan of greasy water and it's set for the next customer.[8]

On the other hand, just as in the United States, there were certainly gradations in the quality of cleanliness and hygiene throughout England and the 352nd's personnel embraced their English cousins regardless. Certainly, they wouldn't have traded places with their brothers-in-arms who were fighting in the other theaters of war.

Indeed, many of the men came to have very warm feelings for their hosts. Fahrenwald, who was so aghast at the dirtiness of English pubs, positively gushed about the kindness of a family that hosted him and Don McKibben after meeting the husband only casually: "He and his wife showed us a fine, relaxing afternoon. We talked over America and England and relative customs and so on, hashed over the war and had a bit of scotch. His wife was very thoughtful and at tea time she served Mac and me one-each poached egg on toast with coffee. A real gesture, that, for the poor citizens get about one egg every six months to call their own. Fine people."[9]

Many of the 352nd's fliers fit the stereotype of the hard-drinking, hard-partying, hard-flying fighter pilot, but some of them didn't. Robert Powell remembered that Lothar Fieg was not a riotous reveler. "His bed was next to mine in the Nissen hut. He was a non-typical fighter pilot— quiet and shy and conservative. He never came to the parties."

"At one point while we were still flying P-47s Lothar was getting a lit- tle flak happy," Powell recalled. "I finally persuaded him go to one of our parties. He was curious and I told him that our flight surgeons mixed up a vat of grain alcohol with fruit juices that we called Thunderbolt Joy Juice. The idea was to have a couple of slugs of that before the trucks arrived with the girls. If you did that, then the girls looked more beautiful. After they showed up you picked one out and gave her a slug or two, took her over to the food and then . . . well, the rest was up to you."

Ultimately, Fieg returned to the States and married his longtime sweetheart.

"After some of these parties," remembered Powell, "we would find one or two of the gals still on the base. They'd often come to the mess hall with a different pilot each day. Finally, when it got pretty obvious, the provost marshal would escort them off the base." Don McKibben's recol- lections supported Powell's: "I remember a stern warning from the Stern Warning Specialists, following a Saturday night party—'Those women have got to be out of here no later than Monday!'"

Fahrenwald recalled how the 486th's party on March 4, 1944 came to an end. "When C-Flight gets back to [the] hut that night, all hell breaks loose. Northrop, who is logging a little dual [having sex], wants the lights out, so Greene and I shoot 'em out with our .45s. Then I spot a big jar of talcum powder on a shelf over Leo's bunk, and while Archy holds a flash- light spot on it, I settle back and take a long, steady bead on it and pull the trigger. Talcum all over, like a burst of white flak, and Leo is not happy. I run outta the hut laughing and Leo empties his .45 in the general direction of my cot and I count seven shots [the capacity of a Colt .45] and return to find my mattress smoldering and my shoes perforated here and there. Fahrenwald spent much of the following morning patching bullet holes with corks and adhesive tape. "Boy do we have the fun, tho."[10]

It is a common and comforting misconception that everyone in every unit in the USAAF got along amicably. However, such a thing was simply outside the capacity of human nature. The pilots of the 352nd Fighter Group were typical. Although they enjoyed great camaraderie there were occasions during which their incompatibilities surfaced. These outward manifestations were infrequent and usually fueled by alcohol.

For instance, Frank Cutler, probably drunk, grabbed a hot poker one evening and waved it under Al Wallace's nose as he slept. Wallace awoke in a fury and flew out of his bed after Cutler. In the ensuing scuffle, Cutler knocked over Wallace's personal photos which further incensed Wallace. It was probably then that Cutler realized he had started something he couldn't finish. Tommy Colby, Willie O. Jackson and Edward Gignac were anxious to prevent a killing and did their best to control Wallace. Still, he pushed through them and crashed his fist into Cutler's head, knocking him down. Cutler fled the Nissen hut and stayed clear until the next day.

Donald McKibben described the primary factor which determined how the 352nd's men mixed and made friends. "Socializing patterns were profoundly affected by the physical separation of the three squadron headquarters around the perimeter of the field, and the custom of assigning members of a flight the same living quarters. It was only natural for squadron mates—and especially members of the same flights—to hang out together, on and off duty." For those reasons, both physical and operational separation, men from one squadron often didn't know those from another very well even though they were part of the same parent organization, the 352nd Fighter Group.

Many of the 352nd's men went to London whenever they could secure a pass. And so did, seemingly, every other American on the island. Because it was often difficult to find sleeping arrangements, the officers of the 486th Fighter Squadron pooled their resources and secured a long-term lease on a hotel suite. There was virtually always someone from the squadron in the city and the suite saw a revolving cast of squadron members, friends and relatives of squadron members, strangers and, of course, women—both professional and casual. Donald McKibben recollected that the suite was perfectly sited for all the activities that interested the young fighter pilots. "It was conveniently located near such eminent bottle club establishments as Chez Marcelle, just off St. Martin's Lane, the New Paradise on Regent Street and the Carlos Club in Grosvenor Square which was only a stone's throw from the U.S. embassy."

Piccadilly Circus was a popular point that offered much of what the young men were after. "There were refugee gals from France as well as the British girls," remembered one of them. He recalled a story that has since become apocryphal:

On one trip to London, we had a brash young second lieutenant with us who was on his first visit—he was among the cockiest of the cocky and always had a smartass answer for everything. As we walked through Piccadilly a gal tapped him on the shoulder and said, "Hello leftenant, would you like to make love? I can show you a good time." He said, "Yeah, how much?" When she told him that it would cost five pounds [about twenty dollars], he said, "Hell no, I came to this country to save your ass, not to buy it!"

King's Lynn and Norfolk were closer to Bodney than London and many of the 352nd's men spent time in those much smaller cities. "We'd drink and chase girls," one pilot honestly recalled. "We were in our early twenties," he remembered. "Aside from flying, that's what we wanted to do." Drinks were easy to find and he recalled that it wasn't too difficult to find a girl. "But finding a nice one wasn't always easy!"

Still, he had some success. "I had a girlfriend in King's Lynn," he remembered. "On pretty much a daily basis the squadron sent a truck out to town in the early evenings to take us out. And we had to be sure to catch it late that night when it returned to take us back to base. If we missed it we were out of luck because there was no way to get back to base other than to hoof it; there was very little traffic on the roads at night. Well, there were times when I'd get otherwise occupied and find myself walking back in the early morning hours through thick, wet fog—it was nearly twenty miles!"

The company of a woman was powerful inducement indeed.

CHAPTER 12

The Enemy Fighters

The enemy aircraft the 352nd's pilots encountered most often was the Me-109. It was the most produced fighter aircraft in history with nearly 34,000 being built. Designed by Willy Messerschmitt, it was first flown during 1935—several years before both the P-47 and P-51. At the time it was unquestionably the world's most sophisticated fighter aircraft. It was a sleek, aerodynamically advanced, low wing, enclosed cockpit, metal monoplane powered by an inline engine. There was nothing in the world like it.

As Germany's primary fighter it was continuously modified to keep it competitive. Indeed, the Me-109K that the Luftwaffe was operating at the end of the war in 1945 had virtually no parts in common with the Me-109Bs that were in service during the Spanish Civil War in the late 1930s. But the modifications forced on it weren't always seamless. A case in point was the armament incorporated in later models. These later guns—and their ammunition—had to be housed in bulbous protuberances that sapped performance and additionally earned it the nickname of "Die Beule" which translated as "The Bump."

The most produced variant of the Me-109 was the Me-109G. Although there were differences in the performance of subvariants, the Me-109Gs generally had a maximum speed of about 400 miles per hour at 20,000 feet, a service ceiling that exceeded 35,000 feet and an armament consisting of two, 13-millimeter machine guns and a single, 20-millimeter cannon—all mounted in the nose. It could also carry two additional 20-millimeter cannon in pods, one under each wing. It was a small aircraft at just under thirty feet in length and with a loaded weight of 6,900 pounds. In comparison, the P-51 exceeded thirty-two feet in length and had a loaded weight exceeding 9,200 pounds.

Captured examples of the Me-109 were evaluated by the Allies against their own fighters. The RAF filed a secret report that compared the performance of the Me-109G-6 against the Mustang Mk III—essentially the British version of the P-51B—as well as other British fighter types.[1] The observations were telling. Overall, the American fighter outperformed the Me-109 but not so dramatically that a skilled pilot could not do well with the German fighter. Further, it must be considered that the RAF might not have been able to maintain the captured aircraft as well as it would have been maintained in Luftwaffe service.

From a practical standpoint the Me-109 wasn't a particularly comfortable aircraft to fly. The report noted: "The cockpit is fully enclosed and rather narrow and cramped for a pilot of more than average size." Although the Mustang's cockpit was not nearly as roomy as the P-47's, it was still reasonably spacious, especially when compared to the Me-109's.

On the ground the Me-109 had to be handled with great care. "The forward view is very poor and this necessitates extreme care when taxying [sic] in the vicinity of other aircraft or obstacles. The brakes are positive but the tail wheel does not caster easily and sharp turns on the ground are difficult. At all times when the engine is run at low revs acute discomfort is felt due to fumes in the cockpit." German ace Heinz Lange's experience confirmed the report's observation that the Me-109 was difficult to handle on the ground: "Its small landing gear made the Bf 109 very sensitive to crosswinds and uneven ground on take off and landing. We had unbelievably high aircraft losses and personnel injuries this way."[2]

The report made the point that visibility from the cockpit was also compromised while airborne. "The forward view is spoiled by the gun magazine bulges on the engine cowling and the thickness of the metal frame of the windscreen. Another factor which makes it practically impossible to see behind is the cramped position in the cockpit. To sum up, the view all round is restricted as compared with the latest Allied types." The report additionally stated that, "Low flying is not very pleasant chiefly due to the poor forward view." The fact that it offered its pilot such abysmal visibility was a marked shortcoming in the Me-109, especially when it is considered that a fighter pilot lived and died by what he saw or didn't.

Where endurance and range were concerned the test pilots rightly declared that there was no comparison; the Mustang dramatically outranged the Me-109. On the other hand, since the Me-109 was a defensive fighter that operated primarily over its own territory, the disadvantage was not crippling. Luftwaffe pilots had the luxury of being able to disengage from combat and putting down at a local airfield or even a reasonably flat pasture or field.

Surprisingly, the German aircraft climbed better than the Mustang. "The Me.109 has a slightly better rate of climb up to 20,000 feet, but between 20,000 and 25,000 feet the Mustang has a very slight advantage." On the other hand, dive performance was important when escape was an imperative. Here, the P-51 had the edge. "The comparison of the respective merits of the two aircraft in dives proved that the Me.109 is steadily out-dived by the Mustang III and as the dive is prolonged the Mustang gains appreciably." This meant that the American fighter could not only escape the Me-109 by going into a dive, but could also, like the P-47, catch the Me-109 in a dive.

The Mustang also outperformed the German fighter in terms of airspeed. At 16,000 feet the American ship was thirty miles per hour faster than the Me-109, and at 30,000 feet it was fifty miles per hour faster. Finally, where maneuverability was concerned, although the two aircraft had identical roll rates, the P-51 showed itself to be better in a turn. The report's authors stated: "Here again the Mustang has no difficulty at all in out-turning the Me.109 in either direction."

However, notwithstanding the report's declaration that the P-51 was clearly superior to the Me-109, the performance of both types varied from individual aircraft to individual aircraft. For instance, an average American pilot flying a tired, dirty and bent P-51 might be at a disadvantage when engaged against a veteran German flyer piloting a new, well-maintained Me-109. Even USAAF pilots flying fresh mounts were not always able to easily outpace the Me-109. John C. Meyer's experience on April 10, 1944 highlighted that fact. On that day, it took him several minutes to chase down an Me-109. "With everything to the fire wall [*sic*], I chased him about 20 miles closing very slowly. I fired intermittently from 700 to 600 yds, range and from 20 to 0 degrees deflection. I observed only occasional hits. Finally the e/a started smoking and crashed into some woods, exploding."[3] It should be considered that Meyer, as the commanding officer of the 487th, certainly was not flying a tired or poorly maintained aircraft.

Several months later, on September 11, 1944, Meyer had another encounter during which the roles were reversed and he was attacked from below and behind by a pair of Me-109s. "I pulled 67 inches for 30 seconds and when I got detonation reduced throttle to 55 inches."[4] After reducing his power to a point that the engine could sustain, Meyer kept a nervous eye on the enemy fighters. "I climbed at 1,000 feet per min. The E/A remained about 300 yards astern and always 3,000 or 4,000 below. Occasionally they would pull up their noses and fire but would then drop behind. They chased me from vic [vicinity] of Kassel to Bonn [approximately 100 miles], breaking off their attack as I reached the Rhine River."

Although both the P-47 and the P-51 were considered superior high-altitude performers, Punchy Powell recollected a mission during which it wasn't apparent: "The highest I ever got was 39,000 and there were still some 109s above me. My airplane was barely flying at that altitude—the controls were like a feather. I took an out-of-range squirt as they dove down at the bombers but saw no hits." As it developed, Powell's aircraft stalled as did the aircraft in the rest of his flight. They were fortunate that day as the Luftwaffe fighters appeared disinclined to engage them. "The 109s were not interested in us; they were after the bombers."

It should also be considered that there were individual aircraft on both sides of the conflict that performed well above their specified parameters. Don Bryan's crew chief, Kirk Noyes, did a bit of special tuning on the engine of Bryan's P-51D, *Little One III*, and it was a spectacular performer. Nevertheless, the thirteen-victory ace once encountered an Me-109 that gave him fits. "On November 2, 1944, I tangled with an Me-109. My aircraft was 20 mph faster than any other aircraft in the group. But that damned Me-109 outperformed me."

Ultimately, the differences in performance between the frontline fighter types of all the belligerents were not very compelling when it is considered that most victories were scored in ambushes or hit-and-run slashing attacks during great wheeling melees where protracted one-on-one combats simply weren't possible. Indeed, anecdotal evidence indicates that good P-51 pilots often had their hands full when faced by competent Me-109 pilots. In short, no P-51 pilot, no matter how accomplished, considered the Me-109 easy prey.

Although the Me-109 was a world-beating aircraft in 1937, the Luftwaffe was nevertheless concerned that it might be outclassed by fighter designs under consideration by other nations. Consequently, it solicited tenders that year from Germany's aircraft manufacturers for a companion fighter. The winning proposal was Kurt Tank's FW-190, a low-wing monoplane distinguished from the Me-109 by its widely spaced landing gear, and especially by its radial engine. Obviously a newer and more modern aircraft, it first flew during June 1939, more than four years after its predecessor.

After an extensive and difficult development period during which it was almost discontinued, the FW-190 underwent significant changes that included switching from the BMW 139 radial engine to the BMW 801. The aircraft finally went operational in France during August 1941 and was immediately successful. Because it outperformed the Spitfire V then in frontline RAF service it caused the British a great deal of consternation and it wasn't until the Spitfire IX was introduced the following year that parity was reestablished. In total, more than 20,000 FW-190s were built. Consequently, aside from the Me-109, it was the German fighter most commonly encountered by the 352nd's pilots.

Like the Me-109, the FW-190 was produced in a number of variants. Because it was larger than the Me-109—more comparable in size and weight to the P-51—it more readily accommodated modifications, and its armament, armor and other features were continuously improved. To be sure, aside from being an excellent fighter it performed quite successfully as a ground attack aircraft when various aspects of its airframe and armament were modified to produce the FW-190F and G variants.

The FW-190A was built in the greatest numbers and varieties. These started with the FW-190A-1 and concluded with the FW-190A-10. The FW-190A-8, which was introduced during the spring of 1944, was the most-produced model. It was just more than 29 feet in length with a wingspan that exceeded 34 feet and a loaded weight of approximately 9,700 pounds. It was slightly faster than the Me-109 and reached 410 miles per hour at 20,000 feet. Although it had a service ceiling above 37,000 feet, it did not perform as well as the Me-109 or its American counterparts at high altitude. However, its standard armament of two or four, 20-millimeter cannon and two, 13-millimeter machine guns was quite good.

Kurt Tank designed the aircraft to reduce the pilot's workload and this was evident throughout the cockpit. In particular, the functions for controlling propeller pitch, engine mixture and throttle were incorporated into a single lever rather than the traditional three. This was made possible by an ingenious electro-mechanical computer. Additionally, the instrument layout was simple and easy to interpret, and the seat was positioned so that the pilot's feet were higher than normal. This feature made it easier to withstand the effects of high-G flight. Further, the bubble-type canopy afforded vision in all directions that was superior to the Me-109's.

Outside the cockpit, the FW-190's wide and ruggedly-built landing gear made landing and taking off much easier and safer when compared to the Me-109. Luftwaffe ace Fritz Seyffardt noted some of these features when comparing the two types. "The difference between the Fw 190 and the Bf 109 [Me-109] was that there was more room in the Focke-Wulf's cockpit and the controls were simpler—for example, landing flaps and trim were electric. Another pronounced difference was the stability of the Fw 190. Thanks to its through-wing spars and wide landing gear the machine was substantially more stable in flight, especially landing on rough fields."[5]

The U.S. Navy conducted a comparative evaluation of a captured FW-190A-4 against the F4U-1 Corsair and the F6F-3 Hellcat.[6] Although the 352nd obviously didn't operate either Navy fighter, the results of the evaluation are instructive and provide valuable insight from a pilot's perspective. Early in the report the test pilots recognized the advantage of the aforementioned single-lever power control: "It should be noted that application of full power in the FW-190 was much easier than in the other airplanes due to the fact that it was necessary to use only the throttle control." The FW-190 was superior, albeit marginally to the Hellcat in terms of speed and rate of climb and roughly equivalent to the Corsair.

Although it was discovered that the FW-190 "rolls with extreme ease at any speed," it also possessed some undesirable flying characteristics. "The FW-190, when in a tight turn to the left and near the stalling speed, exhibits a tendency to reverse aileron control and stall without warning. Similarly, when turning to the right it tends to drop the right wing and nose, diving as a result." Luftwaffe ace Heinz Lange separately commented on this alarming propensity: "A dangerous characteristic of the Focke-Wulf was that in very tight high G-turns it would sometimes, suddenly and with no warning, whip into a turn into the opposite direction. In a dogfight or near the ground, this could have a very bad result."[7]

Indeed, Virgil Meroney, flying a P-47, observed this shortcoming in his encounter report of January 29, 1944. On this mission Meroney led the 487th's Blue Flight against an FW-190 and destroyed it. Meroney was subsequently jumped from out of the sun by another FW-190. "Before he was in range I chopped my throttle and turned into him and he was unable to get a good shot at me. I was able to turn inside of him. After about a 360-degree turn, we were at 5,000 or 6000 feet where he tried to tighten up and stalled out into a violent snapping spin. I was unable to get a shot at the E/A as he disappeared into the overcast at 3000 ft still spinning straight down at such a speed that it would be impossible for him to pull out."[8]

In a turning fight, the FW-190, due to its high wing loading—or relatively small wing area compared to its weight—was seriously lacking in comparison to both the Navy fighters. "Results of comparative tests of turning characteristics showed the F4U-1 and the F6F-3 to be far superior to the FW-190. Both the F6F and F4U could follow the FW-190 in turns with ease at any speed, but the FW-190 could not follow either of the other two airplanes." An additional observation highlights how glaringly poor the turn performance of the German fighter was compared to the Navy fighters. "In a head-on meeting with the FW-190 both the F4U-1 and F6F-3 could be directly behind the FW-190 in one turn."

However, this shortcoming in maneuverability should be taken in context as neither the P-47, nor the P-51, turned as well as the Navy fighters. A report generated by the RAF's Air Fighting Development Unit in March 1944 showed that the P-51 had a slight turning advantage over the FW-190A and a very significant speed advantage of thirty to fifty miles per hour or more, depending on altitude. Likewise the P-51 climbed slightly better than the German fighter and dived much faster.

A comparative test conducted by the USAAF between a captured FW-190A-5 and a P-47D-4 showed that the American fighter was at no great disadvantage.[9] In acceleration comparisons from 210 miles per hour to 275 miles per hour at altitudes of 2,000 and 5,000 feet, the FW-190 outpaced the P-47 and was approximately 200 yards ahead of the American fighter upon reaching 275 miles per hour. But when the test was continued to top speed, the P-47 overtook the FW-190 at about 330 miles per hour "and gained about 2,000 yards very quickly and was still accelerating." Similar results were experienced at 15,000 feet.

In climbs from 2,000 feet to 7,000 feet, starting at 250 miles per hour, the report declared, "The FW-190 climbed faster than the P-47 through the first 1,500 feet, but the P-47 quickly overtook it and steadily outclimbed it by 500 feet per minute." When the same test was held from 10,000 to 15,000 feet, the results were similar: "Again the FW-190 initially outclimbed the P-47 through the first 1,000 feet; however the P-47 rapidly overtook and reached 15,000 feet while the FW-190 was at 14,500 feet."

In diving performance from medium altitude the FW-190 gained a quick advantage but was ultimately caught and surpassed by the P-47. Where turning performance was concerned at airspeeds above 250 miles per hour, the P-47 was again noted to have an advantage: "The P-47 easily out-turned the FW-190 at 10,000 feet and had to throttle back in order to keep from over-running the FW-190. The superiority of the P-47 in turning increased with altitude." But at low airspeeds the report showed that the German fighter was more nimble. "In making the usual rather flat turns in a horizontal plane, the FW-190 was able to hang on its propeller and turn inside the P-47. The FW-190 was also able to accelerate suddenly and change to a more favorable position during the turn."

However, the evaluators discovered that so long as the P-47 pilot did not try to compete at slow speed in a flat turning fight, but rather went into a series of climbs and dives, he could gain the advantage. "In this maneuver, the P-47, which was being pursued by the FW-190 in level flight, attempted to execute a series of climbs, slow turns, and dives which would end up with the positions reversed and the P-47 on the tail of the FW-190."

The USAAF testers believed that, in general, the German fighter was a good machine. "The FW-190 performed nicely in all acrobatic maneuvers, except that the sensitivity of fore and aft controls made low altitude manoeuvers dangerous." But they also discovered the same violent stall tendencies that their Navy counterparts discovered. "This airplane had an extremely bad high-speed stall in turns. This was not so evident in high speed pull-outs, but if trimmed and pulled hard enough, it spun violently straight down without warning." Overall, they believed that the P-47 was a superior machine. "The P-47 with its tremendous firepower, is at least as good as the FW-190 at low altitude. There should be no question about engaging the FW-190 in dog fights at low altitude; but it should be remembered that the FW-190 is a good airplane and has advantages at slow speeds."

Virgil Meroney, the 352nd's first ace, wrote a wartime report in early 1944 and offered that the P-47 was on par with both the FW-190 and the Me-109 in a turning fight. "I feel that it all depends on the situation of the moment. If you are bounced from above you cannot out-dive them since they had more speed to start with . . . Having learned that, I have always chopped my throttle and turned into them, turning in whatever direction I saw them coming from over my shoulder. I have always been able to out-turn them in that manner."

"After that," he continued, "you can, according to the situation, either press home your attack or get the hell out. When attacked by vastly superior numbers of enemy aircraft, I have always found that by turning into them and barrel-rolling into them, it always breaks their formation and I have been able to single one of them out and get him."[10]

As time went on and the P-47 received more modifications—particularly a slightly larger paddle-blade propeller—its performance relative to the FW-190 improved. Moreover, the 352nd's pilots flew at high altitudes—in the P-47's performance sweet spot—when they escorted the bombers. This was precisely where the FW-190's performance was at its worst. And when it is considered that the FW-190 was incapable of diving away from the P-47, the American fighter usually held its own against the German.

The pilots of the 352nd recognized the strengths and weaknesses of both the Me-109 and the FW-190 but did not vary their tactics against them. This was simply because there were so many equalizers in air combat that had nothing to do with aircraft attributes. For instance, the disparities in performance between all the types mattered virtually not at all in the midst of a great, multi-aircraft clash where shooting opportunities were fleeting and there was little chance of protracted one-on-one combat. Another example where the differences in performance didn't really matter was when pilots were ambushed in hit-and-run slashing attacks. Finally, pilot skill was a tremendous leveler.

CHAPTER 13

The Gray Enemy

The Germans were fierce opponents. That being said, the 352nd's pilots dreaded the awful weather over England and northern Europe more than they did their enemy. "I never met a fighter pilot who would admit he feared the Germans," said Don McKibben, "but we were all afraid of the weather." Clouds hid the ground and high winds sometimes drove formations dangerously far off course.

Bad weather was especially treacherous during takeoff and landing; close to the ground there was little margin for error. And when visibility was limited, wingmen were forced into tight formations on the wing of a leader who was flying blind and relying entirely on his instruments. It was hazardous business. Essentially, in poor weather, a flight leader held the lives of his wingmen in his hands. Don McKibben recalled, "We never really talked about it but every wingman dreaded flying formation inside an overcast."

It was a matter of trust on a couple of levels. The flight leader had to trust his instruments implicitly. It was a faith that was sorely tested when, without visual cues, his body—under the physiological effects of vertigo—insisted that his aircraft was in a vertical dive when it was actually straight and level, or that it was in a climbing turn to the right when it was in a gentle descent to the left. This was a phenomenon that all of them had been trained against; nevertheless, practicing under a canvas hood in an AT-6 over the friendly skies of Texas was distinct from real life combat operations in bad weather while at the controls of a high performance fighter with wingmen tucked close aboard. Not only did the flight leader have to keep his aircraft upright and pointed in the right direction, but he also had to ensure that he maneuvered his aircraft smoothly enough so that his wingmen were able to stay with him.

And while the flight leader had to trust his instruments, the wingmen had to trust their flight leader. Vertigo also tore at them; even when they were straight and level it told them that their leader had them in impossibly steep climbs, or in hopeless, diving spirals. But instead of obeying their traitorous senses and breaking away, they had to force themselves to stay in formation.

It was exhausting work. Every tiny movement or correction of the throttle or flight controls required a countermovement. And each countermovement required another countermovement. It was a never-ending series of control inputs that wore pilots out. Punchy Powell recalled one particularly long flog through almost 30,000 feet of clouds. "Finally, one pilot called out over the radio that he'd eat a sack of shit to get out of the clouds. Another guy said, 'You can start right now brother, because my pants are full of it.'"

In the end they all had to trust each other. Not only did the wingmen have to put complete faith in the instrument flying skills of their flight leader, but the flight leader had to have faith that his wingmen would stick with him and not fall away where they might collide with other aircraft or worse, lose control and chop him out of the sky. It was not an unrealistic fear. The wrong combination of control inputs could put a thrashing propeller into an aircraft—and a body—within seconds.

Ted Fahrenwald had a close call in early January 1944. The 486th was recovering from a mission over Europe in poor weather when things turned bad:

> We have drifted to a position squarely behind six other ships, and when their combined propeller turbulence hits us, our formation explodes and we all career violently at crazy angles. I spot Mac [Don McKibben] in his ship, perched up on one wing, and I see that I'm in a vertical bank on the other wing, and heading for an immediate collision. I think I'd best go elsewhere rapidly, so I roll over and gut the stick and presto! I'm all alone. . . . I now go on instruments exclusively and work for a while to get [the] ship under control Finally the needle and ball [are] centered and [I] commence a nice 200 mph letdown. Then I glance up and notice a quarter inch of loose dirt piled up on the glass OVER my head. By this oddity I gather that I've been flying inverted for some time. . . .[1]

After righting himself, Fahrenwald inadvertently put his aircraft into a spin while still in the clouds. He finally recovered his aircraft, descended below the weather and groped his way back to Bodney for a safe landing.

There were times when the 352nd was not so lucky. One of those days was March 8, 1944. The group was ordered to provide escort for bombers returning from a strike on the VKF ball-bearing factory near Berlin. The weather over East Anglia that day was foul, but not bad enough to scrub the mission. Over Bodney there was an overcast layer at 700 feet that reached up to 3,500 feet. Regardless, the group launched a maximum effort that included fifty P-47s and seven of the new P-51s that the 486th was trying out for the first time. Once the squadrons got airborne and formed, the separate four-ship flights eased up into the thick, wet overcast.

Because the 352nd was putting so many aircraft up, and because some of the pilots had transitioned to the P-51, the makeup of the flights within the 486th was rearranged in several instances. Don McKibben was flying a P-47 as the element leader for Henry "Mike" Miklajcyk's flight which was going on the mission as a three-ship. He was on Miklajcyk's right side, while Miklajcyk's wingman, Earl Bond, was tucked tight on his left. McKibben had no wingman. "I had never flown with Miklajcyk or Bond before," he said. "They were both from 'A' Flight, while I was from 'C' flight."[2]

As the three aircraft punched into the clouds, McKibben and Bond nuzzled up to Miklajcyk as close as they dared. Vertigo manifested itself almost immediately and not just in their flight. Ahead and above them, Stan Miles lost sight of his flight leader and eased back on his throttle so as not to inadvertently collide with the other aircraft from his formation. Unbeknownst to him, Miklajcyk, Bond, and McKibben were closing from behind.

"The collision, when it happened," McKibben said, "was like a bad silent movie in shades of gray." McKibben heard nothing over the drone of his own engine, but it was immediately apparent that something was badly wrong when Miklajcyk's propeller lashed into the bottom of Miles's aircraft. "Suddenly, I became aware of the shadowy form of an airplane where it shouldn't be, above and to my left, and numerous pieces of aircraft tumbling about."

Desperate to clear the collision, McKibben snatched his aircraft up and to the right. Miklajcyk, Bond, and Miles disappeared in the murk. Safely away, McKibben immediately directed his attention into his aircraft's cockpit and tried to transition to instrument flight. It was no good; his attitude gyro had tumbled during the violent turn away and was oscillating uselessly. Without the attitude gyro and with no outside visual cues,

McKibben had no good way of knowing whether he was upright or inverted. Had he been high enough he might have been able to sort it out with his other instruments, but so soon after takeoff he was too close to the ground. "Tucked away in some corner of my brain," recalled McKibben, "was information from the P-47 pilot's manual. It stated that the aircraft lost a thousand feet upon entering a spin, and that it lost a thousand feet for every turn it took in a spin. On top of that, it took another thousand feet to recover."

Knowing that there wasn't nearly enough sky below him McKibben hurried to bail out of his doomed fighter. He quickly released his harness and simultaneously reached up with his right hand, unlocked the canopy and slid it back. "I started to step out onto the left wing but was jerked back by my oxygen mask—I had forgotten to disconnect it." Reflexively, he reached up and tore the mask loose from his helmet, leapt into space and pulled his parachute's ripcord.

"I was upside down when the chute opened," McKibben recalled. "The opening shock launched my escape kit from out of its pocket inside my flight jacket and it smacked me right in the eye." Barely able to see out of one eye and with his feet caught in the parachute shroud lines—and still upside down—McKibben thrashed in the clouds to right himself.

He wasn't the only one struggling to stay alive. Miklajcyk's aircraft took a beating from the collision with Miles's aircraft. Like McKibben, he quickly abandoned his ship and parachuted to the ground without injury. His aircraft smashed into a hedgerow but caused no other damage.

Sadly, Earl Bond did not survive. It is impossible to know what happened inside his aircraft but it is quite likely that he turned hard away from the collision and became disoriented. In trying to save his aircraft he might have stayed with it too long. Regardless, he was killed when it smashed into the ground. His body was later pulled from the wreckage.

McKibben's situation improved as he drifted closer to the ground. "I managed to get untangled and upright at about the same time that I dropped out of the overcast," he recalled. "I had barely enough altitude to maneuver away from a paved road and into a plowed field where I made a textbook landing." McKibben's P-47 hit the ground before he did and sprayed flaming aviation gasoline over the area. A thatched roof burned atop a nearby house and smoke curled up from trees in a churchyard. "On the same side of the road as my crashed plane was a house, and a nice lady came out and offered me some tea," McKibben remembered.

A local man, Phillip Taylor, was spreading manure when the three aircraft came down. "I could hear the noise of aircraft above but could not see them as they were flying in the clouds. Then all of a sudden there was a sound like smashing crockery and the planes came diving out of the clouds." The explosions rocked the surrounding countryside. While the sound of the dying aircraft reverberated around him, Taylor caught sight of either McKibben or Miklajcyk descending out of the clouds. "He looked a bit like one of those thistledown seeds."

Surprisingly, Stan Miles stayed with his hacked-up fighter. Miklajcyk's propeller had torn out its hydraulics, killed its engine and sent it plummeting toward the earth. He fell through the clouds and into the clear with little altitude to spare. "I pulled out of the dive right at the treetops and out the side window I spotted a large base with a beautiful runway," he recalled.

With its engine out, Miles's P-47 was little more than a big, heavy, torn-up glider. And not a very good one. Nevertheless he was able to get the landing gear down and glide onto the runway at what turned out to be Hethel, the home of the 389th Bomb Group, a B-24 unit. "They got me out and took me to base operations where I waited until someone from Bodney came to give me a ride back. I never went to the hospital and I certainly didn't visit the officers club as I was greatly saddened and depressed by the events of the day. I was actually in a state of shock for days." Miles's aircraft was scrapped.

The 352nd lost four aircraft before it even reached the English Channel. The group's mission summary narrative was markedly cryptic about the incident: "Two mid-air collisions involving six P-47s going up through overcast after T/O [takeoff]." It noted nothing more. The two victories the group scored over the Luftwaffe later that day failed to offset the toll exacted by the cruel mistress that was the weather. Although the Germans were slowly ground down and beaten as the war progressed, the weather was never defeated.

Kurt Tank sought to address the deficiencies of the FW-190A—especially its high-altitude shortfalls—when he designed the FW-190D. The variant was virtually a new aircraft. Firstly, it used a more powerful inline, liquid-cooled, V-12 engine, the Jumo 213. The installation required a lengthening of the fuselage both ahead of and behind the wing. Prototypes were produced by late 1942 but development was protracted and it wasn't until the late summer of 1944 that the type was fielded.

Nevertheless, the aircraft first flew in 1942 and it is likely that the 352nd encountered developmental or evaluation examples early in 1944 as indicated by the group's mission summary report for February 3, 1944. The 487th Fighter Squadron penetrated to the vicinity of Aurich in northwestern Germany when it spotted the new FW-190s. "This squadron engaged three FW-190s with longer noses and seemingly elliptical wings near Aurich 1150 at 19,000 feet. E/A chandelled into and rolled through squadron formation firing all the while and then split S'd down." The squadron did not score against the new type.

However, Virgil Meroney knocked one down just more than a month later on March 8, 1944, the same day that the 486th lost four P-47s in a mid-air collision. Although Meroney misidentified the aircraft as an Me-109, or an Me-209, it is nearly certain that it was an FW-190. Having shot it up, he pulled alongside it as it burned. "The nose was extra long and big, so it may have been an Me-209 [a type which never entered operational service]. It was painted in the usual colors with dark slate top and light underside, with crosses on both wings and fuselage. In front of the cross on the fuselage was a dash and then some black chevrons pointing towards the nose."[3]

That the FW-190D was encountered by the 352nd prior to being officially introduced into service is further buttressed by an entry in the 486th's historical narrative for May 1944: "A new development seems to be a FW-190; perhaps a new type that may give trouble. It flies high and damned fast, has a longer nose than usual, and is hell to catch."

In truth, the USAAF had been aware of the existence of the new type for some time. Colonel Cass Hough, the chief of the Air Technical Section, wrote a memo to Kepner concerning the new development. The tone of the note suggests that Hough believed the new fighter, which he referred to as the FW-290, was a real threat. "It is readily apparent that the FW-190 with the DB-603 engine (referred to as the FW-290) at War Emergency Power will be *more than a match for anything we can offer* [emphasis in original] up to roughly 26,000 feet. While the P-51B appears to out speed the FW-290 at and above 26,000 feet, it is our opinion that the all around maneuverability of the FW-290 will more than make up for the slight speed deficiency at extremely low altitudes."[4]

Indeed, the confusion about the FW-190D continued into the summer of 1944 as indicated by the following report filed by VIII Fighter Command: "There has been considerable discussion about a long nosed version of the FW-190, which started off when we obtained a document dated 1942, giving details of the FW-190 equipped with a DB-603 engine instead of the BMW 801. To effect this change it was necessary to lengthen the nose-by 3 feet. All through the past winter the story has been very confused. Pilots have reported encounters with long nose 190's, but unfortunately we have never been able to get a combat photograph that could be assessed as such."[5]

When Virgil Meroney scored his fifth aerial victory over an Me-109 on January 30, 1944, he became the 352nd's first ace. Aside from Meroney there were a few other 352nd pilots who were getting a good start toward acedom but none of them had yet notched headline-grabbing scores. However, the 4th Fighter Group, which been operating in England for nearly a year longer than the 352nd, had produced a few high-scoring aces. For instance, Don Gentile had shot down twenty-two enemy aircraft by April 1, 1944, whereas Duane Beeson had seventeen aerial victories to his credit. Gentile's wingman, John Godfrey, had been awarded 9.33 aerial victories by that same date.

The press loved to cover these men and they became heroes in the States. Their stories made good copy. A *Columbus Dispatch* story dated April 9, 1944 led off with a quote that tugged at America's heartstrings: "God Bless My Boy Cries Mother; Wants Flier-Hero Son to Come Home." The article opened with big news that made Mrs. Gentile's emotions all the more touching. "The mother of Capt. Don S. Gentile wept with joy and concern today after learning her son had shot down three more Nazi planes and had been formally recognized as the top American ace of two world wars."

All this attention bothered the head of the USAAF, Henry Arnold. He was worried about the effects of excessive publicity not only on the pilots concerned but also on their comrades. Further, he was worried that the public's morale—and the USAAF's reputation—might suffer if the better-known aces were lost in combat. It had happened already in the Pacific and he was worried about the consequences when the inevitable occurred and one or more high scorers were lost over Europe.

Doolittle and William Kepner, the head of VIII Fighter Command, didn't share Arnold's concerns. Kepner wrote a note to Doolittle that reflected his coldly real perspective on the topic. "A dead hero is of infinitely more value for inspirational purposes than a live average man. A live hero is even better, but in order to achieve the hero status the distinct possibility of the corpse status must be accepted."

For his part, Doolittle appreciated the practical benefits that a high scorer could impart to his comrades, while still acknowledging the fact that he could be lost in combat. He wrote to Arnold: ". . . use them to improve teamwork and to raise the effectiveness of all the fighter pilots. In spite of this, a combat leader must lead to maintain the excellence of his unit and the respect of his subordinates. Some leaders will inevitably be killed."[6] Although these issues weren't relevant to the 352nd during early 1944, they became so on the day before the *Columbus Daily Dispatch* article.

When Virgil Meroney of the 487th Fighter Squadron converted to the P-51B with the rest of the group he was still relatively new to the type on April 8, 1944. On that day, the 352nd flew a mixed escort mission into Germany; the 328th Fighter Squadron flew P-47s while the 486th and the 487th were at the controls of their new P-51s. The escort portion of the mission was not particularly eventful and on the return leg the squadrons dropped down to strafe different German airfields. Meroney spotted a Ju-88 parked at an airfield and after receiving permission from his squadron leader, John C. Meyer, took his Blue Flight down and flamed it.

A short time later, Meroney led his flight against another airfield near Bramsche. There were a handful of Me-410s parked at the far side of the field and Meroney managed to set one afire in the face of fairly heavy anti-aircraft fire. Past the field, his aggressiveness overcame his caution and he committed what would later come to be considered a tactical sin; he wheeled his aircraft around and went after the remaining Me-410s despite the fact that the enemy defenses were fully alert.

Meroney's wingman, Robert Ross, recalled the attack: "My wind screen was covered with oil so I pointed my ship in the general direction of several gun emplacements on the west side of the field. I could not see the results of my attack. Captain Meroney went into strafe again while I circled. I last saw him as he completed his second pass alone."[7]

In the meantime Meroney made good on his intentions and set another of the twin-engine Me-410s on fire, but it cost him:

Then it happened! My engine on fire up to the firewall, and both rudder pedals, and part of my left wing knocked off. She kept ticking over, though. A little hot for comfort, so back on the stick and a hope that I am high enough to bail out. Unable to see for the fire, so out I went, pulling the ripcord immediately. The 'chute opened at tree-top level, pretty close, and I hit the ground plenty hard.[8]

The Germans kept shooting at Meroney. He immediately shucked his parachute and ran for a nearby wood but was forced to surrender when three Germans stepped out from that same wood with their weapons raised. He was returned to the same airfield he had shot up before being sent into the prison camp system a couple of days later.

Meroney, the 352nd's high scorer at the time with nine aerial victories, was also the group's first pilot to be shot down while flying the P-51. Notwithstanding his loss, the 352nd had a good day as it claimed twelve aircraft destroyed on the ground. And although the act of shooting parked aircraft was not imbued with the same romance and glory as aerial combat, the war was not about romance and glory. Rather it was about winning. And destroying aircraft, whether they were on the deck or in the air, was critical to winning.

The next day, April 9, 1944, was Easter Sunday and George Cameron, the group's chaplain, prepared an unusual but inspiring sunrise service on the airfield. In front of his pulpit he arranged rows of 108-gallon drop tanks as seating and positioned P-51s and P-47s as backdrops. More than a couple of hundred men were in attendance as the sun broke above the East Anglia horizon. Cameron was known for the excellence of his sermons and by all accounts, his delivery that morning was exceptional. It closed with a prayer for the pilots and their safe return from that day's mission.

Ted Fahrenwald remembered Cameron's special Easter service:

There was an Easter service up by the control tower this a.m., too, right alongside the C-Flight dispersal-area (!). Three Mustangs were parked to form a background and the chaplain spoke from the wing of one of 'em . . . more daffydills scattered about on the ships' noses, and the ground crews used rows of belly-tanks for seats. Two-thirds of the pilots took refuge in our hut where we sat and drank ale and pondered the devious ways of life. Quite a different setting than that of the service you folks attended, no doubt.[9]

The group was airborne only a couple of hours after the service and despite Cameron's prayers, the mission was a tough one. One of the basic tenets of air combat was that a pilot had to always be aware of what was going on around him. Guarding against an attack from the rear was perhaps the most important—and difficult—element of this principle. The rear quarter was difficult to watch for obvious reasons and was consequently the favored position from which to stalk an unaware pilot. Failure to detect an attack from the rear often had calamitous consequences.

And even the best pilots occasionally dropped their guard. On that Easter Sunday Fred Yochim of the 328th Fighter Squadron participated in a bounce on a handful of FW-190s that were harrying a damaged B-24 near Dummer Lake in northern Germany. "As we started after the 190s they saw us, broke off their attacks and headed for the deck," Yochim remembered.[10] The enemy fighters leveled off just above the ground and Yochim concentrated on the nearest aircraft, leaving the rest of the P-47s in his flight behind. "About that time," Yochim remembered, "a P-47 with a red nose [56th Fighter Group] cut in front of me and began firing on the 190. I saw several strikes. He then pulled up and to the left after firing about 2 bursts; the 190 was still flying with no visible damage."

Yochim gained on the FW-190. "I still had good overtaking speed so I closed to about 400 yards [and] began firing. He was skidding violently. I observed strikes on his right wing and fuselage [and], smoke and flames began pouring from [the] fuselage and right wing root when he struck a row of tall trees."

The enemy fighter hit the ground and Yochim pulled up to the right. It was then that shells slammed into his aircraft; an enemy fighter hit him from the rear. "There was a flash and explosion in my cockpit," he remembered. "I pulled down my goggles and the heat became so intense the aluminum began melting. I unbuckled my harness, opened the hatch and got out. I hit the ground after about one swing rather hard."

The impact with the ground knocked the wind from Yochim and it took him time to regain both his breath and his wits. He removed his flying gear with some difficulty; his oxygen mask and goggles were melted to his face and much of his clothing was burned away. In shock and in enemy territory, Yochim administered first aid to himself and subsequently hid in the surrounding countryside for two days before being captured. He spent the remainder of the war as a POW.

Punchy Powell remembered that day. "I was just returning from a three-day pass to London and didn't fly that mission. When I got back to Bodney I learned that my closest friend, Fred "Pappy" Yochim, had been shot down. I immediately went to the headquarters building where Dick Gates helped me check the teletype reports coming in from the various fighter units."

One of the reports recounted a P-47 getting shot down from behind while chasing another fighter. Important facets of the report seemed to match the 352nd's actions that day. The pilot was seen to bail out of his burning aircraft at very low altitude but the pilot making the report was unsure if the parachute opened in time. "I believed that it had to have been Pappy," recounted Powell, "since he was the only 352nd pilot lost on that mission and had been seen to bail out it gave me a faint hope that he was still alive."

"Pappy and I had gone through all of our flight training together," Powell said. "He was my military role model. He had been in the Army

Air Corps for more than two years before giving up his staff sergeant stripes to become a cadet. He tutored me through my early days in the service and I met his wife when she came to our graduation as pilots and officers at Luke Field. He was my best friend."

Powell felt obliged to get word back to Yochim's wife. "I broke the rules and wrote to his wife, telling her that he had been seen bailing out. I didn't mention that it was at extremely low altitude. She wrote me back, telling me that she appreciated the letter as it was good to have that information before she received the usual telegram which declared him Missing In Action. Knowing the facts made it less shocking to her."

An unusual incident was described by the 352nd's mission summary report for April 9, 1944, the same day that Yochim was shot down. On that day elements of the 487th Fighter Squadron attacked a trio of FW-190s that were harassing a solo B-24 north of Osnabruck. "The 3 FW-190s bounced had 5 to 10 ft. black streamers on tail." What possible purpose the streamers could have had can only be guessed at.

CHAPTER 14

Aces

Gabreski, Zemke, Johnson, Godfrey, and Gentile: these are a few of the dozen or so storied names that head the list of the highest scoring American aces over Europe during World War II. The 352nd contributed several names to this list. Among them was George Preddy, who scored 26.83 aerial victories as the highest-scoring P-51 ace in history. Right behind him was John C. Meyer, who tallied 24 kills by war's end. Preddy and Meyer were numbers three and four, respectively, on the list of USAAF aces from the European theater.

Obviously, at a minimum, it took good flying skills and decent marksmanship to score well. Excellent eyesight was also invaluable. But more than anything else it required opportunities. In other words, it didn't matter how skilled a pilot was if he never had a chance to fire his guns. In fact, it is certain that there were USAAF fighter pilots who were just as skilled as some of the higher scoring aces but who simply never encountered any enemy aircraft. They are forgotten; their names are on no lists.

As fierce as the German fighter pilots could be, they were never ubiquitous and their relative numbers decreased as the war went on. It was ironic that the American dominance during the last year or so of the war worked against the young pilots who were so eager to rack up high scores. There simply weren't enough Luftwaffe aircraft to go around. Indeed, most of the USAAF replacement pilots who arrived during the last few months of the war never encountered a German aircraft in combat.

But it wasn't just the declining number of Luftwaffe machines that worked against the would-be aces. Sometimes, it was their lack of seniority.

If enemy aircraft were spotted it was the flight leader who generally led the attack, while the wingman was expected to hold back and cover the flight's rear. In other words, wingmen often were able to shoot only when there were so many enemy aircraft that the fracas got out of hand, or when a flight got caught on the defensive.

Walter Starck of the 487th Fighter Squadron recalled the role of the wingman in a radio interview: "In some ways, flying wing is as devoid of glory as being a blocking back on a football team. But the man with the ball can't score if the blocking back doesn't take out the interference. Likewise, a wingman protects his leader by watching for enemy aircraft which might attack the leader while he is shooting."[1]

Starck knew what he was talking about; he had played the role of aerial handmaiden himself. "When I flew as wingman last year I never once got a chance to shoot at a Nazi plane and I felt sort of a little 'left out' of the picture. Now that I'm a leader, I'm definitely convinced that a wingman is the key to a successful operations flight." "It is my wingman's responsibility," Starck continued, "to protect my tail when I'm navigating, looking at maps or firing. As a matter of fact, I think one of the reasons I'm still around today is because of the fine work done by a wingman."

In fact, Starck's encounter report of April 10, 1944, underscores that exact point. Leading the 487th Fighter Squadron's Red Flight, Starck dove on an FW-190 southeast of Chateau Thierry. "I began to close on him but at that moment the e/a pilot cut his throttle and pulled into a sharp turn. I was unable to slow down but managed a short burst at him at about 200 yards before I went by him."[2] The German pilot was disinclined to end the engagement at that point. "He then slid in behind me and started firing away at me. Lt. [Harry] Barnes, my wing man came to my rescue and scared him away—thank God! In the meantime, a second FW-190 came sliding into the rear of the flight and Lt. [Robert] O'Nan, my No. 4 man queued up on him and as he was closing, the FW pilot baled [sic] out and the FW 190 crashed.

After downing two Me-109s on May 27, 1944, Robert Berkshire also gave credit to his wingman in his encounter report. "During the entire action my wingman, Lt. [Clifford] Garney, remained with me and at one time herded a 109 off my tail and at another time shook another 109 from an attacking position on him. His actions were without a doubt responsible for the two of us returning."[3]

And of course, as the situation demanded, the 352nd's pilots looked after one another regardless of whether they were wingmen or not. Such was the case on May 27, 1944, when William Furr of the 328th Fighter Squadron was saved by the quick action of one of his comrades. On that day the 352nd encountered a large formation of Me-109s and FW-190s while escorting bombers south of Strasbourg, France. Furr's flight leader led his four-ship of P-51s into a head-on attack against the enemy fighters. "We then went into a dog-fight," Furr recounted.[4] "I fired head-on at an enemy E/A (Me-109) and saw a few hits on his wing. His fire hit me once on the prop spinner."

After passing the first Me-109, Furr wracked his aircraft around behind another. "I fired at a range of 50–100 yds, observing strikes on his fuselage and wing. I then had to pull out to the right to keep from running into him. As I pulled alongside his A/C I saw the pilot jettison his canopy and stand up in the cockpit preparatory to bailing out."

Furr's attention was focused on finishing off the German pilot, and nothing else. "At this time I attempted to get back behind him to get another picture or another burst into him, but before I had time to do this I was hit in one prop blade by a 20-mm shell from behind." Furr, intent on his defeated foe, had become a target himself. "I broke and began evasive action," Furr recalled, "but was unable to shake the E/A behind me. He followed me shooting through about three complete turns." Furr was in trouble; as desperately as he wracked his aircraft around, he was unable to shake the Me-109. That this was so is demonstrative of how closely matched the Me-109 and P-51 were in a turning fight.

Luckily, Furr had comrades close at hand. His friend David Zimms was in the thick of the fighting. "I made four passes at various Me-109s, and finally caught one shooting at Red 4, Lt Furr," Zimms recalled.[5] He tore after the German aircraft. "After hitting the E/A with a few long bursts I closed and saw many hits on the left wing root and fuselage. The E/A then pulled up and [I] got many more hits on the underside of the fuselage."

The German pilot had made the same mistake as Furr, and like Furr, was taken by surprise. Zimms pressed his attack. "I also hit his belly tank which came off and exploded in mid-air; my A/C flew through the flaming residue. At this time the E/A exploded becoming one flaming mass of debris."

Many pilots who were eager for a fight simply had bad luck; they were in the wrong place at the wrong time. A case in point was Don McKibben of the 486th Fighter Squadron. He had been part of the 352nd's original cadre and was widely considered an excellent pilot but he did not score for many months. "The 352nd Fighter Group went operational on September 9th, 1943," he recollected. "In the seven months that followed, I put in about a hundred operational hours, so-called 'combat time.' In all of that time, I never got close enough to an enemy aircraft for either of us to threaten the other. If my flight was protecting the rear end of the bomber stream, it was fairly certain that any German fighters in the area would be concentrating on the lead bomber formations way up ahead, or vice versa."

McKibben's frustration was evident: "I spent a lot of time bird-dogging around in the wrong part of the sky. Of course, I know that sometimes our mere presence helped keep the German fighters away from the B-24s and B-17s. After all, it was called 'escort duty.' I'm sure," he continued, "that the bomber crews did not share my discontent about a lack of action. Still, I felt I should be doing more, if only to balance the books with our taxpayers on two P-47s demolished while in my custody [McKibben flew one P-47 into the water during training in the States and was forced to bail out of another when his flight leader collided with another aircraft while flying through clouds after taking off from Bodney]."

His drought finally ended during a bomber escort mission on April 19, 1944. On that day, he was the element leader—number three—in the 486th's Blue Flight. While the squadron was climbing toward a formation of unidentified aircraft, McKibben spotted approximately fifteen Me-109s diving toward the bombers. Just as he realized that the aircraft the squadron was chasing were P-51s, a lone Me-109 flashed down past his left side. "I called and said I was following him and told the flight to follow me because it looked like the rest of the EA were on, or were headed toward the deck."[6] As McKibben reefed his aircraft around after the Me-109, the German flier winged hard over in a split-S. Upside down, McKibben squeezed a burst of gunfire at the Me-109 but the rounds passed harmlessly behind.

The two fighters plummeted earthward. McKibben cross-checked his altitude and airspeed, and scanned the sky around him. If he wasn't careful he wouldn't be the first fighter pilot bagged while hyper-focused on his target. Too, he had to be careful not to fly into the ground; at high airspeeds and steep dive angles there was a point at which no fighter could be recovered before it smashed into the earth.

All the while McKibben fired short bursts at the fleeing German. Finally, at only two or three thousand feet of altitude he closed to within a hundred yards of the Me-109 as it started out of its dive. "My last burst caused numerous pieces to fall off the airplane," McKibben recalled. "I flew through the pieces and pulled up to avoid collision. I looked back and saw the pilot bail out." Upside down and pilotless, the Me-109 flew into the ground.

McKibben's record was perfect. To that point in his combat career he had engaged only one German aircraft in combat and had shot it down. It would have been impossible for him to have done any better. What he might have done had he had more opportunities is unknowable. As it was, he engaged German aircraft only a couple of more times before he completed his combat tour in September 1944. He finished the war credited with one aerial victory and one probable. It was trained and aggressive airmen like McKibben—lots of them—that kept the Luftwaffe on the ropes from early 1944 onwards.

On the other hand, chance could have brought McKibben into contact with the Luftwaffe much earlier and much more often, and he might have scored many more times. But then bad luck or a momentary lapse in awareness could have cut his World War II combat career short, much as it had Virgil Meroney's on April 9, 1944.

In fact, George Preddy offers a perfect example of how fortunes could change where aerial combat was concerned. A veteran of air combat against the Japanese, he was readily acknowledged by all who knew him as an excellent and aggressive pilot, yet his score didn't reflect these traits during his early combat career with the 352nd. Indeed, Preddy flew more than sixty missions in his P-47, *Cripes A'Mighty*, without scoring a single aerial victory.

Although he did manage to down one German aircraft while flying Ralph Hamilton's *Frances B.*, he might very well have gone home after his first combat tour as a competent but unremarkable fighter pilot. As it was, following the 352nd's transition to the P-51, he started scoring steadily. Anxious to improve his tally, he volunteered for extra combat tours and subsequently went on to make history. Considering Preddy's example, it is interesting to speculate about what Bill Hennon, Don Dilling, Virgil Meroney, and Fremont Miller, among others, might have accomplished had they not been lost or shot down early in the 352nd's career.

Likewise, it is interesting to consider the case of John "Jack" Thornell of the 328th Fighter Squadron. He had joined the Army in 1940 and was a sergeant when the United States entered the war. A well-liked, high-spirited, and friendly man, he started flight training during January 1942 and earned his wings in February 1943. Punchy Powell was close to Thornell. "Jack was very likeable and fun to be around. We used to call him 'Direct Line Thornell' because he always seemed to know what was going to happen before anyone else. It was as if he had a direct line to higher headquarters. We never did figure out who his contact was."

Although he was a good, competent pilot there was no indication during the early months of the 352nd's operational life that he would be a standout in aerial combat. Nevertheless, he scored a victory, his first, on January 30, 1944. After a slow February, he knocked down two Me-109s on March 15, followed by an FW-190 on April 10. Thornell achieved these first four victories at the controls of the P-47.

Following the group's transition to the P-51, Thornell shot down two FW-190s southwest of Kassel on April 19, making him the 352nd's second ace, behind Virgil Meroney. There followed a spectacular month, from May 8 until June 10, 1944, when he shot down ten aircraft on five different days. Particularly interesting was the engagement of May 8, 1944 when the 352nd escorted bombers to Berlin and Brunswick. Thornell shot down two enemy aircraft that day but was jumped by an aggressive Me-109 pilot. Out of ammunition, Thornell called for help and was told by John C. Meyer—tongue in cheek—to ram the enemy pilot. As it developed, Thornell maneuvered to a position only a few feet behind the Me-109. Its pilot bailed out.

Thornell's performance during this period was a brilliant convergence of flying skill and marksmanship on his part, and opportunity on Fate's part. By the middle of June 1944, he was atop the 352nd's scoring list and very high on VIII Fighter Command's charts. And then, by the middle of July, he had completed his combat tour and was sent home, having scored a total of 17.25 aerial victories. His service earned him the Distinguished Service Cross, second only to the Medal of Honor.

It is interesting to note that of the nine different days that Thornell scored an aerial victory, he scored multiples on six of them. When the war ended he was still the third highest-scoring ace of the 352nd. What his tally might have been had he stayed as long as John C. Meyer or George Preddy makes for interesting conjecture.

Statistics reveal a skewed picture of aerial victories within the Eighth Air Force. The Eighth put approximately 5,000 fighter pilots into combat during World War II. Of that number, three out of four—nearly 3,700—never scored an aerial victory. Indeed, only 261, just more than 5 percent, achieved "ace" status by shooting down five or more German aircraft. However, this small group of fighter pilots was responsible for more than 40 percent of the aerial victories tallied by Eighth Air Force fighter crews.[7]

That the aces of all the fighter groups accounted for such a disproportionate share of victories was attributable in part to the factors noted earlier: flying skills, marksmanship, and opportunities. But another very important factor was the difficult-to-quantify characteristic of aggressiveness.

Almost to a man, the aces were known to their comrades as men who were dogged and fierce in the air; they were often described as men who not only did not shrink from a fight, but rather went looking for one. Whereas some fliers were satisfied with simply keeping the Luftwaffe fighters away from the bombers through their presence alone, the aces were more apt to chase the Germans down and kill them. They did this despite the risks that came with freelancing deep over enemy territory.

One of the men in the 352nd who exemplified this sort of aggressive pilot was Glennon "Bubbles" Moran. Moran's father died before he was born in Granite City, Illinois. The youngest of six children, he played football, was a champion wrestler and worked nights at a steel mill to put himself through college at St. Louis University. He was in his freshman year of law school when he went into the Army.

During the spring and early summer of 1944, he was the 352nd's most prolific scorer. A well-liked gentleman, he also aimed to give the USAAF the most value for its money. Moran had a reputation for aggressively searching for, and engaging, enemy aircraft. If he couldn't find them in the air, he looked for them on the ground. And he didn't come home until he was out of fuel. He was so overdue from one mission that when he finally landed, he found that he had already been listed as missing in action. On another, he was unable to taxi back to his hardstand because his aircraft ran out of fuel.

Extracts from Moran's encounter report for the mission of May 29, 1944, show his tenacity. He was the element leader—the number three aircraft—of the 487th's yellow flight. The four aircraft making up the flight were in the vicinity of Gustrow in northeastern Germany, when they gave chase to a formation of more than forty fighters that were harassing a box of bombers at 22,000 feet. Moran reported, "Yellow leader and I each picked out an FW-190 and attacked them. That was the last I saw of yellow leader."[8] Moran dropped the nose of his fighter and dove as his quarry rolled and broke hard for the deck. His wingman, Jule Conard, stuck with him.

The three fighters plunged hard earthward. Moran closed the range on the German fighter and put several bursts into it as they passed through 10,000 feet down to 3,000 feet. "My range was between 200 and 300 yards, my deflection from 0 to 20 degrees. When the E/A reached the 1,000 foot level he half rolled and crashed into the ground. He exploded and burned."

Moran and Conard climbed back up to altitude. At 21,000 feet they spotted a group of bombers to the northeast. The big aircraft were just clearing the German coast and heading over the Baltic near Wogast on their return leg to England. "We were at nine o'clock to them," Moran noted, "and I could see the port guns of an entire box were blinking so I went to the spot with full war power." On arriving, the two pilots found a formation of fifty enemy fighters trailing the bombers from slightly above. Moran reported their position over the radio and then maneuvered to put himself and Conard behind the Germans. A moment later a single Me-109 started a climbing left-hand turn out of the formation. "I thought he had seen us and was breaking away in order that he might be able to come in on our tails," said Moran. "I therefore followed him."

Like Moran's previous opponent, the pilot of the Me-109 went over into a steep dive. And just like before, he and Conard followed him down. While Conard covered their rear, Moran put rounds into the fleeing Me-109 until the German pilot bailed out passing through 1,000 feet. Following their victory, the two P-51 pilots stooged around the area chasing after other aircraft. "I chased two of them," Moran recounted, "but one turned out to be a green nosed P-51 [from the 359th Fighter Group] chasing a FW-190. I then broke from them and spotted an Me-109 who was shooting at a floating parachutist below me at three o'clock."

The German pilot spotted Moran and turned toward him. The two fighters went into a tight spiraling turn down to two hundred feet. "I put down about twenty degrees of flaps and noted that he had about twenty degrees down also. I was then down to about 170 mph." Moran finally outturned his opponent and fired several bursts but didn't score enough hits to bring the German fighter down. As tracers signaled the end of his ammunition, Moran called Conard in to finish the Me-109. "I saw Yellow 4, Lt. Conard, get hits on his fuselage and wings. The E/A then crashed into a field."

Low on fuel and ammunition, Moran and Conard cleared the area and climbed for home.

Not everyone in the 352nd was as aggressive as Moran. Among the more reticent pilots was Harold "Hal" Lund. Lund was senior to most of the group's pilots; he graduated from pilot training class 41-F and flew P-40s in Java during the early disastrous months of the war. After returning to the United States he was eventually assigned to the 352nd. He rose to command of the 328th Fighter Squadron for two brief stints from early to mid-1944.

To the dismay of some of the 328th's more eager pilots, Lund was decidedly not keen to mix it up with the Luftwaffe. "Most of us liked him and wouldn't have called him a coward," recalled one pilot, "but he never went looking for a fight. He just wasn't what a leader of a fighter squadron should have been. The 328th lagged the other two squadrons in aerial victories and a big reason was because Hal Lund was more interested in getting through his combat tour unscathed than he was in killing Germans."

Especially telling is the fact that, as a squadron commander, Lund should have had more opportunities to engage the Luftwaffe than virtually anyone else. Nevertheless, he failed to score a single aerial victory, or even to share in one. Nor was he credited with destroying any aircraft on the ground. Lund was relieved of command of the 328th on July 21, 1944. He eventually returned to the States where he was given command of a training group.

Ultimately, of course, every fighter pilot in the 352nd was different. Each was possessed of a unique blend of attributes and characteristics;

together they made up one of the most potent fighter groups ever assembled. And even if the majority of them never scored an aerial victory it should be considered that simply by virtue of their presence, they were powerful protection for the bombers against the Luftwaffe.

By late May 1944, Col. Joseph L. Mason had commanded the 352nd for a year. He remained its commander for most of the group's wartime career. He kept a sign posted in his office that was particularly appropriate during the time when the group was flying P-47s. "Then shall the right aiming Thunderbolts go abroad; and from the clouds as well as from a well-drawn bow, shall they fly to the mark—Book of Wisdom, Chapter 5, Verse 21."[9]

Because his time was consumed by myriad duties and also because military protocol precluded it, he did not socialize a great deal with his pilots. Nevertheless, what the men did see of him left some generally unimpressed. One recalled, "I didn't really like and respect him. He was a heavy drinker and a womanizer. He was shacking up with the wife of a British lord, Lady Bedingfeld, whom we referred to as Lady Bedding Roll. . . ." Moreover, some believed that he wasn't a particularly good commander, that he was sloppy and that he relied heavily on John C. Meyer to help lead the group. This must have been particularly distasteful to Meyer who was known to dislike Mason considerably.

And while certainly competent, Mason wasn't considered an outstanding pilot. As the group commander he had more opportunities for aerial combat than any other pilot in the 352nd. Although he was ultimately credited with five aerial victories, two of those were for aircraft that he did not shoot down, but which collided into each other while he was leading an attack. Of those five aerial victories, one pilot remembered, "I do know that one of the 486th pilots was really pissed when Colonel Mason took credit for a victory this pilot claimed."

On the other hand, Mason was no wet blanket. On one occasion, John "Jack" Thornell walked out of a party very drunk. He spotted Mason's staff car, slid behind the wheel, and drove off. A short time later, he tipped into a ditch and the car rolled completely over before settling back upright. After stumbling out to survey the damage, Thornell was stunned to see a very groggy Mason crawl out of the back seat. Mason's only comment was that the ride had certainly been a rough one.

Mason was no coward, nor was he incompetent. He led a great many missions and got the group where it was supposed to be when it was supposed to be there. Too, there is no denying the simple fact that the 352nd, under Mason's command, was one of the very best fighter groups in the USAAF. If it was true that he relied a great deal on Meyer or others within the group, it didn't particularly matter. A commander was supposed to use the people and tools he commanded to ensure a unit met its objectives. The 352nd met its objectives and more.

Drop tanks, first used operationally by VIII Fighter Command squadrons the previous year, had proven their worth by the spring of 1944. They had grown more and more reliable as the war progressed, however problems with them were never completely eliminated. The most common issues were tanks that failed to feed, and tanks that failed to release. Of course, if the tanks failed to pass fuel into the aircraft the pilot generally returned to base almost immediately and without incident. However, tanks that failed to drop clear of the aircraft when enemy fighters were spotted put a pilot at a disadvantage. The tanks created drag that penalized performance when it was needed the most. One such occurrence nearly ended in disaster for Glennon Moran of the 487th Fighter Squadron on May 15, 1944 while on a bomber escort mission near Neubrandenburg, Germany. On that day, Moran followed his element leader, Carl Luksic, on a diving attack against an FW-190 that was harrying the bomber stream.[10]

> He [Luksic] closed on the E/A's tail but overshot him. I then chopped my throttle back and tried to slide in on the 190's tail. I fired a short burst at 100 yards with about 60 degrees deflection, giving a ring and quarter lead. I observed no hits. I then began turning with the E/A but due to the fact that my right external wing tank had not released, I could not turn steeply without stalling. The 190 was therefore able to out turn [sic] me and take a good 40 degree deflection shot on me from about 150 yards. He obtained no hits and then broke off and down.

With the FW-190 no longer a threat, Moran and Luksic attacked and destroyed a Ju-88 that had just downed a straggling B-17.

CHAPTER 15

Victory Claims

Every unit of every fighter arm of every air force during World War II claimed that it shot down more aircraft in aerial combat than it actually did. The Germans did, the British did, and the Americans did. So did the Soviets. The Japanese made claims that were so extraordinarily overblown that their fraudulence bordered on magnificent.

Nonetheless, VIII Fighter Command was quite confident with how it awarded credits for aerial victories. "Fighter claims are photographed, then appraised and have been found to be better than 90% correct, for a camera, synchronized to 'shoot' with the guns, is installed in the wings of every fighter plane, and so careful is the scientific appraisal of the claims at Fighter Command that there is a very great degree of certainty of their accuracy, when finally the award of claim is made. On this fact, all who know the procedure, are agreed."[1]

Of course, not everyone agreed, especially when they felt the system was wrong. Clayton Davis of the 487th claimed an Me-109 on January 29, 1944. He chased it in a high-speed dive and knocked pieces off before muscling his aircraft back into level flight just on the edge of compressibility. The German fighter continued straight down into a deck of clouds at three thousand feet. There was virtually no chance that it could have recovered.

After review at the 352nd's parent organization, the 67th Fighter Wing, Davis's claim was disallowed. The 487th felt so strongly enough about the validity of his claim that they appealed the decision in a formal letter, citing Virgil Meroney and Fred Allison as witnesses. They noted that the enemy aircraft had absorbed punishing gunfire, was shedding parts and was out of control when it disappeared in the clouds. Another factor in Davis's favor was that John C. Meyer would never have let the request for reconsideration leave his squadron if he didn't believe it was valid. Ultimately Davis was given credit for the claim.

Four months later, the reviewers made another call that was more cut and dried. Richard Brookins of the 328th dove hard after an Me-109 in the vicinity of Halberstadt, Germany. On the way down he fired a short burst without noting any hits. "Noticing that my IAS was 650 mph, I began to pull out about 6,000 feet and blacked out."[2] Brookins regained consciousness just above the treetops and scanned the area around him for the enemy aircraft. It was nowhere in sight. "I believe the Me 109 crashed as I last saw it going straight down below 5,000 feet. He was turning slightly to the right and seemed to be making no attempt to pull out. As I don't possibly see how he could have pulled out, I make the claim below [one Me-109 destroyed]."

With no reports of gunfire strikes on the enemy aircraft, no confirmation of a crash and no film evidence, Brookins's claimed was sensibly disallowed.

Göring was not impressed by the USAAF's process for assessing aerial victories. After the war, he estimated that USAAF claims were approximately three times greater than actual Luftwaffe losses.[3] In fact, he boasted to his debriefers that most of the Luftwaffe's losses were not due to combat.

According to Göring, an important reason for loss of aircraft was their short range. "A fighter pilot wants to sleep in his own bed. Instead, therefore, of landing at the nearest airfield after completion of their mission, fighter pilots were attempting to reach home base and had to bail out enroute due to lack of fuel. Where four aircraft were lost in combat, forty might crash on the way home."[4]

Of course, Göring's assertion that his fighter pilots lost most of their aircraft while trying to get back to base was a gross exaggeration. But there can be little doubt that most of the Luftwaffe's losses were to non-combat operations. This was certainly the case with the USAAF as two of every three aircraft it lost were destroyed in non-combat operations. The Luftwaffe's aircrews during the last part of the war were much less well-trained and it stands to reason that they experienced a very high mishap rate. Poor weather certainly made it worse.

When a pilot was shot down, the effects didn't end at that instant, at that point, with simply one aircraft and one pilot removed from the immediate fighting. Aside from the operational impacts to the pilot's unit, and the effects on his family and comrades if he were wounded or killed, the downing of an aircraft sometimes produced consequences that were not readily predictable. And occasionally those consequences were borne by those who had no connection to the fighting at all.

An example is found in Carl Luksic's encounter report of April 20, 1944. Luksic was leading the 487th's Yellow Flight when the squadron jumped a dozen FW-190s twenty miles southeast of Paris. Luksic was caught up in a wheeling dogfight with the rearmost enemy fighter. "I finally got in a good burst going straight up and his canopy flew off and flames and smoke shot all over. He then fell off on a wing and spun down from about 5,000 feet right into the center of some big city [possibly Melun], where he blew up and started a big fire in the town."[5] Whether or not civilians were killed is unknown but the point is moot. The nature of air combat was such that there was no way to control incidents of this sort.

Glennon Moran's experience just more than a month later on May 27, 1944, was very similar. Near Strasbourg he got into a hard-turning dogfight with an Me-109 that was curious in appearance due to its orange wingtips. Unusually, the fight lasted nearly twenty minutes after which time Moran hit the German with a short burst of gunfire. "However he continued to turn and dive and climb. He led me down to the deck and between some hills. As we came to a fairly clear spot over a small village, I was able to hit him again. He started burning and as I pulled up over him he exploded and crashed in the village."[6]

Ernest Bostrom of the 352nd's 486th Fighter Squadron scored an aerial victory on September 12, 1944, that offers another instance. *Stars and Stripes* reported: "1/Lt. Ernest O. Bostrom, of East Orange, New Jersey, an Eighth Air Force Mustang pilot, jumped a hot FW-190 pilot near Berlin and was led a merry chase over flak batteries. Bostrom finally closed in on the 'hot rock' and saw him crash and explode into the side of a large apartment house. There wasn't anything left but a gaping hole and powdered bricks." There is no knowing who or what was in the building, but neither Bostrom, nor the German pilot nor its occupants got out of bed that morning with any thoughts that it would be destroyed that day.

One of the reasons that the daylight strategic bombing campaign over Europe was so brutal and bloody was because the combatants were so flexible in adapting their tactics and equipment. The Germans, for instance, tried many different techniques to engage the American bombers. They also experimented with various sorts of weapons, to include rockets and heavy cannons. The Americans continuously refined their fighter escort procedures and simultaneously introduced improvements to their own equipment that increased the range to which the bombers could be protected.

George Preddy acknowledged the dynamic nature of the air war when he prepared the 487th Fighter Squadron's Standard Operating Procedures on April 1, 1944. In it he also noted that despite the continuously evolving character of the fighting, many of the basic precepts of air warfare remained the same. "Our tactics are consistently changing with changes in enemy tactics, changes in our aircraft, strategical [sic] demands, and our own experience and education. However, there are certain fundamentals which have been handed down to us and which have been further proven by our own experience. These fundamentals," he continued, "must be thoroughly drilled into any member of the squadron before he goes on an operational mission."

Chief among these fundamentals, Preddy listed air discipline. ". . . involving the principles of [not] straggling, cross cover, wing man responsibility, and radio discipline." The next precept was, "The fighting heart. The desire to destroy the enemy, to push forward a determined attack. This must be imbued into every fighter pilot; but, I repeat: but, this desire must be controlled through the medium of air discipline." In his next sentence he belied a love of the heritage of America's great west: "The fighting pilot run rampant is like a fine horse that can't be saddled—a source of worry and trouble, a danger, and a waste of good material." Preddy finished his discussion of this matter by noting that, "The combination of fighting heart and air discipline makes up what used to be called the 'pursuit attitude;' it makes a fighter pilot."

He also noted the importance of "continuing education" to the effectiveness—and indeed the survival—of the individual fighter pilot. ". . . it is drawn to the attention of all pilots that they must always be hungry to learn. A pilot with ten thousand hours in the air that thinks he knows all has laid himself open to the whims of the grim reaper. Use the information available. Read publications. They are put out for a purpose."

Preddy then turned his attention to the ultimately practical discipline of aerial gunnery. "The fighter pilot who maintains his position in the formation under all circumstances, who aggressively pursues the enemy, who skillfully follows or leads, is still of very little use if, once having engaged the enemy and outmaneuvered him cannot hit him. Good shooting is the final and conclusive phase of good hunting."

Preddy was right to emphasize gunnery; it wasn't easy. Analysis of P-47 gun camera footage was conducted by VIII Fighter Command to assess the performance of its pilots. The results showed that they typically underestimated the range of enemy aircraft and opened fire much too soon. They also indicated that longer bursts of fire made little difference to the outcome of an engagement; rather accuracy of fire was most important. The analysis described a typical air combat:

> The Thunderbolt pilot opens fire at 500–600 yards which he esti-
> mates to be 300 yards, on a deflection angle of 30 degrees. He
> gives four or five bursts of about a second each, closes to 200
> yards, more closely astern. His channel of fire wavers erratically
> over a two-degree arc, but crosses the line of flight between one
> degree and two degrees astern. He loses much ammunition by
> faulty aim of his bullet stream, which is the chief cause of unsuc-
> cessful attacks, not, as is generally thought, is it due to an insuffi-
> cient density of bullets in the fire pattern. If the pilot closes in to
> about 250 yards, he will get a victory but two thirds of the enemy
> aircraft attacked escape damage.[7]

With respect to range in the context of aerial gunnery, Virgil Meroney's experience was consistent with these observations. He commented on it in 1944 after he became the 352nd's first ace—and the only one to attain that status while flying the P-47. "When I first did any shooting, like a lot of other pilots, I opened up way out of range, and I'm convinced that range estimation cannot be emphasized too strongly."[8]

In fact, no aspect of air-to-air gunnery could be overemphasized. Shooting a moving aircraft from another moving aircraft, especially when both were maneuvering aggressively, was extraordinarily difficult. It was actually an intercept problem that required the shooter to time his fire so that the bullets from his machine guns arrived at a specific point at the exact same instant as the aircraft he was firing on.

The factors that went into a successful firing solution overwhelmed many of the young pilots. For instance, if a pilot did not keep his aircraft perfectly trimmed for balanced flight, the bullets went wide to one side or the other. If the pilot fired from too far away, as most of the inexperienced ones did, the bullets fell short. When firing at an aircraft that was crossing from one side to the other, the pilot had to pull enough lead (rhymes with speed) before pulling the trigger. That is, he had to aim far enough ahead of the target so that it collided with his bullets. To do so required him to accurately judge his target's range, speed, and the angle at which it was crossing his nose. Quite frankly, until the advent of the K-14 gyroscopic gunsight, this was more art than science, especially in the emotive heat of combat.

Very few pilots were skilled at this sort of instinctual "wing shooting." Virgil Meroney, was among those who were. Albert Giesting, Meroney's crew chief, remembered: "It was a real experience to watch Captain Meroney on the skeet range. He was almost casual in his firing stance and yet he knocked one clay pigeon after another out of the sky—and he rarely missed."[9]

But as stated earlier, the majority of the men were not natural marksmen. The smart ones compensated by getting directly behind and very close to their targets. John C. Meyer made no pretenses about his shooting skills. "I am not a good shot," he wrote during the war. "Few of us are. To make up for this I hold my fire until I have a shot of less than twenty degrees deflection and until I'm within 300 yards. Good discipline on this score can make up for a great deal.[10] Virgil Meroney was like-minded. "Usually the e/a tries to hit the deck and kick the ship around while going down. It makes me happy when they do that because then all I have to do is close up and let them have it."[11]

As to the quality of Preddy's shooting, aside from his tally of aerial victories, the observation of RAF exchange pilot Edwin King leaves no doubt that he was an expert shot. "Through my association and flying with Major Preddy, I came to admire his flying skill and his care and dedication for his squadron. I always felt extremely confident when in his company and in comparing him with RAF leaders must put him at the top of my list alongside Squadron Leader [Joseph] O'Meara. When attacking an enemy he showed his perfection by only using sufficient ammunition to achieve the kill."[12]

Punchy Powell recalled that the Germans had a trick or two up their collective sleeves when caught on the wrong side of an aerial gunfight: "Sometimes when we got behind a Jerry he would go into a bank but would step on top rudder so that he'd actually skid even though it looked like he was turning. We were inexperienced when we first saw this and typically took too much lead when we fired."

CHAPTER 16

The Deadliest Gamble

The Germans were deadly opponents, but sometimes the USAAF's airmen visited harm on themselves. Ted Fahrenwald recollected the mission of April 13, 1944, when one of Frank Cutler's fingers was shot away. "You ought to've heard him whoopin' and hollerin' over the radio when he got his finger blowed off! His radio was shot up so that he was transmitting without realizing it (or caring), and the air was full of lively commentary ensuing from his cockpit: '@!__#!!!@@' and then he'd fly up alongside one of the boys and wave his stump gaily at 'em, and follow it up with choice comments relating to the dirty illegitimate Hun who'd done it."[1]

Cutler was interviewed soon after and a news release covered the incident. Cutler described shooting up a parked Me-109 at a German airfield in the vicinity of Stuttgart and then a subsequent attack on a locomotive. "Then it happened," Cutler recalled. "As I pulled up from the engine a bullet came through my cockpit. It blew the index finger off of my left hand. I called in my injury over the radio-telephone, as blood started to splatter all over the damn place. My transmitter was on—and stayed on. That's how the boys heard all the cussing."

Despite his bravado in the interview, there is little doubt that Cutler was in excruciating pain. Although he made light of the incident, his performance belied his skill. "I didn't know whether I'd be able to make the ride back. The finger was gone clean from my hand, resting on the floor of the cockpit. It was my best-looking finger too. It looked as if it had been sawed off by one of the carpenters in my union back home. This was no time to admire it though."

Still deep in enemy territory, Cutler tended the injury as best he could in the cramped, blood-slicked cockpit of his aircraft. "I grabbed the first-aid kit, as the engine started to throw oil as the result of other bullet strikes out there in front of me. I kept the stick between my knees and tried to apply a tourniquet, using the strap from my helmet. No good. I thought of taking to my 'chute, then decided to stick it out."

There was no good or easy way for the stricken flyer to staunch the flow of blood. "I flew this way, with the stick between my knees for two hours. I kept trying again and again to stop the flow of blood. It would let up for a moment and then gush out like beer from a tap." Despite the wound, Cutler kept up with the rest of his comrades. "I kept cussing for two hours. I don't know if that helped or not. The boys tell me I was also laughing and crying. I must have sounded nuts. I don't remember any of that, though I don't think I ever lost consciousness."

Rather than trying to get his ship back to Bodney, Cutler put it down at the earliest opportunity, at RAF Woodbridge. "All I was interested in was getting back to England and landing at the first base I saw, because besides the blood I didn't know what my oil situation was. I finally saw a field, after what seemed like a million years. They tell me I landed *Soldiers' Vote* a little rocky. Next time, I'll do better."[2]

Cutler made a quick recovery and was soon back in the cockpit, one finger short. Of the incident, another pilot remembered that it was actually Cutler's wingman that had accidentally shot off his finger. Reportedly, the wingman hid from Cutler for days, afraid of what he might do; Cutler had a reputation for having a mean streak. Still, he did have friends. Fahrenwald was fond of him. "Frank Cutler's a reckless gent. Excellent flyer and loves death and destruction, same like the rest of us. A vicious temper at times, and at others, a sentimental, philosophical gent. Loves the country as I do and we often wander around poking thru the woods and admiring the beauty of things in general."[3]

That Cutler might have been hit by his own wingman while strafing a target was no real surprise. To prevent such a thing, especially while attacking airfields, the pilots were supposed to hold a generally steady course as they flew their strafing runs. However, particularly attractive targets such as parked aircraft often drew them off their headings like moths to a flame so that their flight paths converged. "It happened all the time," remembered Punchy Powell. "And our gun camera film showed it. Often you could see one or more aircraft pass into the camera frame of the firing aircraft."

Robert Butler, a pilot with the 487th, recounted just such an event that occurred on the same mission during which Cutler had his finger blown off on April 13, 1944. "Flying Yellow 2, I went down on an enemy A/D. I started to fire at a line of E/A parked on the edge of the field and then realized I was endangering my element leader. I swung away and fired a long burst into some buildings at the edge of the field and observed strikes."[4] There is little doubt that at least a couple USAAF aircraft were shot down by members of their own units as they made strafing attacks.

Likewise, the same sorts of incidents occurred during air-to-air combat. Dogfights by their nature were wild, turning free-for-alls during which it was nearly impossible for one person to keep track of every aircraft in the vicinity. Furthermore, the best firing position against an enemy aircraft was directly astern. Accordingly it was the point to which all attacking aircraft converged and more than a few close calls occurred.

The encounter report of John Bennett describes an example. On the mission of December 22, 1943, he dove after an Me-109 that was harrying a B-24. "I attacked it from 300 to 200 yards, firing continuously, observing strikes, smoke and flames, at 200 yds. At about 18,000 feet, my wingman, Lt. McMahan, zoomed past me, and we were both firing at 175 yards until I broke off when the other P-47 got in my sights. The Me-109 was definitely destroyed, for one wing came completely off and in spun down in flames out of control."[5]

Similarly, Henry White nearly shot down a comrade on May 28, 1944, near Madgeburg. On that date, he was chasing an Me-109 as part of a large, confused Lufbery. The Lufbery, named after the French World War I ace, Raoul Lufbery, was simply a defensive circle of aircraft. If an enemy flier dropped into the circle to attack an aircraft, he would immediately come under fire from the pilot behind him.

"He was turning to the left until I bounced him, then he turned right letting me get right up his tail. I pulled the trigger. Just as I did a P-51 came between me and the Me-109 so I broke left to miss him."[6]

And Samuel Dyke expressed frustration for the same reason on June 21, 1944 when he shared credit with Jack Thornell for an Me-410 downed near Dahmsdorf, Germany. "All the time Lt. Thornell was firing while the E/A tried to land. I was next to him but could not fire due to [the] danger of collision." Indeed when considering the multiple mentions of close calls, it is a wonder that midair collisions did not cause a great many losses.[7]

The invasion of Europe was less than two months away by the middle of April 1944, and one of the chief prerequisites for its execution was the neutralization of the Luftwaffe. To that end, VIII Fighter Command, with

Field Order 299, initiated a series of strafing attacks against German fighter bases—code-named Operation JACKPOT—on April 15. This was no secondary effort against targets of opportunity as allowed by Doolittle since his assumption of command of the Eighth Air Force the previous January; rather it was the primary mission of more than six hundred American fighters.

The 352nd's 486th Fighter Squadron, led by Luther Richmond, was tasked with hitting the German fighter base at Vechta in northwest Germany, halfway between Bremen and the Dutch border. At that time it was being used by FW-190s from JG 11 (*Jagdgeschwader* 11, or the 11th Fighter Wing). It was one of three separate airfields the 352nd was charged with attacking that day.

By this time, the 486th had completed its transition from the P-47 to the P-51. Rather than olive-drab paint, Richmond's aircraft sported a natural aluminum finish. This early in the Mustang's career with the 352nd, its nose was not painted in the distinctive blue that would become the group's hallmark a few months later. Of his aircraft's bright metal finish, Richmond recalled, "I wanted the Germans to see me, so maybe we could get together and sort things out. I figured that they would see the silver color from a long way off."

After getting airborne out of Bodney, the 352nd's three squadrons crossed the channel in group formation and stayed together until they neared Dummer Lake. At that point, at 12,000 feet, they split and descended below a solid undercast and headed for their separate targets. Richmond remembered the scheme he formulated for the 486th's attack: "My plan was to pass from about twenty-five miles south of Vechta, to a point twenty miles southeast of it, then head for the deck toward the field with the sun behind us. This we did," he recalled. "I had a section of eight aircraft with me on the deck [White and Red Flights], and eight above [Yellow and Blue Flights] providing top cover."[8] Aside from providing protection, Yellow and Blue Flights were intended to otherwise distract the German defenders with mock dive bombing attacks. They were also directed to photograph the effects of their comrades' strafing runs with their gun cameras.

"As we approached the airfield right on the treetops at about 1355 hours," Richmond recalled, "I was preparing to pull up to three to four hundred feet for the strafing run. I glanced up and saw about twelve FW-190s circling the field at about five hundred feet. I called my men and told them to forget the strafing run and engage the airborne aircraft. The Jerries apparently never saw us, as they were at five hundred feet and we were on the tree tops." It was quite possible that the German pilots were distracted by the top cover flight that Richmond had put over the airfield for that express purpose.

Richmond had never been presented with such an opportunity. "We soon had a number of FW-190's burning on the ground," he recalled. "I remember they were in a rectangle as though the traffic pattern had been transposed to the surface. I had a beam shot at my FW-190, and he half-rolled into the ground. I've never been sure whether I shot him down, or whether he was taking evasive action without realizing how low he was. Things happen pretty fast in a dogfight. Anyway, I received credit for the kill as my wingman [Chester Harker] reported it."

There followed several other fights. Henry Miklajcyk latched onto an FW-190:

I made about a 100-degree turn and went after the FW-190, when he turned to the left and headed southeast. I used full throttle and closed in. I gave him a burst at about 450 yards so he would turn. I saw some strikes, and when he turned he almost lost control due to high-speed wing stall. He straightened out and I gave him another short burst. The canopy fell off and a few parts were flying around. He then turned again to the right and I gave him a two-second burst from 70 to 90 degrees, and saw hits in the cockpit. The ship blew up and went out of control, making a barrel roll just before it hit the deck and exploded.

The fighting continued at a furious pace. Martin Corcoran knocked down two FW-190s and never climbed above 800 feet. Al Wallace engaged a flight of four Me-109s and brought down two of them. He remembered his second victory: "I fired a two-second burst at about ten-degree deflection with no result, probably because he was skidding and slipping. So I stopped firing and carefully slid over exactly dead-astern at about 200 yards. When I opened fire this time, there were very many hits all over the plane and he burst into flames, crashing almost immediately."

By this time, the fight had degenerated into a wild brawl of smaller combats. Richmond climbed above the fray following his score against the FW-190. "After initial contact, we were badly split up and had ballooned up to about six to eight thousand feet. I noticed a German survivor of the dogfight attempting to flee the scene at low level." When Richmond dove on the escaping FW-190 he was fired on by an antiaircraft gun. "I could see his tracers coming up as I passed through about a thousand feet." He switched his attention from the enemy aircraft to the offending gun. "The flak position was right in my sights, so instead of taking evasive action I steadied on my target. Temptation overcame my normally good judgment and I got off a long burst."

Richmond's momentary lapse cost him. "His tracers looked like red golf balls coming up, and normally I would have zigged and zagged a bit so that he would miss. On that day however, the temptation was too great and I held my aim steady as I could see my tracers hitting the flak site." Richmond's predictable flight path made him an easy target. "I felt the ship get hit, and almost immediately a tongue of flame licked back from around my feet and burned my hands quite badly." Aside from the rounds that hit around his engine, others tore into his wing and fuselage. A stream of burning fuel trailed several hundred yards behind the aircraft. Someone called out to warn him that he was on fire. Richmond replied, "I know it!"

He leveled off just above the treetops hoping to evade the antiaircraft guns that continued to pour shells after him. Despite the damage his ship had taken, Richmond was still flying at nearly 400 miles per hour. The fire in the cockpit continued to burn him and turned his hands into what he described as blistered "hams." "Concerned about whether my 'hams' would be of use in bailing out, I struggled with my safety belt and harness and got it unbuckled. All that remained was to pull the yellow canopy release lever. I pulled up quickly intending to zoom up to four to five thousand feet, roll inverted, and fall free. I started up, and pulled the canopy release lever with some difficulty."

The canopy fell away and Richmond was sucked partway out of the cockpit by the pressure differential. "My helmet came off as soon as I hit the slipstream, along with my goggles and oxygen mask. I wound up bent back over the turtledeck with my left foot caught around the throttle quadrant. The parachute straps across my rear were likewise caught on something." Rather than climbing up to several thousand feet, Richmond's Mustang topped out at only a few hundred feet with him flopping helplessly from the cockpit. Then, ever so gently, it nosed over into a gradual descent.

Richmond struggled to free himself from the burning ship before it crashed into the ground. "I managed to squirm down until I was hanging from the left side of the cockpit, and struggled to free my G.I. shoe. I thought of my wife and kids, and said a little prayer, all in a split second. Then I quit struggling, felt my foot slip loose and the heavy web straps rip from around my rear."

Richmond fell away from the stricken aircraft. "Free of the plane at last and floating feet-first on my back, I missed the tail I'd been staring at for a few seconds. All I could hear were the flak guns going off all around me. The trees were going by fast." Although his hands were badly burned, Richmond managed to pull his parachute's ripcord. Traveling as fast as he was, the opening shock was brutal and broke several of his ribs. A few seconds later he hit the ground with tremendous force. "The ground was hard and I hit like a ton of bricks, badly spraining both ankles. There was a burning FW-190 about 150 feet from me, and a flak position a couple of hundred feet in the other direction. Soldiers in the flak position were glancing over at me, and with difficulty, I rolled up my chute attempting to be inconspicuous, but to no avail."

The 352nd's mission summary report recorded none of these details. With the fight still ongoing, there was precious little opportunity to watch Richmond: "Lt. Col. Richmond, 486th Squadron, attacked and destroyed one FW-190 and his ship was hit in the right wing root while strafing A/D immediately after combat. His ship was seen to hit ground and explode."

Soon after his comrades flew away, Richmond was surrounded by German soldiers. His injuries were very painful; holding his hands up eased the throbbing. "A German soldier returned my gabardine flight cap to me, as it had apparently blown out of storage in the cockpit when the canopy was released. As the soldiers prepared to load me into a truck, a German second lieutenant came up and started screaming in my face and patting his pistol. I thought he was going to shoot me, and so did the surrounding soldiers as they started backing off." Unsure of what was being shouted at him, Richmond simply faced down the angry lieutenant.

Gottfried Pagenstert, a thirteen-year-old boy from a nearby farm was one of the first at the scene. He recalled the encounter:

At the same time, a few people from the airfield were standing with a kind of little lorry not far from our farmhouse and went to go get the pilot for prison. Soon after, a fanatical German flak lieutenant came up riding a bicycle. The [bicycle] chain had been coming loose many times. When he arrived he shouted at the pilot. Another man, a courageous sergeant of the Luftwaffe, asked the lieutenant if he knew about the Geneva Convention, and think about what he would feel if he were the pilot? The lieutenant backed off, and the injured pilot was advised to sit in the lorry and was moved away from the place.

Richmond was taken the short distance back to the airfield at Vechta where his wounds were cleaned and dressed. He was put into a small jail cell with a plank bed where he was later visited by the antiaircraft gunner that had shot him down. They exchanged cordial and professional congratulations and Richmond was left to sleep. "That night," he remembered, "my nice warm leather jacket was stolen from under my pillow and I was without it for the duration."

Aside from Richmond, Robert Ross of the 487th Fighter Squadron, who had been credited with four aerial victories at the time, was also hit. The group's mission summary report recorded that his aircraft "was seen to spin twice and burst into flame between Diepholz and Vechta A/Ds. Something came out of his ship which may have been the pilot, but no chute was seen to open." It was later learned that Ross was killed.

In all, the 486th's pilots claimed seven aerial victories in the group's mission summary report. In fact, they had not given themselves enough credit as the Germans tallied eight losses during the encounter—seven FW-190s and a single Me-109. This episode of miscounting during a short, sharp battle over a relatively confined area illustrates the difficulties inherent in scoring aerial victories.

On that same mission, Fremont Miller of the 328th Fighter Squadron was still flying his P-47, *Red Raider*, since the 352nd's transition to the P-51 had not yet been completed. The 328th was charged with hitting the Luftwaffe airfield at Diepholz which was located less than ten miles southeast of Vechta. Miller recalled how unusual the mission was. "We were called out for an early morning briefing and told that we would be strafing only: No bomber escort."[9]

Miller led the 328th's fourth flight that morning. The pilot of the airborne spare was anxious to take part in what was supposed to be a "fun" mission and as the formation reached the continent Miller gave him permission to join his flight rather than sending him back per the normal procedure. The ingress was smooth and after spotting the enemy airfield, the squadron dropped down to treetop level to execute its attack at about the same time that Richmond was leading the 486th against Vechta.

Once the attack formation was set—essentially line abreast—there was little room to maneuver and the pilots generally had to satisfy themselves with whatever target was in their flight path. If a pilot maneuvered too aggressively, he might fly into the fire of one of the other aircraft, or collide with a comrade or even the ground. Miller recalled: "On my side there were not any planes on the ground, only some buildings. I actually had to pull up to get over the building which I was strafing. Before I realized what was happening, the building exploded in my face. Planks and debris shot through the wings of my plane. In the left wing was a big hole and the metal skin was flapping in the breeze."

"I knew I was in trouble." It was a gross understatement

The massive Pratt & Whitney R-2800 radial engine that powered the Thunderbolt was legendary for its toughness; there was not an engine in service that could take more abuse. That fact notwithstanding, it was still subject to the laws of physics. More specifically, in Miller's case, the rules of thermodynamics began to destroy his aircraft's engine. "It carried thirty gallons of oil in a supply tank which was supposed to flow through the engine and be recycled into the tank for use again. But something had broken the oil line and hot oil was coming out of the engine and covering the canopy instead of returning to the oil tank."

In short, the engine was dumping its oil overboard. Miller turned for Bodney. Still he couldn't resist checking on his handiwork: "Before the back of the canopy was completely covered with oil I looked back and could see a huge, black cloud of smoke. The building I had strafed must have contained bombs or fuel."

The oil streamed back and covered Miller's windscreen and canopy with a viscous brown coat that totally obscured his vision. He slid the canopy back and peered out into the windstream but the hot oil that swept into the cockpit compelled him to close it again in short order. It was a moot point anyway as he flew into a bank of clouds that cloaked his aircraft in a blinding blanket of gray.

Miller continued west out of Germany. He composed himself and explained his situation over the radio. Earl Abbott, his commanding officer, called for him to bail out while he was still over land. Although it was likely that he would be captured and made a POW, it was better than the alternative. If the engine failed while he was over the North Sea, there was a real chance—in fact, a 72 percent chance—that he would never be rescued.

Miller didn't want to abandon his aircraft. It was a common phenomenon; if an aircraft was controllable and fire was not a factor, pilots and aircrews were reluctant to leave the familiar closeness of their aircraft even if it was mortally stricken. "I didn't want to disobey his [Abbott's] orders, so I just didn't answer him as if I hadn't heard him." He continued to wrestle with the wounded P-47 as he climbed through ten thousand feet and made his way over the North Sea.

"Flying on instruments had never been one of my best skills," Miller recalled, "but I had to rely on them now." At the same time he had to tussle with his aircraft. The hole in his left wing required right stick and left rudder to maintain straight and level flight.

It was more than Miller could manage. "All of a sudden the instruments went crazy and I was losing altitude fast," he recalled. "If I pulled back on the stick to raise the nose, the engine picked up speed. If I pushed the stick forward I dropped out of my seat." In the gray sameness of the clouds Miller had fallen victim to vertigo and was dropping upside down toward the ground in a high-speed split-S.

"The altimeter was unwinding like lighting and I kept trying to pull the plane through," Miller said. "I knew after I passed the last thousand feet that the odds against me were too great to survive." He pulled on the control stick with all his strength. Then he blacked out.

Unconscious and hurtling uncontrolled through the clouds, Miller was seemingly doomed. His mind retreated reflexively into a series of phantasms: "It was a wonderful feeling, as if I had died and gone to heaven. Beautiful visions, impossible to describe, passed through my mind."

The dreams lasted only seconds. When Miller regained his wits he found that the aircraft had reversed its vector and was climbing skyward through five thousand feet. He quickly regained control and eased the P-47's nose over into level flight. The engine, still losing oil, was nevertheless running. Miller gently coaxed the big fighter into a bank and reestablished a course for England.

Now committed to crossing the North Sea, Miller called Air/Sea Rescue and was immediately reassured by a clear response. In only a moment or two their direction-finding equipment triangulated his position and confirmed that his course and altitude were good. He was directed to make regular calls so that they could continue to update his position.

"Finally," remembered Miller, "the oil stopped running over the canopy so I knew it had all been pumped out of the tank. When I opened the canopy and looked below I saw nothing but water." Only a few minutes later the oil-starved engine finally stopped. Miller eased the nose of his aircraft over in order to maintain flying speed and eke out a few more miles before he had to abandon the ill-fated metal cocoon that was his P-47. There was no longer any question that he was going to spend time in the frigid sea; the critical question was how long he would be in it.

Miller notified the detached voice at Air/Sea Rescue that he planned to jump as he descended through 1,500 feet. They directed him to talk continuously until he bailed out so that they would have the most accurate fix possible. He ticked off his steadily decreasing altitude over the radio and made ready to jump by undoing his lap belt and shoulder straps. Finally, he disconnected from his radio and crawled tentatively out on the wing of *Red Raider*. He braced himself against the icy windstream that whipped at his clothes. An instant later he slid into space.

"Then I counted to ten: Five, ten," recollected Miller. "I looked down to be sure I had the rip cord and gave it a good strong tug. The parachute worked okay but the buckle on the chest strap hit me in the mouth and it felt like it knocked out a tooth, but it was just numb." Miller reached to check his tooth at the same time that he plunged into the heaving water. The parachute settled over him and quickly turned into a wet, cloying and deadly skein. Getting out from under it was paramount; if he became entangled in the shroud lines and dragged under the water, he wouldn't be the first airman drowned by his own parachute.

He had received training against just this sort of event, but splashing down into the North Sea after narrowly averting death in combat was much different than paddling around a pool with squadron mates and instructors. He clawed himself out from under the limp, sopping parachute and inflated both his life preserver and raft. He flailed through two attempts at climbing into the raft before he finally hauled himself out of the water. Then he pulled his knees up to his chest and balanced himself in the tiny dinghy and waited.

And waited. Because he had been speaking to Air/Sea Rescue only a short time earlier he was sure it wouldn't be long until he was picked up. He didn't even bother to bail out the water that sloshed around his seat and feet. After all, his location was precisely fixed before he jumped. It should have been only a matter of an hour or so—certainly no more—before a boat or amphibious aircraft came along.

And he was more than ready to be retrieved; the temperature of the North Sea was a killer. Had he not been able to get out of the water he would have died of the cold within a couple of hours. In the raft he stood a much better chance of surviving but he still ran the risk of hypothermia. "The temperature of the water," recollected Miller, "was about forty degrees and the air was not much warmer." He was dressed in a leather flight jacket and wet wool trousers and shirt. He was cold.

"But I didn't worry," Miller said, "because I knew my boys would go home, refuel and come back to find me." And in fact it was only about an hour later that Miller heard aircraft overhead. They may as well have stayed on the ground; low clouds had rolled in and obscured the surface of the water. No matter how many aircraft were thrown into the search, there was no way to see through the clouds. Still, Miller remained optimistic. "I knew that the ASR people had guided my boys back to the exact spot where I had gone down. Sooner or later the fog and clouds would have to move out and they would see me."

He had a better chance of being spotted by a boat, and indeed he caught sight of a motor launch that passed only a few hundred feet from where he floated. But the weather was so poor that its crew didn't see him. The boat turned away and Miller never saw it again. Through the rest of the day he floated on the cold gray water, listening to the search aircraft overhead. Finally, day turned to dusk and the sound of the search aircraft disappeared. "But I wasn't discouraged," Miller declared, "because I knew they would be back the next day. It never occurred to me that I might die."

The weather grew worse at nightfall. Miller recalled: "The wind came up after dark and the waves were enormous. There was no way to keep my back to the wind. When I got to the top of a wave, the rolling edge would hit me in the face and the water ran down my neck. I was soaked all night."

That he was still alive in the morning was remarkable.

"The next morning the wind let up a little but it was still dark and cloudy and I knew no planes would fly that day," Miller remembered. Some distance from where his raft bobbed in the waves he noted an enormous black bird perched atop a large chunk of driftwood. "He sat there looking at me all day."

Miller had little to do but inventory the small packet of items—butterscotch squares, dextrose tablets, and chewing gum—that comprised the rations in his survival kit. He tried to keep his little craft clear of water and stretched his long limbs as best he could. Still, it was a miserable existence and his feet were underwater most of the time. The cold dreary day ended and the next night passed much like the first.

Miller was still alive the morning following his second night adrift. The huge black bird was still with him. "I knew what he had in mind but I made up my mind to outlast him." This day, like the ones before it, was cloudy and miserable. There were no aircraft overhead but it was as much due to the fact that no one held any real hope that he was still alive as it was to the weather. "My dinghy had lost air and was getting soft. I had a small bellows-type hand pump and I tried to pump some air into the canvas shell but it didn't seem to do any good. That third night was worse that the other two."

April 18 dawned clear enough for a mission. It was uneventful and the 352nd handed its assigned bombers to a newly arrived group and headed for home. As the 328th cleared the coast and started back across the North Sea, Don Bryan called out over the radio: "Let's go down and see if we can spot Big Miller." Most everyone recognized that such an effort would be nothing more than a farewell salute to the memory of a beloved comrade. None of them had heard of anyone lasting in the water for three days. Too, he would have drifted quite a distance during that time so the likelihood of finding him even if he were alive was virtually nil.

Notwithstanding the slim odds, Bryan made a call to Air/Sea Rescue, received a heading, and dropped the squadron down to just a few hundred feet above the wave tops where they spread out. Sixteen sets of eyes scanned the gray water looking for a prize that none of them realistically expected to find.

Then the impossible happened. Miller remembered: "Late that afternoon, after all the planes had gone home, a P-47 came over very low. I waved my arms as hard as I could. I knew the pilot had seen me when he circled and climbed up high enough to where he could contact ASR and report my position."

It wasn't long before a motor launch was on its way. Once it was clear that the boat's crew had Miller in sight, the P-47s pointed for home. "The men on the deck of the launch threw me a rope," Miller said, "and without waiting for them to pull me up, I climbed the rope hand over hand; something I had never been able to do before."

Miller was safe. He had been adrift on the water for more than seventy hours.

The crewmen hauled the near-frozen flyer below decks where they removed his soaking clothes, put him in a set of warm woolen coveralls and fed him broth. Once they had him safely tucked in bed they radioed his particulars to shore. There was confusion in the Air/Sea Rescue chain as it was believed that there was no way that Miller could have still been alive. "I realized for the first time," Miller said, "that my outfit had given me up."

In fact, Earl Abbott, the 328th's commanding officer, met the launch when it made landfall. He was there to confirm that it really was Miller who had been rescued. He recalled that Abbott "turned white as a sheet, as if he saw a ghost. He just couldn't believe I was alive."

Miller was indeed alive but he was at risk of losing his legs. At Royal Navy Hospital, Great Yarmouth, the staff tended him hourly to save his badly frost-bitten limbs. "The nurses," he remembered, "were the most dedicated women I have ever seen. They never complained about anything although they had very little to work with." And his doctor was equally devoted; Miller became his special cause. His feet were kept elevated and fans were positioned to blow cool air on them to keep them from overheating. "My feet gave off so much heat that the nurses would come in and warm their hands on them."

They swelled and turned nearly black. Skin sloughed from them in sheets. "I became an object of curiosity," Miller remembered, "and every day a doctor or two dropped in to see the man who had survived seventy-six hours in the North Sea." The consensus among many of those medical experts was that the circulation would never return to Miller's feet and that they had to be removed before gangrene set in. Eventually, even his doctor reached the same conclusion. Miller was resigned to losing them.

He remembered that the doctor came to visit him on the morning his feet were to be cut off. "He spent a long time probing around just below the ankle bone to see if there was any sign of a pulse. I watched his face intently and I thought I saw a faint smile. He looked at me and said, 'Let's wait one more day.'" On the following day, his circulation improved further as it did on subsequent days. It wasn't long before the danger passed and Miller was assured of keeping his feet.

Strafing enemy airfields was the most dangerous type of mission the 352nd flew. The group lost many more aircraft and pilots in these types of attacks than it did in aerial combat. Several different considerations made this so. First, the airfields were important and the Germans consequently put heavy defenses in place, especially later in the war as Allied attacks intensified. Next, as compared to air combat where both the shooter and the target were moving in several different dimensions, the attacking aircraft flew generally straight courses while the German gunners were stationary. This made it much easier for the gunners to accurately aim their fire.

Moreover, whereas in aerial combat it was generally possible for only one aircraft to attack another at any given time, a strafing aircraft might be taken under fire from many different guns arrayed across an airfield. And because the attacks were generally made in a line-abreast formation, there wasn't much room for attacking fighters to jink, or otherwise maneuver away from gunfire without running the danger of colliding with another aircraft. Too, the Germans sometimes set up indiscriminate, interlocking curtains of barrage fire that the attacking fighters had no choice but to fly through as they crossed the airfield.

Most of the airfield attacks were not specifically assigned by higher headquarters, but were ad hoc affairs performed when the unit went free-lancing after completing its bomber escort duties. For many of the men, although they understood the dangers of these airfield attacks, the sight of aircraft on the ground was too powerful to resist and they were drawn down like flies to honey. This type of aggressiveness meshed perfectly with Doolittle's desire to kill the Luftwaffe wherever it might be found.

Tactics for attacking the airfields varied from one leader to another and generally became more sophisticated as the war progressed. Earlier, it was common for half the attacking force to loiter overhead as high cover, or to fly by the airfield as a distraction. The other half departed the vicinity, dropped to low level, and then turned back toward the airfield while receiving heading corrections from the high group. This tactic sometimes caught the enemy defense by surprise. Later, as the units grew in size, one portion was often assigned as high cover while another suppressed the defending guns and then another executed the actual attack. Sometimes, especially when in smaller flights, there was no pretense at sophistication. Instead the aircraft would "make one pass and haul ass."

The P-47 was irrefutably superior to the P-51 where strafing was concerned. Its eight guns packed much more of a wallop than the Mustang's four, or six, guns, but more importantly it could take much more damage than its replacement. The enormous air-cooled R-2800 engine was not only able to take a tremendous amount of punishment, but it additionally served as a shield in front of the pilot. On the other hand, the sleeker P-51—sometimes dubbed the "Spam Can"—was very vulnerable to hits in its engine's cooling system and sometimes gave up upon receiving the slightest hurt.

Whereas it was inarguably more difficult to shoot an enemy aircraft out the sky, it was more dangerous to shoot one up on a defended airfield. The Eighth Air Force recognized this and kept an official tally of the ground victories scored by its flyers while also making sure that high scorers received recognition in the form of awards and media attention. Nevertheless, it was costly business. Aside from Luther Richmond, the 352nd lost many more men during these types of attacks, including high-scoring aces Virgil Meroney and Carl Luksic.

Besides enemy gunfire, there were other hazards involved in strafing the Luftwaffe's airfields and otherwise flying at low altitude. The 352nd had a good day on April 24, 1944, when it destroyed twenty-eight aircraft on the ground at various airfields. However, the 486th Fighter Squadron gave up one of its own, but not to enemy fire: "Capt. MacKean's plane seen to strike high tension wire and explode approximately twelve miles N. of Augsburg." Robert MacKean, who had destroyed three Me-110s on the mission, did not survive.

Don Bryan, as aggressive a fighter pilot as there ever was, didn't like the odds associated with strafing German airfields. "I went through two tours and 138 missions, and I never shot at an aircraft on the ground," he recalled. "Especially toward the end of the war, the Germans weren't flying because there was no fuel, and the aircraft that were sitting on the airfields wouldn't burn for the same reason—there was no fuel in them. But a lot of our guys were killed by the anti-aircraft guns set up around those fields." There was some wisdom in Bryan's perspective. He was an ace more than twice over, and had flung himself into many aerial battles. That he chose not to challenge fate by attacking heavily defended German airfields is telling.

Fremont Miller returned to Bodney following his release from the hospital. He was there only to recover and was not to return to combat. Nevertheless, he got restless. His feet were only barely beginning to heal and he could do little more than stand on them for short periods of time.

To help him get around, two staff sergeants from the 328th's engineering section, George Wilcox and Victor Hynds, built Miller a hand-powered cart made of bicycle parts. It was dubbed *Red Raider Jr.*, and it no doubt played a role in his speedy recovery. The massively strong Miller was spotted powering himself all over the airfield. He occasionally got overzealous and spilled himself at the very farthest reaches of the base. In those instances, the control tower personnel, who always kept a watchful eye on him, sent someone in a jeep to pick him up, dust him off, and put him back in his contraption.

The fierce gruesomeness of air combat was rarely evident to the pilots of the 352nd. Certainly, they understood what happened when an aircraft exploded or was shredded by gunfire, but the death with which they dealt usually happened at long ranges and high speeds in seemingly limitless skies. And although their .50-caliber machine guns were brutally powerful, most pilots never saw what they did to the human body. Still, there were occasions when the reality of death came close up.

The mission of January 30, 1944, offered an example. Don Bryan of the 328th Fighter Squadron chased down an FW-190 near Emmen and after firing a few ineffective bursts, finally set the enemy fighter's external fuel tank afire. Bryan pulled the throttle of his P-47 to idle when he realized he was in danger of flying past the FW-190. When he finally stopped the closure he was about fifty feet behind the enemy fighter. "I blew his canopy off and got many strikes all over him. While still shooting I ran out of ammunition. He was smoking very badly but I hadn't set him on fire. As I pulled away from him I saw that the pilot's head was hanging over the side of the ship. He was quite dead."[10]

A more gruesome instance took place on April 30, 1944. During the mission Major Stephen Andrew closed on an FW-190 and shot it up badly enough that the enemy pilot jettisoned his canopy and jumped clear. Tragically, he fell directly onto the propeller hub of Andrew's P-51 and was killed instantly. Ted Fahrenwald recalled what happened immediately after: "Well, pal Archy [Lloyd Archibald Rauk] is flying alongside, sightseeing, and inasmuch as this is a gory sight and Arch's stomach is full of party-type butterflies, he pulls off one fur flying boot and upchucks into it and tosses the works overboard. On the way home, then, when over the Channel, Archy figures that one boot is no damn good, so he tosses the other out and down into the briny deep."[11]

As it developed, the body of the German pilot fell clear and Andrew was able to get his ship back to Bodney where bits of flesh, bone and clothing were pulled from the aircraft. Death was very real and very close that day.

Odd things sometimes happened to the pilots for which there simply was no preparation. Such was the case on April 22, 1944, when Clayton Davis was on a strafing spree north of Hanover in a P-51:

I was flying white three and white leader lead [*sic*] us down to strafe an airdrome. On approach I shot up a building and got two Ju-88s taxiing. One I observed hits on, only damaging it and the other [was] destroyed. I saw [it] burning after strikes. Later, I made an attack on a locomotive in the vicinity south of the airdrome and damaged it. As I attacked the locomotive, my canopy flew off.[12]

Regrettably, the narrative ends without Davis commenting on his reaction to the sudden makeover of his fighter into a convertible. It is nevertheless certain that his flight back to Bodney was a wind-whipped and cold one.

The death spiral into which the Luftwaffe had fallen by early 1944 was self-created to a great degree. Chief among its components was Germany's failure to train—or even plan to train—the numbers of pilots it ultimately needed to fight the air war that the United States decided to bring to Europe.

While the USAAF had more than 130,000 trained pilots on hand at the start of June 1944, the Luftwaffe had only a tiny fraction of that number. In fact, from 1940 through the end of the war, the Germans produced only approximately 10,000 single-engine fighter pilots. In comparison, the USAAF graduated 49,503 single-engine pilots during 1943 alone. When it is considered that Germany was fighting not only the United States, but also Great Britain and the Soviet Union, it is not overly critical to characterize its failure to train enough pilots as gross stupidity. If any of the belligerents required vast numbers of excellent pilots, it was Germany.

Whereas the German leadership successfully implemented crash programs to dramatically ramp up the production of aircraft, doing the same with pilots was impossible. Aircraft could be stamped out in prodigious numbers so long as all the resources were available at the right place and time. The Germans demonstrated this during much of 1944 when they manufactured prodigious numbers of fighters despite continuous Allied bombing.

The same was not true of humans. They needed to eat and sleep. They got sick. Each one had a different temperament and a set of characteristics that made him unique. Too, whereas aircraft could be built regardless of the weather, fledgling pilots needed benign flying conditions in which to learn. Europe's weather was miserable during much of the year. And although humans could be pushed, there was a limit to how fast they could learn. Moreover, they needed experience of the type that couldn't be learned as part of a formal training syllabus. Some things simply couldn't be taught and came only from flying regularly over a period of time.

By 1944, the Germans didn't have time. For instance, it still took a year for the United States, with its vast and carefully considered training program—and relatively good weather—to produce a combat-ready, albeit green, pilot with more than three hundred hours of flying experience. The Luftwaffe couldn't match this. Even if it could have, it would have needed to start such a program at the end of 1942 or early 1943. Nothing of the sort was ever implemented.

As a consequence, when the Luftwaffe's leadership recognized its predicament it was forced to cut corners in pilot training. As a result, by 1944, new Luftwaffe fighter pilots started operations with roughly half the flight time and experience of their USAAF counterparts. Worse, they were expected to complete their training while on actual operations.

The result was predictable. Poorly prepared relative to their USAAF and RAF counterparts, neophyte Luftwaffe fighter pilots were quickly killed in combat. Flying accidents killed even more. They were subsequently replaced by less and less well-trained pilots until, by the end of 1944, new pilots were showing up with barely more than a hundred flying hours, only a fraction of which was at the controls of the aircraft they flew in combat.

As a result, an assignment to fly in defense of the Reich during 1944 was akin to a death sentence for a new German fighter pilot. On average, German fighter units defending against the USAAF bomber streams lost more than four of every five aircraft *every single month.*[13] A lucky pilot might survive being shot down two or three times but it was uncommon to escape injury or death on a long term basis. In fact, when *Generalfeldmarschall* Hugo Sperrle surveyed the fighter units of *Luftflotte* 3 during July 1944, he discovered that only the highest ranking commanders, who did not regularly fly in combat, had more than six months of experience while only a few of those who flew regular operations had more than three months of experience. The majority of the pilots had been flying against the USAAF for *less than a month.*

Luftwaffe pilot trainees endured a certain type of hardship late in the war that their USAAF counterparts never had to consider. That is, they ran a small but real chance of getting shot down. Although there is no knowing for certain who was at the controls, a German trainer was bagged by Robert Ross of the 487th Fighter Squadron on April 13, 1944, near Stuttgart. "As we started down from 8,000 feet to strafe this a/d, I spotted an aircraft just above me with fixed landing gear. I pulled up to identify it and saw it was a primary trainer. He was at 1,300 feet when I identified him."[14]

The enemy training plane was like a mouse caught in a cattery; it was unarmed but nimble. Ross had a devilish time trying to pin it down with his high performance fighter. "He saw me at the same time," recalled Ross, "and dove for the deck. I made three passes at him but could not get enough deflection to hit him. On my fourth pass he got behind some trees and I fired through the trees at about forty-five degrees deflection," Ross recounted. "As he came to the end of the row of trees he pulled straight up and fell off on the left wing going straight into the ground where [the] plane disintegrated."

When considering the larger strategic picture, this encounter was consistent with Doolittle's orders. He wanted his flyers to attack and kill the Luftwaffe whenever opportunities were presented. Young German pilot trainees received no special consideration and Allied pilots attacked training aircraft whenever they encountered them.

There was a certain amount of ignorance about the "bigger picture" among the men fighting the war, both on the ground and in the air. Many times the men were kept purposely uninformed by their higher headquarters for security reasons. That is, they were told only what they needed to do their jobs. But for the most part the men were simply too busy, and things were happening too quickly, for them to be fully aware of everything that was happening. And with new units arriving at an ever-increasing clip through the early part of 1944, keeping track of all the players was very difficult.

An example of this is how little the men of the various fighter groups knew about each other. For instance, whereas modern-day aviation historians are intimately familiar with the paint schemes of the various fighter groups, the men who were actually there generally were not. This is illustrated in an encounter report made by Carl Luksic of the 487th Fighter Squadron. On May 19, 1944, he downed an Me-109 near Ludwigslust in northern Germany. "At this same time," he reported, "I saw another 109 shoot down a 51 but other 51s were after him."

"I was rejoined by another 51 with a red and yellow checked nose," he said. "He called me on 'C' channel telling me he was low on gas and wanted to come home. I came home with him."[15] Although Luksic had no idea, the P-51 with the distinctive red and yellow checked nose was from the 357th Fighter Group which went on to generate one of the most distinguished records in the Eighth Air Force, and produced several notable aces to include Leonard Carson, Clarence Anderson, and Richard Peterson. Of course, at that point in the war the 357th had been in combat for barely more than three months and there was little about the unit to distinguish it from any other, except for its markings.

"Especially later on when there were so many P-51 units," remembered Punchy Powell, "I don't remember knowing any of their markings. If we needed to identify them we'd describe them by how they were painted. For instance, during a mission debriefing we might simply say that the aircraft that we saw shot down north of Hanover was a yellow-nosed Mustang and leave it to the intelligence types to figure out what unit it was from." And indeed, the S-2, or intelligence shop, did have a poster that described the markings of all the fighter groups in VIII Fighter Command.

As skilled as the young American pilots arriving from the States were, they still sometimes made mistakes. And making the smallest mistake in the wrong place, especially while flying powerful aircraft in combat, could cost a pilot his life. The encounter report of Robert Sharp of the 328th Fighter Squadron underscores this point:

> I was leading Blue Flt. In the area of Wittenberge I saw an Me 109 on the tail of a P-51 at 23,000 feet. I went in and fired, seeing hits in the wing root and canopy. The Me-109 broke for the deck and I followed. My canopy frosted up and a green-nosed P-51 [from the 359th Fighter Group] took over, firing short bursts, but I saw no hits from his fire. Blue 2, Lt. Carlone, of my flight had followed me and took over from the green-nosed P-51 from another group. Blue 2 fired and got several hits; the e/a started smoking and bellied in about 250 mph. It broke in two and in turning to the left Blue 2 spun in and exploded, probably as the result of a high speed stall. The green-nosed P-51 and I came home together.[16]

Of course, the German pilots also made mistakes. And those mistakes became more common as the replacement pilots the Luftwaffe threw into the fight received less and less training; the exigencies of the air war over Germany, especially the hellish attrition rate, demanded that new pilots be sent into combat as soon as they were reasonably ready. Sometimes reasonably ready was not ready enough as indicated by an engagement that occurred on May 13, 1944.

On that day, Francis Horne of the 328th Fighter Squadron was flying a bomber escort mission when a box formation of approximately fifty Luftwaffe fighters was encountered near Demmin in northern Germany. The enemy aircraft had been unmolested to that point and were positioning themselves for an attack on the bombers. Sensitive to the urgency of the situation, Horne immediately dove on the Germans. "My main effort," he remembered, "being to break up the formation of E/A before they reached the bomber formation."[17]

"I swept from the right back of the enemy formation to about two thirds to the left front corner, firing several bursts." The enormous German formation was unwieldy, and while it might have been effective in massing firepower against the big American bombers, it was ludicrously vulnerable against fighter attacks. The individual pilots making up the huge block of German aircraft were virtually helpless against diving attacks like Horne's. They couldn't maneuver because there simply wasn't room inside the formation to do so. The best they could do was rely on chance and hope that they wouldn't be selected as a target, or in the event that they were fired upon, hope that their attacker was a poor shot.

Nevertheless, it took nerves to stay put and some of the German fliers, as Horne described, simply couldn't do it. "One of the FW-190s broke right when I started closing on him and ran into another FW-190. The right wing came off of the E/A that had broken, and the left wing was knocked off the other E/A and they both started spinning down." As he pulled up and away, Horne looked over his shoulder and saw the rest of his squadron mates savaging the hapless Germans. Horne was awarded credit for the two FW-190s.

Joe Mason, the 352nd's commanding officer, was leading the group that day and also encountered an enormous formation of German fighters. "My flight cut across the arc of their turn and flew through the middle of their formation. I fired as I was going through them, and saw strikes on the wing of one ME 109." Mason found himself all alone when he came out the other side of the group of enemy aircraft.

"I pulled up in a climbing left turn and looked back and down at the bandits. Two of them were spinning down, one with his tail gone and the other with about two-thirds of his wing gone. We had forced this collision of the two 109s when I took my flight through the large formation, the largest I have ever seen." Mason then dove down on a mixed formation of Me-109s and FW-190s.

"I closed on a 190 after a series of short bursts. I set him on fire." Mason pressed after the enemy aircraft. "The first burst had knocked his flap, or some object of similar size, off. Just before he entered a large cloud, smoke, flame and debris came back over my ship. I then pulled up to keep from running through him in the cloud, and came out on top."[18]

Again, two of the enemy aircraft, Me-109s, collided and went down. Mason was given credit for their destruction. These two aircraft, together with an FW-190 that he downed during the same engagement and two earlier victories, gave him a total of five enemy aircraft downed in combat. It was his final tally of the war.

However, it wasn't only the Germans who mistakenly rammed into other aircraft. Marion Nutter remembered the 487th Fighter Squadron's attack on an enormous mass of German fighters that same day: "We swung over their heads and came in on their tails," he recalled. "My closing speed was so great that before I knew it I found myself in the middle of the formation. Shortly before, in the rear of the formation, I observed a 51 crash into the tail of a 109. Both were burning." The mission summary report for the day noted that "One silver blue nose P-51, believe[d to be] Capt. Cutler, 486th Sqdn. seen to collide head on with Me-109 vicinity Tribsees, 1415. Both planes disintegrated."[19]

The pilot of the P-51 that smashed into the Me-109 was Frank Cutler of the 486th Fighter Squadron. The aircraft he destroyed when he killed himself was Don McKibben's *Miss Lace*. Cutler, part of the original cadre of 352nd pilots, was no novice and was credited with 7.5 aerial victories. In fact, he won the Silver Star for his actions a few months earlier on February 20 when he shot down two Me-109s that were attacking a formation of B-17s. And he was recommended for an even more prestigious decoration—the Distinguished Service Cross—for his actions on April 11 when he destroyed three Me-109s in the air and another on the ground.

An aggressive pilot, Cutler was also widely considered a hothead and a mean drunk, a man who was hard to like. In fact, he was sent out of the unit to Ferry Command in mid-November for having gotten involved in "a small-scale knock-down-drag-out brawl."[20] One pilot recalled, "To my mind, Cutler got what he had coming." The 486th's historical narrative for the month of May 1944 eulogized Cutler without recalling his less admirable qualities: "Our top shooting pilot, Captain Frank A. Cutler, didn't return from a mission to Kraesinki in Poland on May thirteenth. The fact that we destroyed nine enemy aircraft that day does not in the least minimize our loss. It will take a good, big man to fill his flying boots." Too, the group's interim history which was filed in the summer of 1944 listed Cutler as one of its outstanding personnel.

It was axiomatic that the men of the 352nd—indeed of any fighting organization—trusted each other with their lives. John C. Meyer demonstrated his faith in George Preddy to a very great degree on May 13, 1944, when the group broke up a large formation of enemy fighters that was readying for an attack on the bomber stream. This was the same mission during which Cutler was killed in a midair collision.

Meyer got into a turning fight with an Me-109 but failed to gain any advantage. After a short time he noted another P-51 on the tail of his adversary, but out of range. Meyer learned that the pilot of the other P-51 was Preddy. Confident in his comrade's flying skills and marksmanship, Meyer pulled his throttle back. As the German flier closed on him, Preddy in turn pulled within range of the German and subsequently blew off his left wing with a thirty-degree deflection shot from two hundred yards.

Their relationship had certainly evolved since the previous year when Meyer restricted Preddy to base for ducking out of an equipment inspection.

CHAPTER 17

Failed Guns
and Varied Tactics

When John C. Meyer returned to the States for a well-earned period of leave on May 14, 1944, George Preddy was designated as the acting commanding officer of the 487th Fighter Squadron. Whereas the enlisted men respected Meyer and readily acknowledged his leadership, they also feared him to some degree. He was exacting, demanding, and often unsmiling. He took his duties seriously and was not reluctant to discipline his men when they did not perform or when they misbehaved. In his defense was the obvious fact that he was leading men in war. In their business a failure didn't result in a lost sale or a slowdown on the production line; rather, failure meant that someone stood a good chance of finishing the day dead.

On the other hand, the enlisted men both liked and respected the more approachable Preddy. Whereas Meyer might have been a stern father figure, Preddy was more like a big brother. Preddy's assistant crew chief, Joseph "Red" McVay explained: Meyer was a tough man with no smile. But the major [Preddy] they loved. He never bragged, and they just loved him. When Meyer went on leave, the major was selected as the acting CO [commanding officer] of the 487th. The top sergeants called all the enlisted men together and said that while the major is CO no one is to foul up. If anybody fouls up—even in London—we're going to tear you apart."[1] None of them wanted Preddy's tenure as their commander to be sullied because of their own shortcomings.

Meyer was among the first of the 352nd's pilots sent home on leave to the States. He did so as part of a recently implemented program. As the time for the invasion approached it was felt that there might not be enough pilots to do the fighting. To that point, a fighter pilot was allowed to rotate home when he accrued two hundred hours of combat flight time. In the 352nd's case, most of the original pilots would have met that requirement at about the time of the invasion.

A pilot shortage catastrophe loomed in VIII Fighter Command. Consequently, the men were given two choices. They could take a one hundred hour extension to their tour while remaining in England, or they could take leave for a month in the States before returning for a two hundred hour extension. Meyer took the longer extension.

Punchy Powell opted to stay in England and complete the shorter extension. "I wanted to get home," he remembered, "but I also wanted to be part of the invasion effort. Even then we knew it was going to be one of the most important events in history. I felt I needed to be there."

Frank Cutler met a woman who came quite frequently to Bodney to visit with him. When he was killed, she started seeing Woodrow Anderson. After he was killed, the officers had the gate guards turn her away whenever she showed up at the base. They likely did so out of a combination of sympathy and superstition.

Göring's flawed leadership of the Luftwaffe manifested itself in astonishingly bad ways. His failures were rooted largely in his personality but also stemmed from a narrow and simplistic understanding of air combat. Although he had been a successful ace during World War I, he failed to appreciate the changes in tactics, techniques, and procedures that had occurred as the science of aviation evolved. The edict he issued to his fighter units during December 1943 reflected his shortcomings. Anxious to inflict the maximum hurt possible on the American bomber formations, he ordered his pilots to avoid combat with the escort fighters at all costs. Instead, they were to concentrate solely on the bombers and ignore the Americans fighters even if they were attacked.

Certainly, it made sense to target the bombers rather than the fighters as it was the bombers that were destroying Germany. On the other hand, the American fighter escorts were virtually ubiquitous up and down the length of the bomber streams and their pilots were aggressive. Consequently, it was difficult for the Luftwaffe fliers to attack the bombers without being molested themselves. And simply disregarding the American fighters gave them the advantage of position and timing over the Luftwaffe aircraft. If the Germans were forbidden to fight, they had to ignore the Americans or flee; it was an excellent way to die.

Eugene Clark's encounter report of May 19, 1944 highlighted this point. Soon after the 352nd's Mustangs rendezvoused with their assigned bomber groups, two large formations of German fighters were spotted. The first numbered approximately forty aircraft and was positioned at three o'clock to the bomber stream, while the second was nearly as large and was flying a few thousand feet above the first. Clark, who was leading the 487th Fighter Squadron, swung around after the lower formation while the 486th Fighter squadron engaged the higher group of Germans.

"Singling out one E/A which I identified as an Me-109, I opened fire," Clark recorded. "I observed hits on the left wing, tail and fuselage."[2] Although he scored hits, the guns on Clark's P-51B experienced the sort of failure so common to the type: "Only my two right guns would fire, which fact threw me into a skid every time I fired. After each burst I had to correct my aim."

Regardless, the reaction—or lack of one—from the Me-109 pilot seemed to reflect a rigid adherence to Göring's directive. "The E/A stayed in formation, taking only mild evasive action," Clark recounted. "Two E/A on either side of him tried dropping back on my tail but my wingman [Charles Ellison] persuaded them to stay put by squirting them each time they dropped back." This lack of aggressiveness on the part of the Luftwaffe fliers was self-defeating. Unmolested, Clark pressed his attack and the enemy aircraft fell into a spin with its landing gear and flaps extended. "As I cocked my plane up on one wing to follow him down," Clark recalled, "I saw him bail out."

There really was no good way to obey Göring's orders. The German fliers could try to crash through the American fighter screens, make one pass against the bombers and dive away. But this approach left them vulnerable to attack themselves, especially as they tried to escape. The P-51 could stay with both the Me-109 and the FW-190 in a dive, and the P-47 could easily overtake both. This meant that the German pilots were invariably attacked from behind—the worst situation possible. When caught thusly, they had few options. Upon reaching the deck they could continue to try to outrun the Americans or perhaps scrape them off by flying low through wooded areas or towns. Another tactic was to fly across an airfield where defending gunners might shoot their pursuers down. Still another tactic was to simply keep running until the American pilots ran low on fuel; this was reasonable against the P-47, but less so against the long-legged P-51.

The encounter report of William Whisner from April 30, 1944, describes his victory over a Luftwaffe flier who unsuccessfully exercised some of these options. The 352nd was escorting B-17s to central France on an attack against the airfield at Clermont-Ferrand. "I was flying Red 3 in a seven-ship section," Whisner recounted.[3] "We were at 17,000 feet at 5 o'clock to the bombers when I saw a lone ship in a shallow dive at about 8 o'clock at 15,000 feet." Whisner made a call on the radio and dove after the unidentified aircraft. The other six aircraft in his flight winged over after him.

As Whisner closed the range in his P-51 he identified the aircraft as an FW-190 and squeezed off a very long-range burst of gunfire from a thousand yards but missed. The enemy fighter steepened its dive and started a turn to the left. "I gave him another burst at about 500 yards, missing again," recorded Whisner. "I noticed my airspeed passing 500 and the 190 pulled out and led me right across Clermont-Ferrand A/D right on the ground." Whisner closed rapidly on the enemy aircraft. He adjusted his rudder trim to null out any aiming errors that might be induced by unbalanced flight. Immediately after, he centered his gunsight over the enemy aircraft and fired from directly behind at a range of only one hundred yards.

"Strikes covered him and pieces began to fall back," Whisner recorded. The two aircraft raced over the enemy airfield at less than a hundred feet with the other six Mustangs of Whisner's flight strung out behind them. The German pilot was doomed. Marion Nutter, Red Flight's leader that day recorded how Whisner shot the Luftwaffe flier into the ground. "I observed one long burst along both sides of the fuselage and canopy. The bandit then went into a stricken sideslip violently at very low altitude and disappeared into the smoke and dust of the field that had just been bombed."[4]

It took a gutsy and confident—or desperate—pilot to turn into a closely pursuing attacker in an attempt to switch from the defensive to the offensive. This was because a pursuer could generally close to within firing range during the turn. Subsequently, the pilot being chased subjected himself to at least one burst of gunfire as he wracked his aircraft hard around into his attackers. Walter Starck's description of his aerial victory over an Me-109 on May 27, 1944, near Strasbourg neatly illustrates this point.

On that date, the 352nd encountered a massive formation of German fighters near the bomber groups it was escorting. "Suddenly, the sky up ahead was filled with a huge glob of planes," Starck, from the 487th

Fighter Squadron, recalled.[5] "They were FW-190s and Me-109s—one hundred, plus." Starck and his wingman found themselves in the center of a Lufbery made up of a dozen German fighters. Starck, badly outnumbered, did his best. "I reefed in hard all the while and was actually making a smaller circle within the 109s," he recollected. "Whenever I started to get [my] sights on one ship, I noticed a flight of 109s ready to come in on my wingman or myself and so had to break off."

Starck saw one of the Me-109s dart out of the circling whirl of fighters and head straight east. He started after the fleeing German, while being careful to stay low in his rear quarter so as to remain undetected. "We flew for about five minutes, wide open throttle," Starck recounted. The German pilot finally caught sight of Starck's P-51 and made a sharp turn to the left. "I tried to cut him off," Starck said, "but he turned the opposite way and we were right back where we started. Then the E/A broke down and made a sharp turn to the left and then to the right. I swung my ship around and as he turned to the right I managed to get in to about 150 yards from him, measured about 90 degrees deflection, and opened fire."

Starck's aim was deadly. "Strikes showed up all over the cockpit in one brilliant mass and the E/A caught fire and did a half roll and spun slowly towards the earth where it crashed in a burst of flames. The pilot did not get out—ever." Starck dropped low and filmed the wreckage of his aerial victory before climbing for home.

One other option the Luftwaffe pilots exercised when conditions were right was to fly into clouds. Once safely inside the gray gloom, they were safe from attack; it was impossible to see more than a few yards in any direction. George Preddy lost an Me-109 to clouds on April 20, 1944, near Beauvais in northern France. After chasing a larger formation of eleven Me-109s, one of the German fighters split from the group and Preddy and his wingman, Ralph Hamilton, went hard after him. "He headed for a cloud," Preddy recalled, "so I opened fire at 30 degrees deflection and 500 yards. I fired until he went into the cloud and picked him up on the other side. I got another burst at him, scoring strikes on the fuselage. He flew into another cloud and I didn't see him again after he entered it."[6]

Three weeks later, on May 8, near Hanover, Germany, Ralph Hamilton had much the same luck. During a hard-turning fracas, Hamilton got separated from his flight leader and attached himself to John "Jack" Thornell; the two of them chased after a handful of Me-109s that were diving on a box of bombers. Both P-51 pilots fired on the same enemy aircraft and Hamilton was forced to pull off sharply to avoid colliding with Thornell. "As I did I picked out another one and took a long burst at the enemy E/A," he recalled. "I pulled up behind him and kept firing at him as we went through some clouds. When we broke out, I couldn't find him, so I went below the cloud cover and rejoined White leader."[7]

Nevertheless, taking sanctuary in the clouds was hardly a Luftwaffe-only tactic. John C. Meyer, the 487th's commanding officer, was one of the most aggressive fighter pilots in all the USAAF and he made no qualms about hiding in clouds. "When attacked by superior numbers I get the hell out of there using speed or clouds or, as a last resort, diving to the deck." He also wrote, "Clouds are very effective for evasive action if there is eight-tenths coverage or better. They are a good way to get home when you are alone.[8]

Frank Greene of the 486th Fighter Squadron was flying bomber escort over Berlin on May 18, 1944. Hiding in the clouds was the last thing on his mind; he didn't even know he was under attack when a cannon shell slammed into his P-51, *Snow White*, sending shrapnel into his cockpit. "Now I know how a guy feels a second before the end. My aileron controls and flap had been shot away from my left wing, sending me down in a tight spin. I never thought I'd regain control, but I did. I noticed however, that if I slowed her down below 140 MPH, she would slow-roll on me and go out of control again."

Greene was joined by Tom Colby. Colby had shot down the enemy aircraft—an Me-109—that had almost bagged Greene. He stuck with Greene as he nursed his damaged ship westward across the continent. "I repeated the Lord's Prayer about sixteen times and somehow I got to the coast of England, but now my troubles were only starting. How could I land at my small fighter field when I couldn't slow my P-51 to less than 140 MPH?

Greene considered bailing out but decided to land at a bomber base where there was a long runway. "I bounced ten times on the cement runway and died a miserable death at each bounce, but when I finally brought her to a stop, without brakes, I felt like thumbing my nose at the meat wagon that was waiting for me."[9]

The excitement of air combat sometimes compelled the pilots to do things that made little sense. David McEntire's actions over Koblentz, Germany, on May 12, 1944, are a case in point. As he finished a strafing run against an airfield, he looked over his shoulder and found an Me-109 directly behind him. McEntire turned hard into his pursuer and soon had him on the run. He fired a burst at the enemy aircraft from five hundred yards. "He caught fire and large pieces fell off the plane. Smoke was so heavy I pulled out to one side to avoid collision and overshot him." Undeterred, McEntire maneuvered himself back behind the enemy fighter but overshot again; the Me-109's engine had stopped. "I pulled off to one side, watched him crash then went down and strafed the wreckage twice using up all my ammunition."[10]

What McEntire's rationale was for expending all his ammunition on an aircraft that was obviously destroyed is unknown. In hindsight it seems especially imprudent when it is considered that he was deep in enemy territory. Too, while he devoted time, attention, fuel and ammunition to punching additional holes in the wreckage of the downed Me-109 he could have been easily attacked himself.

William Furr's actions a couple of weeks later on May 30, 1944 offer another interesting example. He dove into a whirling dogfight west of Madgeburg and was soon spiraling down after an FW-190. "I fired, and as I began firing he bailed out. I was still firing at the E/A when it hit the grd and exploded."[11] It made no sense for Furr to expend valuable ammunition on an aircraft that had no pilot, but he did it nonetheless.

And he did it again a few minutes later. "I then pulled up from my dive behind another FW-190. Another P-51 (U/I) [unidentified] turned in behind him at the same time. This E/A pilot jettisoned his canopy before either of us fired and a few seconds later the E/A began diving toward the grd, then the enemy pilot bailed out." For whatever reason, Furr chose that moment to start shooting at the enemy aircraft despite the fact that it had no one at the controls. "I began firing just after he got out and continued firing until the E/A hit the grd and exploded. However, I didn't hit the E/A with my fire until just before it crashed and blew up." If Furr had a rational reason for shooting at a pilotless aircraft, it has since been lost.

At a meeting with the Luftwaffe's armament board during the spring of 1944, Adolf Galland made it clear how desperate the situation was for his fighter pilots in the West; they were operating at a numerical disadvantage of up to eight-to-one. Further, he acknowledged the high standards not only of the American aircraft but also the training of the American pilots. He declared that something had to be done to change the Luftwaffe's situation. Aircraft losses aside, the extraordinary rate at which pilots were being killed was unsustainable; more than a thousand of his fliers had been lost during the previous four months.

Galland readily acknowledged that there was no way that Germany could ever match the United States in terms of aircraft production. Instead, he offered that the gap could be closed with machines that were technically superior. In particular he had the Me-262 in mind. "At the moment I would rather have one Me-262 than five Me-109's."[12] It was part of an argument he had been making since he first flew the Me-262 a year earlier.

His rationale was compelling and the armament board was convinced. A plan was put together that had a goal of producing more than a thousand Me-262s each month. If such a number could have been produced—and if the pilots to fly them could have been trained—it is likely that the air war over Germany would have developed much differently. However, it was not to be. Hitler quashed the plan.

In fact, when Hitler learned that the Me-262s that had been produced up to that point were not built as bombers he flew into an apoplectic fury that ranked amongst his very worst. He ordered the jets to be made into bombers and readied in time to repulse the coming Allied invasion that everyone knew was coming. Milch, the Luftwaffe's Air Inspector General, was fired soon after. Hitler inserted himself into the production of the Me-262 to such an extent that weekly engine allocations were made at his direction. A further example of his inexpert meddling was his insistence that the Me-262's armament be removed from the nose as part of its conversion to a bomber. Göring pointed out that the aircraft would be unbalanced. Hitler countered that fuel could take the place of the armament. He apparently failed to consider the fact that the aircraft would again be unbalanced when the fuel was burned.[13]

Galland understood better than anyone the potential of the Me-262 to blunt the massive American bomber raids; watching that potential frittered away while Germany was being blasted into rubble nearly drove him mad. He argued vehemently with Göring and anyone who opposed him that modifying the Me-262, a fighter, into a bomber would yield indifferent results.

He was ignored. Göring, ever the sycophant, refused to take the argument to Hitler. To be fair, it is unlikely that he could have swayed the Führer. Indeed, it was forbidden for anyone to refer to the aircraft as a fighter. Rather, Hitler directed Göring to issue an order that it be called the

Blitz Bomber.[14] Galland fumed. "One might as well have given orders to call a horse a cow."

When it was decided that bomber pilots rather than fighter pilots would be transitioned to fly the high performance aircraft Galland correctly pointed out that they didn't have the requisite background. The reply he received was that they were already accustomed to flying with two engines and that "they would quickly learn a bit of shooting." Additionally, they were better trained for instrument flying.

When Galland floated the idea of dividing the production of the jets equally between fighter and bomber units, he was rebuffed. Ultimately, running into obstacles at every turn, Galland sarcastically declared that it would be better for all if the entire idea was dropped and the intended cadre of Me-262 pilots was simply sent on leave until the end of the war.[15] However, sympathizers to his cause—Heinrich Himmler among them—made certain that Galland retained a handful of the new jets so that experimental sorties could be made with them as fighters. Flown by the right sorts of pilots, these aircraft scored small but demonstrable successes against the American bomber streams. These early experiments were invaluable when the decision was finally made in October 1944 to allow the formation of a combat unit to demonstrate the type's potential against the American bombers.

Ultimately, although Hitler's interference created friction that the urgently-needed Me-262 program could ill afford, there were issues with the engines that were at least as hurtful. Aside from obstinate technical problems, strategic metals such as cobalt and nickel were in desperately short supply. After much delay, a type of steel was substituted and the engine was made just barely suitable for operations. The delay caused by this issue calls into question the notion that the Me-262 would have been ready earlier if Hitler hadn't gotten involved.

At the same time that Galland was fighting for the Me-262, his FW-190 and Me-109 pilots were hard pressed to keep up not only with the increasing size of the American bomber raids, but also the greater numbers of skilled escort pilots. An VIII Fighter Command document from 1944 accentuated this point:

From the point of view of quality, the most aggressive fighter units in the Luftwaffe are employed in the West, which is regarded as the hottest of all fronts by most German pilots. It has come to light that one of the recently formed units in the West was asked to volunteer rather than being merely assigned to the new unit. Recent prisoners of war have confirmed that entirely new tactics have had to be developed in the past few months to fight American heavy bombers, and that a first class fighter pilot is required in order to have any success at all against them.[16]

The 352nd's public-relations office was responsible for communicating the exploits of the group's men to the rest of the world. Most of the men who worked in this office were not professional journalists but rather were youngsters straight out of high school who had shown an aptitude and affinity for writing. They worked from a set of guidelines to ensure that the right messages reached the folks back home without providing sensitive information that the enemy might be able to use. Some of their writing was amateurish, some of it was very good and some of it—very occasionally—was inconsistent with what the USAAF's leadership wanted to get into the public media. An example of this sort of release was the one that described the mission of May 21, 1944, when the group hit a number of ground targets near Berlin:

> They proceeded to destroy 22 twin-engined ships and damaged another 13, with Capt. Abbott getting one unidentified twin-engine ship. Then they exploded at least 6 locomotives, and killed approximately 20 soldiers and 25 cows that got in their way as they strafed boxcars, oil cars, factories, a town hall and a railroad station.[17]

The 352nd's commanding officer, Joe Mason, reviewed the proposed release and circled the "25 cows" and the "town hall." Then he scrawled a note on the bottom margin: "For Christ's sake, don't send this out."

Stanley Miles couldn't bring himself to shoot a German pilot descending in his parachute on May 13, 1944. 352ND FIGHTER GROUP ASSOCIATION

Ray Mitchell shot down an Me-109 on December 25, 1944, during the same general melee in which George Preddy was killed by friendly antiaircaft fire. 352ND FIGHTER GROUP ASSOCIATION

Clay Davis was an early pilot with the 352nd's 487th Fighter Squadron. He was credited with destroying one enemy aircraft while flying the P-47 and five while flying the P-51. USAAF

Earl Duncan shared credit for downing an Me-262 on April 10, 1945. USAAF

Ed Heller made the already diminutive Steve Andrew seem even smaller than he was. Frank Cutler is on the left. USAAF

Aircraft were used hard during the spring and summer of 1944. The period immediately following D-Day was especially frenetic. 352ND FIGHTER GROUP ASSOCIATION

The 352nd's briefing room was demarcated with seating areas for all three squadrons. USAAF

352nd commanding officer Joseph Mason (left) and his staff atop a plotting board in the operations section. USAAF

Henry Miklajcyk was an aggressive pilot with the 486th Fighter Squadron. He was credited with 7.5 aerial victories before he was shot down and killed on November 2, 1945. USAAF

George Preddy, history's highest scoring P-51 pilot. USAAF

Ray Littge was credited with 10.5 aerial victories. Here, he is seated in his P-51, *Miss Helen*. USAAF

Henry Miklajcyk with his crew chief, Robert Sprole. USAAF

George Preddy in a staged publicity photograph with other 487th Fighter
Squadron pilots. USAAF

In his letters home, Ted
Fahrenwald captured the
color and life of the
352nd like no one else.
MADELAINE FAHRENWALD

Most of Ted Fahrenwald's
letters home were written
to his sister Caroline.
MADELAINE FAHRENWALD

Virgil Meroney was the 352nd's
first ace and the only one of its
pilots to be credited with five
aerial victories while flying
the P-47. USAAF

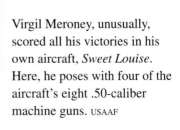

Virgil Meroney, unusually,
scored all his victories in his
own aircraft, *Sweet Louise*.
Here, he poses with four of the
aircraft's eight .50-caliber
machine guns. USAAF

In a staged photo, Henry Miklajcyk describes an aerial clash to fellow pilots from the 486th Fighter Squadron. Miklajcyk was shot down and killed on November 2, 1944. USAAF

After the Me-109, the FW-190 was the fighter most encountered by the 352nd's pilots. Here, an FW-190 makes ready for a mission from an ad hoc airfield in France during 1944. BUNDESARCHIV

The massive P-47 dwarfs Frank Cutler and Willie O. Jackson of the 486th Fighter Squadron. USAAF

Clay Davis claimed four victories (credited with 3.5) on May 8, 1944, while Carl Luksic knocked down five. USAAF

Cyril Doleac with his aircraft, *Ex Lax . . . Shht 'n' Git!* The small port on the wing next to his right elbow is for the gun camera. 352ND FIGHTER GROUP ASSOCIATION

Jim Bleidner was John C. Meyer's armorer through Meyer's entire World War II career. Here, he poses with Meyer's first P-51, *Lambie II*. 352ND FIGHTER GROUP ASSOCIATION

One of the group's P-51s is getting its guns harmonized. 352ND FIGHTER GROUP
ASSOCIATION

Don McKibben's P-51B, *Miss Lace*, with a host of enlisted maintenance men.
The aircraft perished with Frank Cutler when Cutler had a midair collision
with an Me-109. 352ND FIGHTER GROUP ASSOCIATION

These men of the 352nd were credited with 27 aerial victories on May 8, 1944. The Germans would surrender a year later to the day. USAAF

Bill Whisner's *Moonbeam McSwine* late in the war. 352ND FIGHTER GROUP ASSOCIATION

The 486th Fighter Squadron's aircraft prior to the shuttle mission to the Ukraine. All the aircraft but Willie O. Jackson's new P-51D in the foreground are P-51Bs or Cs. 352ND FIGHTER GROUP ASSOCIATION

Handsome Robert "Punchy" Powell strikes a Hollywood pose on the wing of his *West "by Gawd" Virginian*. 352ND FIGHTER GROUP ASSOCIATION

So much activity around a single aircraft was unusual, suggesting that *The Flying Scot* may have been experiencing mechanical trouble. 352ND FIGHTER GROUP ASSOCIATION

Sergeant Nilan Jones was perhaps the best artist in the 352nd. Here, he poses with his stunning rendition of Luther Richmond's wife Jean (also known as "Sweetie) on Richmond's P-47D. 352ND FIGHTER GROUP ASSOCIATION

Early 486th Fighter Squadron P-51s before the application of the 352nd Fighter Group's iconic blue nose paint. This photo likely dates from late March 1944. Luther Richmond's aircraft is in the foreground. He eschewed camouflage as he wanted to be spotted and engaged by enemy fliers.
352ND FIGHTER GROUP ASSOCIATION

The 352nd's pilots created weaving contrails such as these as they protected the heavy bombers. USAAF

The Me-109G was the Luftwaffe fighter the 352nd's pilots encountered most often.
BUNDESARCHIV

Adolf Hitler and
Hermann Göring.

Credited with 17.25 aerial victories,
Jack Thornell was not part of the
352nd's original cadre of pilots, but
was one of its more successful aces.

Armorers reloading a P-51's .50-caliber machine guns. USAAF

A 352nd P-51 over France during late summer 1944. USAAF

After surviving three days in the North Sea—and almost losing his legs—Fremont Miller was sent home to the States. He was credited with two aerial victories. USAAF

There was little that was more rewarding for a ground crewman. USAAF

Francis Horne's *Snoot's Sniper*. Horne flung himself into a huge formation of German fighters on May 13, 1944, causing two FW-190s to collide.
352ND FIGHTER GROUP ASSOCIATION

One of the six German aircraft George Preddy shot down on August 6, 1944. USAAF

Shot up by Glennon Moran on May 27, 1944, this Me-109 crashed into the village shortly after this shot was captured on film. USAAF

The nearly completed control tower at Bodney on the morning of D-Day, June 6, 1944, only hours after Robert Frascotti smashed into it during takeoff.

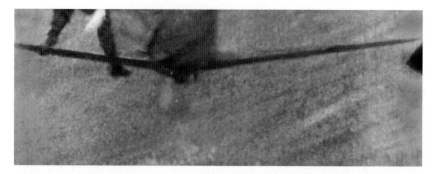

Steve Andrew shot down an FW-190 on April 30, 1944. The pilot, whose legs are visible in this frame, bailed out directly into Andrew's propeller. USAAF

352nd P-47s poised for takeoff out of Bodney. 352ND FIGHTER GROUP ASSOCIATION

Edwin Heller, described as "the Mighty Irishman" by his friend Ted Fahrenwald. USAAF

CHAPTER 18

D-Day

The group's intelligence section recorded the frantic activity immediately prior to D-Day:

> Passing of time wore the glamour of operations a bit thin. Procedures were becoming automatic when the 5th of June, 1944, rolled around. That afternoon Colonel Mason climbed into his P-51 and took off for AJAX [VIII Fighter Command Headquarters]. Upon his return early in the evening he held a hurried meeting with his staff officers. A Tannoy announcement was sent out immediately for all Intelligence personnel, Group and Squadron, to report to Headquarters. No one slept that night nor did they receive much sleep in the two weeks that followed. At 3 AM on June 6—D-Day—the day that signified the beginning of the end of the war in Europe, twenty-nine blue-nosed planes took off in darkness to add their power to the invasion.[1]

Paul Klinger was a cryptographer who worked in the 352nd's headquarters building. He remembered the night before D-Day. "We had codebooks which we used quite frequently and in every month there was always a thirty-second page—we used one page per day of the month. We never used the thirty-second page until one evening when I was on duty." A call came in directing that the page never before used be put into action. "I jumped," recalled Klinger, "and immediately set about decoding the message, which was scrambled. It was the call for D-Day. The message contained instructions for painting the planes and other important information."[2]

If and when it came, everyone, friendly and enemy, knew that chaos and confusion would be part and parcel of the invasion. Among the myriad problems, Allied air commanders were keenly concerned that their aircraft not be mistaken as enemy machines. It was not uncommon for men manning defensive guns to fire on friendly aircraft. In fact, during the invasion of Sicily, more than two dozen C-47s were downed by naval gunfire in a horrific tragedy that killed scores of aircrews and paratroopers. These episodes of what was ironically known as "friendly fire" were never completely eliminated.

Nevertheless, they could be reduced and a number of measures were promulgated to help distinguish friendly aircraft from enemy. One of those measures was the application of invasion stripes to the fighters, medium bombers, and transport aircraft that were planned to be active in the invasion area. Larger, more readily identifiable four-engine bombers were not required to bear the unique markings. The directive required that alternating, eighteen-inch bands of black and white be applied to the fuselage and wings in the order of white-black-white-black-white.

So as to keep from tipping the Germans, the orders to paint the stripes came very late. In many instances crews worked into the early morning hours of June 6; indeed, the paint had not completely dried on some aircraft by the time they took off. The experience of the 352nd was typical. A special crew hurried to each aircraft and marked it with chalk lines. Once that task was complete another crew fell on the aircraft and quickly painted the stripes with brushes, mops, rags and whatever else was handy; there wasn't enough proper painting equipment and the resultant, often sloppy-looking markings, attested to their hasty application.

They closed the bar on the night before the invasion.

Howls went up from the men until the realization sank in. Nothing specific was said but they were told to go to bed early. It was obvious that something big was up. Indeed, the nature of their operations had changed during the previous few days as the Eighth Air Force had sent massive attacks against the Pas-de-Calais region and Normandy. These were on top of the thousands upon thousands of sorties that the England-based Ninth Air Force had mounted during the previous months.

At any rate, the men went to bed. They needn't have bothered. They were almost immediately wakened at 2200 hours (10 P.M.) for what was described as a "maximum effort." Groggy and disoriented they stumbled into their clothes and waited for a ride to the mission briefing. The night was dark and miserable. Rain spat down from low, wet clouds. Fog banked across the field and disappeared only to reappear again. It was weather that made men pray. Mostly they prayed that they wouldn't be made to fly. Ted Fahrenwald recalled their wretched anxiousness: "Not much chatter, but we were all thinking hard and fast, and the same maggoty thoughts nibbled persistently through each of our heads: black night . . . rain . . . low ceiling . . . zero visibility . . . no flare-pots . . . a blind takeoff with 3,000 pounds of high-octane aboard that tiny little Mustang."[3]

Hearts leapt into throats when the briefing map was uncovered. It was the most complex they had seen, crisscrossed with red ribbons and marked with colored lines and boxes and numbers. This was to be D-Day. "Although no one knew exactly when it would be," recalled Punchy Powell, "there was a feeling during the time leading up to it that the invasion might happen any time. Anticipating that, I had extended my tour so that I wouldn't miss it." The day had come; he sat in the hushed briefing room with every other pilot in the group, oblivious to the drizzle ticking on the roof above his head.

The pilots of VIII Fighter Command were tasked with forming a great impenetrable arc to protect the invasion beachhead against the Luftwaffe. Eisenhower and his commanders were taking no chances; the greatest part of the USAAF's strategic air war to that point had been fought to ensure the success of the operation planned for that very day. Virtually every mission, every bomb, every lost life had been spent for the promise of that day. If the Allies failed to establish a lodgment at Normandy the Germans might not be defeated for years. The Luftwaffe could not be allowed to reach the invasion force.

At the conclusion of the main part of the briefing, "Stormy" Gysbers, the group's meteorologist, mounted the stage. Practically speaking, what he had to say didn't matter. The weather was bad, but they had to fly regardless. What did his prognostications and weather-speak and floppy charts matter? Chaplain George Cameron closed the brief with a prayer. If ever the Allies needed God's blessing, it was on that day.

But there was the miserable black night. It wasn't Eisenhower and his staff or Stormy or Chaplain Cameron that had to fly in it. It was McKibben and Fahrenwald and Powell and thousands of young men like them all across England. And none of them relished the thought of launching into the dripping black maw that hung low over the countryside. They were trained. They were well-trained. But very few of them had much real experience flying through the sort of night-mess that spat down on them as they slunk out of the brief and to their respective pilot huts.

The 486th Fighter Squadron was scheduled to take off first and the time came for its pilots to man their aircraft. Notwithstanding the newly-applied black and white stripes that ringed their wings and fuselages, the blue-nosed Mustangs looked ghostly-beautiful, dripping wet and silvery in what little light found its way to the hardstands. Ted Fahrenwald likened them to shiny little tropical fish.

The pilots climbed into their cockpits and the crew chiefs strapped them in. They waited in the damp, peering across the black of the field. Some of them wondered if they had time to unstrap and squeeze a few more drops of urine from their bladders; some of them wondered if the weather might improve; some of them wondered how they would all grope their way into takeoff position without someone getting chopped to bits; some of them wondered at the hum of the aircraft already airborne from different bases and some of them wondered if they would live to see the next day.

In a break with normal operations, a red flare spluttered from the control tower high into the dark and wet. At once, the 486th's P-51s huffed and barked and spun themselves to life in a gratifying staccato growl that soon steadied to a comforting thrum. A few minutes later the squadron's aircraft began their awkward, waddling taxi to the takeoff funnel. All pretense of order came apart in the dark and some flights failed to assemble while tagalongs joined others; few of them made it to their proper place in line. Fahrenwald found himself at the head of the entire mess as part of a three-ship. According to the brief, they were supposed to take off in four-ship formations:

> By the darting flames of their engine exhausts I could make out the dim identifying letters painted on the fuselage of each ship. So Pappy Gignac and McKibben and I were together, and we three were hogging the slot reserved for the Colonel's flight. That, however, was tough titty, because it was too late now to monkey around trying to get organized. We ran up our engines and it was time to go, and I didn't want to push that throttle at all. My instruments glowered greenly at me like the winking, blinking, luminous eyes of a whole pack of pussycats racked up in a blacked-out bookcase.

But they did go. With their throttles pushed up, the pilots of the first three Mustangs felt their aircraft bump along the muddy grass on a north-easterly heading as they picked up speed. Gignac's mount hit something slippery that spit him off to the side. Fahrenwald, on McKibben's wing, jockeyed his throttle to stay in position until the two of them finally lifted off. They both drew a collective breath as they raised their landing gear and put precious altitude between themselves and the ground.

Behind them Martin Corcoran swung his four-ship into takeoff position.[4] A string of lights intended as a takeoff aid had been torn away, presumably by Gignac, Fahrenwald or McKibben. Without the lights, and failing to check his compass, Corcoran aligned the flight too far to the right. Not noting the mistake, he advanced his throttle and started his takeoff roll. To his right, Donald "Red" Whinnem rolled with him as did Robert Frascotti who was next in line to the right. Carleton "Bud" Fuhrman was on Frascotti's right wing. Unknown to any of them, Charles Griffiths had mistakenly tacked onto Fuhrman's right wing and was also taking off. Corcoran's four-ship was actually a five-ship.

Meanwhile, Fahrenwald tucked himself tightly to McKibben's wing, anxious not to get separated in the murk. "We banked into an easy turn to port," Fahrenwald recalled, "and I glanced back to the field and all of a damned sudden a horrible, billowing explosion half-blinded me, and I knew automatically what it was: a Mustang, a maximum load of high-octane and one of the boys, all gone to glory in a puff of flame." Below Fahrenwald and McKibben, every man on the ground gaped horror-stricken into the brilliant pyre.

Robert Frascotti was dead. On the errant heading, Corcoran's flight hurtled at high speed to the edge of the airfield where a new control tower was under construction. Corcoran and Whinnem passed to the left of it as they lifted airborne. Fuhrman passed it to the right. Further right, one of Griffith's wheels struck a pole on a nearby volleyball court but he was unhurt. Frascotti, in the center of the flight, smashed into the tower with a blinding yellow-white blast.

None of them really knew what had happened. Corcoran and Whinnem were ahead of Frascotti when he hit the tower and Whinnem guessed that perhaps the field had been attacked. Fuhrman thought that someone had dropped their external fuel tanks and they had exploded. Likewise, Griffith's had no idea what had created the brilliant flash.

Regardless of what happened, the group still had to execute its mission. The assigned sector was patrolled and little took place that was noteworthy. To a man, all the pilots marveled at the incredible numbers of ships at the beachhead and on the English Channel. Likewise, as the sun rose it revealed massive formations of aircraft. All of it was in action that day to ensure that the invasion force did not fail.

George Arnold led a flight over the beaches of Normandy that very early morning as night gave way to day. "One of the things I saw—and I reported it—was what looked like a huge balloon. It was about twenty thousand feet above our area. I didn't know if it was a German secret weapon, or what it was, but I didn't want to get too close and besides we didn't have the time or the gas. So I just reported it and didn't hear anything more about it. But I'm positive it was there—a big, big balloon over the beachhead.[5]

After his flight landed back at Bodney, Donald Whinnem was especially hurt upon learning that Frascotti had been killed. Frascotti was well-loved in the squadron, a jokester and a fantastic athlete. He and Whinnem had been best friends since starting flight training early in their military careers.

Whinnem remembered: "When I returned to Bodney and they told me what had happened to Bob, I went over to the Parachute Room in one of our Nissens and had a cry for myself. Willie O. [Major Willie O. Jackson, the 486th's commanding officer] came and found me and told me that he understood what I was going through. He said that I was posted for the next mission that day, but that he would scratch me so I would not have to fly. I told him no, that I wanted to get back and fly and keep going or I probably wouldn't again. I think I flew three missions that day, and there were lots of missions for that whole week. Everyone was really good to me."

On subsequent missions that day, the 352nd was charged with getting behind the beachhead and bombing or strafing anything they could find that was German. The group hit vehicle traffic, marshalling yards, rolling stock, armor and troops. The USAAF's commanders were particularly satisfied at the Luftwaffe's seeming impotence; only two aircraft managed to get through to the beachhead and they did no damage. A flight of FW-190s appeared over Rouen and the 328th's Red Flight shot down two of them, but the feared Luftwaffe counterattack never materialized.

The ground crews at Bodney worked as they never had before. Aircraft were refueled, rearmed and sent airborne again as quickly as possible. The men were in good spirits. It was a historic occasion and they were part of it. Moreover, the invasion—if it was successful—signaled the beginning of the end. And they would get to go home when it ended.

Nevertheless, a number of them were felled in their tracks just after midday. The complaint was nausea and abdominal pain. In fact, so many men were stricken that it caused some of the afternoon missions to take off with fewer aircraft than planned. The culprit was later learned to be a bad batch of rice pudding that had been served at lunch.

Ultimately, the tempo picked up again in the late afternoon and into the evening. The last sortie landed just before midnight; some of the pilots had flown three sorties and spent more than fifteen hours in the cockpit. But it had been a hugely successful day. The group flew 116 sorties in support of the greatest invasion in history. Losses were much lighter than anticipated. Robert O'Nan and Robert Butler of the 487th Fighter Squadron were both shot down by flak. Butler managed to parachute near the beachhead and returned to Bodney shortly thereafter. O'Nan was captured and spent the rest of the war as a POW.

The rhythm of operations continued on June 7 at a breakneck pace that wore at the pilots and the aircraft. In fact, four of the sixteen aircraft that took off with the 487th Fighter Squadron on a midday mission aborted. Things got worse from that point.

The 487th's report was cryptic: "Lt. Mulkey crashed 1 mile N. Bury S. Edmond at 1055; Lt. Garney last seen 50 mi. ne London 1525 at 3000' coming down thru overcast. Lt. Hall last seen at 1400 at 500', at Q6539."[6] What likely occurred is that Mulkey became disoriented in the clouds after takeoff and spun out. Or he suffered an engine failure. Likewise, Garney probably fell victim to vertigo as he descended back through the clouds during the return. Hall was hit by flak and killed. The loss of the three men marked a black day for the 487th. But in context, it was a drop in the bucket compared to the carnage that was taking place on the ground in Normandy.

The group actually lost a fourth man that day, one of their cherished and seasoned veterans. Edward "Pappy" Gignac, who had been promoted to major and made the 352nd's operations officer, led a group of 486th pilots on a predawn sortie. As Ted Fahrenwald described, the mission was fairly unremarkable:

> That old renegade, sharing our hatred of instrument flying, led us well: winding us up through many narrow, dark corridors in the fog and up through a dozen evil little cloud decks, and we headed for France on-top, on-course and on-time, and at our estimated time of arrival peeled off through a hole and went hunting. Unable to spot any live game, we vented our rage on a small-town railroad yard and on a highway bridge—in the center of which Pappy laid a 500-pounder with neatness and precision. We clobbered a couple of lone trucks and went home for breakfast.

"Not being slated for the next flight," Fahrenwald recorded, "I slept in a chair in the pilots' hut, and as I snoozed Pappy led his last squadron to France—or to anywhere, for that matter." The P-51s of Gignac's flight growled mightily as they lifted clear of the airfield, formed and then winged eastward toward Normandy. The sweet din didn't disturb the dozing Fahrenwald in the slightest.

The surrounding sky to the southeast of the beachhead was clear of enemy aircraft and Gignac led the 486th's flyers to a railroad siding at Trappe where they dropped pairs of 500-pound bombs. Once the flight was free of the heavy ordnance, Gignac took it hunting. A short time later near the town of Voisin-le-Bretonneux the pilots came upon a large group of German tank transporters and other heavy trucks. Gignac didn't hesitate as he called for the flight to set up a racetrack pattern and immediately started down in an aggressive strafing attack.

Such a tactic was a double-edged sword. Its benefit was that it was orderly and lessened the chances of a tragic midair collision when pilots simultaneously chased after the same target. On the other hand, it was somewhat predictable which made the aircraft easier to track for the gunners on the ground.

Nevertheless, the blue-nosed fighters wheeled and dived on the convoy, shredding the vehicles with their .50-caliber gunfire. The volume of the antiaircraft fire increased as the enemy gunners recovered from the surprise attack and got their weapons into action. Following the second round of passes a call came over the radio asking Gignac if he planned to continue the attack. He called back: "I can't, I'm on fire."

Gignac's right wing was ablaze. Too low to bail out, he hauled back on the control stick and exchanged his airspeed for altitude preparatory to jumping clear. The silvery P-51 slowed as it topped out at 2,000 feet, staggered and tipped nose down. An instant later it exploded.

The young man, the blooded veteran, the winner of the Silver Star who was remembered by his hometown as a hellion "in the nicest possible way," was gone.

Ted Fahrenwald didn't want to fly on June 8, 1944. It was another dark, wet, early morning. The brief was at 0200 and takeoff was scheduled for 0300. The German reinforcements pouring into Normandy had started moving by night and hiding by day to preserve themselves against the seemingly innumerable formations of roving Allied fighters. Consequently, intent on catching the enemy troops in the open right at sunrise, higher headquarters directed predawn launches.

Fahrenwald had a bad feeling about the mission. It was to be his hundredth; it was a number to which a great deal of superstition had been attached—at least in his own mind. "As a matter of record," he recorded, "one of our finest pilots, Bobby MacKean, had simultaneously acquired a Silver Star and a tombstone while strafing an airdrome in southern France—on his 100th mission."

"So I shuffled past the flight surgeon and sniffed and dragged a leg, but he wouldn't take notice at all," Fahrenwald remembered. He tried a more direct tack: "Tonight I don't want to fly any more, and if you make me go you'll be sorry." The flight surgeon was unmoved.

Fahrenwald gave up on getting out of the mission and scuffed his way through the damp to his aircraft where he found his crew chief, Sergeant Robert German, asleep in the closed cockpit. Fahrenwald woke him and the two traded places—German helped him strap into the snug little cockpit. "Came the time and I wound 'er up," he recalled, "but that Merlin engine wouldn't kick over: the prop ground around and around and I thought, while mentally rubbing my hands together: Ahhhh . . . Kismet! Maybe the bastard will never start, I hope!"

German would have none of that nonsense. He quickly connected a battery cart to Fahrenwald's aircraft, *Joker*, and the engine burst to life. A few short minutes later, Fahrenwald joined the rest of the 486th's Mustangs as the blue-nosed ships rolled across the dark grass field and lifted into the night.

The squadron climbed into the clear and spread into a line-abreast formation as the first hint of dawn pinked the eastern sky. Racing across the channel, they skimmed just above a shimmering cloud deck until, just west of Paris, they spiraled through a hole and went hunting. Below them, elements of the Wehrmacht looked for hiding places in which to spend the coming day.

The weather grew increasingly better as the dawn turned to day and it wasn't long before a column of nearly forty heavy vehicles was spotted bending around a corner of a gravel road toward a patch of woods. Immediately one of the 486th's pilots dropped a pair of bombs that exploded at the head of the line. Trapped, the German soldiers could do little but get out of the way while the rest of the 486th's Mustangs wheeled overhead and made their attacks.

Fahrenwald added his own bombs to the maelstrom and took stock of the scene: "A dandy disaster below! Trucks afire, long parallel banners of black smoke drifting across the fields, and the road all shot to hell with

bomb craters. Now some of the boys were down on the deck beating
things up with machine guns, and the traffic pattern was out of this world,
with Mustangs streaking in fast from every point of the compass, tracers
crisscrossing, ships chandelling up all over the sky and at all angles."

Fire discipline seemed to be wanting amongst his adrenaline-stoked
comrades and Fahrenwald wasn't particularly anxious to throw himself
into the teeming tumult. Instead, he arced around the periphery of the
slaughter and spied half a dozen large trucks half-hidden in hedges. He
and his wingman sprayed the trucks and road lengthwise with machine
gun fire and set up for another run. "With an evasive, skidding wingover
we went in broadside to the column, flying nearly abreast, each flaming
our targets. My guns seemed to be perfectly harmonized, coming to a
sharp focus some three hundred yards ahead of my ship; and any target
caught in the focal point was automatically a dead duck."

After shooting up another truck, Fahrenwald made ready to leave—he
was about out of ammunition and "wanted a bit to travel on." It was time
to go. "But untouched below," he recalled, "sat the great grand-daddy of
all Jerry trucks, so I thought I'd better shoot it up, just a little."

He did. It was carrying ammunition and it blew up precisely as he flew
over it. The shock wave rolled his aircraft inverted and rocketed him skyward. Fahrenwald regained control of his wits only after he regained control of his aircraft. He rolled upright and continued his climb and leveled
off at four thousand feet. "I had control of the ship and the engine instruments were normal," he recalled. "My wings were bent and beat up a bit:
the skin was wrinkled and a lot of odds and ends from the disintegrating
truck had holed through."

Fahrenwald wasn't sure exactly where he was: "Having been preoccupied in cleaning my fingernails during briefing, I didn't know just where in
the hell I might be, but figured that a course of due north would be as good
as any." He was steady on course for only a short time when the engine
began to go sour. He made some minor control adjustments and it seemed
to recover for a short time before getting decidedly worse.

"Then the whole damned engine froze up and the tired old prop,
with ironic finality, stuck up in front of me like a V-for-Victory symbol."
Black and white smoke and orange flames reached back from the engine
toward the cockpit. Fahrenwald had to get out of the aircraft before it
exploded. After calling out a quick farewell to his squadron mates over
the radio, he unsnapped and disconnected everything that attached him
to his beloved Mustang. Then he grabbed his cigarettes, pulled the nose
of the aircraft sharply up, jettisoned the canopy and jumped clear of his
stricken ship.

Only a second or two later, the aircraft fell off to one side and neatly ladled him out of the sky and right back into the cockpit, trapping his leg under the instrument panel. At the same time it continued tumbling out of the sky. Almost automatically Fahrenwald extracted his leg, pushed away from his Mustang once more, and pulled the ripcord on his parachute.

The opening shock nearly knocked him unconscious and tore away his rubber dinghy and survival gear. "Upon regaining vision, curious and simultaneous impressions were noted: I saw the unfortunate *Joker* strike the ground in a little clearing, to explode with a terrific orange flash; then there came the fascinating and amusing sight of a profusion of little gadgets all about me in the air—bits of rope and colored cloth, tin cans and tiny packages, as though a bomb had burst in a junk-peddler's cart below me."

Fahrenwald was giddy that he was still alive. He reached into his jacket, pulled out a flask and took a couple sips of bourbon. On sliding it back into his pocket he considered his situation. "I looked down between my dangling feet and it seemed awfully high to be minus an airplane: some five hundred feet of nothing between toe and treetops."

On getting closer to the ground he noted that he was being blown—and fast. He was unsettled by his next realization: "Then, in the direction of my drift, I saw a camouflaged German airdrome upon which I calculated I'd land, whether or not I wanted to."

George Preddy was temporarily leading the 487th Fighter Squadron during the D-Day period while John C. Meyer was away in the States. It was a time of furiously demanding operations, and the 487th—not including the other two squadrons—lost five pilots during the first three days. Still, Preddy bore up well. He wrote a letter home to his parents that tried to blend an optimistic confidence with the import of what was going on over Normandy:

> We all hope this big invasion will be a success and everybody in the air is doing all that is possible to aid the men on the ground. We have the highest respect for those boys, and it is our duty to them to clear the way and protect them from the Luftwaffe.
>
> We feel proud of our leaders and confident of their ability. Although nobody doubts that the Luftwaffe and the German Army are strong and the fight will be tough. I don't think there is any doubt that we can beat them.

The invasion is a big moment for the English people and one they have been waiting for, for years. They are taking it in their customary calm, quiet manner.

All of the pilots and ground crews in the Group are doing a superb job and we are succeeding in doing considerable damage to the enemy.

I hope all are well at home. I'm getting along fine and feeling very good.

Lots of love,

George[7]

Harold Stanfield was an armorer with the 486th Fighter Squadron. He recalled an especially hectic episode that illustrated the hectic work pace typical of the days following the invasion. "Often when our planes returned from a mission, other pilots were being briefed for the next one and ground crews had to hurry to get the planes serviced and rearmed. At times, the pilots were on their way to the planes while the ground crews scrambled to get them ready."[8]

On this particular afternoon Stanfield and his comrades wrongly thought that their workday was over after several missions had been flown. "Word came to 'D' Flight that a maximum effort bombing mission was scheduled for immediate takeoff," Stanfield remembered. But there were only three armorers available to load two, five-hundred pound bombs on each of the flight's six aircraft.

And the pilots were already on their way to the aircraft. Stanfield and the other two armorers—Dick Linn and Robert Long—enlisted the help of every man on the flight line to hang the bombs from the wings, install the fuzes and attach the arming wires.

"We fuzed the last bombs with pilots in the cockpit and engines running," he recalled. "As the planes taxied toward the takeoff area, we ran with them removing pins from fuzes and installing arming wires." As they ran and worked, the men stuffed the pins into their pockets. They finished the job just as the pilots swung their ships around for takeoff.

It was a standard requirement for the armorers to count the number of fuze pins after the aircraft were armed; it was essential that the number of pins matched the number of bombs. The pins were a safety feature and if they were not removed the bomb could not explode. To send an aircraft into harm's way to deliver a bomb that was little more than dead weight was a terrible waste. In this instance it was a moot point as the aircraft were already winging their way toward Normandy.

Nevertheless, Stanfield remembered that the armorers followed procedures. "When we reported to the armament shack," he said, "Emory Noland was there to count the pins. It took us several minutes to round them all up since our fatigue uniforms and jackets had about eight pockets. As Emory's count reached twelve, we were all relieved."

Stanfield's account makes the point that the pilot was only one person at the tip of a very long spear. That spear included men whose tasks were varied but critical; their specialties ran the gamut from dentist's assistant to radio technician to aircraft mechanic and everything in between. It took a lot of good men doing a lot of good things to win an air war.

In fact, there were just under two thousand men stationed at Bodney at any one time. The enlisted men and non-flying officers of the 352nd totaled about 800 against about 100 pilots. Aside from the 352nd, there were a host of specialty units on Bodney to support them that counted about 1,000 men on their rosters. So then, only about one in twenty men on the base was a flyer.

William Reese flew his first dive bombing mission during this time on June 10. "If you can imagine, no one in the squadron had ever dive bombed and our first mission was to go out and bomb a bridge in France next to a little town."[9] Like air-to-air gunnery, dive-bombing was an exacting science. In order to hit a particular point on the ground, the aircraft had to be at a precise airspeed, altitude, and dive angle—and in trimmed and balanced flight—when the bomb was released. Most of the 352nd's men had never trained for it.

Reese watched as the first flight dove toward the bridge and released its bombs. Rather than hitting the bridge, they hit the town. The second and third flights had no better luck. Reese's flight, the fourth, was the last one to attack the bridge "By the time that our flight went in," he recalled, "we decided we had to change something. We went in at a higher angle and finally put that bridge out, but it was a fiasco of the first order."

Reese described another bombing mission that highlighted how little the pilots understood the bombing they were doing: "When it came my turn to drop the bombs, only one bomb came off and the other stayed on the plane. I couldn't get rid of it so we joined up in formation and headed back home. I think most of us were under the impression that when you armed the bombs something was pulled out of the bomb so it was hot from then on, but I thought, what the hell, and put the switch back in the de-arm position."

Reese's flight leader descended into the traffic pattern at Bodney and made a combat approach which included a violent, near-vertical turn over the field while putting down the landing gear and flaps just before dropping onto the grass. Reese followed him through the maneuver. "As I came in on final, I saw the planes in front of me all of a sudden take off in all directions. They didn't quite touch down, and then they just gave it full throttle and took off again. I was wondering what all that was about and started to make my flare to land. I noticed that I went over an object in the field, but I went ahead and landed." As it developed, the "object" he noticed was the bomb he had hauled back from France. It had come loose during his approach and—because he had de-armed it—had not exploded.

There were of course many ways to die in the sky over Europe and Nelson Jesup of the 487th Fighter Squadron described one of those in a letter home describing his mission of June 11, 1944. This was during the hectic period following the Normandy invasion when all stops were pulled to not only support the troops on the ground with bombing and strafing missions, but also to continue with bomber escort missions. Jesup was making his way back toward Bodney at low level over France with two other comrades:

> There we were barreling along as we approached a small bridge and, just as we got over it, bombs dropped by B-17s above the overcast started hitting the bridge . . . we went all through the flame and smoke and debris and our planes were tossed around by the terrific explosions under us. I thought I'd 'had it' as we say, but I got out of it with a beat-up airplane. Thought I would have to bail out for awhile but I managed to get it back. There was one hole in the leading edge of my right wing that you could put your head in.[10]

CHAPTER 19

To the Other Side

Operation FRANTIC was born out of the Tehran Conference of November 1943. Although the focus was on much larger issues, it was there that Arnold persuaded Stalin to go along with a shuttle mission concept that had American bombers flying out of their bases in England and Italy, attacking targets deep in Europe and then continuing to Soviet bases in the Ukraine. From there, they would fly more missions before returning to their bases. It was an idea that had been brewing in USAAF circles for several months.

Arnold had great hopes for the idea. Firstly, the bombers could penetrate deeper into Europe than they could if forced to turn around and return to their home bases. Second, the raids would confuse German defenders; after attacking the bombers on their inbound legs, the Luftwaffe fighter pilots often landed and rearmed in order to attack them on their homebound routes. The shuttle concept foiled that practice. Beyond that, with the potential to launch attacks in three directions—east from England, north from Italy, and west from the Soviet Union—the Luftwaffe would be forced to thin its defenses in order to cover all the approaches into Germany.

But perhaps more important were the political implications. Although he wasn't naïve about Stalin or the Soviet Union, Arnold—and President Roosevelt—hoped that a closely coordinated and executed air campaign might increase goodwill and understanding between the two uneasy allies. Further, Arnold hoped that it might make possible the establishment of American bases in Siberia from which to attack Japan. Moreover, the raids would be a visible and tangible demonstration to the Soviets of the American commitment to the fight against Nazi Germany. For his part, Stalin hoped to get American equipment. In particular, he wanted some of the massive new B-29s that the United States was beginning to field against Japan.

Tens of thousand of tons of American material and equipment flowed into the Ukraine beginning in early 1944. Working together, the Americans and Soviets prepared three separate bases; Migorod and Poltava for the bombers, and Piryatin for the fighters. The Soviets insisted, despite American protests, on providing the air defenses for the three bases. The Americans weren't convinced the Soviets could do a credible job. Ultimately, the Soviets won the argument. This was typical of the relationship between the two allies during FRANTIC; the Soviets held all the cards and the Americans usually gave in to their demands rather than jeopardize the entire scheme.

None of this was overly important to the men of the 486th Fighter Squadron when their commanding officer, Willie O. Jackson, and George Hampson went to VIII Fighter Command headquarters just a few days after the Normandy invasion. "On their return," Don McKibben recalled, "although nothing of the plans under foot [sic] were divulged, we all knew something big was at hand. All preparations for a long, protracted mission were made and eighteen pilots and eleven enlisted men were selected."

It was to be the second series of shuttle missions. The first had been flown by the Fifteenth Air Force out of Italy on June 2, 1944, with Ira Eaker aboard the lead ship. The target was a marshaling yard at Debrecen in Hungary. On arriving, Eaker and the crews were welcomed by Soviet officials and the press, and then Eaker was whisked away to Moscow for high-level talks. A second mission was flown from the Ukrainian bases on June 6, against the Galati airfield in Romania. Three days later the Fifteenth's units left for their bases in Italy, hitting the Foscani airfield in Romania along the way. Except for its novelty—and the fact that things went more or less according to plan—this first effort was unremarkable especially as the targets that were hit could have been struck from Italy.

The 486th was scheduled to escort a shuttle mission on June 16, 1944, alongside the 4th Fighter Group out of Debden. The 486th's pilots flew their aircraft to Debden on June 15 but the mission was cancelled and they returned to Bodney two days later. "After several days of false alarms and dry runs," recorded Don McKibben, "our squadron was ordered to Debden the evening of 20 June. We drove through the chilly grey morning of the 21st to be briefed for 'the Russian Deal' and after looking at the foul overcast that hung 200 feet over the field, hardly a man would have been eager to fly if this hadn't been the big show we had sweated out for so long."[1] Notwithstanding the poor weather over England, the 486th took off with the 4th Fighter Group under the leadership of the 4th's legendary leader, Colonel Donald Blakeslee.

"Colonel Blakeslee's navigation was faultless and at exactly the briefed minute," remembered McKibben, "the red-nosed ships of the 4th Group and our own blue-nosed planes swung over the bombers and began weaving out to the side and over the glistening B-17s." After hitting the Schwarzheide synthetic oil factory near Ruhland and another target at Elsterwerda, the bombers reformed into two tight boxes. McKibben waxed almost poetic: "There's something dignified and majestic about a large formation of our bombers plodding through the sky and, knowing we were flying over territory never before visited by American aircraft, a certain pride was felt by all our boys." McKibben also noted that some among the 486th's contingent of enlisted men were manning waist guns aboard the big bombers. "We didn't intend to let the enemy get a crack at our crew chiefs."

Warsaw was more than fifty miles to the formation's rear when the Luftwaffe finally showed in the form of fifteen Me-109s. The German fighters never got close to the bombers as both the 486th and the 4th tore after them. The 486th knocked down four for no losses while the 4th shot down one but lost one of its own. That the Germans took so long to attempt an intercept was serendipitous. Had they attacked early and forced the escorting P-51s to jettison their external tanks before they were empty, the bombers might have been forced to turn around or make the trip unescorted.

The American pilots looked down on landscapes the likes of which they had never seen. "Now and then our course took us over what had been a Russian [Ukrainian] village but was now a cluttered heap of rubble," McKibben recollected. "Tank tracks had chewed the earth and shell blast had laid it bare." Farther into the Ukraine, the Mustangs dipped their wings and arced away to the south and their designated base at Piryatin while the bombers continued east toward their airfields at Mirgorod and Poltava under the protective wings of a newly arrived escort of Soviet Lend-Lease P-39s.

The four P-51 squadrons had been airborne for more than seven hours when Blakeslee led them over Piryatin exactly on time. McKibben remembered, "You could sense the relief in Colonel Blakeslee's voice when he said, 'Well, boys, here's the end of a perfect mission.' Well, it wasn't quite perfect and a 4th Group boy didn't help matters any when he staged a minor accident on the lone steel mat runway and held the remainder of us in the air for twenty minutes."

After getting safely on the ground, the American pilots were trucked to debriefing tents where Russian girls poured coffee and fed them white bread and jam. McKibben remembered a particularly attractive young woman with whom the pilots flirted, calling her "gorgeous." She knew a few words of English and teased them in return: "Nyit, Nyit. Americanski pilot handsome."

Ken Williams recalled that, at least in a basic sense, communicating with their hosts was not too difficult. "I tried to converse with the people by sign language mostly. I could speak no Russian and they could speak no English, and yet they explained to me the operation of an antiaircraft gun and I very easily explained to them how my airplane operated. Their politeness and willingness to take us in and give us all they had regardless of the cost to them showed their true sense of hospitality."[2]

The pilots were put into tents for the evening. McKibben recalled what happened:

> That night we had just gotten settled into our sacks when all hell broke loose around us and we peered under the edge of the tent to see ack-ack breaking in the sky above us and searchlights groping through the night. We just layed [sic] there and took in the show. That is, until a couple of flares broke into brilliance directly over our tent area. There was a sudden rush of half-dressed and undressed figures making for the slit trenches at the end of our row of tents. . . . Meanwhile, tracers from the field defences were trying to shoot out the Jerry flares and as the parachutes got lower to the ground, the Russians depressed their guns until the tracers were coursing between our tents and directly over our heads.

McKibben and his comrades were on the periphery of an air attack of historic proportions. Although the Germans had failed to interdict the bombing mission as it crossed Europe and passed into the Soviet Union earlier that day, a reconnaissance variant of the He-177 dogged the bombers to their bases and took photographs. Although the German aircraft was spotted, the Red Air Force failed to intercept it and Soviet authorities forbad the American fighter pilots from pursuing it. Following the He-177's return to Minsk, the Luftwaffe readied a raid that included He-111s, Ju-88s, Me-109s, and FW-190s.

The German force, which numbered approximately 150 bombers, hit the airfield at Poltava just after midnight on June 22, 1944. Soviet air defenses were so pitiful that the Luftwaffe crews bombed and strafed the airfield for more than two hours without loss. Other than trying to engage the raiders with light antiaircraft weapons and a handful of Yak fighters, nothing was done to contest the admittedly brilliant German attack. Again, the Soviets would not permit the American pilots to take off after the raiders.

The Luftwaffe attack was a remarkable success that left forty-three B-17s aflame and damaged twenty-six more. Perhaps worse was the loss of nearly half a million gallons of high octane fuel; it had been transported into the country at a dear price and it was turned into a spectacular pyre that lit the airfield with a hellish orange pall. Additionally, the bomb dump was hit and most of the munitions were destroyed. Never before had the USAAF suffered such losses on the ground. Miraculously, only one crewman was killed.

Bill Reese was scheduled to go on the shuttle mission but his aircraft was taken by the 486th's operations officer, Donald Higgins, when Higgins's own aircraft went sick. As it turned out, with most of the squadron gone there was no one to care if Reese went to London. "This was during the time when the V-1 buzz bombs were coming over," Reese recalled. "I just couldn't get over being fascinated with those things. They sounded like an outboard motor buzzing along. And then, all of a sudden, they would get quiet and pick up a glide angle of about 45 degrees. Whatever it hit exploded on impact."

Reese recalled that the English were very well-practiced at getting under cover as warnings were sounded. "Usually, when heading for the bomb shelters they met the Americans going out to see what was going on. It was really fascinating watching the buzz bombs at night, especially when the flak was trying to shoot them down while you could hear their distinctive 'putt-putt' and see the exhaust flare. Then it would get quiet and you would see a big explosion. It was really kind of exciting!"[3]

Stunned by the German attack on Poltava, the Soviet and American authorities evacuated the remaining aircraft and crews. The 4th Fighter Group was sent to the airfields at Chuguev and Zaporozhe, while the 486th and about forty bombers were sent to Kharkov. McKibben recollected the move: "Kharkov airport was on the outskirts of the town and as we circled to land, we could see that the city was very modern with the straight, simple lines of its tall office buildings and apartment houses reflecting the evening sun with a rose-orange glow. But looking closely, we could see that many of those buildings were gutted. The fighting had passed here only a few months before."

Several days passed with the 486th's pilots shuttling from Kharkov, to Piryatin, to Chuguev and back to Piryatin. McKibben recorded a number of interesting observations. At Kharkov he noted that the American presence caused quite a stir. "Formations of men and women soldiers gaped as we passed and drew up in front of a large brick dormitory." Inside, the men were seated and fed. "Awe-struck and blushing, girls began bringing us course after course of dinner. They led off with a raw, pickled herring. Some of us struggled with it for a while and others, not wanting to offend our hosts, quietly slipped it into their flying suits to be disposed of later."

McKibben also noted the character of the people. "Everyone we met was pleasant and tried his very best to make us feel at home, despite the obvious hardships they were under." And, "Despite the desolation surrounding them, these people are undoubtedly the singingest, dancingest race we have ever met. All the time we were there [Kharkov] an accordion played Russian melodies while the American officers and GIs danced with the girls in the dirt square or in the large hall which served as a movie house during the evening." Furthermore, the young pilots couldn't help but notice the females among their hosts: "The women were attractive, though not beautiful and long after we left Russia those buxom belles were the source of great wonderment on the part of Americans who had only known English and American girls. Compared to those Russian beauties, our girls are flat chested indeed."

Leonard Gremaux shared his perspective of the Russian woman: "Lots of them are pretty rugged individuals but they seem to be pretty nice. Having had no close associations—dammit—with any of them, I can't say much, though. They're sure doing a big job. One girl stood guard on my plane for exactly eleven-and-a-half hours. All of them work hard."[4]

Because of the chaos caused by the German attack of June 22, and rising tensions between the Soviets and the Americans, no missions were flown until the Americans departed for Italy on June 27, 1944, and bombed the oil refinery at Drohobvos, Poland on the way. The raid was uneventful for the most part, although Carleton Fuhrman took off late and was jumped by a pair of Me-109s as he hurried to catch up with the formation. The Germans opted to disengage from the hard-fighting Fuhrman when the 486th turned back to rescue their comrade.

The P-51s landed at Lucera without incident. The following day they made the short flight to Madna at the edge of the Adriatic. Sunny southern Italy was a wonderment to the 486th's pasty pilots. Where England had been relentlessly gray and wet, Italy featured brilliant topaz skies and a golden sun that warmed the bones. McKibben recalled their priorities: "As soon as we had landed, dispersed our airplanes and given directions to the mechanics for their servicing, we struck out for the beach. We were to spend every afternoon for the next week on that beach. By the time we left Italy we all had a dark brown tan."

The airfield at Madna was home to the 52nd Fighter Group. McKibben's envy was evident when he described the routine of his Italy-based counterparts. "Italy was a flyer's paradise. Clouds were the exception, rather than the rule as they are in England and the pilots could count on a mission every morning. Returning from their mission a little after noon, they were automatically released for the rest of the day, which was spent on the beach."

In fact, the fliers from the FRANTIC effort had several days off until July 2. The target was Budapest, Hungary, and a large force of fighters rose to meet the American attackers. It was one of the few times during the war when the 486th finished a fight on the wrong side of the ledger. Although Donald Higgins knocked down an Me-109 and shared an FW-190 with a 4th Fighter Group pilot, Lester Howell was shot down when he chased after a group of fighters alone.

Steve Andrew also went down when his engine stopped running over Budapest. With characteristic calmness, he broadcast his situation. McKibben recalled: "He asked for the wind direction and told his flight to strafe the airplane as soon as he had landed it and gotten clear. He glided a few miles toward the semi-friendly Yugoslav border and made a perfect belly landing. His flight saw him get out of the ship, wave, and run like hell. They set his ship on fire."

An uneventful raid was flown to Arad, Romania, the next day and the trip back to England was made on July 5; the bombers hit the railroad yards at Béziers, in southeast France, along the way. Although the bulk of the 486th's pilots made it home that day, others were delayed for mechanical or other reasons and they straggled back in smaller groups or alone.

Ed Heller was left behind in Piryatin. His rudder had been shot up during the initial sortie from England. It was ready in time for the trip to Italy but a series of other mechanical problems left him stuck in place for nearly three weeks. During that time he was feted by his Russian hosts at an event where he was the only American present. "Anyway, the guy running the show started offering toasts," Heller recalled. "They filled my water glass full of vodka and we started drinking in honor of President Roosevelt. Heller took a sip of his vodka. "The pilot next to me intimated that that would never do; bottoms up, he inferred. So I steeled myself, grabbed the left side of my chair with my left hand, and poured the stuff down with my right."

The next toast was to Churchill. Heller couldn't refuse. Neither could he decline to drink to Stalin. "After that the going was really rough. I remember getting up from the table and being bid good night. The moment I hit fresh air I fell flat on my face."[5]

He started home in late July and nursed his sick aircraft to Tehran where he promptly came down with dysentery and was held up for another two weeks. After recovering he made his way to Casablanca after taking a couple of days to sightsee in Cairo. At Casablanca a jealous general snatched his aircraft from him and he was subsequently sent back to Bodney via Air Transport Command.

Although the 352nd's pilots didn't participate further, several more FRANTIC missions were flown. The last took place in September and was a botched supply drop to Polish forces in Warsaw. Despite the painstaking planning and backbreaking work the USAAF invested to make the shuttle concept a success, the Soviet leadership killed it through malicious pigheadedness. Virtually every move the Americans made was stymied, blocked, delayed or otherwise obstructed by Soviet obstinacy. It was clear to the Soviets that the American raids were not critical to the war in the East. And in truth, they were correct. The same raids could have been flown from bases in England or Italy. Nevertheless, for the thousands of American men who participated, the experience was one of a lifetime.

During the war, every family of every serviceman was fearful of the telegram boy. Western Union telegrams from the Secretary of War delivered news that loved ones had been killed or were missing. Such information changed the lives of millions of Americans. On June 22, 1944, Ted Fahrenwald's brother, Frank, received such a telegram. His breezy, cavalier and devil-may-care brother had gone missing in air combat. It hardly seemed possible to him that he could be gone:

THE SECRETARY OF WAR DESIRES ME TO EXPRESS HIS DEEP REGRET THAT YOUR BROTHER FIRST LIEUTENANT HAS BEEN REPORTED MISSING IN ACTION SINCE 8 JUNE OVER FRANCE. IF FURTHER DETAILS OR OTHER INFORMATION ARE RECEIVED YOU WILL BE PROMPTLY NOTIFIED.

CHAPTER 20

Longer Legs and Longer Missions

Many of the 352nd's pilots remembered the relatively limited range of the early P-47 as its chief shortcoming. Not a few of them preferred the dangers of air combat to the cold-sweated anxiety of crossing the North Sea with nearly empty fuel tanks. To them, the P-47 simply didn't carry enough fuel. Their recollections were not without merit as more than a few Thunderbolts fell into the English Channel or the North Sea with empty fuel tanks.

But many of the longer-ranged P-51s were lost for the same reason. The explanation was simple: Because the P-51 carried enough fuel to go farther and stay over enemy territory longer, its pilots were logically tasked to go farther and stay over enemy territory longer. Consequently, when bad weather—especially clouds and strong headwinds—came into play, accurate navigation became difficult and the pilots often wasted precious fuel trying to find their way home.

This was the case on July 19, 1944, when William Wilson of the 328th Fighter Squadron was lost. The mission summary report for the day noted: "Lt. Wilson, 328th Sqdn. Last heard from vicinity Lille, approximately 1145, when he reported that he was out of gas and was baling [sic] out." As it developed, Wilson came down on dry land and was made a POW.

Wilson's loss foreshadowed a catastrophe that befell the 328th two days later on July 21, 1944 when the squadron experienced its worst losses of the war. On that day the 487th Fighter Squadron downed three Me-109s while the 486th and 328th were not able to get engaged. Upon turning for home the three squadrons encountered unusually stiff headwinds as well as an undercast that obscured the ground. Ultimately, five pilots from the 328th went down into the North Sea and another two put down on the English coast after only barely making landfall. Of the five who went into the water, David Zimms and Elmer Dubay bailed out and were rescued by an American minesweeper.

George Middleton's diary included a brief note on the mission: "Munich. Winds aloft change on return [and] blew us out over the North Sea. No radio contact. In sight of land but ready to bail out. Landed at RAF field with little gas left. Lost seven planes and three pilots."[1] The 352nd's mission summary report completed later that day held out hope for the three men who went into the water and were not immediately rescued: "Lts. [Richard] Casper, [James] Lanter and [Robert] Lampman, 328th Sqdn are NYR [Not Yet Returned] at this time but may have landed in England. Last heard from N/O Wash but have no definite fixes on any." Sadly, no trace of the three fliers was ever found. The weather did to the 328th what the Luftwaffe never could.

The 352nd's mission summary report for July 29, 1944, reported an encounter that suggested the Luftwaffe might have been experimenting with tactics and camouflage schemes intended to spoof or confuse the Americans: "2 ships, Red Flight, 486th Sqdn, were separated from group and were bounced by 75 Me-109s in vicinity of Munster, 1115, 20,000 ft. E/A were all silver and flying P-51 formation, peeling off in flights of four, but did not press attacks."

Because this was nothing that the Luftwaffe subsequently practiced to any degree, it is difficult to ascertain what actually took place. It is quite possible that the encounter occurred just as described and that the pair of 486th pilots had been attacked by a large formation of unpainted Me-109s. But the possibility also exists that the two fliers had been mistakenly bounced by other P-51s, and that they had in turn misidentified the attackers. This possibility is particularly attractive because the attackers used American formations and did not press their advantage despite their overwhelming numbers. Still, it is hard to believe that all parties would have misidentified an aircraft type which they were all flying themselves. In the end, the encounter was little more than interesting.

In the days following the invasion the fighter groups flying escort out of England were assisted by a relatively new technology. In fact, two, giant, handmade Microwave Early Warning (MEW) radar sets were delivered to England earlier that year and made operational in time for D-Day. Technically designated AN/CPS-1, these sets provided information on enemy fighter formations that previously would have been unknowable. They also proved invaluable at tracking V-1 missiles inbound to England beginning in June 1944. Moreover, they provided intercept data for night fighters, assisted aircraft in finding ground targets and gave headings to lost pilots. Tests showed they could detect an aircraft flying at 16,500 feet at a range of 177 miles. Aircraft flying at higher altitudes could be detected out to a distance of nearly four hundred miles.

Each MEW was massive and required more than fifty personnel to operate and maintain it. Nevertheless, it was relocateable and could be disassembled in two days, transported in sixteen trucks and then reassembled in two more days. At its heart, it had five PPI oscilloscopes so that different controllers could direct separate formations. The controllers grew more effective as they gained experience and the MEWs—supported by a complex network of control centers, smaller radars, and other equipment—soon became an integral part of the air campaign.

An early example was detailed in a report filed by the 487th Fighter Squadron on June 8, 1944, while operating over France: "Proceeded to area arriving 1120 at 8,000'. Searched for targets, directed by controller to go to Le Mans, as 100 FW 190s were on A/D [airdrome] there." The mission was a success whereas before the advent of MEW the squadron would have continued to snoop around the countryside, perhaps finding nothing worthwhile to attack.

Pilots occasionally disappeared during combat for reasons that were never determined. During a big fight, it was difficult to track everyone and losses sometimes went unnoticed until the clash was over, or even until long after the group returned to Bodney. Although enemy action was most likely responsible for the majority of the losses, the reasons for others were never discovered, as sometimes they disappeared on missions during which the enemy was never encountered. This was the case with the 352nd's first combat loss, William Alm, who disappeared without a trace on the mission of September 14. Any number of factors caused these men to go missing, including mechanical failures, fuel starvation, or hypoxia caused by lack of oxygen. Nelson Jesup on July 8, 1944, highlighted this point in a letter home:

> I developed a leak in a gas line and gas was spraying into the cockpit. . . . It got so bad that even with my oxygen mask on (I was at 22,000 ft), I was getting sick and having difficulty breathing. I was almost to the French coast when I turned back toward England and I had decided to bailout after sticking it out until I got closer to the English coast where Air-Sea-Rescue boats could pick me up. I unfastened my safety belt, shoulder straps, oxygen equipment and switched over to the emergency channel on my radio and called in so they could get a fix on me. I was about to climb out when for some unknown reason the gas spray stopped and I stayed with it and got home—with a beautiful headache.[2]

Another example occurred a month later during the mission of August 5, 1944, when the group claimed five Me-109s between 1115 and 1215 during a big scrap while escorting bombers south of Hamburg. However, no one knew what happened to Don French, or Clifford Wilcox. The two lieutenants simply failed to return to Bodney. The mission summary report was scant on details about their fate: "Lt. French, 486th Sqdn, last seen w/o Stade 26,000 ft, 1154. Lt. Wilcox, 487th Sqdn, joined 328th Sqdn as a spare and was last seen at Madgeburg, 23,000 ft, 1255." As it turned out, French claimed two Me-109s before being shot down and captured. Wilcox was later learned to have been killed.

Another loss that is difficult to explain occurred just a week later on August 12, 1944, when Gerald Thurman jumped out of his P-51 over the English Channel after an uneventful escort mission over France. The group's mission summary report recorded: "Lt. Thurman, 486th Sqdn, last seen when he bailed out of a/c, reason unknown, 30 mi. s/o Selsey Bill, 8,000 ft, 0915—no chute seen." Thurman was never found.

Why Thurman bailed out of his aircraft is difficult to guess. From the scant details in the mission report it is apparent that he did not communicate with anyone from his flight, or with Air/Sea Rescue. This fact suggests that he had a radio failure of some sort, either with the actual radio box or with the microphone in his mask or the circuitry in between.

Another curious aspect is that he bailed out at eight thousand feet. This was more than enough altitude—even had the engine failed—to have gotten much closer to the coast where rescue was more assured. He could have safely taken to his parachute at only a thousand feet, or even used that last bit of altitude to close the distance to shore before ditching the aircraft. This suggests that the cockpit was not habitable, most likely because of fire, although no mention of fire or smoke was made in the mission summary report. At any rate, Thurman was somehow compelled to abandon his aircraft. That his parachute failed sealed a tragic end for what had obviously been a very bad day.

Chaplain George Cameron served in China as a Marine prior to attending seminary and being ordained, so he wasn't a simple deliverer of Sunday sermons. Rather, he knew and understood the trials and difficulties that the 352nd's men experienced. And he was very active in ministering not only to their needs but also to those of their families.

One of his causes that the men supported with vigor was to buy a $1,000 war bond for the children of each pilot that was shot down and killed. The bonds were intended to help pay their college tuitions after they graduated from high school. The bonds were obviously very well received by the widows. The chaplain at Camp Leonard Wood in Missouri delivered one of the bond's to the widow of Gerald Thurman. He took time to write Cameron: "I wish I had the ability to write you how very appreciative Lt. Thurman's wife was for the bond. She is anxious that all who had any part in this work to be assured that it will be used in the education of her child. Allow me to express my great admiration of the splendid work you are doing along this line."

Cameron was ever-inventive in his fundraising schemes but one approach he tried during a two-day period was to simply play musical favorites on a phonograph in the mess hall in exchange for a donation. The effort captured the attention of *Stars and Stripes*, which recorded how Cameron's concept was turned on its head: "Recently, one Joe offered ten shillings for a Sinatra disc. After the chaplain had dropped the note in the money-box, someone offered 15 shillings if The Voice were not heard. Cameron returned the ten bob to the original bidder and didn't play the record." As it turned out, of the 150 pounds that Cameron raised during the two-day event, most of it was paid to him by men outbidding others to not play particular songs.

Cameron was also the likely inspiration behind the charitable efforts of the 352nd's enlisted men. As hard as they worked, and as important as that work was, they understood full well that they were not in daily danger. Rather, it was their infantry brethren that were giving up their lives to take Europe back from the Nazis. Recognizing that, and wanting to do what they could, the 352nd's NCO club purchased two $500 War Bonds. Of these, one was given to the son of an infantryman killed in combat, while the other was presented to the daughter of another. Goodwin Klinetob spoke for his comrades when he said: "We'd like the infantry to know that we sure appreciate what they're doing."

CHAPTER 21

Clearing the Table, Clearing the Sky

George Preddy's nickname when he was a boy was Mouse. By the summer of 1944 he was a leading ace and was known as Ratsy. In many ways it seemed to fit. He liked to gamble and craps was a favorite game. Moreover, he was good at it. Indeed, he named his different aircraft not for his mother, or his girlfriend or sister or anyone else. Rather, he had them emblazoned with his good-luck cry at the craps table; whenever he threw the dice, he shouted, "Cripes a'mighty!"

On the evening of August 5, 1944, Preddy hit it big at the craps table at Bodney's officers club. By the end of the night he had taken everyone's money and in fact collected shirts and jackets and other uniform items from those who owed him more money than they had. But the various pieces of clothing were secondary to the $1,200 in cash he won. It was the equivalent of several months pay.

Preddy also hit it big at the bar. It wasn't unusual. Like many of his peers he drank with abandon when he celebrated. And because the next day's weather was expected to be too poor for a mission he didn't moderate his intake. By the time he crawled into bed that night, Preddy was good and drunk.

He was wakened a short time later. The bombers were headed to Berlin and the 352nd was tasked with escorting them from Hamburg to Berlin and part of the way back. Preddy was scheduled to lead it; he hadn't been asleep even close to long enough to get sober. In fact, his drunkenness hadn't even had time to transition to a hangover. Meyer stopped by to check on him and on seeing how drunk he was offered to take the mission for him. "No, damn it," Preddy replied. "I'll take the mission. It's my turn."

Preddy checked the mission details and made ready to brief the rest of the group. Finally, with the pilots from all three squadrons in place and ready to take notes, he mounted the briefing platform and began. It didn't go well. Still drunk, he stumbled off the platform more than once as he reeled off the mission particulars and his expectations for that day's effort. The 352nd's commanding officer, Joe Mason, leaned over to Meyer and noted that Preddy was still bombed. Meyer assured him that there was still time to get him in shape to fly. Whether Meyer, a stern disciplinarian, would have been so sympathetic if it were another pilot is not knowable. But certainly the idea that he would help a drunken man to lead the entire group was inconsistent with what might have been expected.

Nevertheless, during the time between the end of the briefing and the takeoff, Preddy was led off and made to breathe pure oxygen. It was widely believed that the unadulterated gas caused the body to metabolize alcohol more quickly. In reality, its effects were largely psychological.

Still, when it was time, Preddy climbed into his aircraft and led the group airborne without incident. In all likelihood, considering his high-spirited and social nature, and additionally considering the number of missions he had flown up to that point, it wasn't the first time he had flown while hung over or drunk. As it developed, the weather was fabulous with nothing but a few high scattered clouds. Notwithstanding the spectacular conditions, Preddy vomited what remained of the previous night's celebratory libations. Around him, the 352nd's blue-nosed Mustangs arced gracefully over the bomber stream.

That the Luftwaffe showed up in strength made the scenery all the more spectacular. However much this might have been the one mission during which Preddy hoped not to meet the enemy, it was not to be. "I was Group Leader," he recorded in his encounter report.[1] "We were escorting the lead combat wings of B-17s when 30-plus Me-109s in formation came into the third box from the south. We were a thousand feet above them so I led White Flight—consisting of Lt. [Sheldon] Heyer, Lt. [Cyril] Doleac and myself—in astern of them."

Preddy dropped down and singled out an Me-109 toward the rear of the enemy gaggle. He opened fire from 300 yards and noted hits around the cockpit as the German aircraft caught fire, rolled over and fell toward the earth. "At this time," Preddy continued, "Lt. Doleac became lost while shooting down an Me-109 that had gotten on Lt. Heyer's tail."

With Heyer still on his wing, Preddy pulled up behind another Me-109 and opened fire. Just as the first one had, this Me-109 also caught fire. "He went spinning down and the pilot bailed out at 20,000 feet," Preddy recalled. He looked over his right shoulder and saw Heyer blasting another German out of the sky.

Between the two of them Preddy and Heyer had knocked down three enemy fighters in short order. The truth was, as Preddy noted, that the German pilots were not fighting back. Rather, according to their orders, they were refusing combat with the American fighters and trying to get at the bombers. This was noted in Preddy's report: "The enemy formation stayed together taking practically no evasive action and tried to get back for an attack on the bombers who were now off to the right."

Preddy and Heyer pressed their attacks. Preddy flew up close behind another Me-109 and gave it a burst. "He went down smoking badly and I saw him begin to fall apart below us." Preddy and Heyer were joined by a four-ship of P-51s even as they continued to hack away at the enemy formation. Preddy struck again. "I fired at another 109 causing him to burn after a short burst. He spiraled down to the right in flames. The [German] formation headed down in a left turn keeping themselves together in rather close formation," recounted Preddy.

He started the day drunk but nevertheless knocked down four enemy aircraft. Still, he wasn't finished. "I got a good burst into another one causing him to burn and spin down." He went after one more German. This pilot was the only one who fought back that day:

I got a short burst at the Jerry but missed. It was just the two of us then, and after I missed he had the edge on me. I went into a steep climb into the sun and as he tried to follow me I could see him firing everything he had. He couldn't stay with me in that climb and dropped off. Then it was my turn again. I got behind him, and he must have known then that his game was up. Before I could get in a shot I saw him fumbling with the hood above his head, trying to get out. When I hit him, the plane quivered a bit and started down, but he was out by this time, so I saw him float down without bothering him.[2]

Preddy made an uneventful flight back to Bodney where he made a fast, loud, low-level victory pass before pitching up and landing. He was met at his hardstand by his ground crew along with John C. Meyer and many of the 487th's officers and men. Physically, despite the fact that several hours had passed since he had gotten airborne, he was still miserable. In the few photos that were taken after he landed he appeared subdued, even wretched, and not at all excited at having shot down six enemy aircraft.

If Preddy wasn't excited, at least in his hung over condition, VIII Fighter Command certainly was and made certain that his exploits were well-publicized. His single-sortie score was a record at the time and the next day Bodney was overrun by a host of newsmen, photographers and commentators. He was compelled to reenact his return to the airfield and he beat up the base with victory rolls and other aerobatics. After landing and taxiing back to his hardstand, the welcome of the previous day was reenacted. All of the action was filmed and the footage was later combined with portions of his gun camera film to make a short publicity feature of the sort that was so popular during the war.

George Preddy bought a war bond with the $1,200 he won at the craps table the night before his record-setting mission. He promptly sent it home to his mother. Edwin King, an RAF exchange pilot who often flew on Preddy's wing remembered the gaming that went on at Bodney's officer's club. "Much gambling took place in the Club—craps on a special table, bridge and other card games. I joined a bridge game until I found out the amount of the stakes. What I thought to be per hundred turned out to be per point!" King was astonished at the amounts his American friends were wagering. "I then had to drop out as one British pound per point was most often the stake and well beyond my pocket."[3]

By the late spring of 1944, the latest model of the P-51, the P-51D, began showing up at the 352nd. The most obvious difference from the earlier models was the teardrop, or bubble canopy. It allowed the pilot an unobstructed view in all directions—an advantage that was invaluable in aerial combat. It did create a bit more drag. This additional drag, along with other considerations, caused it to be—technically—two miles per hour slower than the P-51B. In operations the difference was unnoticeable. Other factors such as the mechanical state of the engine and the trim of the aircraft could cause much greater degradations, regardless of whether an aircraft was a P-51D or P-51B.

Another significant improvement was the addition of one more .50-caliber machine gun per wing, for a total of six. It increased the aircraft's hitting power by half again. Moreover, the wing was slightly redesigned and one of the benefits was that it was possible to install the guns upright; gun jams were virtually eliminated.

The version of the P-51D that was built at North American's plant in Dallas was the P-51K. The two aircraft were virtually identical except that the P-51K had an Aeroproducts propeller rather than a Hamilton Standard propeller. The Aeroproducts propeller was considered substandard by some pilots and crew chiefs and was often replaced by a Hamilton Standard. The 352nd operated only a relative handful of P-51Ks.

Other improvements continued to be incorporated into the P-51. One of these was an anti-G system. Losing consciousness during hard maneuvering, also known as "blacking out," was a constant hazard for fighter pilots during air combat. This type of aggressive flying put the pilot under the stress of multiple Gs, or multiple times the force of gravity. Depending on the individual and his physical disposition on any given day, a pilot might experience a partial loss of consciousness and blurred vision under as few as three Gs. Most pilots blacked out as Gs exceeded five, although a number of factors influenced how resistant an individual was to the effects of high-G flight. As a rule, short, stocky, muscular pilots were able to withstand the effects better than their taller, leaner counterparts. Too, a well-rested and well-fed pilot was generally more resistant than a sleep-deprived pilot with a hangover.

Regardless of the causes and effects, losing consciousness during air combat was dangerous for obvious reasons. Jack Diamond of the 487th Fighter Squadron recalled an episode: "I made a quick turn to pull behind an enemy fighter that made a fast pass across our formation." The maneuver was too much and Diamond blacked out. Luckily he was unmolested during the brief period when he was unconscious. "When I regained my sight there was not another plane around. All I could do was head west and keep a sharp lookout for enemy planes."[4]

Karl Dittmer, also of the 487th, had a similar experience. He chased an Me-109 that went into a steep dive. "In a few moments I found my bird porpoising in the dive. I remember using both hands to try to recover from the dive. The next thing I recall is returning to consciousness with my right leg kicking or twitching, a spasm common to a complete black out. I noticed my airspeed indicator was pegged on the dial, and the large hand on the altimeter was making a complete revolution every two seconds or so. The small hand indicated we were climbing through 20,000 feet."[5]

Beginning in the summer of 1944, replacement aircraft began arriving with anti-G systems. The pilot wore a special set of tight fitting trousers, or chaps, with bladders sewn into the lower abdomen, thighs and calves. This "G-suit" was connected to the aircraft with a hose. A pneumatic system in the aircraft metered air into the G-suit as the aircraft went into hard turns.

This air inflated the bladders inside the suit and caused it to tighten around the pilot's lower body consequently slowing the movement of blood out of the brain. Fitted properly, a suit could increase a pilot's G tolerance by about twenty percent which was enough to provide a real edge in air combat.

Another device introduced late in the war was the AN/APS-13 tail warning radar, or radio set. It was mounted in the tail, or vertical stabilizer, of the P-51 and projected a cone of radar energy to the rear. When an object, namely an aircraft, penetrated that cone, it reflected the energy back to a receiver which triggered a red light and a warning bell in the cockpit. It was intended to alert the pilot when an enemy aircraft approached unseen from the rear. In practice it was not well-liked as it was triggered by friendly aircraft as often as not when the formation maneuvered or changed positions. If the aircraft was low enough the system could also be set off by the ground. Jack Diamond recalled one instance when it sounded an alert and, "scared me to death. I racked the plane around in a hard left turn while looking for an enemy plane coming up on my tail." He saw nothing. "Finally," he said, "I spotted two wing tanks floating down below me." Another P-51 had dropped its external fuel tanks and they had fallen behind Diamond's aircraft and triggered the tail warning radar.[6]

The drudgery, pettiness and nitpickery of military life have been bemoaned by the rank-and-file soldier ever since fighting became organized. This trivial-mindedness reached a zenith during World War II when enormous masses of men—some not necessarily the brightest—had to be organized and led. Regulations, occasionally absurd, governed nearly everything. An example from the 352nd's parent organization, the 67th Fighter Wing, was posted in the daily bulletin of August 20, 1944. Typed in capital letters, as if to lend the message greater import, it was typical of the sort of bureaucratic inanity that grated against men of common sense:

THE ONLY AUTHORIZED COLOR FOR BICYCLES IS LUSTRELESS OLIVE DRAB. ALL GOVERNMENT ISSUE BICYCLES THAT ARE NOT PAINTED TO CONFORM WITH THIS WILL BE IMMEDIATELY PAINTED WITH AN APPROVED LUSTRELESS OLIVE DRAB. FOR IDENTIFICATION PURPOSES THE NAME OF THE INDIVIDUAL TO WHOM THE BICYCLE IS ASSIGNED MAY BE PAINTED ON THE REAR FENDER.

It is ironic that the Supreme Allied Commander in Europe, Eisenhower, did not send his messages in capital letters.

More reasonable was the oft-repeated admonition in the daily bulletin that warned against violating blackout regulations: "The O.D. [Officer of the Day] has again reported that blackout regulations are not being complied with by various units on this station. Several violations have been reported recently and it is directed that all organizations exert every effort to insure [*sic*] that blackout regulations are more rigidly adhered to."

The proper marking of laundry was also a regular on the daily bulletin hit parade: "The Station's laundry service is being impaired through the fact that personnel are neglecting to mark their clothes properly, or to use a regulation ticket on their bundles. All unit supply rooms will take immediate steps to see that all clothes (particularly fatigues) are properly marked. . . ." It is easy to make light of the issue, but certainly sorting through disorganized bundles of stinking laundry was no easy task. And it was a necessary one.

One can't help but wonder what painful or frightening episode must have occurred to motivate the following message in the group's daily bulletin for August 23, 1944: "All personnel are advised that the old type prophylactic known as 'V-Packet' might be harmful to the individual if used. This packet has two tubes [prophylactics]. Only the new type prophylactic known as 'Pro-Kits," and having a single tube, is to be used. All personnel having the old type V-Packet in their possession will turn them in to the nearest medical dispensary as soon as possible." No doubt this message raised more eyebrows than the normal run-of-the-mill administrative notices carried in the daily bulletin.

Then there were postings that made absolutely no sense whatsoever: "Circular 19, ETOUSA, 1942, requires American pedestrian personnel to walk on the right side of the road facing oncoming traffic. This regulation is dangerous and grossly violated by American personnel. All personnel will be given adequate instructions on this matter to help minimize this existing danger."

The millions of men the United States put into uniform came from all walks of life and possessed a broad spectrum of talent. The 352nd, like many units, counted a number of very good musicians among its ranks. Sometime after the unit's situation at Bodney had stabilized they were issued instruments, music, and stands and were formed into a band. Paul Klinger was a member. "We called ourselves Little Joe's in honor of Colonel Joe Mason. This proved to be very beneficial. Colonel Mason eventually took all of us off all duties and told us to do nothing but practice and play at dances."

The men of Little Joe's did exactly that. "We played weekly at King's Lynn Red Cross and were paid one pound, plus all the food we could consume," Klinger recalled. "The English girls flocked around the band stand and kept us happy in playing our music. Ward Gammet played the best with a pitcher of beer on the floor ready for consumption. We played at many Red Cross clubs and American and British officer's clubs."[7]

That Mason was able to spare enough men to create what was essentially a professional dance band was due to a number of factors. Firstly, planners early during the war were conservative when they developed the table of personnel required to staff a fighter group. No one had ever done it before on such a scale and they played it safe; when setting out to win a war, it was better to have too many men than not enough.

Too, a phenomenon occurred that was articulated nicely by the official history of the 352nd's communication section: "As men became proficient at their work . . . fewer men were required for a given job or installation, with the result that the personnel problem gradually disappeared almost entirely." This turned out to be the situation with virtually all the specialties that were required to run the squadron.

And it wasn't just the dance band. The 352nd fielded sports teams that regularly traveled to other bases to play. In fact, the group's football team—the Mustang Blues—was the lightest in the European theater of operations. Yet their superb passing attack and vicious tackling saw them to a 4-2-1 record for the 1944 season.

The aircraft the 352nd flew—P-47s early on and P-51s later—were rugged but not unbreakable. And it wasn't always apparent when they were about to fail. For instance, a hard landing might create a hairline crack in a wing spar or other structure without showing any external indication of damage. Likewise, a hard turn at high speed might cause the aircraft similar injury. Nevertheless, it would often fly perfectly well until the accumulated stress of many more sorties caused catastrophic structural failure.

This was apparently the case on August 6, 1944. The 352nd was escorting bombers in the vicinity of Lüneburg, Germany, when it was caught up in a running engagement with Luftwaffe fighters. Charles Cesky of the 328th Fighter Squadron filed an encounter report that described the disastrous failure of a squadronmate's P-51:

I noticed that the Flt Ldr's wingman [Walter Gehrke] broke suddenly following an Me-109. I followed down with him til at approx 17,000–18,000 feet alt[itude] Lt Gehrke's wing broke off of the A/C and he started spinning. I last saw this plane at 16,000 feet when I passed him in pursuit of the Me-109. I stayed astern of the enemy A/C going straight down until at 6,000 feet the pilot of the enemy A/C bailed out; the enemy A/C hit the grd and exploded about one and one-half mi from where Lt Gehrke's plane crashed. I did not fire at the E/A.[8]

Walter Gehrke was likely pinned inside his aircraft by centrifugal forces and did not get out of the doomed aircraft.

Another example occurred on November 27, 1944, when the 352nd was tasked with an unusual mission. It was to attack a wooded area where oil was believed to be stored. The plan was for the pilots to drop partially full external tanks into the woods, and then set them afire with their guns. Walter Smith of the 487th was flying as the element leader of the last flight when a formation of Me-109s was spotted prior to the target area at 30,000 feet. The 352nd's pilots dropped their tanks and attacked immediately.

"My flight leader got the next-to-last Jerry," Smith recorded, "and I went after the last one."[9] As Smith closed on the German fighter, it stalled in the rarefied air and fell into a spin. Smith followed the Me-109 and saddled up behind it as the German pilot regained control of his aircraft at 15,000 feet. "I started firing and saw strikes around the cockpit and smoke start coming from his engine. Just as his canopy flew off, my plane gave a vicious snap and continued snapping to the left, completely out of control. I believe the left wing came off."

With no way to regain control, Smith released his canopy and safety belt and was immediately thrown clear of the aircraft. His comrades never saw him jump as indicated by the day's mission summary report: "Capt. Smith was last seen at 1200, 23,000 ft in a flat spin after losing left wing—no chute seen." Smith descended safely in his parachute, was captured and spent the rest of the war as a POW.

Later during the war the aircraft were equipped with G-meters, or counters, that the mechanics could use to determine if especially high Gs were sustained during a flight. If so, special inspections were required to ensure that the aircraft was still flyable. Although these inspections demanded extra effort, they helped lessen the chances that pilots might be sent into combat in broken aircraft. No doubt, these efforts saved lives.

Ted Fahrenwald made it back to Bodney unannounced on August 20, 1944. After bailing out deep inside France on June 8, he'd had enough adventure and drama to write a book. "I wandered into the Club and it was just suppertime. I swaggered into the dining room and took a grinning look at the long table where sat the reckless remnants of my infamous squadron, all stuffing their ugly faces with Spam and Sprouts." The men looked up at him, stunned. "Bottle-Arse Leo tore himself away from a trough-full of swill just long enough to growl: 'Christ Almighty! The gaw-dam Jerries won't even have him!' And he bucked his head down and flailed away at his supper with a fork in either hand."[10]

Fahrenwald was sent home to the States. At the time, the USAAF was hesitant to put pilots back into action who had been shot down and helped by the Maquis. It was feared that if they went down again and were captured they might be forced to give up the names of those who had helped them.

CHAPTER 22

Summer with the French

The fighting in Normandy had been brutal since D-Day. After establishing a tenable beachhead immediately after the invasion, the Allies were stymied for several weeks before breaking out at the end of July. At that point, they chased the German Seventh Army and the Fifth Panzer Army south to the town of Falaise. There, during the middle of August 1944, the Germans fought desperately to keep from being encircled.

The fight, which became known as the battle of the Falaise Pocket, was savage butchery. Allied air units, in particular the Ninth Air Force and the RAF's Second Tactical Air Force, shredded the Germans wherever they were found. Thousands of German vehicles were destroyed and the roads were choked with the stinking corpses of dead soldiers and draft horses. Occasionally, units from the Eighth Air Force—including the 352nd—were assigned ground attack missions to keep pressure on the Wehrmacht. They often ranged far beyond the battlefield to interdict German reinforcements and supplies.

Bill Reese of the 486th Fighter Squadron was on one of these missions during the early afternoon of August 17, 1944. The flight of seventeen Mustangs stumbled across a handful of railroad cars parked at a siding next to a small French village; the encounter report does not record its name and it is likely that the pilots didn't know exactly where they were.

"So we set up a pattern and started shooting up the freight cars," recalled Reese.[1] "What we didn't know was that for some reason Jerry had some heavy machine guns set up in the area and, after my first pass, I got clobbered—smoke coming out of the engine which immediately started to lose power. I zoomed up to about five hundred feet and tried to roll back the canopy, but couldn't as it must have been hit and jammed. I wasn't very enthusiastic about bailing out anyway, so I looked for a place to belly-in."

Reese could find no good place to set down and committed to setting down in a small meadow surrounded by trees. As he hauled his burning ship through a turn toward the tiny little field his engine quit. "I could see the field as long as I was in a turn, but once I started in on my final approach, all I could see was smoke and flames, and I couldn't sideslip because I was too low—couldn't even see out the side of the canopy because of the smoke, so just held a gentle glide until I felt the prop tickling the ground and then held it there until the plane settled on the ground."

The Mustang slid smoothly for a short distance then bucked violently twice before it abruptly stopped, covered in dirt and grass. Luckily, the cloud of dust and debris smothered the fire that had been working back from the engine. Nevertheless, Reese had not come through the crash unhurt—his Mae West was covered in blood. "I felt my face after taking off my helmet and goggles, and it felt like my nose covered my face cheek-to-cheek. A flap of skin was hanging down over one eye, and that was when I found I had a fair-sized wound on my forehead."

Aside from putting out the engine fire, the crash also freed his canopy and Reese cranked it back easily. "As I climbed out of the plane, I noticed my metal gunsight mount was broken, so I guess I proved once and for all how hard my head was!" Reese walked away from his broken ship as the other three aircraft from his flight circled overhead. "Strangely enough, although I was in somewhat of a daze, I felt no pain at all . . ." It took him a short while to realize that his parachute and Mae West were still attached. "I ditched these in some bushes and started on toward a wooded area."

Low on fuel, his flight flew away and left Reese on his own. Almost immediately, two trucks full of German soldiers drove into sight. "To give you an idea of my mental state," Reese said, "I just stood there and watched as they drove up to the plane. I guess they didn't see me or assumed I was a farmer. Anyway, I finally turned around and walked into the wooded area and when I approached the other side I started realizing I was not being very cautious."

Reese heard the sound of wood being chopped and forced his wits into place. He moved slowly to the edge of the woods and spotted a farmer with an axe. Hiding in the brush he watched the man for perhaps half an hour before he came out of hiding. "I really needed a drink and some cleaning up," Reese remembered. "I had a hanky tied around my forehead, was dressed in an A-2 jacket, olive drab wool shirt and pants, and combat boots, and for the last time in this war I was unarmed—no gun, no knife. The farmer spotted me as I stepped out of the woods, but he didn't run, just kept on chopping."

The Frenchman said something in French and Reese responded in English, saying that he was an American. The farmer understood nothing except that Reese was American. Nevertheless, Reese used his hands to communicate that he was thirsty. The other man had no water, but grabbed an empty wine bottle and strode to a spring hidden in a small copse of trees in the middle of the field. "He held the empty wine bottle under the water until it filled, but as I started to grab it he held me off and held the bottle up to the sky, shook his head, poured the water out and filled it again." Reese took a close look and noted small wriggling creatures. The farmer emptied the bottle once again and after two more attempts was satisfied that the water was clean enough. Reasoning that he had been inoculated "for just about everything," Reese drank the water and suffered no ill effects.

Reese pulled his escape kit from his jacket. Aside from money and other small items he remembered that it included a collection of silk maps and an "asshole" compass, "because that's where you hid it if captured." The two men studied the maps. "I knew I was in France, but where exactly escaped me," recalled Reese. After a short time the Frenchman oriented himself and showed Reese that they were near the town of Épagne, about a hundred miles east of Paris. Reese thanked the man and headed northwest toward the Allied lines.

After coming upon a paved road and following it for a short time Reese approached a bridge near a small village. Not wanting to expose himself on the bridge, he took time to observe it. He saw nothing, started across and was immediately surprised by a woman and her daughter. "All three of us were kind of shook up," he recalled, "and they hurried on across the bridge ahead of me. About the time I got across the bridge, here came a little girl on her bicycle—she took one good look at me, turned around and rode like a bat out of hell away from me."

Reese was certain that the child was intent on alerting the Germans, yet he still continued carefully along the road. "About a mile out of the village, I saw a man coming riding a bicycle. He didn't look too threatening, so I stayed on the road. As he came opposite me, he slowed and said, 'American?'" The downed American flyer acknowledged the Frenchman's query whereupon he was hustled off the road, into the brush and admonished to stay put until help arrived.

"Sure enough, in a little while he came back with another man and a spare bike which I got on, and the three of us took off down the road and away from the village," Reese recounted. At another village he was taken into a kitchen at the rear of a tavern where he was given a pillow and blankets and made to lie down. "I was beginning to feel like it had been a full day and, believe it or not, they got a doctor to attend my wounds." The doctor told Reese that his nose had been broken lengthwise, but that it would probably heal without any complications. He additionally treated the wound with sulfa powder before bandaging it.

It was night by then and the tavern was doing a good business. "We could hear a lot of commotion in there," Reese said, "and one of the Maquis—and to this day I can't believe he did this—opened the door a crack so I could see into the barroom, and it was full of German soldiers in uniform drinking beer. I'm sure the smile on my face would have been described as sickly."

Shortly after, another Frenchman rushed into the kitchen and raised the alarm. Reese recalled: "It seems the Germans had originally thought I had perished in the plane, but later on had found my parachute and Mae West. They found my tracks leading to that wooded area and had lined up about 100 soldiers abreast, armed with machine guns, and they marched through the wooded area gunning every dense thicket they found and were now searching all the villages in the area."

His rescuers rushed Reese to a barn and hid him in a hayloft where he remained undisturbed. The following day he pedaled a bike back to Épagne with a Maquis escort where he was given over to the care of the town's mayor and his family. Reese remembered them as Papa and Mama Doizlet and their teenaged sons Andre and Henri. "Every day I witnessed feats of bravery and love that I will remember and cherish to the end of my days."

Reese remembered that Papa Doizlet was nervous and anxious. He and Henri had unexpectedly come upon three German trucks on the evening of the day Reese had been shot down. The father and son team destroyed them and killed 26 soldiers. Papa was upset because they had been explicitly instructed by their contacts in England to use their explosives against trains alone.

Reese was especially touched by Mama Doizlet. "Two things I really remember about Mama—her cooking and her love for everybody around her, but especially for Papa. She knew that each morning that she said goodbye to Papa might be the last time she would see him, so her goodbye kiss in the morning was a sexual experience by itself—two old folks kissing up a storm." Reese remembered that the reunions at the end of the day were even more amorous.

He also recalled that the French Resistance seemed ubiquitous. He remembered that the local gendarme stopped by the Doizlet house regularly. "The first time I saw him he was in the house before I was aware of it and, of course, I thought I was in big trouble, but he laughed and gave me a hug instead. About then, Papa came in and the gendarme handed a small bag he had brought to Papa." The bag held explosives to replace those that Papa and Henri had used against the German trucks.

The Allies completed their liberation of Paris on August 25, just more than a week after Reese had gone down. During that time and through the rest of August and into September Reese enjoyed a somewhat relaxed and bucolic life at the Doizlet house. Another downed airman, a Canadian bomber gunner, was secreted into the house and Reese recalled that he genuinely enjoyed the other man's company. "Having someone to talk to did make the time pass faster."

As it appeared that liberation was imminent, the elder Doizlet brought out a store of champagne and cigars that he had cached early in the war. The champagne had kept well but the cigars were somewhat desiccated. "Papa felt the time had come to start enjoying them," Reese said, "so we had champagne with every evening meal, and I had one very dry cigar every evening."

Reese recalled how a flight of P-47s caught a convoy of German trucks and put on a show for his hosts and their neighbors. "We all ran to a nearby hill and sat down and really enjoyed the ensuing actions. The P-47s had about ten trucks trapped on the road, having destroyed the lead and trail trucks and were setting up a pattern to take care of the rest." The display of firepower left an impression. The eight .50 caliber machine guns in each aircraft combined to literally lift and scoot the big German trucks, effectively turning them into junk. "The destruction was complete," Reese said, "and I know the P-47 pilots got a kick out of the people up on the hill jumping up and down and cheering them on. When they left they flew over us and rocked their wings."

Although the Germans were on the run in that part of France, it was still a dangerous time. Reese recalled: "The Maquis were ordered to try to hold the two cement bridges in our area—one at Épagne and the other at the little village upriver that I had crossed on the day I was shot down. Papa decided that the time had come for the Maquis to come out of hiding and disguises. They would have to man the bridges and fight for them."

While the women and children were moved to safety, Reese was assigned to escort a German spy—a female who had been working as a prostitute in the area since 1939. With Papa's Llama .45-caliber pistol, Papa's son Andre and another teenager, Reese took the woman four or five miles toward a Maquis hideout, before settling down for the night. The woman's hands were bound and her ankle was tied with a rope that was attached to Reese's wrist. "She was about thirty years old and could speak some English and was quite confident that this was all a mistake. Thank God she didn't try to get away."

The small party made it through a forest to the Maquis hiding place the next morning. Reese was stunned by what he found; an expansive log structure that looked as if it belonged in the American Wild West. "A stockade with a ten-foot log wall around what looked for all the world like a fort. It was really large with stables and barns on the ground floor and living quarters above, and the place was alive with about sixty or seventy wives and assorted children. Some of the women were armed, and all were very curious about us." As the first American that many of them had seen, Reese was a welcome validation that his countrymen were on their way.

After tucking into a huge meal prepared by the makeshift fort's older women, Reese and Andre took their prisoner to a nearby river so that she could wash. "As she finished," he recounted, "our little gendarme came strolling up, said something to Andre and smiled at me, took one look at our spy, let out a scream and piled into her with both fists going." Stunned, Reese hesitated for a moment. "I finally decided this was my prisoner, grabbed him by the collar, lifted him up and off her and said, 'No!'"

The woman was a bloody mess; the gendarme had ripped her pierced earrings free and bashed up her nose and mouth. Reese later learned that she had betrayed the gendarme's brother to the German SS and that he had been tortured to death. "When his relatives buried him, you could no longer tell that he had been a man, but since no other Maquis had been arrested, it meant he had not talked."

The Germany spy was back in the river tending to her cuts and bruises when another Maquis came out of the woods talking excitedly. Andre translated for him: German soldiers were nearby and Papa Doizlet wanted Reese to shoot the woman. After the previous couple of days she knew too many of the Maquis and Doizlet did not want to take a chance that she might return to German hands.

Reese wasn't ready to do such a thing. He pretended that he didn't understand what Andre was telling him to do. "While we were talking, the Maquis went up to her, shot her five times, dumped her body in the river, said something to Andre and took off." It was time to guard the two bridges.

Most of the men—about thirty—were dispatched under Papa Doizlet's command to protect the bridge at the little village north of Épagne. "They set up along the bank of the river and of course all the women and children from the villages were already at the stockade except for four or five old folks who couldn't travel and one eleven- or twelve-year-old girl who wouldn't leave her grandfather."

Reese was sent with the Canadian and a group of poorly-armed youngsters to protect the Épagne bridge. "I couldn't believe some of the weapons the teenagers had—pitchforks, a shotgun with a broken stock held together with wire, some rusty antique rifles with three or four cartridges. Reese had the Llama pistol and seven or eight hand grenades, while Andre had a Sten submachine gun. The Canadian had a decent rifle as did two of the grown men.

It didn't matter. The Germans never showed. "About 1400 that afternoon, we heard heavy firing from the other bridge; however, neither friend nor foe—not a single soul came down our road," remembered Reese. "About an hour later, a Maquis came running down from the other bridge and said we were all to come help."

There had been a sharp fight that sent the Germans in retreat. Reese recalled the scene: "We cautiously approached the village and our worst fears were realized. The old folks had all been shot and the little girl tied to a bed and repeatedly raped, blood all over, she was in deep shock, conscious but her mind a complete blank. We cleaned her up and the Maquis took her to the doctor that fixed me up, but the last I heard, they did not expect her to live."

The episode had a pronounced effect on Reese's perspective of the war. "From this point on, every time I turned my machine guns loose, I would be smiling, really enjoying it, no matter who or what was on the receiving end, as long as I thought it was German."

An American jeep with two soldiers drove into Épagne the next day. Reese and his Canadian friend and the rest of the town turned out to see them. "The two soldiers were engineers scouting for Patton's tanks and were lost and very surprised to find we had two bridges intact." The soldiers agreed to take Reese back to friendly lines. "It was really a happy, sad farewell with much hugging and kissing as I really did feel like part of the Doizlet family, and I felt that they considered me their American son."

Reese was in London three days later during the second week of September 1944. There, he was debriefed about every aspect of his time in France. "I also had a complete physical—no permanent damage, but I still had a pretty good knot on my forehead." Although he was given a new uniform, the bump on his head kept him from being fitted with a hat—there was none large enough.

Reese remembered that one helpful saleslady at the Oxford Street Selfridges—unable to help him—apologized and advised him to "keep his

pecker up." Reese couldn't hide his surprise. "I guess she realized something was lost in the translation by the expression on my face. She quickly
explained that in England that expression meant to keep a stiff upper lip."
In the end, he went against regulations and did without a complete uniform. "The flight surgeon wrote a letter excusing me from wearing a hat
around town and soon every MP in London knew who I was."

Reese found letters waiting for him. One of them was from his father,
dated September 8, 1944, when in fact—unbeknownst to his family—he
had already been returned to American control. The contents of the letter
are representative of the hopes and fears and faith in God that many parents of American servicemen shared.

Dear Son:

On Wednesday of last week we received a telegram from the
Adjutant General of the Army, informing us that you had been
reported missing in action over France since August 17. I don't
need to tell you what a shock this was to us. Although we had
known, of course, that you were facing grave danger every day,
we had been unable to realize that some day such a message
might come to us. Somehow, we had just instinctively felt that
you would come through all right—that your marvelous training,
fine physical condition and natural level-headedness, plus your
and our faith in God's protecting care, would pull you through.
We still feel that way. That's why I'm writing you this letter, and
why Betty has continued to write—so there will be a few letters
from home on hand to greet you upon your return. I probably
shall not write again before we hear further from or concerning
you, as I know that you will communicate with us just as soon as
you can. . . .

During this time—about ten days—Reese had plenty of time to relax
in London. "I collected some back pay, all I had to do was call in once a
day, so it was party time. I also did some sightseeing and shopping. It
seems everywhere I went I ran into somebody I knew and they immediately had to buy me a drink—or drinks—and hear my story."

Because of his experience, Reese was given orders back to the States
but he didn't want to go. "I really had some conflicting feelings about this.
I sure enough wanted to see Betty again, but I also had an entirely different viewpoint on this war. By turning down my chance to come home, I
felt almost fatalistic about ever coming home, but I had to do it and I did."

In fact, Reese was one of the first airmen to evade who was allowed to stay in combat. The most important reason was the fact that the people who had aided him were safe behind American lines and could not be easily harmed by the Germans in the event that Reese was ever shot down again, captured and forced to give up their names.

Reese was one of more than five thousand Allied airmen who were shot down over France and safely returned to England. Their return was made possible by thousands of "helpers" who were part of the polyglot of groups—including the Maquis—that comprised the French Resistance. These helpers lent their aid at tremendous risk not only to themselves but also to their families and villages. Indeed, the penalty for such activities imposed by the German occupiers was death. Still, their contribution to the Allied war effort was real and significant, and one that endeared them forever to the flyers and their families.

Reese was one of more than a dozen 352nd airmen who were shot down and evaded. After returning to duty he flew his next mission on September 25, 1944. It was more than three weeks before his twenty-first birthday.

CHAPTER 23

Taking Care of Business

Many of the missions the men flew in the P-51 exceeded four hours while a few of them lasted an additional two or even three more hours. Flights of this length posed biological issues. Of course, there was the stiffness and pain that came from sitting in a small, cramped space for such an extended period while flying in dangerous skies. Likewise, the cold often made men miserable. And flying for a long time at high altitude in an unpressurized cockpit degraded their alertness and reflexes in subtle ways. Finally, the often urgent need to urinate was not to be discounted as a significant discomfort.

Exacerbating this last issue was the fact that many of the men drank one or more cups of coffee prior to going flying. Despite the fact that they were young—and had healthy bladders—the pilots still emptied them as completely as they could before they flew. Punchy Powell recalled: "We always took that last-minute piss on the tail wheel before each mission. That was a must."

To facilitate the execution of this very basic bodily need, the aircraft was equipped with a rubber relief tube that was vented to the outside. The business end, shaped like a funnel, was tucked away on the cockpit floor when not in use. When the need arose, the pilot unfastened the tube from where it was clipped, inserted his penis in the funnel and did his business. The urine traveled through the relief tube, down the length of the fuselage, and out the exit port located at the bottom of the empennage, forward of the rudder.

This was in theory. The reality was often quite different. First, the men flew over enemy territory during a significant portion of their missions and were frequently too busy to bother with their bladders. Another issue was the fact that, especially when escorting the bombers, they were flying in tactical formation. Doing so with a handful of genitalia wasn't easy or advisable. But the biggest challenge was their clothing. It was very difficult for them to remove their gloves and paw through layers of flying gear in the extreme cold. Finding and extracting a private member shrunken by hours of sitting in the cold was a real challenge. "Getting John Henry ready for action was not easy," Powell confirmed. "We usually wore long underwear, our olive drab GI shorts and our GI wool pants." Likewise, Bill Reese noted that he never even tried: "Too many clothes and my hands would have been very cold out of my heavy gloves!"

These observations were underscored by Don McKibben's recollection of the only instance in which he tried to use the relief tube. He attempted it while flying at 30,000 feet in a P-47 over Germany:

The sky was brilliant blue, outside air temp was minus 50 degrees Fahrenheit and I had to negotiate through several layers of clothing while in a seated position. This required the use of three hands: one to hold the relief tube, one to unzip flies and search for the elusive body part, and a third to keep the aircraft from careening all over the sky. Just as I thought I had everything lined up and was starting the offload, I had to free one hand to level the aircraft. There was no stopping the stream, which missed its mark and sprayed the cockpit. The urine, steaming at approximately 98.6 degrees Fahrenheit, at that altitude, instantly turned to frost that coated the inside of my canopy. Suddenly, I was flying blind on a bright, sunny day. I was busy with the defroster control when someone called out on the radio, 'Bogies at 3 o'clock high.'

Not wanting to be caught in a fight with his barn door(s) open, McKibben scraped with a good deal of vigor at the glaze on the right side of the canopy. Only when he cleared a small peephole and saw that the bogies were friendly fighters did he breathe a little easier. A short time later, his aircraft's defroster finally cleared the rest of the canopy

"There was also a sort of unwritten rule that if you used the relief tube, you were responsible for cleaning it," remembered Powell. "That might have been another reason that we didn't use it more often." There was the additional issue that the men didn't like putting their private parts where those of others had been.

And there were other considerations. Urine was sometimes trapped in the tube during a flight and didn't have time to evaporate before the aircraft flew again. It subsequently froze and blocked the tube when the aircraft got airborne and climbed to altitude. Or, if it was clear during the first use, trapped urine often froze and precluded a successful second use. Don Bryan recalled an incident:

> The first time you used it at any altitude was okay. The problem came when you had to do it two or more times and the temperature was 20 or 30 below freezing [at high altitude] there was a good chance that the tube would be frozen. Most of time if you got down to smoking altitude [below about 10,000 feet] the blockage would melt. One time I had to use it a second time when I had been above 20,000 feet for the entire mission. It was frozen and I pretty well filled it up. I was holding it in my left hand waiting until I could drop down to smoking altitude when some SOB yelled BREAK!! I dropped it and grabbed the throttle.

Bryan made it safely back to Bodney; by then, the dropped tube full of urine had been forgotten. It remained so until the next day when Kirk Noyes, the crew chief for Bryan's ship, *Little One III*, climbed into the cockpit and closed the canopy to perform some maintenance tasks. Bryan remembered that the weather was cool but the sun was strong and he was outside enjoying it with several other pilots. It didn't take long before the stink of urine drove Noyes out of *Little One III*. Angry, he stomped over to where Bryan sat with the other pilots and demanded to know "what the hell happened." Bryan recalled that, "It took a bit, but I did manage to cool him down."

Powell recollected that the only time he used the relief tube was to prove a point as much as anything else. "In our squadron [328th] we vowed that the first time we flew over Berlin we would urinate on it. Of course, at high altitude it vaporized immediately, but at least we could say that we had pissed on Berlin."

Just as the long missions were hard on pilots with less than heroic bladders, they were also hard on smokers. They were forced to go much longer without a cigarette than they otherwise would have. Smoking was not a good idea while over enemy territory for all the obvious reasons, but it was also quite literally impossible as a cigarette simply would not burn in the rarefied air of high altitude.

Clarence "Spike" Cameron remembered his nicotine cravings: "I couldn't wait to get down to a lower altitude once we were on our way home. I'd light up just as soon as we got below about ten thousand feet where there was enough oxygen for a cigarette to stay lit. I don't think anything ever tasted so good."[1] He wasn't alone. During the 1940s, more than two of every three males in the United States were smokers and the rate was at least that high in the 352nd. "Pretty much all of us smoked," remembered another pilot. "It was not just a social thing, but it was also part of the fighter pilot image."

CHAPTER 24

Unheralded Heroics

It is undeniable that courageous feats in battle sometimes go unheralded for any number of reasons. As the combat history of the 352nd spanned the most violent period of the air war, it is certain that the bravery of at least a handful of its men went unrecognized. Such was nearly the case with Joseph Broadwater of the 328th Fighter Squadron.

Broadwater was assigned to the 352nd during July 1944 and his performance during the remainder of the summer was satisfactory but not particularly remarkable. He was with the 328th on September 12, 1944, when the group navigated to a point northwest of Madgeburg and attached itself to the 351st Bomb Group, a B-17 unit, at the front of the bomber stream.

Although the focus that day was on hitting a selection of six different oil targets, the mission was intended to provoke a sizable Luftwaffe reaction as much as it was to cut Germany's oil supplies. Accordingly, the route that the 351st Bomb Group was assigned—at the head of the 94th Bomb Wing—was a circuitous one that passed through some of the most heavily defended parts of Germany. Thomas Clarke, the radar navigator-bombardier aboard the lead B-17, recalled how his fellow crewmen went wide-eyed upon seeing the mission map during the briefing. "We looked at the general route map on the briefing board, somewhat shocked. One pilot said, 'some clown put up that crazy route to scare us.'"[1] He was wrong and the 351st took off on schedule.

It wasn't long after the 352nd established itself overhead the 351st when word was received that some of the trailing bomber groups were under attack. Clarke took comfort in the blue-nosed Mustangs that arced overhead. But much to his dismay, they didn't stay. "Some sonofabitchen [*sic*] pilot back there called in panic, 'We could use some help back here.'"

Clarke was crestfallen when the air commander cleared the 352nd back to the fight. "I thought, Christ, we're dead ducks." His spirits plummeted further when he realized that only a single P-51 remained behind as a radio relay to the rest of the 352nd. Clarke recalled this with some bitterness: "In spite of the briefing we all received, this fighter commander overhead had a knee-jerk reaction and took all of his fighters to the rear, without a hope in hell that he could get back to the front to fight for us. . . ."

Soon after, Clarke recalled that the sky to his front appeared to be "full of specks." When the commander aboard Clarke's bomber called out the aircraft, the pilot of the lone P-51 responded: "I see them, and I'm going forward to check it out." The pilot also called back to his 352nd comrades and directed them to return immediately.

Over the intercom, the top turret gunner aboard Clarke's ship counted aloud the number of fighters in the enemy formation. He stopped after reaching seventy and then called out: "Sir, our fighter is attacking the German formation! He has rolled over and is attacking them from their rear. He is flying formation with them. He has exploded one, now another one. . . . Oh, they blew him out of the sky!"

Although the P-51 pilot had knocked down only a pair of the enemy fighters, their formation was disrupted and it took time to get formed again. During that period, elements of the 352nd returned and tore into the mixed force of Me-109s and FW-190s. Although the 351st Bomb Group lost six B-17s to all causes, it is likely that their losses would have been much worse had it not been for the aggressive P-51 pilot that was their sole escort.

Because Broadwater had been alone, no one in the 352nd knew what happened to him. When he didn't return he was simply listed as missing. Typically, the bomber and fighter units did not communicate with each other and the heroics of the lone Mustang pilot were soon forgotten by all except Tom Clarke.

It wasn't until several decades later that Clarke, who had felt especially indebted to the unknown Mustang pilot ever since that day in September 1944, sleuthed out his name. An exhaustive review of relevant documents convinced Clarke that his hero could have been no one other than Broadwater. And so, only just barely, Joseph Broadwater's selfless actions escaped the pitiless maw of obscurity.

The 352nd, excluding the thousand or so personnel making up Bodney's service units, counted nearly a thousand men on its rolls. It was a large organization and it was impossible for any one person to know every other. Aside from the fact that it was big, the 352nd was also dynamic and its composition changed constantly as new personnel arrived and old hands departed. As an example, the command of the 328th Fighter Squadron changed ten times. Some of those men were lost in combat and, in fact, combat losses were a chief contributor to the flux in the unit's pilot roster.

Broadwater's case is instructive. He flew his first sortie with the 352nd, a check flight, on July 28, 1944. On July 30th he flew an orientation hop and subsequently flew three more administrative flights before his first combat sortie on August 17th. It was less than a month later, on September 12, that he was shot down and killed. And so, the 352nd's roster changed once more.

Of the ten combat missions Broadwater flew during his short tenure with the 352nd, his logbook shows that seven of them were bomber escorts. His typical descriptions of these escorts included the words, "dry run," meaning that there was no enemy fighter activity. This was indeed the nature of bomber escort missions; for the most part they were tedious, bone numbingly cold flights that nonetheless demanded sharp vigilance for those increasingly infrequent instances when the Luftwaffe fighters attacked. Yet Broadwater's story validates the fact that it took only one of those instances for an airman to die. He was shot down during his first encounter with the enemy.

The various mission types the 352nd flew were assigned unique names. A *Ramrod* was a pure bomber escort mission. A *Rodeo* was a bomber escort mission intended to provoke a response by the Luftwaffe. A *Rhubarb* was a fighter-only mission generally flown at low altitude; it was intended to shoot up targets of opportunity, both air and ground. On *No Ball* missions, the fighters escorted bombers against German missile sites, whereas *Chattanooga* missions went after the German rail infrastructure.

New pilots were obviously necessary to take the places of those who were rotated home or shot down. The perspectives of the old hands toward the newcomers were varied and depended on their own experiences and personalities. Don McKibben's attitude was fairly typical. He had been part of the 352nd since the beginning and had seen many of his friends, including Ted Fahrenwald, shot down.

> As for replacement pilots, I think it was generally true that the veteran pilots greeted newcomers within the following construct: First, the guy earned his new assignment, and deserved all the cooperation and assistance I could give him to help him adjust to the outfit. Second, aside from what he deserved, he would be expected to cover the ass of whoever he was assigned to fly with. Me, for example. Third, I would offer and maintain an arms-length friendship. Having lost many classmates and close buddies up to that point, I wasn't enthusiastic about adding another good friend to the list.

Ribbons and medals and other personal military decorations are representations of a man's worth, of what he has accomplished, of where he has been and of what he has been a part of. Napoleon declared, "A soldier will fight long and hard for a bit of colored ribbon." It was true long before Napoleon's time and it is still true today. And it was certainly no different during World War II.

In the late summer of 1944, having completed his two combat tours with the 352nd, Punchy Powell was sent to fly a desk at the 66th Fighter Wing's headquarters at Sawston Hall. "Because I had newspaper experience as a civilian they used me to screen all the news releases coming from the various fighter groups in the wing. It was a boring job and I didn't get to fly that much."

Consequently, Powell was delighted one day when the wing's commanding officer, Brigadier General Murray Woodbury, asked around his staff to see who had experience flying P-51s in combat. "I told him that I was qualified in the Mustang," Powell remembered, "and he asked me if I would fly with him the next day to observe one of the wing's fighter groups attacking a German airfield. I agreed right away."

"The next morning we met on the flight line of one of the fighter groups," Powell recounted. "The general let me know what the specifics for the flight were. We weren't going to actually attack the airfield with the rest of the group, but rather we were going to fly overhead and watch."

Powell and Woodbury took off separately from the rest of the group and timed their flight so as to arrive just before the attack was scheduled. "We climbed to 30,000 feet," recalled Powell. "It was equivalent to being in a foxhole in the sky—there was just about nothing that could touch us up there. In fact, we were so damned high that we could hardly see the attack. The airplanes looked like ants."

In any event, the flight was little more than a sightseeing excursion. "The trip back was uneventful," remembered Powell. "When we landed and got out of our planes I started filling out our paperwork and asked the general how he wanted to record the flight. He told me to mark it as a training mission; that made perfect sense to me as we really didn't do much."

Three weeks later the wing staff was called out to parade formation in their Class A uniforms. Powell remembered being stunned when Woodbury was called forward. "They awarded him the Distinguished Flying Cross for that mission," he recalled. "I was so pissed that I really wanted to go into his office and say, 'General, if you wanted a DFC that bad, I could have given you one of mine and we could have saved the gas we used that day.' But I was smarter than that and kept my mouth shut."

No doubt, undecorated as he was and surrounded by youngsters like Powell who were bedecked with hard-won awards, Woodbury felt inadequate. He used his imagination to turn the mission into something far beyond what it was, something that merited special recognition. "If that mission earned him the DFC," Powell recalled with disgust, "then logic says it should have been recorded in my logbook as a combat mission. Instead, it was logged as a training flight."

Human nature being what it is, it is certain that Woodbury was not the only officer who abused his authority in the same manner.

CHAPTER 25

To the Sound of the Guns

Sometimes it wasn't possible to make the distinction between aggressiveness and foolhardiness until after the event. Richard Brookins toed that fine line during the big air combats of September 27, 1944. He was flying as Don Bryan's element leader when a massive formation of 150 enemy fighters was spotted heading for the bomber stream. Although Brookins pushed his engine to the limit, he was left behind as the rest of the flight raced to intercept the enemy fighters before they reached the bombers.

Brookins's attention was caught by a second group of German fighters. "I saw a box of 60 FW-190 and Me-190s [sic] at nine o'clock and approx 1,000–2000 feet above me. There was no support behind me and being alone I turned up and into them. I was too busy to fire as I went through them."[1]

The Germans scattered, probably as much to avoid a collision as for any other reason. "Most of them spread out," recalled Brookins, "some split-essing and some climbing. As I passed them I rolled over on my back and followed and [sic] FW-190 down. I closed fast and gave him a short burst from 200–100 yds. The E/A exploded in flames and broke up into several pieces." Brookins watched the enemy pilot leap from the stricken aircraft and saw his parachute blossom at 16,000 feet.

Although he had been absurdly outnumbered, there is an argument that Brookins's attack was not as imprudent as it might have seemed at first blush. First, he likely caught the enemy flyers by surprise when he tore through them; they had little chance to respond to his attack. And more importantly, they ran an enormous risk of colliding with each other if they turned to chase him down. Some pilots liked the idea of being out-numbered because they were presented with targets wherever they turned, whereas their opponents had to be careful not to shoot each other.

Although they flew in the same skies, the Eighth Air Force's bomber and fighter crews flew two different wars. The bomber crews were charged with the heavy work; it was their bombs that blasted the guts out of Germany. That fact was not lost on the Germans and they did everything they could to destroy as many bombers—and the men who flew them—as they could. Essentially, the bombers and their crews were targets.

It was a hateful existence. In most cases it was fate rather than skill that determined which crews survived. Certainly they could create some of their own luck by flying good tight formations that maximized the fire-power of their defensive guns against the Luftwaffe's fighters. Or they could react with speed and efficiency when their aircraft were damaged. But it was sheer chance that determined which flak burst hit which bomber, or which formation of bombers was targeted by the German fight-ers. These were things that the bomber men could not control and many fine men were blown out of the sky through no fault of their own. That being the case, the very act of climbing into their aircraft, mission after mission, was a very special sort of bravery.

And they loved their fighter pilot counterparts. An official study con-ducted after the war noted this fact:

> Fighter pilots who were troubled with misgivings about the worth of escort work had only to head to the nearest bomber field to learn that their big brothers regarded them as knights errant whose very presence sent spirits up and losses down. . . . To combat crews, few sights were lovelier than the prancing of friendly fight-ers around bomber formations during the quiet stretches of a mis-sion, or more breathtaking than their sudden appearance—deus ex machina fashion—at an instant of ultimate extremity. Bomber crewmen who had ever stared straight at an onrushing FW-190 for long seconds before catching sight of a P-51 on its tail would not soon forget the emotions of that moment.[2]

Naturally, the nature of the air war was different for fighter pilots like those of the 352nd. They were hunters; their job was to protect the bombers by shooting down other aircraft or chasing them away. And their fate was largely in their own hands. If they were ambushed by an aircraft they didn't see, it was their own fault. If they were outmaneuvered and outgunned by an enemy fighter, it was largely because their own skills were wanting. Certainly bad luck in the form of mechanical failures or unlucky flak bursts played a role in their survival, but to a much lesser extent when compared to the bomber crews. It must also be considered that as the sole occupants of their aircraft, fighter pilots did not have much time to dwell on the bad things that might happen to them.

These factors combined to have an interesting effect. Eighth Air Force surveys showed that three of four fighter pilots desired a second combat tour after completion of their first. This stood in dramatic contrast to the responses of the bomber pilots which showed that only one of four desired a second combat tour. What makes these results ironic is the fact that fighter losses during this period actually exceeded bomber losses.[3]

This data notwithstanding, fighter pilots generally had an aggressive perspective on their duties. It was common in the 352nd for the pilots to wait around the operations area in the event that a special mission was called or another pilot came off the schedule for one reason or another. Fahrenwald wrote home that the pilots were forced to take time off: "Get two days off every ten days and can't fly on our days off. New rule the boss put in because we wuz all hangin' around moaning and trying to get on a milk-run mission when we wuz supposed to be relaxing somewhere." In an oblique reference to the partying that many of the pilots engaged in while on their days off, Fahrenwald noted, "If that two days off is relaxation, then somebody better dig out his dictionary."[4]

Don Bryan recollected the same attitude. "We had to be told we *couldn't* go. We wanted to go on missions, we wanted to fight. I remember I used to get mad when I was told I couldn't go out on a mission." In fact, Bryan was told he couldn't fly on September 17, 1944, when virtually all the Eighth's fighter groups were committed to protecting the Allied airborne forces dropping into the Netherlands as part of Operation MARKET GARDEN. Those parachute- and glider-delivered forces were charged with fighting a new route through the Low Countries and into northern Germany.

"I found out I wasn't scheduled to go on the mission because my airplane wasn't ready," Bryan recalled. "I rushed down to talk to my crew chief, Kirk Noyes, and he wouldn't give my airplane to me. He said it was due for a hundred hour inspection and it couldn't fly. And everything else that could fly was already assigned to other pilots."

Bryan didn't give up. "I saw that the two squadron hacks, a pair of war-weary P-51s that were kept around for odd jobs, were still on the field.

I went to see the CO to talk him into letting me go out with them." The 328th's commander, John Edwards, told Bryan that if he could scrape up two more aircraft to make a flight of four, he could go.

"I got another pilot from the 328th, then called over to the 486th and got hold of Bill Whisner; he wasn't scheduled either. He called over to the 487th and was able to scrounge up two more aircraft and another pilot to make up the rest of our four-ship." The four pilots, on their own, were able to do pretty much as they pleased. With Bryan in the lead they made their way across the North Sea and over Holland where USAAF C-47s threaded their way toward their drop zones through wicked pockets of antiaircraft fire.

"We parked ourselves overhead the route and I saw a C-47 towing two gliders get hit by an eighty-eight," Bryan remembered. The 88 millimeter cannon was the standard German antiaircraft weapon. And it was deadly. "The Gooney Bird went down in flames and the gliders went down with him—their pilots must not have released the tow cables. There were at least fifty men killed by just that one gun."

"That really made me angry," Bryan remembered. "There were dozens of good men dead because of that single gun." Still, try as he might, he and his ad hoc flight couldn't find the antiaircraft gun and its crew. "It was somewhere in the brushy fields and patches of woods below us, but the Germans were expert at camouflage and we couldn't find it." Exasperated, Bryan started to lead the flight away in search of other targets. "Then," he recalled, "I saw another C-47 with two gliders get hit in the same area. And again, both gliders went down with it." For whatever reason, the glider pilots were unable to separate from their tow aircraft.

Livid, Bryan whipped his flight around to renew his search for the gun. "The Germans manning that gun knew better than to shoot at us," he said. "We could kill them—the Gooney birds could not." Still, the four pilots had no more success finding the gun than they had earlier. "I was really frustrated," Bryan remembered. "If we had been able to find that gun earlier, the men with the second C-47 and its gliders would have still been alive. And it really bothered me that the glider pilots didn't release their cables; I couldn't understand why they let themselves get pulled down by the Gooney Birds."

Bryan spotted a third C-47 as it approached the area with another pair of gliders. "I dropped down low behind it and followed in trail as it flew the same route as the other two C-47s," he recounted. Just as before the transport was hit by the big gun. "But this time, I had him," remembered Bryan. "I saw the muzzle flash when he fired." While the doomed C-47 and its two gliders fell to earth, Bryan hauled the nose of his P-51 skyward, dropped his wing tanks and prepared to dive on the enemy position.

"As I dropped my nose down," he remembered, "the engine quit. When I released the wing tanks I had forgotten to switch the fuel selector to the internal tanks." Unperturbed by the sudden quiet, Bryan kept his eyes on the enemy gun as his aircraft closed the range. Finally, he pulled the trigger. "I opened fire and really let them have it."

Bryan finished firing, pulled his aircraft away from the gun and reached down to the fuel selector switch. The engine caught and a few seconds later was roaring at full speed. "I never worried about that engine," he said. "I knew it would start." The three other pilots joined Bryan and together they made repeated firing passes. "The gun was hidden along a fence line and the four of us strafed it and everything around it. We found some trucks and wagons and troops—we really chewed the place up. No one there was going to shoot down any more Gooney Birds."

"It was the only time I fired my guns in anger," Bryan said. "So many dead boys because I couldn't find that gun."

Following the initial troop insertions, the following message was received from Major General Paul Williams, the commander of IX Troop Carrier Command: "The officers and men of troop carrier command express sincere appreciation to the men of VIII Fighter Command for their splendid cooperation in our common effort under difficult weather conditions and in the face of determined enemy opposition. Please convey my personal appreciation to all members of your command."

John Evans was a bomber pilot who completed his tour on the day prior to the Normandy invasion. "Throughout my thirty missions in B-24s I never once saw an enemy fighter, though I did see plenty of flak." Even so, his aircraft never suffered any real damage.

"I certainly did not want to return to the United States and get back into the training command," he recalled, "so I applied for a tour in fighters." When asked which type of fighter he wanted to fly, he told his commander with just a touch of sarcasm that he had seen plenty of P-38s land at their base with an engine out, but that he had never noticed any single-engine fighters recover with a dead engine. Ultimately, he was assigned to the 352nd's 487th Fighter Squadron and was excited at the prospect of flying the sleek, blue-nosed Mustangs. That excitement notwithstanding, his luck finally failed him. On September 25, 1944, he had to bail out over

Frankfurt when his ship developed coolant trouble and the engine died. He spent the remainder of the war as a POW.

During 1944, aside from training new fighter pilots from scratch, the Luftwaffe sourced experienced fliers from wherever they were available. Pilots who had been removed from service for various reasons were brought back, bomber pilots were converted and instructors were pulled from the flying schools. Stripping the flight schools was a particularly desperate and self-defeating move as it simply exacerbated a problem that was already bad.

Hermann Buchner was charged with getting a disparate group of these fliers ready for combat. He had been a successful ground attack pilot flying FW-190s on the Eastern Front and had scored forty-five aerial victories against the Soviets, and a single B-17 during a brief stint in Romania. During the summer of 1944 he was posted as a flight instructor to the airfield at Prossnitz, Austria, where he was given twenty pilots from various backgrounds and an equal number of FW-190s.

Buchner remembered that he pushed the men at a brutal pace. "Now things were happening fast and we flew four or five practice operations per day." Although the men were slated to fly the FW-190 in the ground attack role, Buchner emphasized the more difficult skills of aerial combat. "The men were learning quickly. Many of them had flown no operations for a long time and had been away from the front for too long. Some of the Staff Officers complained to me . . . about the way the flying was being carried out. They were of the opinion that Schlachtflieger [ground-attack pilots] should not be fighter pilots."

Indeed, the attitude among some of his trainees was poor. "Some had had enough of the whole thing, but there were also those who did not want to go to the front, at least not so quickly. The actual situation at the front meant that the pilots of the Schlacht groups had to learn the tactics of the US fighters."[5]

One notable example of a Luftwaffe fighter pilot who was returned to service late in the war when he might otherwise not have been was Walther Wever. He was the son of the Chief of the Air Command Office of the same name who had been killed in an aircraft crash in 1936. The younger Wever started flying combat operations on the Eastern Front during 1943 and had been credited with forty aerial victories by the summer of 1944. On July 10, 1944, he was shot down by ground fire and badly

injured, losing one of his feet to amputation. After several months of recuperation he started flying again and returned to combat operations during
February 1945 as an Me-262 pilot. He was subsequently shot down and
killed in aerial combat on April 10, 1945.

A four-ship flight from the 487th Fighter Squadron was downed by
enemy fighters on September 23, 1944. It was the greatest loss suffered by
the 352nd in air-to-air combat. Clarence Johnson, Phanor Waters, Joe
Ayers, and John Clark were jumped somewhere in the vicinity of Almelo
in the Netherlands. The paucity of information in the group mission summary report indicates that no one knew what happened to the four pilots:
"Capt. Johnson, Lts. Waters, Ayers and Clark, all 487th Sqdn, Red Flight,
last seen Hengelo, 1700. Last heard on RT giving position Aimelo [*sic*] at
1730. Nothing further known."

Of the four pilots, only Clark survived. "We were flying the normal
four abreast formation at about 1500 ft when we started to get a lot of fire
from the ground. We then dropped down to 500 ft." The four blue-nosed
P-51s—with their wing tanks still attached—started an easy righthand
turn. After arcing through nearly a full circle Clark caught sight of a flight
of eight FW-190s bearing down on the four-ship. "I pushed everything to
the wall and started a sharp right turn and continued to turn right, but the
'190 behind me continued to fire and he finally got inside of me"

The enemy pilot's aim was good and Clark's Mustang was soon
aflame. He shucked the canopy, stood up and was sucked clear of the burning wreck that had been his fighter. His parachute opened only just before
he hit the ground, badly injuring a leg, and he was captured soon after.[6]

The FW-190s were from 5./JG 26. Gerhard Vogt—a forty-victory ace
at the time—was credited with two of the 352nd's flyers while Wilhelm
Mayer was awarded credit for another. The fourth Mustang was smashed
in a collision with *Fähnrich* Maximilian Busch, who was killed. Vogt was
an exceptionally accomplished pilot who had scored all his victories in the
West, his first in November 1941 before most of the pilots in the 352nd
had even entered the service. Mayer also was quite experienced, having
been credited with twenty aerial victories since the spring of 1943. Both
Vogt and Mayer were killed in air combat during January 1945. Vogt was
shot down in combat with Spitfires while Mayer was killed by Mustangs.

Notwithstanding the 487th's loss of four pilots on September 23, there
was little the Luftwaffe could do to counter what the sky over Europe had

become. The Americans had turned it into a place over which they exercised complete control whenever they wanted.

In fact, by the middle of 1944 the chief factor limiting USAAF bombing operations was no longer the availability of men and equipment, but rather the one thing that the Americans could not control. That one thing was the weather. Still, as the war progressed, weather was not as significant a consideration as it had been earlier. Radar bombing had progressed to the point where the big bomber streams could strike their targets through the clouds nearly as accurately as they could when the sky was clear. Consequently, if conditions were clear enough over England and en route into Germany, the bombers were launched even if clouds obscured the target area.

And if the bombers went to Germany, so did the fighters. The lessons driven home over Schweinfurt on October 14, 1943, were never forgotten and the big ships went nowhere without protection. Sometimes numbering more than a thousand, the American fighters were modern, fast and well-armed, and they were flown by aggressive, well-trained, and supremely confident pilots. And even if they were not as experienced as some of the most seasoned German fliers, it didn't matter. There were so many of them that the odds simply ran out against the Luftwaffe veterans. One old hand after another was killed in the bloody butchery that was the air war over Europe.

One of these German veterans was Gerhard Loos who was credited with ninety-two aerial victories, of which fourteen were scored in the West. He was shot down while flying an Me-109 near Rheinsehlen, Germany, on March 6, 1944. After successfully bailing out he fell to his death when he released his parachute harness too early while drifting toward high voltage lines. Another was Emil Bitsch who was on combat operations against the Soviet Union from June 1941 to August 1943, and was subsequently transferred to the West. During his actions against the Soviets he was credited with 104 aerial victories. He scored only four more from August 1943 until he was shot down and killed by a 352nd P-47 on March 15, 1944. Wolf-Dietrich Wilcke was credited with 162 aerial victories—25 in the West—during 732 missions. He was shot down and killed by P-51s on March 23, 1944. Karl Heinz-Kempf had been on combat operations since 1940 and had 445 missions and 65 aerial victories—17 scored in the West—under his belt by the time he was shot down and killed over Belgium on September 3, 1944.

These men are only a small sample of the many high-scoring Luftwaffe flyers that were downed during 1944. Although they were among the best in the world, they were simply overwhelmed by enormous numbers of good Allied pilots flying superb machines. And not to be discounted as a contributing factor was the fatigue that dogged them due to the gruelling operational tempo. Basically, they flew until they were killed.

It is also worth noting that many of these men tallied impressive scores on the Eastern Front against the Soviets but failed to score similar successes in the West. This is indicative of the differences in training and tactics between the Red Air Force flyers and those from the United States, Great Britain and the Commonwealth nations. Although these differences—and the reasons for them—might be debated at length, the incontrovertible fact was that the Soviet pilots were simply not as good as their counterparts in the West. Rather, the fighter units in the West, of which the 352nd was representative, handled the Luftwaffe on much better than even terms.

The Allies started moving tactical air units onto airfields in Normandy almost immediately after establishing a lodgement. The primary purpose for doing so was to get as close as possible to the troops they were supporting. A secondary benefit was that they could recover aircraft that were low on fuel or damaged. Pilots that might have been lost while crossing the North Sea or English Channel could land safely on the continent. It was an advantage that was leveraged immediately and regularly. The 352nd released a story on September 13, 1944 that described one such occurrence when John C. Meyer landed at an airfield in Belgium that had just been abandoned by the Germans:

> When he climbed out of his cockpit he saw that four other 51 [P-51] pilots were in the same fix. The Germans were still shelling one end of the nearest town, so going for help on foot was impossible. It was suggested to pool all the gas, so for four hours the five pilots drained their tanks and helped pour it into Col Meyer's *Petie*. With 35 gallons, Col. Meyer took off for Brussels, where he refueled, sent help to the others and then took-off for his base in England. The other pilots were luckier. They stayed overnight and were guests at a champagne party given by the local townspeople.[7]

Cy Doleac had a similar experience that same month. His tanks were nearly empty when he set down at an airfield. He had no idea where he was although he knew he was very close to the front lines. "I no sooner touched the ground," he recalled, "when hundreds of people sprang from the woods and surrounded the plane and covered me with flowers. I had a helluva time trying to find out where I was, but one fellow who could speak a little English told me I was in France, near the Belgian border, and that the Germans had left three days before."

A guard was quickly posted around his aircraft. "I was the first American they had seen, so men, women and children insisted on kissing me on both cheeks. When I told them I was from New Orleans, they were rather surprised I couldn't speak French."

Doleac validated the "small world" hypothesis when he went looking for fuel and crossed paths with a gasoline convoy from the Royal Canadian Air Force. "It stopped when I hailed it and who should jump out but an old RCAF chap I knew when I flew with them." The Canadians lent a helping hand and plenty of fuel, and he was ready to fly back to Bodney by early the next morning. "All my well wishers came back to see me take off, but insisted on autographing my plane. I've got enough names and addresses to last me for a long time."[8]

Most of the aircraft flown by USAAF crews in combat carried personalized markings or nose art. The practice was fairly free-wheeling and the range of artistry included cartoon characters, clever depictions of everyday objects or simple names. But among the most popular subjects were women. Wives and girlfriends were generally depicted with some measure of decorum and sensibility while those from popular culture or the imagination were often painted more indiscreetly as nudes or semi-nudes. These renderings were generally censored only when commanding officers felt that they crossed the line from artistry to pornography. And what was acceptable in one unit might not be in another. For instance, a P-47 with a bare breasted beauty painted on its nose was transferred to the 352nd from a unit that was transitioning to the P-51. Colonel Joe Mason directed the artwork's removal.

Ted Fahrenwald was characteristically glib when he wrote home about naming his aircraft. "Still pondering name for my ship. Considered naming each gun for a gal, but there are but eight guns and I don't want to play favorites." Don McKibben had no trouble christening his P-51B. He named it for the lissome *Miss Lace* from Milton Caniff's comic strip, *Male Call*. Except for the fact that she was merely a cartoon character, there was nothing to dislike about *Miss Lace*; as a physical specimen, she embodied the very finest female attributes. "Our squadron artist, Sergeant Nilan Jones, expertly painted the beguiling figure on the right side of the aircraft," recollected McKibben.

Often, the pilot had his nose art and victory markings painted on the left side of the aircraft, while the right side was generally reserved for the crew chief. However, McKibben broke from tradition to ensure that the greatest number of people had an opportunity to appreciate *Miss Lace*'s features. "When parked on the ground at Bodney, between the perimeter road and the woods, only the right side of the airplane was visible to the folks passing by. I figured the critters in the woods on the other side would have no interest in the view."

There were times when two pilots shared the same aircraft. In those instances one pilot claimed one side for his artwork, while the second pilot personalized the other. Punchy Powell's first aircraft was one of these split-personality cases; he shared a P-47 with Jamie Laing. "Jamie was one of the original pilots and the plane had been assigned to him before I arrived at the unit. Since we didn't have enough Jugs at that time for all the pilots, Jamie and I shared that plane. I had my nose art, *The West "By Gawd" Virginian* on the right side while his art, *Jamie Boy*, was on the left.

For no reason that anyone could remember, Cy Doleac christened his aircraft *Ex-Lax . . . Shht 'n' Git!* When Princess Elizabeth of the royal family visited Bodney in May 1944, she was escorted to the flight line where she was intended to see Bill Whisner's aircraft, *Princess Elizabeth*. It had been named in her honor especially for the occasion; it was the only aircraft available that hadn't already received artwork. Someone with a daring sense of humor parked the princess's aircraft next to Doleac's. Doleac's ship, with its off-color moniker, was moved to a less prominent position only barely in time to keep from embarrassing England's future monarch.

The artwork, if it required something more than simple stenciling, was generally performed by talented enlisted men. In units the size of the 352nd there were usually several who had worked as professional artists before the war. Punchy Powell recalled: "There were several pretty good artists among the airmen, some better at lettering than illustrating, but each squadron had a few of these especially talented men. The pilots usually compensated them in some way, typically with a bottle of scotch or something of that sort rather than cash."

Aircraft were usually renamed when they were passed from one pilot to another. This happened when the original pilot was rotated out of the squadron, or was given a new aircraft, or was shot down while flying a different aircraft for whatever reason. George Preddy's P-51, *Cripes*

A'Mighty 3rd, Serial Number 44-13321, is an excellent example. After Preddy went home on leave during August and September 1944, the aircraft was given to Malcolm Stewart, who renamed it *The Margarets*. Only a short time later, on September 15, it was passed to Marion Nutter, who renamed it *Sexshunate*, a play on words on Section 8 of United States Army Regulation 615-360. This regulation prescribed the conditions for discharge due to mental unfitness. Nutter scored three aerial victories in the aircraft, and Ray Littge scored one. Ultimately, this aircraft scored more victories than any other P-51 in history. It was destroyed when Walter Padden was shot down and killed while flying it on a strafing mission on April 16, 1945.

Frank Cutler was altruistic about his aircraft's name. He eschewed the notion of a sexy female image or a sobriquet dripping with innuendo. Rather, he christened it *Soldiers' Vote*. He explained his reasoning in a news release: "If a man has the right to die for his country, that man certainly has the right to vote." At the time, the voting age was twenty-one. Many of the men doing the fighting had yet to reach that still-tender age.

Personalization of aircraft sometimes went beyond nose art. Charles Cesky, an ace with the 328th Fighter Squadron, painted the wingtips of his aircraft bright orange so that his wingmen could better see them when flying formation in fog and clouds.

CHAPTER 26

Grinding through the Fall

George Preddy was sent home on leave during the late summer of 1944 and spent September at home in Greensboro, North Carolina. No longer was he "Mouse," the diminutive big-eared boy who ran a small concession stand at the War Memorial Stadium. Rather, he was Greensboro's favorite son, a genuine war hero and the nation's leading ace in Europe.

It never went to his head. Although most veterans home on leave were left to their own devices, Preddy was, whether he wanted to be or not, a wartime celebrity. He obligingly made personal and radio appearances as directed by the USAAF, and attended community functions as requested by proud hometown citizens. Ironically, the biggest of these was held at the same stadium where he used to hawk candy and soft drinks. And he had a knack for giving his interviewers full accounts of air actions against the Luftwaffe without coming across as self-important.

During this time he and his family also visited his younger brother Bill who was undergoing fighter training at Venice Army Air Field in Florida. The two were permitted to take a pair of P-40s and engage in mock combat. The younger Preddy gave his much more experienced older brother quite a tussle. George told Bill, "Boy, you're ready to take on the best the Luftwaffe has to offer, but just don't get too cocky!"[1] Preddy was impressed not only with his brother's native ability but also with the training that he and his peers had received; they were obviously much better prepared for combat than he had been early in the war.

Preddy also announced his engagement to his Australian girlfriend, Joan Jackson. The two of them hadn't put eyes on each other for nearly two years but had maintained their relationship via mail. Such a thing speaks to the queer exigencies imposed by the war. Aside from the difficulties of communicating by letter was the added consideration that those letters were sometimes a couple of months or more old by the time they made the transit from one theater of war across the globe to another. It is also interesting to speculate about Preddy's reasons for such an unusual engagement; he was a gregarious sort who very much enjoyed the company of women. And he had certainly enjoyed that company since leaving Australia for the United States and England. Regardless, the engagement was very real and very public.

Rather than staying in the States where he could have drawn just about any assignment he wanted, Preddy was anxious to get back into combat. Later he declared, "I sure as hell am not a killer, but combat flying is like a game and a guy likes to come out on top. I'm not aiming for any particular score, I just want to finish the job here in Europe so I can go back to the Pacific. I'd like to get another crack at the Japs and also see my fiancée in Australia."[2]

Although Preddy was modest, it is likely true that he would have liked—just as virtually all his comrades would have—to shoot down many more enemy aircraft. There was no denying the excitement of air combat and its risks; Preddy surely thrived on it to some extent. Too, there was little to rival the feelings of very close camaraderie that developed in a fighter unit at war. Finally, there was the undeniable fact that Preddy was a very good fighter pilot and that most men enjoyed doing that at which they excelled.

Much has been made of the fact that German fighter production figures increased significantly during the late spring and summer of 1944. This was indeed the case. The Germans, under Albert Speer, dispersed their aircraft manufacturing industry into much smaller plants and shops that were difficult to destroy from the air. On the other hand, Göring noted in postwar debriefings that the fabrication quality of the aircraft declined as the numbers produced increased.[3] Further, the production numbers included damaged aircraft that were repaired and returned to service by the manufacturers.

Typically, aircraft that sustained damage that was not repairable at the airfield were returned to the factory to be rebuilt. Aircraft that sustained damage greater than 60 percent were salvaged and scrapped. Although his knowledge of such things was probably incomplete, Göring said that the repairs of damaged aircraft varied from 500 to 900 per month.[4]

Moreover, the increased numbers of aircraft produced, new-built or remanufactured, really didn't matter because Germany wasn't training enough new pilots to fly them. Pilot training tailed off to virtually nothing by the fall of 1944 and fuel shortages precluded almost all flying except for combat. It was a situation that simply couldn't be sustained.

Camaraderie and friendships in combat grow to an extent not easily understood by those who have never experienced it. This solidarity in arms was exhibited by a trio of P-51 pilots of the 355th Fighter Group based out of Steeple Morden. On October 3, 1944, Henry Brown, one of the Eighth Air Force's leading aces, was shot up while strafing the Luftwaffe airfield at Nordlingen. Unable to keep his ship airborne, Brown bellied it into a large pasture. Fellow ace, Charles Lenfest, arced around in a slow turn, lowered his flaps and landing gear and readied to set down in the field.

The 355th had successfully executed a "piggyback" rescue nearly two months earlier on August 18 when Royce Priest landed in a wheat field to pick up Bert Marshall. Lenfest hoped to repeat that success and landed not far from where Brown's aircraft slid to a stop in the muddy meadow. Brown ran toward his ship as Lenfest taxied toward a good takeoff point. The rescue attempt came apart when Lenfest's P-51 became stuck in the soft ground.

Nevertheless, fellow pilot Alvin White was not deterred and he also set down in the field intent on lifting out at least one of his comrades. It was for naught. By the time he landed, Brown and Lenfest were already running through a nearby wood and never saw their would-be rescuer. With no reason to stay, White took off again whereas Brown and Lenfest were eventually captured and made POWs.

Elements of the 352nd had a front row seat to the botched rescue as delineated in the group's mission summary report for the day: "P-51 seen to belly in on grass field, 1220. Another P-51 seen to land in same field but a/c's wheel[s] stuck in ground. 3rd P-51 landed and took off again. Undetermined whether this a/c picked up anyone. Other P-51s then strafed 2 A/C on field—A/C believed 355th Gp."

But the 355th's fliers weren't the only ones from VIII Fighter Command who set down on the continent that particular day. Among the details of the group's mission summary report was this cryptic note: "Capt.

Bennett—487th Sqdn—Injured, extent unknown—Believed landed in France. Lt. Ross—487th Sqdn—Believed landed in France." The report was never designed to provide detailed narratives, but the story associated with these two lines underscores the fact that many interesting incidents were buried in the officialdom of virtually every mission summary report.

On this day, the point was made that air combat demanded the most of its participants regardless of whether they were seasoned veterans or green neophytes. Russell Ross was the latter. He flew on John Bennett's wing in a borrowed aircraft on his first escort mission. Over France, they climbed through a layer of clouds. When they broke clear they spotted a gaggle of Me-109s above them. "We immediately ascended in order to engage them," Ross recalled.[5] "Suddenly a flak shell burst close to Major Bennett and struck his aircraft. He took a hit in the left shoulder and began to bleed profusely. Afraid of losing consciousness, he told me he needed to land."

The two of them made three separate attempts to penetrate down through the clouds and into the clear. Each time they failed. "The soupy cloud cover and our close proximity to the Seine River Valley and its surrounding hills heightened our sense of peril," recalled Ross. "After the third try, Major Bennett gave me permission to return to England." But low on fuel, Ross had no choice but to stay with Bennett.

"On the fourth try we broke through the clouds and found ourselves in the valley, flying parallel to the river. On either side of us we could see the hills disappear back up into the overcast. "Shaken, hearts in our throats, we followed the river and searched for an accessible landing site." Bennett had little choice but to try and set his aircraft down onto a small, wet, level piece of ground. Ross circled overhead and watched. "He had to jump a fence, but he landed successfully. The aircraft rolled almost to a complete stop. At the last moment, one wheel caught a shell hole and the plane nosed over onto its back." Fortunately, Bennett wasn't hurt any further. Ross watched a group of Frenchman pile out of a small truck and pull him clear. "The major stood and waved at me, so I knew he was in good hands."

Ross didn't want to chance a landing in the same field. "I found a pasture full of sheep and buzzed them several times to herd them out of my path." He set his aircraft down with no problem and was met by four Frenchmen. "They were interested in the number of swastikas that decorated the cowl of the airplane. Laughing, they patted me on the back and shouted over and over again, 'Boches Kaputs!' I couldn't speak French, so I was unable to tell them I hadn't made the kills."

Both Bennett and Ross had put down in Allied-held territory. Bennett was taken to a hospital where he received good care. Ross was delivered to a B-26 base where he spent the night. He returned to his aircraft the next day with an airman and fifteen gallons of fuel. It was enough for Ross to get back to the B-26 base where he subsequently took on enough gas to get back to Bodney.

His homecoming was mixed. "Upon arrival I reported directly to [Lieutenant] Colonel [John C.] Meyer who was very concerned about Major Bennett and his whereabouts. He then chewed me out for landing in the field with my gear down." Meyer had a point. Although the aircraft would have been damaged in a belly landing, it would have been far less likely to overturn as Bennett's aircraft had. "Still," Ross continued, "I was relieved to be home, and I felt proud, knowing I had returned the airplane intact. When I reported this fact to the aircraft's pilot he was not happy. He said, 'You mean you had a chance to get rid of that dog of an airplane and didn't? I've been trying for a long time to get rid of that thing.'"

"It sure took the wind out of my sails," remembered Ross.

Personnel from this Station are not complying with the Station Order which states that the gas mask will be worn, adjusted to the face, between the hours of 1000 and 1030 on Thursdays of each week. Unit C.O.'s and Department Heads are responsible for enforcing this order and will see that it is strictly complied with by personnel of their command or department.

In fact, a chemical warfare unit was stationed at Bodney. It was not needed, but based on experience from World War I the Army was organized so as not to be unprotected in the event the belligerents resorted to gas warfare. That being said, the VIII Fighter Command recognized the situation for what it was. "The vast expansion of our Air Force required the building up of the chain of military organization right on down the line. The consequence was that, in order to justify some of them, sections were attached which had no real function and very little work, others were absolutely useless, and their officers and enlisted men idle and discontented. Chemical warfare for example, became nothing but a Thursday nuisance when they sounded the weekly gas alarm for a half hour. The rest of the week they had nothing to do." This observation was made during the same period that the bulletin was published.[6]

The following Business Establishments are placed "OFF LIM-
ITS" to all persons of this command, effective immediately:

Mrs. Ethel May Horne Residence, Old Weston Road, Kinwick,
Huntingdonshire.

The Railway Inn, Sharnbrook, Bedfordshire.

No. 155, High Street, Huntingdon, Punts.

So long after the fact it is difficult to know with certainty why these
places were put off limits. It might have been that they had abused the pay-
checks of naïve American servicemen, or were fronts for prostitution or perhaps because the owners had previously had bad experiences with Americans.

This last explanation was certainly a real possibility. Far from home
and in a strange and exciting new place—and being young men who often
drank too much—the Americans were known to occasionally misbehave.
This was noted both in England and at home in the United States. The *New
York Post*'s Leland Stowe noted "The GI is at best when facing the worst.
But when they go on leave they frequently are not nice at all. On average,
the Americans are a sadly undisciplined lot and by European manners their
manners are pretty bad."

Further evidence that American troops were not always on their best
behavior is provided by a message carried in the 352nd's daily bulletin. "It
has come to the attention of this Headquarters that a recent wave of malicious destruction to British telephone pay stations has been occurring in
the small villages of this area. Evidence and apprehensions substantiate the
fact that the vast majority of this damage is caused by American personnel.

On the other hand, these same men made up for their faults in other
ways. Harold Denny wrote in the *New York Times*: "He's not the best soldier in the world—far from it. But he probably is the best fighter." Denny
also noted another characteristic invaluable in soldiery: "He can't stand
being beaten."

The air war that was part of the Allied strategy for defeating Germany
demanded air bases on a scale never seen before or since. The new instal-
lations that were so quickly created across all of eastern England required
expansive stretches of open ground. Consequently, it was only natural that
virtually all of them were located in the countryside.

And pheasants, those most favorite of game birds, were ubiquitous across all the countryside. Many of the men of the 352nd grew up hunting and were excited at the prospect of sharpening their shooting eye and, at the same time, bringing fresh game to the unit's mess. Yet, East Anglia was not Kansas, West Virginia or Wyoming. Whereas the game the Americans grew up shooting was on public land or belonged to property owners who welcomed hunters more often than not, the English pheasants belonged largely to the King of England.

Clarence "Spike" Cameron recalled an incident that underscored these differences. "We had seen pheasant all over the fields surrounding the airbase," he remembered.[7] "These were wheat and barley and oat fields, but the English called it corn, which was different to us. Anyway, a handful of us checked out some shotguns and headed off the base to go shooting."

The young pilots found game and started shooting right away. "It wasn't long," Cameron said, "before an English farmer came running across the field waving his arms at us. He said, 'You can't do this—these are the King's pheasants! They belong to the King!' Well, one of our guys said, 'Fuck the King.'"

The affront stung the Englishman, yet he kept his composure. "He, of course, had an English accent," said Cameron, "which always amused us. He said, 'I say, you shouldn't talk about our king that way. It's not polite. After all, we don't talk about your president that way.'" The Americans blinked at the man who had just upbraided them, then burst out in guffaws. "I'm not sure why," Cameron recalled, "but all of a sudden, we found the whole situation hilarious—we couldn't stop laughing."

Cameron's experience was one that was repeated in variations many times over throughout East Anglia during the war years. Americans poached the King's game just as soon as they arrived. Nevertheless, the crown was actually quite generous to its American guests. Soon after they arrived in England, arrangements were made for the men to obtain permits that allowed them to take game legally within certain constraints. Still, the Americans continued to make petty poaching forays through the end of their time in England despite regular admonitions against it.

The notice in the 352nd's daily bulletin for September 9, 1944 was typical of the many different iterations that were regularly posted during the unit's stay in Bodney. "A complaint has been received from the agent of Clermont Hall that personnel of this Station are shooting game on the Clermont Estate. All personnel of this station are warned against poaching on this Estate and will be punished severely if apprehended."

George Preddy was given command of the 328th Fighter Squadron on October 28, 1944, shortly after returning from the States. The 328th was a good unit but since the departure of Everett Stewart earlier in the year it had been led by a series of commanders for relatively short stints. While not bad, some of the commanders might have been best described as adequate. Further, few of them were in the position long enough to establish the sort of real leadership that Meyer embodied at the head of the 487th—a unit he had stewarded since early in the 352nd's existence. Consequently, the 328th's score in aerial combat lagged the tallies of the 486th and 487th. It was believed that Preddy's aggressive nature might be just the sort of medicine the 328th needed. Fighting talent aside, considering Preddy's drinking and off-duty shenanigans, the decision to put him in charge also represented a risk on the part of the 352nd's leadership.

It was a good decision. Ray Mitchell recollected Preddy's first meeting with the pilots of the 328th as their new commanding officer. "I had a good impression of George because I had heard a lot about his past exploits in the South Pacific as well as in the ETO. So our expectations were great for George before he came. In his first meeting with us he seemed to be more cold and calculating, kind of quiet. When he talked, he had something to say; it wasn't just idle chatter. Everybody respected him, but it took a while for us to get acquainted with him and know what to expect of him."[8]

Art Snyder, Preddy's new crew chief recalled: "Within a day or two of taking command, he gathered the squadron around a bomb shelter, and he got up on top of the shelter and gave a short talk as to what we were there for. I vividly recall him saying that the main thing we were there for was to shoot down the Hun."[9]

Preddy led the 328th with vigor and the squadron's performance and morale improved. In fact, less than a week later the 352nd got into a tremendous melee on November 2, while escorting the bombers to Merseburg. The group was credited with downing 38 enemy aircraft, of which 24 were shot down by the 328th. Both tallies were records for VIII Fighter Command up to that point. Preddy himself was credited with downing an Me-109 that day. Although the 328th's fantastic performance could hardly be attributed in its entirety to Preddy, it was an indication that the combat leadership of the unit was no longer a cause for concern.

However, the responsibility of command didn't change Preddy's mischievous nature. He was still a drinking prankster. After a night of partying, Preddy sometimes sneaked into the quarters of other ranking officers and tipped them out of bed as they slept.

By the fall of 1944, it was overwhelmingly apparent that the Luftwaffe would not be able to stop the USAAF's raids by continuing the same sorts of operations it had maintained since the Eighth Air Force began operations during August 1942. Counter to what Adolf Galland had hoped more than a year earlier, the Me-262 was still not operating in numbers big enough to be meaningful. Something different had to be tried.

Galland put his hopes in a desperate plan he dubbed *der große Schlag*, or "The Big Blow." No longer would he dutifully send his undertrained fighter pilots up to be butchered even before they intercepted the bomber streams. That practice had degenerated into nothing more than a meat grinder that yielded few results.

Instead, he envisioned a plan whereby the Luftwaffe would curtail operations long enough to husband a force of up to three thousand fighters. Then, when conditions were right, especially the weather, at least a couple thousand of those fighters would be launched against the American bombers. Subsequently, as the fighters recovered they would be quickly refueled and rearmed in order to keep both the escorts and the bombers overwhelmed.

For the first time in a very long time the tables would be turned and the Germans would outnumber the Americans. Galland hoped to destroy 400 to 500 heavy bombers in a single day and was ready to accept similar losses to his own fighter force, to include up to 150 pilots. By inflicting such a blow, he hoped to stymie the daylight bombing campaign long enough to buy some time. What might be done with that time was uncertain, but it was better than being bombed to death.

The plan had potential. However, in order to build such a great reserve of fighters, ongoing operations had to be scaled back. Instead, the Luftwaffe's leaders could not resist the temptation to use the burgeoning force prematurely. That was the case on November 2, 1944, when Galland sent almost 500 fighters after a bomber force that numbered more than a thousand.

Although the number of fighters was impressive, it fell far short of the critical mass that was needed to stop the bombers. Moreover, the weather was poor and the German flyers struggled even to make contact with the bombers. In the end, the attempted interception was an utter failure and the Allied fighter pilots had a field day.

It is a fact that the human character—in all its varieties—has remained virtually unchanged since prehistory. Certainly, a person's nature is influenced by family and culture and society but the basic innate qualities that make a person what he is are largely ingrained. That being the case, the men who fought World War II were, at their core, of the same cloth as their forebears and descendents.

William J. Stangel of the 328th offers an interesting example. A native of Thief River Falls, Minnesota, he joined the Royal Canadian Air Force in 1941 before the U.S. entered the war. He was transferred to the Royal Air Force and served in England before being commissioned into the USAAF during 1942. He was a gregarious and charming man who was quite comfortable with the ladies. In fact, by the time he joined the 352nd in August 1944, he had been married at least four times. Such a number of marriages was remarkable, but what was even more extraordinary was that Stangel had never been divorced. In fact, Stangel was a serial bigamist.

It didn't affect his performance in the air. Stangel had a big day on November 2, 1944 during which the 352nd knocked down a record 38 enemy fighters; it was the same day that Galland had launched five hundred fighters. Stangel was leading the 328th Squadron's Red Flight. The squadron blew apart when it encountered a massive formation of German fighters estimated at more than a hundred. Stangel pitched his flight into the battle and singled out an aircraft. His short burst of fire missed and he overshot the first fighter and climbed toward another, an Me-109. Its pilot threw open his canopy and bailed out. Stangel picked out another aircraft, fired, missed and overshot once more.

There followed a short, slashing engagement during which Stangel failed to score. Nevertheless, opportunities were plenty. "At this time I engaged another E/A," he reported.[10] "We started into a few quick turns and finally ended up in making head-on passes at each other." This fight lasted longer than was normal; whereas many aerial clashes were typified by aircraft taking quick shots at each other and then diving away, Stangel and his opponent, an Me-109 pilot, stayed at each other.

"At last we were closing directly head-on. There wasn't time to roll either way so I dropped the nose a bit more and it seemed we were about to hit when I pulled the trigger with a short burst." Unsure of the effects of his gunfire, Stangel reefed his Mustang hard up into a climbing left-hand turn and twisted around in the cockpit. "I saw this E/A pull up a bit, start to roll on his back and then dive vertically to the ground and explode."

Still the fight wasn't over. Another Me-109 flashed in front of Stangel and he took a quick shot, missed, turned left hard after it and lowered his flaps ten degrees to tighten his turn. Still thinking clearly, Stangel looked back to clear his tail and caught sight of squadron mate Eugene James to his left along with a pair of Me-109s closing on him from behind. "I pulled the stick right into my stomach," Stangel recalled, "and almost stood my A/C on its tail." James tried to climb with Stangel but his aircraft was unable to keep up and he fell into the path of the pursuing Germans. Stangel recounted what happened next: "The nearest E/A dropped a bit to clear Lt. James and collided with the second E/A. Both E/A went down; the pilot of one EA bailed out." It was a big day for Stangel. These were his first aerial victories. He claimed two individual victories and shared credit for the two, mid-air victims with James.

Aside from Stangel, the day was a big one for several other 352nd pilots. One of those was Arthur Hudson, also of the 328th Fighter Squadron. He was number two in Major Earl Abbott's White Flight. Abbott, the 328th's commander, led his flight down from over 27,000 feet onto a group of Me-109s that were setting up for a plunging head-on attack on a formation of bombers; Hudson followed Abbott down.

Abbott singled out an Me-109 and shredded it as the opposing groups of fighters plummeted through the bomber formation. At the same time a German pilot overshot Hudson from behind and flew out in front of him. "I maneuvered onto his tail and began firing at 10,000 feet altitude and followed him down firing to 6,000 feet. I got many good hits above the trailing edge of his wing."[11] The Me-109 smoked and caught fire as it fell through an undercast.

Hudson followed Abbott through a complete circle but lost him when his leader punched into the clouds. Diving through the undercast Hudson had no luck finding Abbott but got lucky when another Me-109 dropped through the clouds in front of him. The young P-51 pilot recognized an opportunity when he saw one; he followed the German into a hard left turn and opened fire. "I got many strikes on the wing and fuselage," Hudson recalled. "He then jettisoned his canopy and bailed out at 2,000 feet. His chute opened just as he hit the ground."

Still anxious to find some friends, Hudson climbed back through the clouds. There, rather than squadron mates, he spotted another Me-109. "Climbing up towards him, I engaged him in a climbing turn but stalled out and flipped over." The German pilot tried to dive away but Hudson recovered his aircraft and gave chase. The enemy pilot went back into a climb with Hudson on his tail then reversed direction and pointed earthward once more. "I began firing in the dive," Hudson noted, "and he then bailed out."

Hudson found himself below the clouds again and once more he powered back up through them where, again, he spotted another Me-109. The two pilots spiraled down through the clouds as each tried to gain an advantage on the other. Finally, the German flyer tried to make a break. "I chased him to the deck for about three minutes," recorded Hudson, "and caught him as he started turning to the left. I took a burst and got a few hits in the turn." Hudson subsequently misjudged how fast he was closing on his quarry and almost overran him. Instead, he lagged the German's turn, gained some separation, then reengaged. "I got hits on his wing and something came off of his aircraft causing him to flip on his back and crash into the ground, exploding."

Hudson had no time to celebrate. He quickly checked his tail and discovered another Me-109 closing into firing range. He turned hard right and the enemy pilot fired an ineffective burst at him as they passed almost head-on. Quickly reversing his turn to the left, Hudson tacked on to the other fighter's tail and opened fire. "I started firing but only one gun would fire, and as I was overrunning him I pulled up into the clouds. . . ."

This time Hudson stayed in the protective gray of the clouds until he was well clear of the area. Only then did he climb and head for home where he landed uneventfully. For the day's work he was credited with four aerial victories.

Arthur Hudson was killed by ground fire less than a month later on November 27 while strafing an airfield.

During the massive air battle of November 2, 1944, many of the 352nd's pilots were using the new K-14 gunsight for the first time. For all practical purposes, it was an American version of a British design—the Ferranti Mark IID computing gyroscopic sight—that took much of the guesswork out of the black art that was aerial gunnery. The brains of the K-14 were housed in a mechanical analog computer that took into account the motion of the firing aircraft and automatically calculated the proper lead required to hit a target with any sort of angular crossing component. In reality, this was virtually all targets.

The manual for the K-14 described its advantages in the opening paragraph: "As you adjust the K-14 gyroscope gunsight, it automatically gives you the correct lead and shows you the range of the target. In other words, it's the answer to the poor deflection shooter's prayer. Though exceedingly complicated internally, the sight is easy to operate with a little practice."

The sight itself was made up of a glass reflector plate upon which six illuminated diamonds, arranged in a circle, were projected. At the center of the circle of diamonds was an illuminated dot, or pipper. If the gunsight was set up correctly, and the target aircraft was within range, the pilot had only to fly his aircraft so as to put the pipper over the target and pull the trigger.

Operating the sight was not difficult. There was a span scale on the front of the sight which the pilot set to match the wingspan of his target. In practice, most pilots set this at just over thirty feet which approximated the wingspans of both the Me-109 and the FW-190. Some variants actually had markings on the scale for the types of enemy aircraft likely to be encountered. A twist grip on the throttle handle controlled the size of the circle of diamonds. As the pilot twisted the handle fore or aft, the size of the circle increased or decreased. The pilot's objective was to match the target aircraft's wingspan with the circle defined by the inside points of the six diamonds. Once that was done, with the pipper over the target aircraft, the pilot had to wait approximately one second before pulling the trigger in order to allow the gunsight computer to stabilize. Following that short interval, a two-second burst of machine gun fire was recommended.

So long as the pilot was able to hold his aircraft steady for a short time prior to pulling the trigger, the K-14 was very accurate. However, if he had to constantly whip his aircraft around in order to get or keep the pipper on the target, the primitive computer had a difficult time keeping up and the firing solution was not as accurate. Likewise, the sight was not good for quick snapshots. Nevertheless, used properly, the K-14 could be deadly.

Charles Rogers used it to claim two Me-109s on November 2, 1944. "I was using a K-14 sight and I got the first E/A with a deflection of approx 65 degrees and 400 yds range; the second E/A at approx 45 degrees deflection and 300 yds range. I think the K-14 sight is very good for high deflection shooting and long range."[12] Rogers thought right. Scoring those hits would have been very difficult with the earlier fixed sight.

Don Bryan remembered that the pilots didn't get much training or instruction on the K-14 gunsight. "We really didn't know much about it until the first time we took it into combat." Although some of the group's pilots had been using the new gunsight since September, Bryan didn't get a chance to test it in combat until November 2, 1944.

On that day Bryan led Yellow Flight on an attack against a large formation of Me-109s. "By the time I could get in position for my bounce, about 10 to 15 of them had started down on the bombers; the others were preparing to start down."[13] After Bryan nosed over in pursuit it took only a short time before he was in position to fire. "I closed to about 100 yards on one of the Me-109s. Using my K-14 sight for the first time, I got only a few strikes."

The fight degenerated into a huge, frantic brawl characterized by hard turns, snatching reversals, and gut-wrenching climbs and dives. It was the sort of air combat during which pilots, for the most part, were able to fire only short, high-deflection bursts lest they become targets themselves. It was also the sort of fighting that the K-14 was not designed for.

It was only when the fight dispersed and aircraft were arcing through the sky in ones and twos that Bryan had an opportunity to be impressed by the K-14. After downing his third aircraft, Bryan was joined by Milton Camerer and started climbing back toward the bomber stream. As he passed through 10,000 feet, he spotted two Me-109s at 5,000 feet. He rolled into a split-S and attacked the trailing fighter: "I had only two guns firing as I made my attack. I opened fire at about 500 yards and hit the enemy aircraft very hard around the fuselage and wings." With only the two guns Bryan's accuracy with the K-14 against the non-maneuvering German was still lethal. "The enemy aircraft snapped into a very violent spin to the left and went through the undercast in flames and spinning."

Bryan next turned his attention to the other Me-109, which, like the first, was not maneuvering. By this time, he had only one operable gun. Despite the fact that firing a single gun tended to yaw the aircraft and destroy its aim, Bryan closed to eighty yards and destroyed the enemy fighter. It was in situations like these, where both the firing aircraft and the target were relatively stable, that the K-14 excelled.

The experience of Bryan's wingman Francis Hill during this fight reinforces the assertion that the performance characteristics of the different frontline fighters were only part of the equation that accounted for success in aerial combat. During the fight Bryan and Hill were bounced by a formation of enemy fighters. "I called Don [Bryan] on the RT and he made a violent break," Hill remembered.[14] "In following him, I blacked out at the top of a chandelle and never did rejoin him. There was an awful lot of action for the next ten to fifteen minutes."

Hill remained unmolested during the few seconds that he was unconscious. Soon after awakening he was joined by Charles Goodman and the pair threw themselves after two four-ships of Me-109s. "We went into a fat-assed lufbury [sic], and then I found out that the Me-109 could turn as tight or tighter than we could. The old circle got tighter and tighter until I snapped out and went into a spin somewhere around 25,000 feet." Even with his aircraft out of control, Hill still maintained his composure. "There was a cloud layer about 5,000 feet below so I let the old girl wind up. I figured those eight bastards behind me couldn't do much damage so long as I kept spinning."

After falling into the cloud layer, Hill used his instruments to recover from the spin. Back in control of his aircraft, he climbed again, looking for Goodman. "All was peaceful and calm with the exception of one lone

Me-109. He didn't see me, and I was able to climb up behind him . . ." Hill gunned down the unsuspecting German from directly behind. It was his first aerial victory. That he was able to do so had absolutely nothing to do with any sort of performance advantage that the P-51 did or did not have over the Me-109.

Nelson Jesup of the 487th Fighter Squadron scored his first aerial victory during this fight. He tacked onto a formation of about fifteen FW-190s as they dove on the bomber stream. As he closed the range he selected his target. "With each squirt [burst of gunfire] I observed strikes and pieces flying off the e/a. He rolled over and bailed out. By this time I had two Jerries on my tail but I managed to finally outrun them. I was alone and had to head home as my engine was running rough from the long period it had been operating at high speed."

Back at Bodney, Jesup's squadron mates shared his excitement at having scored. "It sure felt good when I came over the field and saw the boys who weren't flying lined up outside the hut. They knew by the way I buzzed the field for landing that I had gotten something and they jumped all over my plane banging me on the back. . . ."[15]

Karl Dittmer completed a tour as a B-17 pilot a few days before D-Day and talked himself into the 352nd's 487th Fighter Squadron rather than going home. On the 352nd's big day, November 2, 1944, he was flying his brand new P-51D, *Dopey Okie*, on the wing of Sanford Moats. "Things were uneventful until we were over Holland, headed for home."[16] Moats spotted an Me-262 and started after it with Dittmer in tow.

"The German pilot was no dummy," Dittmer recalled. "We could cut him off in the turns and get closer, but as soon as we approached gun range, he'd roll out of his turn and pull well away from us. We played with him for several minutes. I think Sandy was hoping we'd run him out of fuel. The Kraut may have been attempting to do the same with us."

Moats and Dittmer eventually gave up the chase. Dittmer checked his fuel. "Whoo boy! Not so good. I called Sandy and told him how much I had. By then we had the Zuider Zee in sight, and were as close to England as we were to the nearest airfields on the continent." Moats called Air/Sea Rescue and got a steer to the closest field in England.

After they crossed the English coast, Dittmer started a descent through the clouds. "After sweating a few moments, I broke clear of the clouds and that's when my engine sputtered and quit. I looked to my right first, since one can't see much looking forward, and saw an airfield with paved runways a couple of miles or so just off my right wing." It was a B-24 base and Dittmer saw several of the big bombers in the landing pattern. "I pulled the bird up into the clouds to slow her down, since my airspeed was rather high. Then I shoved the gear handle down although my airspeed was well above gear-lowering speed." Dittmer pulled the nose of his aircraft back up, stomped hard on the right rudder to reverse his turn, dropped out of the clouds and headed for the runway.

He slipped his powerless, blue-nosed P-51 between a pair of B-24s and just as he was touching down was caught in the wake turbulence of the bomber in front of him. It lifted the little fighter up and right and then shoved the nose down. "I found myself looking at grass," Dittmer recounted. "I remember pumping the stick back against the left aft stops while pumping the left rudder against its stop. I thought, hell, I'm going to mess up my brand new bird. There was no way she could recover, but she did. She righted herself a fraction of an inch above the grass, skidded over to the center of the runway and touched down like a feather. Then, my knees started to shake."

The massive fighter forces that Galland prematurely committed on November 2, 1944, presented the 352nd with an opportunity unlike any the group had ever experienced. In fact, the 352nd's pilots were credited with thirty-eight aerial victories—twenty-four by the 328th Fighter Squadron alone. Both were records at the time for the European theater of operations.

Although the German fighters succeeded in knocking down twenty-six bombers that day, it was far short of what was required to slow the American steamroller. And it had cost the Germans 120 aircraft and 70 pilots—almost 5 fighters per bomber. Still the Luftwaffe leadership failed to appreciate the lesson it had been dealt. Rather than marshalling 2,000 or 3,000 aircraft as Galland envisioned, the force was frittered away during smaller efforts in the latter half of November.

The declining quality of Germany's pilots became more and more evident as the war progressed. William Halton of the 487th noted the docility of the Luftwaffe's fliers in his encounter report of 27 November 1944, nearly a year after Göring had declared that his German fighter pilots were forbidden to chase the American fighters: "The 109s seemed confused and not at all aggressive," he recalled.[17] "When we contacted them they had the initial advantage of altitude and did not use it. After they had allowed us to neutralize their advantage, they took no evasive action whatsoever except split-S-ing for the deck and permitting us to close in on them."

In fact, John C. Meyer noted the degradation of the Luftwaffe fliers nearly six months earlier in his encounter report of May 8, 1944. He shot down three German fighters that day and was wholly unimpressed with the fighting qualities of the men he defeated:

> Although E/A seemed aggressive and skillful against our bombers they were conspicuously lacking in these qualities when engaged by our fighters. Mere aggressive acts on the parts of one or two of our fighters against superior numbers would cause the enemy to abandon his mission and break up his formation. The run of the mill German pilot [is] notable in his lack of initiative, following his leader in too tight formation in all circumstances. They are also often ready to bail out at the slightest provocation.[18]

Meyer's observations were consistent with the order Göring had issued late the previous year—that his fighters must avoid combat with the American escort fighters at all costs. Or they may have been a simple reflection of the poor training and low morale of the German pilots. Regardless, if cornered they should have been expected to fight to the utmost of their abilities. It was this failure, or inability, to fight that Meyer seemed to find so striking. In particular, he noted how readily the Luftwaffe fighter pilots jumped from their aircraft; many of them bailed out before shots had been fired. Indeed, Meyer frightened a German flyer out of his cockpit the same day he made his observation. He recounted the event in his encounter report: "As I was fast closing on tail end Charlie, without firing a shot, he leveled off and bailed out."[19]

The 352nd's pilots observed this behavior time and time again, particularly during the last year of the war. In fact, Charles Cesky of the 328th Fighter Squadron received credit for two aerial victories on two separate occasions over Luftwaffe pilots that simply bailed out before he could bring his guns to bear. On November 27, 1944, Cesky chased an Me-109 down through an overcast near Hanover, Germany. "When he leveled off at about 5,000' under the undercast, I turned into him with about a 30-degree deflection. I withheld my fire, and was about to press the trigger when the pilot of the E/A bailed out."

A month later, on December 25, 1944, Cesky and his flight engaged a four-ship of FW-190s. After shooting down two of the Germans he latched onto the leader: "Proceeding on to the leader of the E/As I followed him around in a tight spiral until at four thousand feet the pilot of the E/A bailed out and the plane crashed."[20] The fourth and final member of the FW 190 flight abandoned his ship as Cesky's wingman, Alvin Chesser, was about to open fire on him.

In fact, this behavior was noted by VIII Fighter Command in the fall of 1944:

> A new phenomenon began to appear clearly in the period follow-ing D-Day, with all its symptoms of a rapidly declining morale in the Luftwaffe. Probably the first indication of it was seen, with a great deal of incredulity, as early as February 21, 1944, when Capt. J. W. Wilkinson, of the 82nd Squadron, 78th Group, dove on an ME 109; when the P-47 was still 800 yards away, the Hun pilot opened his canopy and bailed out. But on May 19, 1944, another Nazi did the same thing for 1stLt. Paul C. Holden, 83rd Squadron, 78th Group, when he dove on the enemy, following an attack on our bombers by 20 single-engine fighters, an attack which the 78th Group broke up. In view of the still presentable G.A.F. [German Air Force] aircraft status it would seem reason-able to suppose that the Hun was finally suffering from a chronic shortage of properly trained pilots. After these first two incidents many began to be noted, no less than 10 were noted in May, and 5 more in June.[21]

The Me-262 finally started operations during the summer of 1944, albeit in very small numbers and mostly with operational testing units. Although it was temperamental, the new jet offered eye-watering perform-ance. Its top speed exceeded 550 miles per hour and its rate of climb was far better than any of the Allied types.

And it packed a mighty wallop. Intended to knock down bombers, it was equipped with four 30-millimeter cannon and, later, 2.2-inch rockets. Although the cannon had a fairly slow rate of fire, it took only two or three shells to knock down one of the big American bombers. Indeed, the USAAF's leadership was extremely wary of what the Germans might be able to do with the new type if they fielded it in numbers. In fact, Spaatz wrote Arnold during the summer of 1944 and declared that he feared the Luftwaffe might regain the initiative in the air war should the German jet become widely operational.[22]

The Me-262 was still relatively new when the 487th Fighter Squadron, led by John C. Meyer, had a prolonged encounter with one on November 9, 1944, near Lake Dummer. The Luftwaffe pilot was determined to down a straggling B-17 that was guarded by two flights of Mustangs from another fighter group in close escort, and the 487th in detached escort.

Although the 487th's Mustangs were hopelessly outclassed by the speed and climb rate of the jet fighter, Meyer put his greater number of aircraft to work with good effect. He deployed the sixteen blue-nosed Mustangs across a broad front so that the Me-262 pilot—fast as his aircraft was—never had a clear approach to the lone bomber. Whenever he maneuvered to set up an attack from one direction, Meyer pivoted his line of fighters to cut him off. Ultimately, after a twenty minute exercise in probing and blocking, the German fighter pilot left without scoring any hits on the bomber.

Meyer subsequently wrote a comprehensive statement that described the encounter and additionally included his personal observations. Where other squadron leaders—out of laziness, ignorance, or lack of interest—might have left off making an official report, it was typical of Meyer that he took the time and energy to craft and forward such an important document. It is also a measure of the man that his insights relative to the new jet were so remarkably accurate.

Of course he noted the much greater speed and climb rate of the Me-262. In describing the relative differences between the jet's performance and that of the P-51 he used typical aviation terms but also put them in a practical context when he wrote: "Me-262 is able to fly around the outside of an apple by the time a P-51 flies through the core."

He also made an observation that would not be immediately obvious to someone who had not seen the jet from multiple aspects: "The Me-262 viewed head-on looks remarkably like a P-51 with combat tanks [external wing tanks]. This, plus speed of closure, makes identification from this perspective extremely difficult." Certainly, when viewed from head on, the jet engines slung underneath the German fighter's wings might easily be mistaken for the external fuel tanks of a P-51.

Meyer was obviously impressed by the Me-262. Further, he believed that the German pilot could have broken through his screen of Mustangs and destroyed the bomber had he only been more aggressive. In summary he wrote that, "A good team of sixteen (16) P-51s is just about an even match for a single Me-262 from a defensive point of view. Offense is out of the question, the enemy aircraft having all the initiative." It is telling that in the section of the report that called for tactical recommendations Meyer wrote, "None." Other than numbers, the USAAF truly had no good counter to the Me-262.

CHAPTER 27

More Mistaken Identities

Notwithstanding the extensive aircraft identification training that the 352nd's pilots received, the vagaries of human eyesight, the similarities between different aircraft types and the emotions of combat combined to ensure that cases of mistaken identity persisted through the war. William Fowler's experience on May 8, 1944, was fairly typical. After knocking down an FW-190 northeast of Brunswick, he became separated from his flight leader and after motoring about for a bit joined with another pair of 352nd P-51s. "The three of us bounced a Me-109 and another ship which looked like an FW-190. As we closed in, the supposedly FW-190 pulled up as if to drop back in on our tails so I pulled up to make an attack on him."[1] Fowler gave the other aircraft a good look before he squeezed the trigger. "As I came into range I identified him as a Yellow nose P-47 [361st Fighter Group]. I joined with him and we started home. The two of us ended up in a group of P-47s on the way home, with whom I came home."

On June 12, 1944, Glennon Moran might very well have shot down an RAF fighter. The 487th filed a report that day describing its action near St. Jacques, France. "Major Preddy and Lt. Moran had combat between 18,000 and 8,000, destroying one each. Lt. Moran's 109 was painted slate blue, with RAF circles [roundels] on wings."[2]

It is extremely doubtful that a German fighter would have carried RAF markings as it would have been doubly likely to have been shot down; Allied fighters would have attacked it because it was an Me-109 while German fighters would have attacked it because it carried RAF markings.

Considering the aggressive nature typical of fighter pilots, it is highly unlikely that an Me-109 thusly painted would have been left unmolested by either side. What probably happened is that Moran misidentified an RAF fighter and shot it down.

These cases of mistaken identify were not unique to the USAAF. John Bennett recounted an incident that occurred near Nordhausen, Germany, on September 11, 1944, that illustrates this fact. After a scrap with an Me-109 he and Alden Rigby started a climb to rejoin the bomber stream. "We reached 5,000 feet and were in a climbing turn," Bennett recorded in his encounter report, "when I saw another plane get on my wing-man's tail."[3] Bennett alerted Rigby who identified the other aircraft as another P-51. Bennett wasn't satisfied. "Despite his assertion, it looked like a Hun to me, so I reefed my plane in as sharp as possible to the left and observed the Bogie to be an Me-109."

Bennett directed Rigby into a hard turn and simultaneously started after the German. "The Hun was about 200 yds. away from my wing-man and smack on his tail. Why the Hun never fired on my wing-man I don't know, unless he thought Lt. Rigby was another 109 chasing me, because Lt. Rigby was flying a P-51B, which was painted olive drab, and had on it an old type canopy. I was flying a new P-51D, with no camouflage paint and with a bubble canopy." As it developed, the encounter ended in a draw when the German dove away into a cloud layer.

Later, the group's mission summary report for November 2, 1944, noted another instance of mistaken identity: "9th FC [Fighter Command] Mustangs camouflaged with orange spinners made repeated passes at our a/c in target area and W/D [withdrawal], also simulating enemy a/c characteristics." It is difficult to know what the intentions of the other fighter group were. Too, it is likely that the 352nd's pilots misidentified the parent organization of the other aircraft; it is probable that they were from the Eighth's 357th Fighter Group which flew aircraft that were painted with red and yellow checked noses.

And it wasn't only the pilots who had difficulty distinguishing enemy from friendly aircraft. Antiaircraft gunners were similarly challenged. This was particularly true when the P-51 first began operating over Europe. John C. Meyer noted this while attacking airfields near Stuttgart on April 13, 1944, and recorded his observations in his encounter report. "Approaching the field I observed several flak towers and gun emplacement. The field seemed to be well defended, however as on other occasions I saw German troops who made no move to man their guns or take cover.[4] I believe this is due to their difficulty in recognizing the P-51 from the Me-109." Meyer had the same experience a short time later while strafing a Ju-52 transport aircraft at another airfield. "Again, the problem of recognition seemed to confound the Huns, for as I attacked the Ju-52 the crews turned and watched me, but made no move to seek cover until I started firing."

Indeed, the Luftwaffe noted the same issue in a message intercepted during the spring of 1944: "They [USAAF fighters] imitate the landing procedures of German fighters or effect surprise by approaching the airfield in fast and level flight. The difficulty of distinguishing friend from foe often makes it impossible for flak artillery to fire on them."[5]

An episode occurred during the mission of November 21, 1944, which revalidated how the problem of proper identification confused friend and foe alike in the unconstrained, three-dimensional, whirl of air combat. On that day Karl Waldron of the 487th Fighter Squadron was William Whisner's wingman. The two of them had earlier joined with John C. Meyer and his wingman after Meyer's number three and four aborted.

Meyer spotted a formation of enemy aircraft southwest of Merseberg at 29,000 feet. He immediately led the flight in a series of climbing turns from 23,000 feet. "We closed in on them," Waldron recalled, "and they didn't drop their tanks, thinking possibly that we were friendly."[6] Regardless of what the enemy pilots thought, Waldron's lead, Whisner, went immediately to work. "Captain Whisner knocked down two and while he was knocking down his third I started firing at a FW-190 that was off Captain Whisner's left wing." Waldron's shooting was good. "I stopped firing when his entire left wing section fell off and the E/A snapped over and spun down. I was using the K-14 sight which proved darn good. I was shooting at 10-degrees deflection."

The fighting became confused. Waldron hung with Whisner while Whisner chased after another FW-190. At the same time Waldron put rounds into a different FW-190 arcing high above him. Immediately afterward he was attacked from above and behind by another German pilot. "While trying to break from this E/A," Waldron recalled, "I spotted a P-51 high that I decided to join."

Still pursued by the enemy aircraft, Waldron skidded, twisted and turned as he clawed skyward toward the other P-51. "I then spotted another 190 at 2 o'clock," he recounted. "I looked back at the Jerry on my tail, when suddenly I saw him pull off my track and point his nose at the other 190 to my right, giving him several bursts. The 190 under attack exploded and the attacking 190 broke for the deck."

As it developed, Waldron was awarded credit for the two FW-190s that he took down with his own guns as well the third FW-190 for which he unwittingly set up a "bait and switch." He later told *Stars and Stripes*:

"The guy on my tail must have been new because he mistook the 190 in front of me for another Mustang and fired a long burst, sending his Nazi pal hurtling down in flames."

But it certainly wasn't just the Germans who made those sorts of mistakes. Earlier in the year, on May 12, 1944, the 352nd's mission summary report noted: "U/I [unidentified] P-51s bouncing from 31,000 feet in Frankfurt area forced group to drop tanks early." And prior to that, on March 26, 1944, the mission summary report recorded a similar incident in which P-47s attacked other P-47s: "Flight of 7 P-47s marked either CY or CV bounced Blue Flight 328th Sqdn, S/E St. Quentin. Their No. 3 man fired his guns from approximately 250 yds." Evidently the guilty party was a poor shot as the report makes no mention of any damage.

The incident above is also interesting for a different reason. It indicates that the writers of the report had no idea what the squadron markings were of the other fighter units operating out of England. Or they lacked the motivation to research them. This is evident because the CY markings mentioned above were carried by a squadron from the 55th Fighter Group, a P-38 unit. A P-38 would never be mistaken for a P-47 and so the markings had to be CV rather than CY. Those letters were carried by the 368th Fighter Squadron of the 359th Fighter Group.

So then, it was a pilot from that particular squadron that had fired on the 328th's Blue Flight. Because the 352nd's summary report failed to report any such details it might be concluded that such incidents simply weren't very important in the context of everything else that was happening.

Colonel Joe Mason turned over command of the 352nd to Col. James Mayden on November 17. The changeover was fairly seamless. The 352nd had been hard at war for more than a year by that time and the men knew their business; there was little that needed changing. Ultimately, the group continued to pile up successes under Mayden just as it had with Mason at its head.

Walter Starck was one of the 487th Fighter Squadron's original pilots. A solid performer, it nevertheless took him several months until he was credited with his first aerial victory on February 10, 1944. During the fall of 1944 he finished his first combat tour and returned to the States for a month of rest and relaxation. After returning, he almost became an accident statistic. Anxious to get back into flying fettle, Starck took his P-51 on several local sorties during which he practiced landings, low flying, aerobatics and such.[7]

On one of these flights he encountered a small RAF utility aircraft typical of those used for spotting artillery strikes. His account is illustrative of the varied ways that the young USAAF flyers killed themselves outside of combat. "I noticed it had British markings," Starck recalled of the little airplane, "And he was ready for me. You can imagine the 'battle' that ensued." Starck wrestled his high performance fighter up, over and around the nimble little spotter craft. It was like using a sledgehammer against a house fly. "The British pilot had great skill," Starck recalled, "and managed to break away from my thrusts time and again."

The ill-matched duel went on. "Of course, I was not to be defeated," Starck continued. "I did all sorts of things to get on his tail—chopped throttle, reduced airspeed, alternately dropped and then raised flap to make sharper turns." Although the little RAF aircraft still proved elusive, Starck was pleased that his flying skills seemed so sharp. "Then 'it' happened," he remembered. "I noticed that the control column was loose, as though all the cables had come off. No resistance of any kind."

Starck checked his airspeed indicator. It read 62 miles per hour. At such a low airspeed, his aircraft had essentially stopped flying. "I immediately pushed the power on to its fullest and milked the flaps up slowly, all the while making sure I maintained straight and level flight. I think I even stopped breathing so as to not shake the airplane." The P-51 finally horsed itself and Starck out of danger. Afterward he was so shaken and embarrassed by the incident that he never shared it with his squadron mates. Sadly, there were many young USAAF flyers who never shared the stories of their airborne high jinks not because of nerves or shame, but because they simply didn't survive them.

Nevertheless, during his career with the 352nd Starck notched more than a hundred combat missions and had knocked down a total of four Me-109s as November 1944 was drawing to a close. On November 27, he flew what was supposed to be—and ultimately was—the last mission of his second combat tour. Starck's experience that day was instructive: In the world of combat aviation, skill was sometimes not enough to trump bad luck.

On that day, the 352nd was tasked to strafe an oil depot. However, near Merseberg, Germany, the group was vectored by a controller onto a large formation of enemy fighters. It wasn't long before a formation of nearly seventy-five aircraft was spotted. Starck, who was leading the 487th's Red Flight, took up the chase. "I saw a flight at 10 o'clock high heading for the deck," he recounted.[8] After shoving everything to the firewall, Starck closed on the fleeing Luftwaffe pilots. "I singled out the last Me-109 but before I opened fire the pilot jettisoned his canopy and bailed out. The aircraft began to spin and then fell apart."

Starck continued after the Germans as they dived for the ground. "I tagged onto the next Me-109, adjusted my K-14 sight and opened fire at 300 yards. Strikes showed on cockpit, fuselage and tail. The E/A turned sharply, began to spin and broke to pieces. I saw no chute."

Starck picked another target as the enemy fighters made a gentle heading correction to the right. "I set the K-14 sight just right," he remembered, "and opened fire at 150–200 yards." Strikes showed on the fuselage and tail section. The tail section came off and flew into my accessory section." Starck didn't note it in his encounter report, but the sound of a large part of his third victim smashing into the underside of his P-51 must have been unnerving.

The aircraft was badly damaged. "Coolant poured out onto my windscreen," Starck reported. "I broke away and headed for home." He nursed his aircraft as best he could and tried to keep the engine's temperature down by pulling back the RPM while simultaneously pushing up the manifold pressure. It worked for about ten minutes but it wasn't enough to clear Germany. "By this time the engine temperature was quite high," Starck remembered. "Fire broke out and I had to leave the ship."

The 487th's commanding officer, William Halton, remembered Starck's radio call: "Shortly after I broke off combat, I heard Capt. Starck, who was leading Red Flight, call on the R/T and say that he was hit and was heading for friendly territory but that he thought that he was going to have to leave the ship. He wished all the boys luck and said that he had gotten two 109's. Nearly everyone in the squadron likewise heard Capt. Starck say this."[9]

Starck later recalled his radio transmission: "Why I did not tell him there were three E/A, I do not know. When I had time to think, I recalled all three but that was of little concern to me at the time." It is possible that since the first enemy ship went down without ever having been shot at, Starck's mind treated it differently in the excitement of the moment.

Regardless, Starck had to leave his ship immediately. "To do this," he recorded, "I had to clear all my hose[s], wires, and belt, stood on the seat, rolled the ship on its side, popped the stick forward and flew out, well clear of the ship." Starck, knocked down by an aircraft that he had personally shot out of the sky, fell toward the earth. "I delayed opening my chute," he recalled, "for a few thousand feet."

When he finally pulled the parachute's ripcord, it dealt him a blow that was consistent with the wicked turn his luck had taken. "When my chute opened, the left harness buckle hit me in the jaw. That's all I knew until I woke up. My chute was in a tree top and I was suspended a foot above the ground. Civilians came up just then and took me prisoner."

CHAPTER 28

To the Continent and Tragedy

Galland's "Big Blow" was gutted by the German chiefs. Hitler, Göring, and even Galland himself simply did not have the discipline to hold the Luftwaffe's fighters in reserve until an overwhelming number were ready and in place. Instead the promising force was committed piecemeal and was subsequently mauled by American pilots who were only too ready and able to rack up impressive scores. By the end of November 1944, the German fighter force was an anemic wreck.

Nevertheless, the Luftwaffe's leadership made plans for an audacious effort to support Hitler's Ardennes offensive. Hitler intended to launch a winter offensive to punch a hole in the Allied lines and smash through Belgium to Antwerp. Once Antwerp was taken, he aimed to capture or destroy as many Allied forces as he could preparatory to suing for a favorable peace. The plan, which had been in the making for several months, was risky in the extreme. For it to have any chance at all the American and British air forces had to be weakened, if not actually neutralized.

Consequently, Luftwaffe staffers headed by *Generalmajor* Dietrich Peltz, the commander of II *Jagdkorps* (II Fighter Corps), drafted a secret scheme for a massive, coordinated, early morning strike to simultaneously hit more than a dozen different American and British air bases in France, the Netherlands and Belgium. The plan was given the code name *Bodenplatte*, a term that described ground prepared for artillery.

To achieve the maximum amount of damage and confusion, the raid was planned to coincide with the start of the ground offensive on December

16, 1944. A mixed force of approximately 1,000 FW-190s and Me-109s was scheduled for the attack. If the Allied air forces could be crippled for even a week, the chances that the Germans might succeed in reaching Antwerp would be dramatically increased. However, if the American and British air forces were left to savage the German army as they had since before the invasion, the offensive would surely fail.

The concept of a surprise attack on the Allied bases was also consistent with what the largely undertrained Luftwaffe fliers could actually accomplish. Whereas air-to-air combat demanded considerable flying and gunnery skills that took time and experience to develop, it was much easier for novice fliers to strafe stationary targets on the ground. If luck was with the German pilots and they were able to catch the Americans and British on the ground, they stood a good chance of inflicting meaningful damage.

But the weather on the morning of December 16 kept virtually everyone on the ground, Allies and Germans alike. *Bodenplatte* was postponed. Nevertheless, the German ground assault took place on schedule and the American forces were taken completely by surprise. The Wehrmacht gained ground quickly, especially as the Allies couldn't bring their airpower to bear. When the weather cleared somewhat the following day the Luftwaffe committed its aircraft and crews as the situation on the battlefield demanded. But there was no massive air attack; rather, air operations over the Battle of the Bulge, as the great clash came to be called, developed into a steady, bloody grind.

The fighting was a brutal shock for the Allies. Prior to the attack it seemed that the war was nearly over. In fact, the situation grew so desperate that the Ninth Air Force, whose mission it was to fly tactical support sorties for the troops on the ground, was augmented by units from the Eighth Air Force. The 352nd Fighter Group was part of that augmentation and was placed under the command of IX Tactical Air Command.

The commander of the Eighth Air Force, Gen. James Doolittle, exhorted his airmen to take the fight to the Germans with great ferocity:

> The enemy is making his supreme effort to break out of the desperate plight into which you forced him by your brilliant victories of the summer and fall. He is fighting savagely to take back all that you have won and is using every treacherous trick to deceive and kill you. . . . So I call upon every man, of all the Allies, to rise now to new heights of courage, of resolution and of effort. Let everyone hold before him a single thought—to destroy the enemy on the ground, in the air, everywhere—destroy him.

Don Bryan remembered preparing for the group's movement to the continent. They were ordered to an expeditionary airfield in Belgium, Y-29. "We had all of December 22 to get ready," he recalled. "We were told that we had to wear our dress uniforms—pinks and greens—rather than our normal flying clothes. It was supposed to be a simple ferry flight to Y-29 from Bodney, and once we got in the area the Ninth Air Force radars were supposed to give us vectors into the airfield." The pilots received no good explanation as to why they were required to fly in their dress uniforms. As it developed, they had little idea how long they would be gone and most of them packed whatever clothes and personal belongings they could fit into their aircraft. On December 23, the 487th and the 328th were ready for the flight.

Bryan recalled that Earl Abbott was leading half of the 328th—sixteen aircraft—that day: "Just after engine start we were told to shut down and stay in our aircraft. I saw some personnel climb onto the wing of Earl's aircraft and give him something. Once they stepped down Earl ordered us to start up and told us we had a mission." Shortly after takeoff, Abbott aborted and passed the lead to Bryan before returning to Bodney. "The big problem was that Earl had all the code words," Bryan recounted, "and once we got over the continent the radar stations wouldn't respond to our calls."

Returning to Bodney was not an option for Bryan. "We cruised around for a while and then Hank White called and said 'Yellow Lead [Bryan] you have two FW-190s closing on you—I'll tell you when to break.'" That Bryan didn't maneuver immediately indicated how much trust he had in his squadron mate. "I switched to internal tanks and got ready. When Hank called for the break, we did in-place 180-degree turns."

Coming out of his turn, shed of his drop tanks, Bryan caught sight of the enemy aircraft. "Just before I opened fire the FW turned over on its back and jettisoned its canopy. The pilot hadn't gotten out when I fired. My first burst hit him square in the belly." Bryan fired more rounds at the enemy ship without observing any more hits. It didn't matter. The enemy aircraft continued down, slammed into the ground and exploded. Bryan's wingman, William Sanford shot down the second FW-190.

Bryan eventually took the formation into an airfield that turned out to be A-84 at Chièvres; it was in Belgium near the French border. After landing he parked next to a P-47 from the 361st Fighter Group, a Ninth Air Force unit. "It was the dirtiest aircraft I had ever seen," he recalled. The Ninth Air Force units flew hard and often, usually from primitive airfields where maintenance was difficult. Consequently, aircraft cleanliness was not a priority.

Bryan noted two pilots standing next to the P-47 who were nearly as filthy as it was. "After I filled out my flight record, I put on my hat, climbed out of *Little One III*, walked up to them and said, 'Hi, where am I?' One of the pilots looked at me in my dress uniform, glanced over at *Little One III* gleaming in the sun, then looked back at me and said, 'God damned Eighth Air Force,' and walked away. I never had a chance to tell him that we normally didn't wear dress uniforms on combat missions."

Punchy Powell arrived back in the United States that same day. His time in combat was over and he felt pride as the ship glided past the Statue of Liberty. "It was a moving and happy moment for me," he recalled. Moving and happy it might have been, but it had no lasting impact on the young fighter pilot's cockiness when he stepped off the ship a couple of hours later. "At the bottom of the gangplank was an American Red Cross gal," he remembered. "She gave us a wonderful smile and spoke to each of us as we stepped onto the dock. She looked at me and said, 'Welcome home, Lieutenant, what would you like that we can give you?' I was a typical smartass fighter pilot and I said, 'A quart of real American milk and you—and not necessarily in that order.' She just laughed and said that she could take care of the milk, but that the other might be a problem."

From that point, Powell had thirty days of leave and he started immediately for home. "It was the morning of December 24 when I reached Roanoke, Virginia, after an all-night train ride," he recalled. His fiancé, Betty Wiley, attended college there. "She met me at the boarding house where she lived. When my taxi pulled up she came running down the sidewalk and gave me a wonderful welcome, kissing me and hugging me like she would never let me go."

"She insisted on watching me shave," Powell remembered, "and then we went to the railroad station and took a train to our hometown, Thorpe, West Virginia. After being overseas for a year and nine months, it was wonderful to be home to experience the love and warmth of Betty and my parents and hers—and all of our families and friends. It was a glorious Christmas Eve."

The 328th and 487th Fighter Squadrons finally made it to Y-29 on the same day, December 24, 1944, that Powell and Betty Wiley arrived at

Thorpe. Y-29 was a barebones airfield near the Belgian village of Asch, southeast of the town of Genk. It had been carved out of a pine forest only the previous month by the 852nd Engineer Aviation Battalion and consisted of a pierced steel planking (PSP) runway of a few thousand feet, with similar taxiways and hardstand parking for about 150 aircraft. The 366th Fighter Group from the Ninth Air Force, operating P-47s, had been operating at the airfield for almost four weeks when the 352nd arrived. Living in well-worn tents that did nothing to keep out the cold gave the men a partial appreciation for what their infantry counterparts were enduring in less protected conditions during one of the coldest winters in living memory.

Albert Giesting had been Virgil Meroney's crew chief but since the previous April when Meroney was shot down and made a POW, Giesting had been promoted to flight chief, responsible for a number of aircraft. He remembered the living conditions in the tents at Y-29. "I made up some cots which was done by folding our blankets of which we had only two in the middle of the cot and covered it with the shelter half [small personal tent] to keep everything dry when the frost—about two inches thick—that formed on the roof of the inside of the tent would melt during the day. The shelter half kept everything dry." Clothing issues were nonexistent: "Getting dressed was no problem as you wore everything you had. You slept with it as well as worked with it."[1]

There were no showers or washrooms at Y-29. The men shaved and washed their hands out of their helmets as best they could and simply went without showering or bathing. However, after a week or so, arrangements were made for the men to wash their stink away. Richard Brock recalled: "I do remember that while we were at Y-29 we would go in G.I. trucks around sundown to a coal mine and use their showers. The facility was very nice with a white tile interior and was very clean, not at all what you would expect at a coal mine."[2]

Likewise, arrangements were made to take some of the misery out of the living conditions. "We were all about to freeze to death, both day and night," recalled Brock, "so Colonel Mayden had everyone to make a list of the personal items they needed from Bodney and give it to him. He then went to Paris and got a C-47, flew to Bodney, and returned with our personal items as well as a planeload of blankets, bed rolls, and etcetera. After that we kept reasonably warm."

The roster of the 352nd and all its various support units at Bodney numbered nearly two thousand men. The effort at Y-29 used only the most essential personnel. The 352nd took less than two hundred men, of whom seventy-five were pilots. The remainder were maintenance and other support troops. If there was a requirement for some sort of special material support or aircraft part it was flown in from Bodney. Too, pilots were easily rotated back to Bodney for rest. Likewise aircraft, so long as they were flyable, were ferried back to Bodney if they required maintenance beyond what the cadre at Y-29 could perform.

Indeed, Dick DeBruin remembered: "Almost daily one or two P-51s would fly to Bodney to exchange pilots, deliver important papers, or pick up aircraft parts." This was actually an efficient way to maintain operations. It was common that an aircraft would not be flyable for want of a critical item not readily available at Y-29. It was much more expedient to dispatch an aircraft to Bodney to retrieve it than it was to order it through official channels. And as DeBruin recalled, other messages or materials could also be readily delivered.

The cooks did the best they could in tents that were not designed as kitchens. Preparing meals was difficult and getting pots and pans and dishes clean was even more so. Ray Mitchell appreciated the effort: "The cooks did their best in snowy weather near zero. They came up with some interesting meals. The one thing I remember the most was that they went into the community and came up with a few fresh eggs for the pilots lucky to be on missions that day."[3]

Owing to the expedient way in which it was put into service, the airstrip at Y-29 offered no cover to the men working on the flight line. Whereas they had built warming huts at Bodney out of the wooden crates in which the external fuel tanks were shipped, there was neither time nor material at Y-29. Consequently, working on the aircraft was sheer misery. Cyrus Reap, the chief maintenance officer, remembered, "Frostbite was a big problem because the men were working and getting fuel on their hands and the evaporation of that in the cold caused a lot of frostbite."[4]

Richard Brock recalled how the men improvised to fight the cold. "We would light a match to a five-gallon can of 100-octane gas to keep our feet from freezing. One day about four of us guys were standing around one of these lit cans of gas when we saw Lieutenant Colonel Jackson coming straight toward us and we all figured we were in for a good chewing out for burning the gas. However, he asked if we were staying warm and when we told him we were he said, 'If anyone comes and tells you to put the fire out, just send them to me.' No one ever complained about it."

The Luftwaffe did what it could to add to the misery. A harassment raid, typically flown by a single Ju-88, was sent to Y-29 virtually every night. These intruders occasionally dropped bombs, usually well off target. Still, it was unnerving. A 487th history noted the reactions of the 352nd's officers and men who had never known what it was like to come under attack as Bodney had never been bothered by the Germans: "Being garrison troops from way back, pilots and ground personnel—especially the groundhogs—were more unnerved by the American ack-ack being thrown up around them than by the enemy planes overhead."[5]

On December 25, 1944, George Preddy was scheduled to lead a flight from the 328th Fighter Squadron on the 352nd's second patrol of the day. The mission was a sweep, intended to keep the sky over the battlefield clear of the Luftwaffe. Preddy briefed the mission particulars to include routing, radio frequencies, expected enemy air activity and the weather. Following the briefing, Preddy smiled and hiked up his trouser legs to show off his red socks to the rest of the pilots. He laughingly referred to them as his fighting socks.

Art Snyder, Preddy's crew chief, remembered that morning. "The major [Preddy] used to give me his watch to hold for him while he flew combat missions. But that morning when I preflighted his plane I noticed the cockpit clock was out of order. So when he came out to the plane, I mentioned this to him. He said, 'I'll just take my watch with me.'"[6]

At the same time that Preddy's pilots were readying for the mission that morning, the pilots of 6./JG 27—part of II./JG 27—were doing the same thing a hundred miles to the northeast at Hopsten, Germany. Fritz Koal was among them. He had been flying Me-109s with the unit since the summer and had seen service all over eastern and southern Europe until 6./JG 27 was moved to Hopsten in November. During the short time between the move and late December the unit took a beating and Koal remembered that readiness "went down rapidly."

He recalled how the mission of Christmas Day 1944 was planned. "We were to stop Allied bombers from attacking German units in the Battle of the Bulge area. The 5./JG 27, 7 and 8./JG 27 were to engage the bombers while 6./JG 27 was to cover them from above."[7] As it developed, 6./JG 27's *Staffelkapitän* was unable to fly, and Koal was directed, as the next most experienced pilot, to lead the unit. He had turned twenty only two days earlier.

The sixty or so aircraft comprising II./JG 27 got airborne about mid-day with Koal at the head of 6./JG 27. "The cold skies were blue and we could hardly spot a single cloud," he recalled. Once joined, the *Gruppe* climbed to about 29,000 feet and Koal took his unit a few thousand feet above them. Thusly arrayed, the formation headed to the battle area.

Preddy had already led his pilots airborne out of Y-29. The ten-aircraft formation climbed at full throttle through the clouds in two-ship elements. Leveling at 15,000 feet, Preddy took the pilots on a patrol that offered no action for nearly three hours. During that time the pilots grew inured to the uncharacteristic static that filled their earphones. The radios had been poorly tuned since arriving at Y-29. Notwithstanding the interference, the flight still maintained contact with their radar controller. James Cartee was Preddy's wingman that morning. "I was flying Ditto White Two," he recorded in his encounter report. "Near the end of our patrol, Ditto White Leader [Preddy] was vectored to a point slightly S/W of Coblenz where bandits were reported."[8]

Preddy led the patrol to a fight where P-51s and Me-109s were already engaged. He called over the radio, "Looks like they started without us; let's join 'em."[9] Ray Mitchell, Preddy's number four, remembered the scrap. "Preddy had just finished his transmission when the radio was filled with screaming about the beginning of a fight and I saw an Me-109 coming down from my left not far from behind [James] Lambright. I attempted to call Preddy but the radio was jammed with chatter. My only choice," Mitchell continued, "was to break from the flight and get in behind the Me-109 before it got in range of Lambright. I let up slightly until I was sure of the Me-109's position and then went full throttle to get in behind it and set it on fire. The canopy came partway off and the plane went down out of control."

Mitchell looked over his shoulder. "I discovered an Me-109 on my tail and made such a hard left turn that it became a high-speed stall and I went into a spin. I stayed in the spin for a while to make sure that I was no longer a target, and then pulled out." Mitchell's recovery was a wrenching one. It registered nine Gs—well above the P-51's operating limit.[10]

While Mitchell covered the flight's rear, Preddy threw himself into the melee and was soon turning hard with an Me-109. "After several turns," Cartee recalled," Major Preddy was gaining on the 109 when another 109 cut in front of him. He gave the latter 109 a burst. I observed many hits, the canopy came off and the pilot bailed out. Major Preddy immediately swung back to the first 109 and after about another turn got on him. He got numerous hits and this pilot also bailed out."

Fritz Koal was part of the fighting. "When we reached the target area we saw bunches of Mustangs attacking the *Staffeln* below us." Koal called for an attack, started down, and looked over his shoulder to make certain that his pilots were following him. "My very high speed brought me down there faster than I would have expected. I was in a perfect position and opened fire on a Mustang."

Koal noted several hits on the American aircraft but had no time to press his attack. "At that moment my ship was hit hard by enemy fire and I could not see what happened to the Mustang I was chasing." With his aircraft out of control, Koal jettisoned the canopy and struggled against negative g's before he was able to leap clear. It is quite likely that Koal's Me-109 was the first aircraft that Preddy knocked down that morning.

The fighting was over almost immediately. Cartee described the remainder of the mission. "Getting a new vector, we continued toward Liège, where bandits were reported on the deck. We were a three-ship flight now, a white nosed P-51 having joined up." The third P-51, an ad hoc wingman, was flown by James Bouchier of the 479th Fighter Group. The 479th flew a bomber escort mission from England that morning and was caught up in a melee during which it scored fifteen aerial victories while losing three pilots of its own. Somewhere along the way, Bouchier was spit out of the fight and attached himself to Preddy and Cartee.

The three of them were southeast of Liège at 1,500 feet when they spotted an FW-190D flying low over the ground below them. "Major Preddy went down after him," recalled Cartee. "The 190 headed East at tree-top level. As we went over a woods, I was hit by ground fire. Major Preddy apparantly [sic] noticed the intense ground fire and light flak and broke off the attack with a chandelle to the left. About half way through the maneuver, at about 700 ft his canopy came off and he nosed down, still in his turn. I saw no chute and watched his ship hit. Flak and tracers were still very thick."

George Preddy, history's top-scoring P-51 ace, was dead. And tragically, he had been shot down by his own countrymen. Determining with certainty who killed him is impossible. The American army was thick in the region and it was well protected by antiaircraft units. Eyewitnesses spotted Preddy chasing the FW-190 and remembered that the antiaircraft fire was so thick that the tracers arcing through the sky looked like a "whole field of golf balls." Preddy, at only a couple of hundred feet, was seen to clear his aircraft as it fell inverted. His parachute never opened.

Ironically, a pair of Me-109s roared low overhead the scene a couple of minutes later. Not a gun was fired.

Aside from Preddy, Bouchier was also shot down; he bailed out and survived. Cartee's aircraft was also hit. In fact, a burning tracer round punched into his cockpit and fell down around his feet where he tried to stamp it out. Once he landed back at Y-29, Cartee was surprised to see the group commander, Colonel James Mayden, waiting at the parking mat. "Mayden had probably gotten word that there was a mishap. His first question was 'Where is George?' The whole outfit was upset at the loss of Preddy."[11] Art Snyder recalled watching the rest of the patrol taxi back to the parking area. "Then I recall this one pilot—I can still see the picture in my mind—went by with his thumb down. I knew what he meant—that the major had had it!"

It was only after he landed that Ray Mitchell learned that Preddy had been killed. The news was heartrending. As he made his way back to his tent he was invited by a comrade to share a Christmas dinner. In his melancholy, the fact that it was the Christmas holiday had completely escaped Mitchell. "It had been that kind of a day," he recalled.[12]

That Preddy had been shot down by American forces wasn't made public immediately. *Stars and Stripes* carried a story on his death and simply noted that he had been killed by antiaircraft fire: "In the ensuing chase, ack-ack spat from a wooded area, tearing Preddy's plane apart and sending it down in flames."

Fritz Koal's eyes were injured during the fight that morning. The twenty-year-old who had led 6./JG 27 into battle was only returned to combat during the final two months of the war. He scored three aerial victories.

It is manifest that each of the men that made up the 352nd was a real person, with real hopes and dreams as well as friends and family that loved them and that they loved back. And great aspirations aside, they also endured typical complaints and deprivations while at the same time they enjoyed simple day-to-day pleasures. The letters they wrote home reinforce that point. Excerpts of those written by Carl Tafel Jr. of the 487th Fighter Squadron are instructive. A native of Louisville, Kentucky, he arrived at Bodney in time to fly missions in support of the Normandy invasion. Later that month, June 29, he wrote a letter to his parents.[13] After sharing what he could about the missions he was flying, he described his life at Bodney:

> Instead of losing weight as I expected to over here, I believe that I am gaining a little. We get plenty to eat and in between meals we have snacks at the line of cheese sandwiches, cookies, etc., and at night we usually have a few more of everything. Our exercise consists of volley ball every once in a while and ping-pong. What a life.
>
> Crap games are very few now as the end of the month usually finds everyone waiting for pay day. When they do play pounds are treated as if they were dollar bills instead of being worth four dollars.
>
> We have three cocker spaniels here on the field, and they are really cute. Two are brown and one black. I take this one out walking every once in a while and he runs himself to death over the field chasing birds. His name is Ratsy, and he belongs to one of the boys in the squadron however he is more or less the squadron mascot.
>
> Three of the boys left for the states today as they had finished their operational tour. We all just sat around and were envious, but it is something to look forward to.
>
> Love to all.

Nearly six months later, on December 3, 1944, Tafel wrote of his exasperation at not having yet scored in the air. "You have no doubt been reading about the terrific fights that are going on in the air over Germany. We have been in on just about every one, but I have yet to get a confirmed victory. I seem to be in the top cover flight all the time when we get into a scrap or else I have to break off to get a Hun off my tail." He also bemoaned the miserable weather. "Right now it is raining and blowing like the devil. We are limited to four blankets as the boys at the front need the rest so we feel the cold more than ever in the morning."

Tafel also confirmed the importance of cigarettes to their daily lives. "Received a carton of cigarettes from Uncle Joe and Aunt Lucia so please thank them for me as I don't have their address. We are having a shortage of smokes over here so they came in handy. Don't get me wrong, I still don't indulge, but I gave them to my crew chief who can't get any as only combat personnel is allowed to buy them."

A few days later, on December 8, Tafel wrote his parents again and registered a gripe that was nearly universal. "As usual the mail situation is terrible. The letters that are getting through were written in Oct. I don't know the reason, but I do know the mail is slow. I got a package from you today." He also described the V-2 rocket which was then terrorizing London. "The V-2 is a very nasty weapon as you have read and so far we have no way to combat it except bombing the store houses where they are kept. I have seen a number of them go up but it is impossible to catch them as they are faster than sound as you know. Had one hit close to me in London and was very queer as you hear the explosion and then the sound of it coming."

As he was in his previous letter, Tafel was again preoccupied with staying warm. "Went to London the other day for just one day. Saw several shows, did a little shopping, and came home. Have been running low on heavy socks to fly in so I bought some as well as some heavy pajamas as we sent all but four blankets to the boys at the front and it isn't enough to keep warm at night." He closed the letter with a postscript typical of a young man: "Please send some more stuff to eat."

Again, in his letter of December 11, 1944, Tafel wrote of the cold. "The weather is cold and wet as usual. Germany has lots of snow on the ground, and it is mighty cold in the air. The other day my heater was a little off, and I was so cold I couldn't bend my knees. It is times like that when you welcome a fight to get your mind off the discomforts of the weather."

He also wrote of girls. He mentioned that he had seen a number of "good shows," including *Bathing Beauty* with Red Skelton and Esther Williams. "About all a show needs is a few good looking girls along with their legs, and it will be a success. Right now there seems to be an unusual number of young girls being featured, and it makes everyone homesick as the devil. Some of the boys I fly with are only twenty and for the last two years instead of having a good time dating and dancing they are worried about chasing a German through the sky at 400 or 500 MPH."

On December 21, 1944—at the height of the Battle of the Bulge—Tafel wrote only a very short note to his parents: "Do not worry if you get no letters from me for a few weeks or so. If you look at the papers you will see what is happening in the front lines, and it so happens that we are going to try and throw our weight into stopping the drive." He closed the note with one sentence. "Will let you know as soon as I am able to about my part in the counter push."

On December 26, 1944—the day after George Preddy was killed—the 487th dove to assist a formation of P-47s being attacked by Me-109s west of Bonn. The group's intelligence section filed a report the following day: "Lt. Tafel, flying with Capt Hamilton, with squadron engaged ten-plus Me-109s. His plane was seen to get hit and catch on fire." Tafel was shot down and killed. His aircraft crashed near Liers, Germany, and the Germans buried his body in the cold ground next to the wreckage.

CHAPTER 29

Making History

Immediately after arriving in Belgium, the 352nd's pilots took advantage of the radar units that had come ashore during the invasion of Normandy. The radar sets these units operated—a combination of fixed and mobile types—tracked aircraft up to 100 miles or more away, depending on a number of factors, including the type and condition of the equipment, the weather and the altitude of both friendly and hostile aircraft. The units that dealt directly with the fighters were called fighter control squadrons and were tasked with tracking both friendly and enemy aircraft formations. With this information, they vectored fighters to enemy formations, or provided warnings when German aircraft were in close proximity. The radio callsigns of the units with which the 352nd worked most commonly were Marmite, Sweepstake, Sediment, and Nuthouse.

However, the technology was still in its infancy and virtually no one in the USAAF had more than a few years experience working with it. Too, the equipment wasn't always reliable; Identification Friend or Foe, or IFF, devices aboard the USAAF aircraft didn't always work, or sometimes pilots forgot to turn them on. Consequently, mistakes were not infrequent. In fact, many of the formations the USAAF fighters were sent to investigate turned out to be friendly. Still, it was certainly better to have the radar units available than not.

And often enough, the pilots were vectored to bona fide enemy targets. Indeed, that was the case on December 27, 1944, the day after Tafel was shot down. On that morning, the 487th was scheduled to patrol along a route from Liège to Verviers, to Frum, to La Roche. The group's

OPFLASH report indicated that the radar units were on top of their game: "Sweepstake instructed squadron to ignore briefing. Vectored to 20 mi SW Bonn vic/o (F1927) 1115 hrs. Fight on in two separate altitudes from 8000 ft to deck. Sqdn split up half to Bonn half to Mauen. 12-plus FW-190s headed west on deck in formation. Combat ensued radius 5–10 miles of Mauen from 1115 to 1125." In the engagement that followed, the 487th claimed sixteen enemy aircraft.

Ray Littge was credited with three of them. He described the reaction of the German fighters when they spotted the 487th: "They started a loose Lufberry [sic] to the left and my wingman, Lt. Ross, and I got behind the last boy in the Lufberry. I got strikes on his wing and tail, and he immediately snapped over to the left hit the ground and exploded."[1] Littge and Ross lost little time in moving up the line of German fighters where Littge attacked another FW-190 with virtually the same result. "I got behind another one," Littge recalled, "and got many strikes in the cockpit and wing root area. He rolled over on his back and went into the ground."

By this point, all but one of the FW-190s had been shot down or had cleared the area. Littge recounted latching onto the one remaining German fighter: "I got strikes on him several different times. He straightened out, jettisoned his canopy, and started pulling up. Then an unidentified P-51 came down on him from above, and got several strikes as the pilot of the E/A bailed out." It had been a big day for the 352nd; aside from the sixteen victories claimed by the 487th, the 486th tallied an additional six.

The missions that the 352nd flew out of Y-29 were markedly different than the bomber escort missions that had made up the bulk of its flying since the summer of 1943. The sorties from Y-29 were shorter and generally more exciting—and perhaps more dangerous. They were the sorts of missions that were typical of what the Ninth Air Force pilots had been flying in support of the Allied armies since D-Day. Many of the 352nd's pilots embraced the change and Don Bryan was among those. "For me," he recalled, "the move to Y-29 was a dream come true. There were no more of those long, dull, escort flights, which admittedly were marked with occasional moments of terror. At Y-29 we didn't have to concentrate on saving fuel. And we had radar control to vector us to targets and to help keep us clear from attacks. They were short missions and at least two per day."

Although the weather offered opportunities for the execution of *Bodenplatte* during the first two weeks following the start of the Ardennes offensive, the German high command did not put the plan in motion. However, with the Wehrmacht bogged down in a frozen stalemate toward the end of December, and with favorable weather forecast for the near term, the decision was made to try the attack in concert with a renewed push on the ground. Cryptic orders were sent to nine *Jagdgeschwadern* (fighter wings). At that point in the war, these units were intended to be equipped with approximately 275 aircraft each, however they were not at full strength.

Additionally tasked was a *Nachtjagdgeschwader*, a night-fighter wing. Ironically, for a mission that was intended to strike targets on the ground, only one *Schlachtgeschwader* (ground-attack wing) was tapped. A *Kampfgeschwader* (bomber wing) was assigned pathfinder duties for the fighter wings.

The orders included the codeword "Varus," which meant that the operation was officially on, and "Teutonicus," which authorized commanders to brief their men and ready their aircraft. A final codeword, "Hermann," was paired with a date and time—1.1.45 and 0920—indicating the exact minute at which the airfields were to be attacked: January 1, 1945 at 9:20 a.m. Immediately upon receipt of the orders, the Luftwaffe commanders set their men to work at a redoubled pace.

The Luftwaffe's *Jagdgeschwader* 11 (JG 11) was given the task of attacking Y-29. The unit had been formed in April 1943 and spent much of its short life fighting the American daylight bombing offensive over northern Germany. It was the deadliest assignment in all the Luftwaffe. In fact, just one of its *Gruppen*—III./JG 11—lost sixty-five pilots during 1944 alone. Its other Gruppen suffered similarly, if not as badly.

Major Günther Specht had led JG 11 for seven months by the end of December 1944. Specht was a hard-bitten Prussian who nonetheless was not only respected but also liked by his men. He had been part of the pre-war Luftwaffe and scored his first two aerial victories while flying an Me-110 against RAF Hampden twin-engine bombers on September 29, 1939. As a point of reference, of all the 352nd's officers, only James Mayden, the commanding officer, had been in military service when Specht scored his first aerial victories. John C. Meyer didn't even enlist as an aviation cadet until October 1939.

Specht spent his wartime career in the West. It had been hellish. One of his eyes was blown out and he was shot down several times. Recovery from his various injuries kept him out of the fight for a total of more than two years and most of his comrades from early in the war were dead. Nevertheless, he tallied an impressive total of thirty-four aerial victories, seventeen against four-engine bombers. Since taking command of JG 11, he flew as much or more than any pilot in the unit. There were few real fighting men in the Luftwaffe who were as experienced and talented—and long-lived—as Specht.

Still, JG 11 was a shambles. Since it had been formed the majority of the unit's pilots had been replaced many times over. It had been especially hard hit during the intense fighting that characterized the two weeks since the start of the Ardennes offensive on December 16. Indeed, during just the last half of December 1944, JG 11 suffered 142 aircraft destroyed or damaged and 33 pilots killed or unaccounted for. Further, more than two dozen pilots were wounded. Overall, the Germans lost more than 350 fighters during just the three days from December 23 to December 25. After years of fighting a war during which replacements were inadequate to keep pace with losses, there were few fliers left in the German Air Force that could be counted as experienced by American standards.

Detailed orders for *Bodenplatte* finally arrived at JG 11 on December 31, 1944, and the various commanders at the unit's different airbases—Gross-Ostheim, Darmstadt-Griesheim, and Zellhausen—briefed their pilots later that evening.[2] Exhaustive instructions, together with photographs of the target area, were intended to help make up for what the individual pilots lacked in experience. Following the briefs, many of the pilots were ordered to make the night an early one. At the same time the unit's ground crews continued to work at a frenetic pace through the bitterly cold night in order to get as many aircraft ready as possible.

Dick DeBruin, the 352nd's supply and transportation officer, remembered New Year's Eve and how he and some of the other officers took advantage of an ad hoc bar that the 366th Fighter Group had set up at Y-29. "After our evening meal on New Year's Eve, Meyer [John C.] said, 'Let's go over to the 366th area for one drink and then to bed.' I drove one of the Jeeps, and a group of us went for one drink. He [Meyer] appeared to be very calm that evening and one could imagine his thoughts were about the next morning."[3] In fact, Meyer was anxious to get a patrol up early the next morning. He had been badgering higher headquarters for permission to do so, but had yet to received it.

JG 11's pilots were up before daylight. Dawn, when it came, was icy cold. The sun reflected through a thin, crystalline haze that turned the sky nearly white. The pilots ate breakfast and received their final briefs while the ground crews struggled to make a few more aircraft serviceable. Ultimately, the various JG 11 units were able to get just more than sixty aircraft and pilots ready for the mission.

Shortly after 0800, the pilots of JG 11's staff flight—*Stab* JG 11—got their four FW-190s airborne out of Darmstadt-Griesheim with JG 11's commander, *Major* Günther Specht, in the lead. Six other FW-190s from I./JG 11 followed. The mechanics had outdone themselves; a total of sixteen flyable fighters remained behind with no pilots available.

Specht led the other pilots northeast toward Frankfurt to rendezvous with the rest of JG 11's formations. To the east of Frankfurt, a Ju-88 navigation ship took off from Zellhausen and twenty Me-109s from II./JG 11 quickly lifted off and trailed behind it. Once the formation was assembled, it also headed toward Frankfurt. South of Zellhausen at Gross-Ostheim, 31 FW-190s formed behind another Ju-88 and likewise set course for the rendezvous point.

The pilots of the Ju-88s and of the different *Gruppen* of JG 11 caught sight of each other over Frankfurt. They joined with little problem; the Ju-88s pushed to the front with the FW-190s of Stab and I./JG 11 heading the formation of fighters. The FW-190s of III./JG 11 followed with the Me-109s of II./JG 11 bringing up the rear. The string of just more than sixty aircraft headed northwest at less than two hundred feet in order to evade detection by Allied radars. Their route took them across the Rhine at Koblenz and over the front lines about twenty miles east of Aachen. At that point the twenty Me-109s of II./JG 11 climbed to just more than a thousand feet to give cover to the FW-190s.

Unlike many of the other groups flying to their targets at that very moment, JG 11 didn't lose any aircraft to friendly antiaircraft gunners. Still, it took a beating before it ever reached Y-29. After crossing over the lines into Allied-held territory Specht's formation ran a seemingly endless gauntlet of light and medium antiaircraft fire. Of the sixty or so aircraft that made up the attacking force, two Me-109s and two FW-190s were shot down. Several more aircraft were hit. A few miles northeast of Asch, the two Ju-88 crews, their jobs complete, left the pilots of JG 11 to finish the route on their own. Now at the head of the formation, Specht squinted over his left shoulder toward Asch and then took another look behind him at the men and aircraft that made up his *Jagdgeschwader*. A moment later he led the formation in a sweeping left turn to the southwest and toward the target.

The route from that point took JG 11 toward Y-29 but it also took it nearly over the top of Y-32 at Ophoven just a few miles north of Asch. Y-32 was occupied by the RAF's No. 125 Wing which was composed of four Spitfire squadrons. The field, virtually in front of them, drew a large number of JG 11's pilots like moths to a flame. That they mistook it for Y-29 would work to the 352nd's favor.

Albert Giesting was up early on January 1, 1945. "It was very cold when we got up at about five and went to the line to preflight the planes. The pine trees where the tents were at were covered with snow and some would fall down on your neck as you walked through them."[4]

The flight line, out of the cover of the trees, was even more frigid. "On the line," Giesting recalled, "the wing and engine covers were frozen and hard to remove. After plugging in the battery charger to heat up the batteries we checked the coolant and started the engines with a maximum effort." Normally, Giesting would have supervised the crew chief of each aircraft and lent a hand where required. But some of his crew chiefs hadn't yet arrived from Bodney and he was shorthanded.

"I was on my second preflight," he recounted, "and had the safety belt around the stick to check the mags [magnetos] when the guns began to fire; the pilot from the previous evening had left the gun switch on." Giesting had unwittingly sent nearly two hundred heavy machine gun rounds a half mile or more somewhere into Belgium. "I expected to have to make a trip in to see Colonel [Lieutenant Colonel] Meyer but he never said a word about it. I guess he figured we were doing the best we could, and we sure were. The armorers were a little mad as they had to get out and clean the guns and add some ammo—about thirty rounds per gun."

While the 352nd's aircraft were readied, eight P-47s from the 366th Fighter Group's 391st Fighter Squadron took off past them. The time was 0842. They were slated for a short dive bombing mission and were expected back at Y-29 in less than an hour..

By that time, Meyer was getting himself and eleven pilots from the 487th Fighter Squadron ready for a quick patrol. Meyer, at about 0800, had finally received permission from IX Tactical Air Command to fly the mission. He was ordered to have the squadron back no later than 1000 in order to be ready to fly a bomber escort mission at noon. "Col. Meyer hit back for the 487th's ready room, picked eleven other pilots, and told them they were going with him—on a routine flight."[5]

One of the JG 11 pilots who attacked the RAF base at Ophoven was Georg Füreder. After spreading out with the rest of the formation he pulled up and dove on the airfield. "My approach was too steep to engage the fighters on the east side of the airfield, so I aimed at four or five C-47s in the north-west corner," he said After making his firing run, Füreder wracked his aircraft around in a hard reversal to make another pass at the airfield. As he did so he was startled by tracers ripping past his aircraft. He was further surprised to find a brace of P-47s—one of them firing—directly behind him.

"I pulled sharply to port and his rounds passed astern of my plane. My pursuer and his No. 2 gave up the chase and headed off west. I started after them, then broke away for a final run at the airfield heading south."[6] Füreder recalled that several RAF aircraft were afire at Ophoven before he left the area. Additionally, scattered fires marked the wreckage of several German aircraft that were knocked down by Ophoven's anti-aircraft guns.

The P-47s that attacked Füreder were part of an eight-ship flight from the 366th's 390th Fighter Squadron. Led by Lowell Smith, they had taken off from Y-29 only minutes earlier on a ground attack mission. Soon after getting airborne their attention was caught by antiaircraft fire coming out of Ophoven and they immediately spotted the JG 11 aircraft. Discounting the uneven odds they dumped their bombs and rockets and attacked the enemy formation at once. Over the next thirty minutes the 366th's pilots shot down eight of the attackers. More importantly, their attack, together with the confusion caused by the misidentification of Y-32 as Y-29, delayed JG 11 enough for Meyer to get the 487th airborne.

Carl Galloway was John C. Meyer's crew chief. "When we arrived at Y-29," Galloway recalled, "he decided to leave his chute in the plane. I suppose he thought it would save some time for a fast takeoff. Later he asked me to take it to the operations hut after each flight and he would pick it up when he came out to fly."[7]

But on January 1, 1945, Meyer arrived at his aircraft without his parachute. He had forgotten it and sent Galloway after it. Upon returning Galloway helped Meyer into it and got up on the wing of his aircraft as Meyer lowered himself into the cockpit. "As we were getting straps in place," Galloway remembered, "everything seemed normal. No rush. Our plane was parked with its nose to the west. As I was standing there I looked to the east and what I saw must have frightened me. Colonel Meyer asked me, 'What's wrong sergeant?' I told him to look in his rear view mirror."

What Galloway had seen was the start of the German attack. "When he [Meyer] saw that, he told me to jump," recounted Galloway. "I heard him give the order to the others as he started the engine. There was no warm-up and he taxied out and took off at once."

Al Giesting's recollections coincided with Galloway's. "When the pilots came out for the patrol mission," Al Giesting remembered, "they didn't seem to be in a hurry as they were waiting for a sort of fog and frosty haze to burn off. About nine o'clock, they started and the P-47s [366th Fighter Group] took off first and went off toward the northeast in the direction of the slag heaps that were out that way." It was only a few minutes later that the action started. "I heard a big explosion," Giesting said, "and looked toward where the P-47s were and they were dropping their bombs. Then I noticed a lot of planes coming. About this time, the 487th must have seen the same thing and started to take off all bunched up."

Meyer was in a hurry as were his pilots behind him. Giesting remembered the crush of P-51s that went hurtling down the runway: "If the front one [Meyer] had cracked up, the whole bunch would have had it as they were almost prop to tail, but they all got off okay and the battle started, as by this time the 109s and 190s were over the east end of the field."[8]

Meyer, with his guns already armed and his gunsight on, lined up on the northeast-southwest oriented runway, gunned his engine and started rolling to the northeast. As he lifted clear of the runway he slapped his landing gear handle up and spotted an FW-190 just above the trees crossing from his right to left. He made a mild heading correction and fired his guns; the enemy fighter rolled inverted and went down in a flaming explosion. It had happened so quickly that Meyer's landing gear doors hadn't even closed before he fired his guns.

Meyer's encounter report described his downing of the enemy aircraft in a very matter-of-fact fashion. He took no literary license and his description does nothing to highlight how very remarkable the feat really was. "Leading twelve ships of the 487th Squadron taking off to the northeast from Y-29, Belgium. Immediately upon getting my wheels up I spotted 15-plus 190s headed towards the field from the east. I attacked one getting a good two-second burst at 300 yards, 30-degree deflection, getting good hits on the wing roots."[9]

From the ground, Richard De Bruin described Meyer's victory:

J. C. [Meyer] was gaining speed as he passed me and I turned ninety degrees right to watch his takeoff. He was starting his climb and his wheels were not fully retracted. To my astonishment and disbelief I saw an enemy fighter plane on the deck flying directly across the path of J. C.'s takeoff. J. C. immediately fired his weapons and hit the fighter which was a German FW-190. It crashed in flames in the middle of our airfield. . . . Before, I could only imagine what our pilots did while in an air battle. Now, I was a spectator watching in person from the ground one of the greatest fighter air battles.[10]

Alex Sears, Meyer's wingman, likewise was caught up in the fight almost immediately. "One Me-109 came at me head-on and we made several passes at each other, both of us firing. On the third pass I got some strikes on his engine and shot part of the tail section away. He started burning and went into a lazy spiral and crashed."[11]

Having downed one FW-190 just after taking off, Meyer engaged another almost immediately after. He chased it southwest for approximately ten miles, nearly to Liège. "On my first attack I got good hits at 10 degrees 250 yards. The E/A half-rolled and recovered just on top of the trees. I attacked but periodically had to break off because of intense friendly ground fire. At least on three occasions, I got good hits on the 190, and on the last attack the E/A started smoking profusely and then crashed into the ground. Out of ammunition, I returned to the field, but could not land as the field was under attack." Meyer was jumped by Me-109s on two separate occasions while he waited for the fight to clear at Y-29, but managed to dodge his attackers.

Ray Littge along with Meyer and Sears was one of the first pilots airborne. He started climbing and before he was able to join with anyone else found himself in the middle of the fight. "I picked out a 190 flying at 3,000 feet, and made one turn with it to the right. I got strikes on the wing roots and cockpit. He snap-stalled to the right, recovered, then snapped again, and hit the ground and exploded.[12]

Littge then chased after an FW-190 at low altitude. After he scored a few hits the German pilot started maneuvering aggressively but was unable to shake the P-51. Rather than fleeing east toward Germany the FW-190 pilot headed west with Littge—now out of ammunition—still in pursuit. "He took me almost to Paris," Littge noted, "when he started climbing, and at approximately 3,000 feet he bailed out in Allied territory." Rather than flying back to Y-29 after the long chase, Littge landed to refuel.

Wayne Stock was a crew chief with the 486th. That morning he was in the cockpit of *Miss Ginny* as he ran the engine through a power check. "I was sitting there when the control stick, which was fastened between my legs with the safety belt, started violently shaking. I looked off to my left to find one of the other crew chiefs wiggling an aileron to let me know that there was something going wrong. I turned around and saw that the sky was full; it looked like a swarm of bees."[13] Unconcerned, Stock continued with the engine check until the stick started shaking again and another aileron wiggler gestured for him to get to cover.

"And there they were—all over the place," Stock remembered of the German attackers. "I started walking towards our tent city in the woods toward the mess hall and turned around to see a German aircraft coming straight at me." Stock raised his carbine to shoot at the diving aircraft and then thought better of it. "By that time he had picked up his nose and was headed off toward the woods. Two P-51s were right on his tail and he was nailed very shortly back beyond us."

A short time later Stock botched a running dive into a gun emplacement where some of his comrades were already taking cover. "I got quite a laughing at from the other guys." The laughing turned to rapt attention as the men watched the 487th shoot down the attacking Germans. Stock remembered that "some were smoking and some were tumbling."

Henry Cottrell, an armorer with the 328th Fighter Squadron recalled that morning. He and his comrades had ushered in the New Year the previous night from the sparse comfort of their tents which were located in the fir trees a couple of hundred yards away from the flight line. "Stewart had a couple of bottles of Calvados [French apple brandy] which we soon disposed of. At twelve o'clock, Stewart took out his .45 and emptied a clip in the air to celebrate. After that we fell into our bedrolls and went to sleep."[14]

Cottrell was still asleep when the Germans attacked. "I awakened to the sound of gunfire. I thought that Stewart was shooting his .45 again. Then I realized that it was more than that." Cottrell kicked himself off his cot and leapt to his feet. "I grabbed my carbine and ran down the path to the field. A German plane flew over me and I fired at it. I emptied two clips. The pilot waved at me—I can still see it in my mind. As this was going on I could see the planes taking off and starting to fire as they got airborne; it sure was something to see."

Richard Brock was working in the cockpit of one of the 486th's aircraft when the attack started; he scrambled out when he looked up and saw a crew chief gesticulating at him. "I got out and ran and laid down in the ditch along the perimeter road. When I looked up and saw a lot of men laying in the ditch, I realized we were a perfect target for strafing so I jumped and ran to an area where there was a lot of brush piles and there I found a foxhole large enough for one more guy." Safely tucked out of the way, Brock and the rest of the men watched the unfolding fight.[15]

Marion Nutter was a 487th pilot who wasn't on the schedule that morning. He remembered the battle in a letter home to his brother Bob:

I was walking out of the operations tent about quarter of nine and heard someone holler, 'Hey, a dogfight!' and he pointed at the horizon towards Germany. There, zooming and turning just above the trees were P-47s, 109s and 190s going at it tooth and nail. The first thing we knew the fight had moved right over our heads. My squadron, as luck would have it, had just then taken off and was already in the scrap. . . . By then two of our boys were on one of them and the Jerry almost spun in trying to get away. He recovered right on the trees and zoomed away from the field in a steep turn. Right there one of our boys nailed him and he dropped his nose and went straight in a huge orange ball.[16]

Alden Rigby was at the end of the runway that morning, assigned as White 4. "I think all of us knew that we had to get off the ground and instinct simply took over," he recalled. "No choice—our chances were slim-to-none."[17] Certainly, the odds might have been a bit better than that, but Rigby made an excellent point; as closely packed as the 487th's aircraft were that morning, they made an excellent target. A couple of well executed strafing runs could have turned the squadron into a flaming fiasco. But the Germans failed to do that and they paid dearly.

"It was a relief even to get airborne," remembered Rigby. "It was also a relief to know that the folks on the ground were friendly—this probably helped to give us a very aggressive attitude." Indeed it was quite unusual that the 352nd's airmen were engaged in aerial combat over friendly troops. And certainly this was the first time they had ever fought over their own airfield.

A minute or two after getting airborne—just a few miles east of the airfield—Rigby spotted an FW-190 preparing to fire on his flight leader, Ray Littge. Rigby called for Littge to break left and he responded with a hard turn that gained him a few precious seconds, "I did not see him again until after the action," Rigby remembered.

He didn't waste any time and immediately fired a forty-five-degree deflection shot at the FW-190. Bullets streamed into the German aircraft's wings and cockpit. "The E/A rolled over and went straight in from about 500'."[18]

"I broke sharply to the left," recalled Rigby, "and noticed another FW-190 headed east on the deck. I dropped down on his tail and my gun sight went out so I fired a long burst until I noticed hits on his wing roots.

He started pouring black smoke and lost altitude until he crashed in the trees." That Rigby was able to hit the enemy aircraft without a gunsight was no small feat. Simply visualizing a straight line from the aircraft to the target was difficult enough. Judging the range and computing the right amount of deflection, or lead, was nearly impossible.

Alone, Rigby raced back toward the airfield where he spotted a P-47 in a hard circling fight with an Me-109. "The P-47 fired a short burst and I noticed a few strikes on the tail section of the 109. The E/A seemed to tighten his turn and as the P-47 mush[ed] to the outside, I cam[e] in from beneath and fired a long burst, noticing hits on his wing. Coolant came out. The E/A crashed into an open field."

In a span of only minutes, Rigby had knocked down two FW-190s and an Me-109; he had shot down two of those without an operable gunsight. Still, he wasn't finished. "I started circling the field to make a landing because I was almost out of ammo. I investigated what seemed to be another fight a mile or so to my right. I pulled into the fight with two other 51s. One 51 fired at the E/A and scored hits. The 109 broke in my direction and I fired the remainder of my ammo at him, scoring at least one hit in the cockpit. The E/A dove straight into the ground."

Without ammunition, Rigby finally decided that he was finished. Whereas just more than a week earlier he would have had an hours-long trip back to England, on that morning he was able to make his approach to landing almost immediately. He set up behind one of his squadron mates: "The 51 ahead of me drew some ground fire on his low pass and victory roll." Rigby was a fast learner: "I decided against any celebration in the air. It was a good thing the AA [antiaircraft] troops on the ground were not that great, or more friends than the enemy would have 'bought the farm.'" With four victories fresh under his belt, Rigby landed unmolested.

In almost an exact replay of Rigby's first victory that morning, Dean Huston, flying as Yellow 4, also found himself protecting his flight leader immediately after taking off. "I was about 300 yds astern and above Lt [Sanford] Moats when a FW 190 started to crawl up behind him. Lt Moats was already engaged with another ship and I told him to break left."[19] Moats reacted to Huston's call. The FW-190 pilot also pulled left, but not hard enough to get into a firing position. At the same time, Huston pulled down hard under the enemy aircraft and then hauled the nose of his P-51 back up, firing a three-second burst. "Hits were observed all over the wings and fuselage," Huston recorded, "with flames resulting immediately. He went into a dive from about 2,000' and crashed into the grd. I saw no chute."

Sanford Moats, who had been saved by Huston's timely call, recollected the start of the melee. "As I took off, I spotted about fifteen-plus

FW-190s at 100 feet coming from three o'clock on their way to make a pass at the air strip N of our field. At the same time I noticed approx 15 Me 109s flying top cover at 3,500 feet just below a thin cloud layer."[20] Moats recalled that two of the low-flying FW-190s turned hard into him and Huston. They all entered a Lufbery to the left while the antiaircraft gunners on the ground below fired indiscriminately into them.

"I closed on the tail of the first 190," remembered Moats, "and looked back to see a 190 closing on the tail of my wingman." He called for Huston to break just as the other FW-190 began to fire. With Huston momentarily out of danger he turned his attention back to the enemy aircraft to his front. "I then fired a short burst at 300 yds and 30 degrees deflection at the 190 ahead of me, observing strikes in the cockpit area and left wing root." The German fighter caught fire and flew into the ground; the pilot did not escape.

Richard DeBruin described the panic that followed as the German fighters—increasingly pressed by the 487th's pilots—continued their strafing attacks: "Everyone on the ground, which included about sixty or more pilots, just on our side of the field, scurried for shelter. It wasn't funny at the time, but later we laughed because some hid under fuel trucks."[21]

By that time the rest of the 487th's twelve-ship flight was airborne. "Approx 50 E/A were in the vic," recounted Sanford Moats, "and the entire area was full of friendly flak." The next aircraft he targeted was an FW-190 strafing a nearby marshalling yard. "He broke left and started to climb. I fired a short burst at 200 yds and 20 degrees deflection, observing a concentration of strikes on both wing roots and the cockpit. Both wings folded up over the canopy of the E/A and he went straight in. The pilot did not get out."

Moats went after another enemy fighter almost immediately. "I continued my left turn and rolled out slightly above and behind another 190 which broke left." Again, he fired another brief burst of gunfire and saw hits on the German's fuselage, canopy and left wing root. The canopy fell away as the aircraft caught fire but the pilot failed to parachute clear before crashing into the ground.

Moats had knocked down three enemy fighters in quick succession but there was still no shortage of targets. He found himself alone and caught up in a mixed formation of Me-109s and FW-190s headed east away from the airfield. "They split up and I picked one 190 who broke into me. We made several head on passes and I pulled up and came down on his tail, firing a two-second burst, observing strikes from wing tip to wing tip. He leveled off and hit the deck." As the enemy fighter hunkered down at low level and raced east toward Germany Moats continued to peck at him. "As we passed over Maastricht, I fired a short burst that exploded his belly tank, and my aircraft was hit by 40-mm ground fire."

Notwithstanding the damage to his aircraft, Moats continued to dog the enemy fighter as they raced low over the countryside. "At this time I had only one gun firing and the E/A kept taking violent evasive action on the deck as we crossed the front lines." Still, he continued after the German and finally pulled above and to the right of the ragged enemy ship. He waited just a moment before making another attack that scored hits around the wing root. "The enemy aircraft broke left, pulled up slightly, and dove into the ground. The pilot did not get out."

Nearly out of ammunition, Moats navigated back to Y-29 where he was immediately fired on by the airfield's antiaircraft guns. If the loss of Preddy to friendly fire had made an impression on the antiaircraft units at Y-29 it was not apparent. "A lone Me 109 made a pass across the field and I made a pass at him. He broke into me and I fired my remaining few rounds of ammo at 90 degrees deflection and 100 yds range." Just as the pilot Moats had previously shot down had made a run for Germany, this one also fled east. However, unlike the earlier pilot, this one successfully escaped Moats.

His ammunition spent, Moats returned to Y-29 and parked himself overhead where his presence might deter more Germans from attacking the field. "Another Me-109 came by and I followed him through a couple of barrel rolls but could not shoot as I was out of ammo. He went straight up, chopped throttle, tried to get on my tail, couldn't, stalled out, recovered, and split S'd at 1,500 feet, barely pulling out above the trees." This German pilot was skilled but not so skilled that he was able—on that morning—to fight more than one adversary at a time. Moats remembered: "Another P-51 came into the area at this time and shot the E/A down four miles northeast of the field."

The other Mustang was piloted by Henry Stewart. Stewart had gotten off to a slow start that morning. Soon after getting airborne he climbed to altitude to give cover to his lead, William Halton, but the antiaircraft fire was so heavy he was forced to turn away. "When I broke I ran into a 109. I made a few turns with him but could not get into firing position."[22] Stewart disengaged with the German fighter and almost immediately latched onto another: "I followed another 109 up through the clouds at about 150 mph but could not close and almost spun out." Having unsuccessfully turned with two of the German fighters, Stewart went after a third. "I came back down and went around with another 109. I fired but did not observe any strikes."

Notwithstanding his lack of success, the hapless Stewart stayed in the hunt; he was nothing if not persistent. "I then came back toward the field and tagged onto another 109 headed toward our field. I closed on him and pulled the trigger, nothing happened. My knee had shut my [gun] switches off. I got them back on and fired. I got a few strikes, we started turning over a slag pile and Capt. Whisner came along and clobbered him."

If Stewart was frustrated, he remained undeterred, and a few moments later, his doggedness finally paid off. "I came back toward the field again and saw two P-51s chasing a 109. The 109 broke, I cut my throttle and slid in behind him at about 100 yds and 100' off the deck. I fired and observed many strikes. The 109 went straight in and exploded."

In Stewart's case that morning, success bred more success. "I pulled up to 2,000' and started a turn. I saw another 109 on the deck headed E[ast]. I closed my throttle again and dove behind him. At 150 yds range I opened up and got many strikes on the wing root and fuselage. The 109 went straight into the ground."

Stewart was on a roll. It was at this point that he spotted Moats, who was out of ammunition, tangling with the skilled Me-109 pilot. Stewart recalled: "I started back toward the field and picked up another 109 on the deck, 51 chasing him. The 51 broke and I dove down on the E/A, our alt being about 100 feet. He turned and I followed him E[ast]. I closed to 150 yds and fired, getting strikes all along the right side of the plane. Coolant came out and the 109 crashed into the ground."

William Whisner, who had earlier shot down one of the fighters that Stewart had been chasing, remembered that the fight was a free-for-all from the very beginning. "We didn't take time to form up, but set course, wide open, straight for the bandits."[23] Whisner noted the 366th's P-47s were already engaged, and also spotted a large formation of FW-190s at 1,500 feet with a number of Me-109s above them. "I picked out a 190 and pressed the trigger. Nothing happened." Whisner hadn't yet armed his guns. Whereas, the pilots had plenty of time to complete their combat checks when they were flying out of Bodney, such was not the case on this particular morning.

"I reached down and turned on my gun switch," Whisner recollected, "and gave him a couple of good bursts. As I watched him hit the ground and explode, I felt myself being hit." Whisner whipped his aircraft around in a hard climbing turn to the right and saw another FW-190—guns ablaze—very close behind him. "As I was turning with him, another 51 attacked him and he broke off his attack on me."

"I then saw," Whisner recorded, "that I had several 20mm holes in each wing and another hit in my oil tank. My left aileron control was also out. I was losing oil but my pressure and temperature were steady." Such damage would normally have compelled a pilot to turn directly for home, but Whisner was already there. "Being over friendly territory I could see no reason to land immediately, so turned toward a big dogfight and shortly had another 190 in my sights. After hitting him several times, he attempted to bail out, but I gave him a burst as he raised up, and he went in with his plane, which exploded and burned."

Soon after knocking down the second enemy fighter, Whisner found himself engaged with a third, an Me-109. This fight taxed Whisner's skill and lasted much longer than was typical. "We fought for five or ten minutes," he recalled, "and I finally managed to get behind him. I hit him good and the pilot bailed out at 200'. I clobbered him as he bailed out and he tumbled into the ground."

Calls came over the radio that the airfield was getting strafed again and Whisner raced in that direction. "I saw a 109 strafe the northeast end of the strip. I started after him and he turned into me. We made two head-on passes, and on the second, I hit him in the nose and wings. He crashed and burned east of the strip." Whisner chased after several more enemy fighters without success and finished the day with four confirmed aerial victories.

Whisner's wingman, Jack Diamond, never had a chance to get joined and in fact did not immediately see the fight. "I saw aerial activity around an airfield [Ophoven] a few miles away and I thought it must be an enemy attack. It was soon every man for himself. I kept searching the sky for planes and called Whisner three times to let him know I was not with him."[24] Whisner didn't respond to Diamond's calls. Alone, Diamond took off after an FW-190. Chasing the German pilot at very low altitude, he scored hits on his fuselage and wings and sent him crashing into the trees. "As I followed he flew into the ground at a low angle and pieces of the plane flew off everywhere. I looked back as I zoomed over but saw no explosion."

Diamond hurried to get away from the ground. He then spotted another FW-190 and dove immediately behind him. "I moved in so close that my plane was bouncing up and down violently from his prop wash." Diamond squeezed off burst after burst of gunfire but was unable to bring the enemy aircraft down. He briefly considered hacking at the enemy fighter with his propeller but quickly dismissed the notion. Finally, low on ammunition and without any friendly cover, Diamond gave up on the fleeing German and turned back toward Y-29.

The fight was still going on when the eight P-47s from the 366th's 391st Fighter Squadron entered the standard landing pattern at Y-29. This was the same flight that took off at 0842 on a ground attack mission before the battle started. Tom Colby, a pilot with the 352nd's 486th Fighter Squadron, remembered that he and seemingly everyone else on the ground tried—without effect—to warn them off by waving, pointing and shouting as the aircraft came in to land toward the southwest. "All the P-47s landed successfully thanks largely to a .50 caliber battery located in the 366th Fighter Group area. This battery was located near the control tower. Every time a Jerry approached a P-47 which was wheels down on his downwind leg, this gun fired tracer in front of the Jerry and behind the P-47, effectively scaring off the German."[25]

The action over and around the field was mayhem. Giesting remembered, "There was so much going on that one guy couldn't possibly keep track of everything. The guys were cheering like they were at a ball game."

After knocking down the FW-190 that was chasing Sanford Moats early in the fight, Dean Huston was hard after another German when his pursuit was cut short: "I was on the tail of a 109 at low level fairly close to the field when my 51 was hit by gunfire. I looked around and nothing was on my tail so I continued for a few seconds and then happened to glance at the oil pressure gauge and it was reading zero!" Huston hauled his aircraft in a turn toward the airstrip, dropped his landing gear and flaps and got his ship on the ground just in time. "I touched down," he recalled, "and the engine froze as I was rolling down the runway."

Albert Giesting recalled seeing an unfortunate German pilot safely bail out from his aircraft, only to have his parachute catch fire.

Nelson Jesup was one of the last 487th pilots to get airborne that morning. He firewalled his engine and as the aircraft broke ground he raised his landing gear and nosed over slightly to accelerate just a few feet above the runway. It was then that he noted an Me-109 with a blue propeller spinner coming directly at him. An instant later the German fighter passed close aboard down his left side only twenty feet above him.

At the edge of the airfield, Jesup pulled the nose of his fighter nearly vertical then chased an Me-109 into the clouds before losing sight of it. He played cat-and-mouse with a couple more enemy fighters before spotting an FW-190 climbing into the clouds. At 4,500 feet, both aircraft topped out with Jesup in trail of the German. He took a long range shot at six hundred yards without observing any hits. "At 400 yards I fired another burst and observed a cluster of strikes in the region of the cockpit. He slowly rolled off to the left and went down through a hole in the clouds in a spiral and went into the ground. I did not see the pilot get out."

Following his aerial victory, Jesup went back above the clouds to try his luck again. There, he was mistakenly attacked by an RAF Typhoon. Having sustained no damage his descended back through the clouds and returned to Y-29.[26]

William Halton scored once that day. "I fired at one [FW-190] at zero degree deflection and he spun in and exploded in some woods." After unsuccessfully using the remainder of his ammunition to shoot down another FW-190 he gave up and headed for Y-29. "I was attacked three times by 109s but managed to evade them. The enemy pilots were very eager. The 109s gave me plenty of trouble."[27]

The action over Asch that morning was compact and fought at low altitude. No other air battle during all the war was comparable. Many of the men later remarked that the action over Asch that day seemed almost staged—as if for a motion picture. Marion Nutter recalled in a letter home to his brother: "I had always wanted to see a dogfight from the ground and I certainly got my wish. A movie couldn't have done better."[28]

Its deadly nature aside, the 487th's history of the event noted that the battle had the same feel as a big sporting match. As the pilots returned, mostly for lack of ammunition, the men on the ground rushed them, "cheering like alumni at a Notre Dame–Army football game."[29]

Meyer, after having led what was indisputably one of the most successful air actions in history, taxied back to his parking spot. His crew chief, Carl Galloway, remembered that Meyer—almost immediately upon arriving at Y-29—had considered that such an attack might one day come. "J. C. [Meyer] had told me that I should dig a foxhole as it might come in handy someday. Well, I never did. When he came back the first thing he wanted to know was did anyone get hurt? I told him no. Then he wanted to know why I didn't dig the hole. No excuse. He said, 'You dig one, and make it large enough for the two of us. This is an order.'" Galloway got the hole carved out of the frozen ground in short order.[30]

The fighting over and around Y-29 that day involved more than combatants. A Belgian woman who lived in Asch at the time recalled: "We fled to the cellars because the bullets hit the walls of our house. In our street, a six-year-old girl was killed and two boys were badly wounded by the bullets. On the territory of Asch, three planes crashed. When everything was over, we went looking to the wrecks. We saw parts of bodies being gathered to put in bags. That made quite an impression on us."[31]

Few German recollections of the fight over Y-29 exist. This is partly because many Luftwaffe records were lost, but is primarily due to the fact that so many of the pilots who participated simply didn't survive the war. However, a few accounts do exist. The deadly, wheeling fight was recounted by *Oberleutnant* Paul-Heinrich Dähne: "At 09.20 hrs we engaged many enemy fighters which had just taken off. The dogfight was very hard and unforgiving. Several enemy fighters were shot down. However, several of our own were also shot down."[32] In fact, the pilots of JG 11 mistakenly claimed to have knocked down four P-51s, four P-47s, an RAF Typhoon, and an additional unidentified single-engine aircraft.

Actually, the only American aircraft shot down in the melee was a P-47 of the 366th Fighter Group; its pilot survived. That Dähne understated JG 11's losses and grossly overstated the American losses was due in part to a natural bias in favor of his own side. But it was also attributable to the fact that the fight had been so confusing and chaotic. More than a third of JG 11's pilots were lost and most of the others scattered to whatever bases they could reach, or crash-landed on the German side of the lines. The attendant confusion combined with the fact that operations continued unabated at a chaotic pace meant that the Luftwaffe had little ability to accurately recreate what had truly taken place. "I, for myself," Dähne recalled, "was just able to reach friendly territory with a badly battered aircraft." Ironically, Dähne, who had scored more than ninety aerial victories against the Soviets and three in the West, was killed in a flying accident just before the war ended.

JG 11 was clear of Y-29 before 1000 that morning. Although several of the 487th's pilots landed early due to damage or fuel exhaustion, others stayed airborne for a while longer to provide cover for the airfield. The group's OPFLASH report for the engagement was sent the same day and was, considering the nature of the clash, fairly accurate. It noted that the 487th got airborne at 0921 that morning and that all aircraft were down just more than two hours later at 1127. It also recorded that twenty-three enemy aircraft were destroyed for the cost of one aircraft damaged. The narrative is fairly short, and the takeoff time is slightly at odds with the takeoff time noted earlier in the report:

> Squadron was on runway preparing to take-off on above patrol [Grebenvoich to Laacher Lake and return to base] when bandits approached from the northeast. Squadron took-off head on into the e/as [enemy aircraft] and combat ensued in the immediate area from 0915 to 0945 and within a radius of 15 miles of the base. At least ten e/as were seen to go down in the immediate vic/o [vicinity of] the field. E/as were active all along the northern front lines and as far west as Turnhout. Intense friendly ground fire caused our aircraft to break off attacks in many cases.

The report also described the enemy pilots as "Very aggressive and appeared to be of a higher calibre than pilots engaged in recent missions."

The German attack did virtually no harm to the 352nd. Only one of the group's P-51s was hit. Cyrus Reap was the senior maintenance officer at Y-29 and recalled the damage: "The strafing planes hit one of our parked 51s and ignited the fuel strainer in the wheel well. Our fire truck was try-ing to put out the fire by shooting foam into the air scoop, thinking it was the engine, but corrected this and extinguished the blaze." For this nig-gling bit of damage, the Luftwaffe paid a very dear price.[33]

Not only were the non-flying personnel of the 352nd treated to the sight of their unit scoring an incredible victory literally in front of their eyes, but they were also exposed to the horror that was often part of the tri-umph of aerial combat. Richard DeBruin was directed to help with the dis-covery and identification of the enemy pilots so that a graves registration team could bury them. He recalled one of the crash sites: "We located the remains on a field less than a mile from Y-29. The aircraft, an Me-109, was completely destroyed by fire and the pilot's torso was lying on the ground with the head and limbs severed and spread over the area. It was not some-thing I cared to observe."[34]

Many of the 352nd's men chafed to investigate the still smoldering German wrecks. After being released from duty in the afternoon, Albert Giesting and a pair of fellow mechanics headed toward one of the German crash sites. "The plane hadn't burned but had plowed a big ditch and thrown the pilot clear. It looked like he was a very young kid but dead any-way." Dean Huston's recollection was nearly identical: "A group of us walked out to the area just east of the strip where a German fighter had augured in and the body of the pilot was still there. I remember feeling that he was barely out of high school. I will never forget it, or that day."

Perhaps the dearest loss sustained by JG 11 was that of the unit's com-mander, Günther Specht. It is impossible to determine who killed him or how, but he was dead nonetheless. Many of the downed German pilots—and their aircraft—were burned beyond recognition or literally blown over the countryside. Chet Harker, a pilot with the 352nd's 486th Fighter Squadron recollected that some of the pilots and airmen were sent into the area around Asch for the gruesome task of collecting bodies or body parts in order to process them according to military procedure. "We were given bags and told to pick up anything, uniforms or body parts that could be returned to the Germans for subsequent identification. As I recall, one of the people in my group found the sleeve of a German pilot with the severed arm still inside."[35]

The body of Specht, along with those of several other German fliers, was never found or identified. Ultimately, the loss of old hands like

Specht, who should have been leading from a headquarters, underscores how desperate the Luftwaffe was for seasoned pilots.

Art Snyder was another of those who wanted to see a wrecked German aircraft firsthand. "Among the many dogfights that we were able to witness, one was close at hand and the Jerry was skimming over the ground up and down with a P-51 on his tail." The Mustang finally caught the enemy aircraft with a short burst of gunfire and knocked it into the ground. Snyder recalled: "This was about a mile from the strip, so the next day a couple of us walked out to where the crash was and looked at the pilot who looked not to be over twenty. I thought of taking a souvenir and managed to get the tail wheel off; why I took that, I don't know."[36]

The news of the events at Y-29 on January 1, 1945, spread quickly. Newspaper and radio reports in the States were out almost immediately. Even Walter Starck learned of it even though he was a POW at the time. His engine gave up a few weeks earlier on November 27, 1944, when he ran into pieces of an aircraft he had shot down. "I was already in Stalag Luft I at the time. But we heard of it within hours of the happening. Each night, after 8 P.M., a 'secret' paper with the latest news of the war happenings came out of nowhere. One of those papers had the news of the outstanding performance of the Yanks, courtesy of the BBC."[37]

However, news traveled quickest through official channels. And the officials at the ends of those channels reacted quickly. Richard Gates, an officer with the 352nd's operations shop, the S-3, recalled: "That afternoon, a silver, twin-engine aircraft circled Y-29 and landed. A short time later, someone yelled 'ten-hut!'"[38] The 352nd was visited by none other than the commanding general of the U.S. Strategic Air Forces, Gen. Carl Spaatz. With him were Lt. Gen. James Doolittle, Lt. Gen. Hoyt Vandenberg, and Maj. Gen. Pete Quesada. The generals toured the area, met the men, and were thoroughly briefed on the very big day. Doolittle recorded his visit to Y-29:

> When we approached for a landing at the fighter field, we saw a bunch of German fighter planes lying all around the area. The field group commander [presumably John C. Meyer], a very eager chap, was to have flown a group patrol mission at 10 A.M. However, he decided to send up and lead an early dawn patrol and had just become airborne when the German planes came over intent upon destroying his planes on the ground. They were easy meat for our boys, who destroyed a couple of dozen then and there. It was a reward for a group commander who was an eager beaver.[39]

What had been a banner day for the 352nd was stained by a singularly tragic event. Richard DeBruin remembered watching a formation of the group's Mustangs flying to the west of the airfield in the afternoon. "This flight encountered some British Royal Air Force Typhoons. Suddenly one of our P-51s shot down a Typhoon, killing the British pilot." DeBruin recalled that both the Typhoon pilots and the 352nd's pilots landed at Y-29 and that, "There was quite a discussion among the pilots involved after they were on the ground."[40]

It was Francis Hill of the 328th who had shot down the Typhoon pilot, who was actually Flight Lieutenant Don Webber of Royal Canadian Air Force (RCAF) Squadron 183. Hill was devastated at his mistake. Art Snyder recalled talking to Hill: "He said everybody was talking on the radio and hollering 'bandits.' He lined up on this one and gave a short burst; immediately he knew what he'd done and said he felt like jumping out."[41]

The Canadian pilots were angry, and with good reason. Unfortunately, at that stage in the war it was not unheard of for USAAF pilots to mistakenly attack their British and Commonwealth counterparts, whereas the opposite did not happen quite so often. For one, the Americans had stopped camouflaging their fighters and instead left them in an easy-to-distinguish bare metal finish. On the other hand, the RAF and Commonwealth air forces still painted their aircraft in palettes that, from a distance, were not dissimilar from those that the Luftwaffe used. The RAF and RCAF markings, or roundels, were distinguishing features, but were sometimes too difficult to make out at long range or in certain light conditions, or if a pilot was overeager.

Moreover, pilots from the Eighth Air Force were not used to encountering other Allied aircraft deep over Europe. Rather, they were accustomed to escorting heavy bombers at high altitude deep into Germany where other friendly fighters were seldom seen. Consequently, the sight of camouflaged aircraft often put American pilots immediately at the ready.

Of the accidental downing, a supplement to the 352nd's operational report for January 1, 1945, dated January 2, provided few details: "Sediment and Sweepstakes [radar controllers] reported bandits over base area. In subsequent confusion Typhoon was shot down as FW-190." In a separate OPFLASH report the group recounted the 328th's bounce of the Typhoons in just slightly more detail: "Uneventful control of above area [St. Vith to Bonn to Duren and return to base] on Marmite [radar] control. No e/a seen. Flying control, SWEEPSTAKES and SEDIMENT reported bandits in base area and squadron returned in search of bandits. Lt. Hill shot down Typhoon which was identified, in be [sic] confusion, as a FW-190."

Albert Giesting had an interesting recollection about the incident. "I don't know if it's true but I heard Meyer burnt the film out of the P-51 camera."[42] It is impossible to determine the veracity of what Giesting heard. There is no record that Meyer, Hill, or anyone else denied responsibility for the Typhoon pilot's death. If it was true, perhaps Meyer felt that showing the film would have been a morbid or unseemly act; that there was nothing to gain by viewing the mistaken killing of an Allied airman.

Notwithstanding the tragic death of the Typhoon pilot, there was still considerable revelry that night. But later, things took an ugly turn when William Whisner, who had shot down four German fighters that morning, got out of hand. Whisner had been with the unit since virtually the beginning and had been very close to George Preddy. Like Preddy, Whisner sometimes drank more than he should have. John C. Meyer recounted what happened.

Bill sat dejectedly drinking Coke amidst the gala partying of the remaining participants in this day's events. Bill had had a serious brush with the Group Commander about three months before. He caused a hell of a scrap over at the Officer's Club and struck a high-ranking visiting officer. Under ordinary circumstances if it had been anyone else but Bill, he would have been court martialed right then. The command was becoming fed up with his periodic soirees, and he had been told in no uncertain terms . . . that the next time would be the last. . . . Bill, since that date, had not touched a drop. However, it seemed to me that this occasion was an exception, and after arranging with two of the burliest of our Group to be his watchdogs and take responsibility for keeping him out of trouble that night, Bill joined the fun. It was not too long, however, before he was on the road he had travelled so many times before, and the watchdogs stepped in. This medium-sized youngster, however, was a wild man, driven crazy by his drink, and a battle royal ensued, glasses were broken, furniture wrecked, and whiskey bottles smashed. . . .[43]

Stories and wild conjecture about the attack were rampant among the men at Y-29 and other Allied bases. Richard Brock recalled: "There was a rumor that an autopsy was performed on one of the German pilots and it was determined that he was a teenager and was high on some sort of drug to give him the courage for such a desperate mission. It was also rumored that he was a colonel."[44] Of course, the story was absurd but it was an indication of the sorts of unfounded reports that made the rounds in an environment where it was difficult—and not particularly necessary—to keep every person informed of every aspect of a wide-ranging war.

Luftwaffe operations on the morning of January 1, 1945, suffered generally from the basic inability of its flyers to execute a mission according to plan. The pilots were so inexperienced that a significant number of them simply became lost on the way to their targets and never found anything worthwhile to attack. Too, coordination with the antiaircraft units was poor and many aircraft were mistakenly shot down while still over German territory. Still, not withstanding these failures, and despite the fact that the Germans were absolutely annihilated at Y-29, *Bodenplatte* did score some successes at other Allied bases.

Although records are sketchy, the German attackers that morning destroyed approximately 350 Allied aircraft and damaged many more. In fact, at A-90 near Metz-Frescaty, more than two dozen P-47s were destroyed. But because almost all the aircraft the Germans destroyed were parked, the raid killed virtually no Allied airmen. To be fair, the point was moot. At that point the Allies could field whatever number of aircraft and crews were needed to successfully prosecute the war. Indeed, the total American aircraft manufacturing rate had been scaled back since before D-Day.

Ultimately, *Bodenplatte* did not achieve its objectives. Although the raid did cause some measure of panic, it had no appreciable effect on the ground campaign and the Allies recognized it for the desperate action it was. It cost the Luftwaffe approximately three hundred aircraft, but worse, it cost more than two hundred pilots killed and captured. These pilots, especially the more experienced leaders, were not replaceable at that point in the war. For this reason historians have typically criticized the operation as reckless, ill-conceived and bordering on stupid.

In this instance, the Luftwaffe leadership deserves more credit. The aircraft and crews that were lost as part of *Bodenplatte* would have been destroyed and killed anyway; the air war over Europe had turned into an overwhelming and ruthless grind that the Allies dominated. And it is absolutely certain that the inexperienced pilots that made up the bulk of the Luftwaffe would never have destroyed so many Allied aircraft in aerial combat. Simply put, the Germans chose the best method available to them to cause the most damage they could. In the end, they simply did not have enough aircraft, experienced pilots or luck to make *Bodenplatte* a success.

Just as they had been while stationed at Bodney, the men were given passes off base while in Belgium. The local economy was in tatters and it lurched along on a combination of currencies, scrip and barter. Cigarettes were a classic medium of exchange. Staff Sergeant James Bleidner recalled one episode: "I had a day-pass to go to Brussels but I had no money. I didn't smoke, but I always drew my ration of cigarettes. On that occasion, I had three boxes of cigarettes and had a wonderful day at a fine restaurant, bought some art and saw the sights."

CHAPTER 30

Finishing the Fight

Punchy Powell married Betty Wiley on January 4, 1945. "A few days later we were flying from Washington, D.C. to New York City and the flight attendant handed me a copy of *Newsweek* magazine. Reading it, I discovered that Fate had taken our top ace. George Preddy was killed on Christmas. It was a sad thing to learn on my honeymoon."

Some of the 352nd's pilots were with the unit for only very brief periods, usually not by choice. One of those was Thomas Lauderdale. He arrived at Bodney late in 1944. "On my first mission I saw an airplane explode from flak. In my excitement I used up my oxygen and had to fly home at lower altitude." Nothing at all happened on Lauderdale's second mission. "On my third trip," he recalled, "we flew at 37,000 feet, dragging in the clouds."

At such high altitudes, the fighters handled very sluggishly, and when Lauderdale reached down to switch fuel tanks, he accidently descended into the clouds. By the time he collected his wits and climbed back above them he found that his flight had left him behind. He was alone and lost. When he finally found his squadron mates, he was so excited that he let his airspeed get out of control; he sped past them before finally slowing enough to rejoin them.

All of these miscues were typical of newly-joined pilots. They had to assimilate and adapt to procedures and techniques that the old hands developed gradually as a group. Lauderdale was sent from Bodney to Y-29 on January 2, 1945, the day after *Bodenplatte*. "It was snow, frozen ground, thawed ground, and mud. I had a very thin cot on which I spent the night. Cold. I went to a pub, but being the new boy in the crowd I only had one beer. One of our bunch went out and tried out his sidearm on the side of a railroad embankment."

On January 5, Lauderdale flew his fourth mission and was hit by ground fire over a railroad yard. "I thought it [his aircraft] was going to burn but every time I thought I should bail out I was over a ridge." He finally made it back to friendly lines where he put the aircraft down in a crash landing. "The infantrymen who picked me up reassured me that I was on the right side."

Although he was back in friendly hands Lauderdale was also badly injured. He went into surgery and stayed in the hospital until he was well enough to ship back to the United States where he arrived after VE-Day. He subsequently spent two more years in various hospitals until he was finally released. "I'm sorry I never made it to Berlin," he recalled somewhat ruefully.[1]

George Preddy's younger brother Bill arrived in England during early January 1945. He was a strong, handsome, well-liked young man who had been a top performer all through flight training. And he had achieved his dream of flying fighters. He was assigned to the 339th Fighter Group at Fowlmere where he flew P-51s.

He had moved about so often since leaving the States that he didn't learn of his brother's death until January 22, 1945, nearly a month after the fact. The following day he wrote a letter to his parents.

What I have to say now is difficult to explain because I hardly understand it myself. There is no use to say not to grieve for I know that is impossible. It is useless to say try and forget, for we can't and shouldn't. We should remember, but in doing so we should look at it in the true light.

A man's span on this earth is not measured in years. Above all, that is least important. To find happiness, success, and most important, to find God is the Zenith of any man's worldly activities. I think a man has not lived until these things have been achieved . . .

Yes, George knew a full, rich life. He surely reached out and touched the face of God many times.[2]

Virtually all of the 352nd's pilots had watched, with a mix of morbid fascination and horror, as bombers were blown out of the sky, usually by flak. There were plenty of opportunities as the Eighth Air Force lost more than four thousand bombers. "It was so awfully sad," Punchy Powell recalled, "to see a bomber come apart, or start down, and see only two or three, or sometimes no parachutes at all. And yet you knew that there were men trapped alive in there—that very instant—falling to their deaths."

One of the 352nd's RAF exchange pilots, Edwin King, recalled the horror of watching the big bombers being blown out of formation. "Although I had enjoyed my attachment [to the 352nd] and had learned a lot, I found it hard to come to terms with witnessing these large bombers being shot down and, on so many occasions, being unable to prevent it. That we stopped the slaughter being even greater is without question, but it still hurt."[3]

Sometimes the stricken bombers made it safely back to the ground, but very few 352nd pilots saw it close up. William Reese of the 486th was one of the lucky ones. It was in early 1945 when he volunteered to fly sensitive papers to a headquarters element at an airfield in Belgium. Reese remembered that the control tower directed him to quickly clear the runway as there was a battle-damaged B-17 close behind him. "I pulled off the runway and swung the plane around so I could see what was going on. I also made sure that I could taxi off into the grass if the B-17 headed my way."[4]

"I could hardly believe what I was looking at as that poor plane approached the runway," recalled Reese. "The nose where the bombardier sat was gone—just a gaping hole." The left outboard engine, number one was gone; it had literally been blown off the wing. The engine next to it, number two, was still running. The right inboard engine, number three was smoking and its propeller was feathered. The number four-engine was also feathered and on fire.

"Parts of the wing on my side were missing, and as the plane stopped in front of me, I could see there were holes in the fuselage well over a foot in diameter, and part of the vertical stabilizer was missing." Reese was incredulous at the damage the bomber had sustained. More incredible was the crew. The bombardier's head had been blown off and it landed in the copilot's lap; not surprisingly, the copilot went into shock. "The pilot had to fly that bird solo," Reese described, "and only with one leg because the other one was badly damaged with shrapnel. Only two crew members were still able to walk about after landing." As much combat as he had seen, Reese described that crew's performance as the most remarkable he had ever encountered.

As the American armies raced east into Germany during the closing months of the war they were directly supported by Ninth Air Force units operating fighters in a ground attack mode, as well as medium bombers such as the B-26 and the A-26. In turn, P-51s from the Eighth sometimes flew cover for the Ninth Air Force aircraft. Clarence "Spike" Cameron of the 486th recalled one of those missions: "We were flying top cover for a group of P-47s as they strafed and bombed some ground targets."[5] Although Cameron and his squadronmates were not attacking targets on the ground, they still had their hands full. Not only did they have to keep an eye on the P-47s flashing below them, but they also had to maintain their own formation, fly their aircraft and keep an eye on the surrounding skies.

Things occasionally slipped through the cracks. Cameron was watching the P-47s do their work when he turned to take a quick glance ahead. "There," he remembered, "only a few hundred feet in front of me, and only a hundred or so feet above me—and coming straight-on—was an Me-109." Cameron noted the enemy aircraft's gray propeller spinner at about the same time he heard and felt a crashing boom directly behind him. A 20-millimeter shell from the enemy fighter exploded into his fuselage and took out his radio. Moreover, his left rudder pedal flopped underfoot; the control cable was shot away.

"It was a good thing my radio was out," Cameron said. "I was so mad I couldn't stand it, and I shouted every curse word I could think of." Mad or not, with his rudder partially shot away, he had no chance of getting turned around in time to catch the streaking German. In fact, the enemy pilot flashed through the 486th's formation and escaped unscathed. Likewise, Cameron returned to base unharmed save for a case of badly ruffled feathers.

This incident underscores the point that although the Luftwaffe flyers were not as numerous at that point in the war as they had been several months earlier, they still counted aggressive men in their ranks. It also brings home the truth that the smallest measures of distance or the briefest intervals of time made an enormous difference between life and death in air combat. When it is considered that Cameron's aircraft and the Me-109 had a closing velocity that exceeded several hundred miles per hour, and that the cannon shell had been traveling close to a thousand feet per second, the multidimensional physics that put it into Cameron's fuselage were virtually identical to the physics that would have put it into his cockpit. In effect, he was saved by a digit that was three or four places to the right of a decimal point.

This sort of luck was on Cameron's side one other time. "We spotted a huge number of German aircraft parked at an airfield late in the war," he recalled. "I was really excited at getting an opportunity to rack up a big score."

The 486th's pilots dropped down for their strafing run. "We were really low—only about twenty feet or so," Cameron recalled. "Then, as we got close, we could see that the airplanes were wooden decoys mounted on sticks!" The antiaircraft guns positioned around the enemy airfield were already firing; Cameron lifted up just a few feet and his aircraft was hit almost immediately by a 20-millimeter cannon round. "There was a loud explosion on the left side, just behind my cockpit," Cameron recalled. Notwithstanding the hit it sustained, the aircraft stayed flyable and brought him safely back to base.

"We found a hole blown in the fuselage fuel tank right behind the cockpit," Cameron recalled. "Why it didn't explode, I have no idea." Again, the distinction between the dynamics that put the enemy shell into the fuselage rather than into his body was so small as to be insignificant on paper. In real life, however, it meant that Cameron stayed alive.

The group's operational report for January 22, 1945, described an incident that highlighted the dominance of Allied airpower during the last year of the war. On that afternoon the group's squadrons flew separate patrols out of Y-29 on a route that started over St. Vith in eastern Belgium then took them about seventy miles into Germany to Laacher Lake southeast of Bonn, thence northwest to Brühl, then east to Düren. The report from the 328th noted: "Marmite [radar control] noted no targets but [the squadron] sighted an airdrome near Bonn F-6149 and saw twelve FW-190's and Me-109's preparing to take off. . . . When E/A sighted our A/C they turned back into the dispersal area."

Despite the spare description, much can be read into this non-event. The German fliers were obviously not looking for a scrap. Whatever the state of their training or morale, the decision of the formation leader to taxi his group back to the cover of its dispersal area showed good common sense. Even had the German pilots been well-trained and eager to fight it would have been foolhardy to take off with the P-51s ready to pounce with an altitude, airspeed and positional advantage.

Likewise, the 328th's leader that day, Earl Abbott, exercised thoughtful restraint when he didn't dive immediately into the attack. If the enemy pilots had spotted the squadron's Mustangs, there was no doubt that the antiaircraft gunners defending the airfield had detected them as well. Although the German fighters themselves would have been easy targets, strafing through the fire of forewarned and ready enemy gunners would have surely cost the 328th an aircraft or two. The return on investment— particularly that late in the war—wasn't worth the risk, at least not to Abbott.

Sadly, Abbott, one of the group's original pilots, disappeared two days later while leading the 328th's White Flight on a bounce of two Me-109s near Wahn, Germany. One of the German fighters was downed while the other escaped. Neither Abbott nor his aircraft were ever seen again.

By the end of January 1945, the last of the war was in sight. Neverthe- less, the 352nd still took losses that hit the men hard. The fratricide of Preddy the month before was particularly demoralizing. It was just more than two weeks later that the indomitable John C. Meyer was gone. On January 9, he was en route to Paris to make a radio broadcast when he stopped in St. Trond, Belgium, to visit a friend. There, the staff car in which he was travelling was hit by a trolley. Meyer was injured so badly that his leg was almost amputated. He was subsequently evacuated to Paris and then to the United States, where he eventually made a complete recovery.

The 352nd's contemporaneous narrative history for the month recalled the impact on the unit:

His accident coupled with the death of Major Preddy on December 25th has dealt the 352nd a blow which is felt, not only opera- tionally but by each individual personally. Together, the major and the colonel had destroyed a total of seventy German planes both in the air and on the ground. Each of them had led the Eighth Air Force active fighter pilots at succeeding intervals and between the two had been awarded three DSCs, four Silver Stars, fifteen DFCs, twenty-three Air Medals and two Purple Hearts. Added to the loss is the fact that Major Abbott was reported KIA on January 24th. He was last seen peeling off to chase a 109 near Julich, Germany.

The 352nd left Y-29 for Chièvres, Belgium, on January 27, 1945. Officially known as Y-84, it was a permanent airbase built by the Belgians during the 1930s on the site of a World War I airfield. After its capture by the Germans in 1940 it was considerably improved with additional runways, hardstands and permanent buildings. It was used extensively by the Luftwaffe during the next several years and was consequently attacked repeatedly by both the Eighth Air Force's heavy bombers as well as the Ninth's medium bombers.

Regardless of its damaged state, it was big enough to accommodate all of the 352nd, and the elements that remained in Bodney made their way to Chièvres during the first half of February 1945. The men were thrilled. After more than a year and a half at Bodney, the new base was exciting as was the new language and the notion of being on the continent where ground combat was actually taking place. Moreover, the beer was more familiar to American palates, traffic drove on the correct side of the road and the women were attractive and friendly. Too, the majority of the men were billeted in beautiful old chateaus.

The group flew its first mission from the new base on February 2, 1945.

Engine problems, although infrequent, continued to plague the 352nd into the last few months of the war. First Lieutenant Frederick Powell of the 486th Fighter Squadron flew what turned out to be his last mission on February 3, 1945. As was typical, the day's orders had the 352nd providing bomber escort. "We'd only been airborne about forty-five minutes and hadn't yet met the bombers when my engine just quit. It was like someone had flicked a light switch—it hadn't been running rough at all."[6] Powell switched fuel tanks as he turned west toward the Allied lines. The engine still wouldn't start. "I tried everything I could think of," he recalled, "but nothing worked."

Powell didn't have enough altitude to make it across the lines and was forced to put the aircraft down more than five miles short of friendly territory near the town of Goch. "I was lucky to find a good field and when I landed I slid into a pond that was about a foot deep. I had flown right over a German antiaircraft unit and they came running towards me, so I put my hands over my head and climbed out onto the wing." Powell lost his footing and fell face-first into the pond; it was a Chaplin-esque mishap that disarmed his captors with its humorous absurdity. Powell recalled that the Germans, "laughed so hard that they didn't shoot me." Instead, they asked him to help scavenge the fuel from his P-51.

Of course, his comrades knew nothing other than that he hadn't been injured when he set his aircraft down. The mission OPFLASH report offered only a terse note. "Lt. Powell crash landed at E9144 1115. Reported that he was OK on R/T."

"They ended up treating me all right," Powell remembered. "I wasn't abused or pushed around or anything." A guard took the wet and bedraggled American flyer to a nearby airbase where he spent the night. "I didn't speak German," Powell said, "and my guard didn't speak English, but we both knew high school French so we were able to communicate." The following morning Powell and the guard left on foot for the German interrogation center in Frankfurt. "We had walked about a half mile when my guard motioned for us to turn around." The two trudged back to the airbase where the German checked out ammunition for the gun with which he was guarding Powell. Then, properly armed, the guard set off again with Powell in tow.

"We ended up at his home that night," Powell remembered, "where he fed me, including apple strudel which tasted quite good." The two eventually caught a train in Dusseldorf which brought them to Frankfurt. There, while walking through the bomb-ravaged city, Powell's escort was accosted by a local jail guard who insisted that Powell be shot. Powell's guard refused to do so and ultimately delivered him to the proper authorities. Powell stayed a POW only until April when he was liberated near Moosburg by George S. Patton's Third Army.

It was natural that the character of the 352nd changed month-by-month during the latter stages of the war. Virtually all the original pilots had rotated home and were followed by many of the pilots who had arrived later. And then there were the men who were gone because they were shot down and captured or killed, or lost in accidents.

The appearance of the group's aircraft changed as well. Gone were the invasion stripes of the summer of 1944; they were ordered removed in successive stages from late June 1944 through the end of the year. Rudders were painted in bright colors that coincided with their normal flight assignments, and old personal markings were replaced with new ones as aircraft were handed from veteran pilots to new arrivals. Carlo Ricci got to the 352nd late in the war and inherited an aircraft with a tremendous history. The aircraft was serial number 44-15041 which had been John C. Meyer's personal mount as *Petie 3rd*. Meyer had used it to tally ten aerial victories including two scored during the New Year's fracas at Y-29.

Following Meyer's injury and his subsequent return to the United States during January 1945 the aircraft was assigned to James N. Wood. Wood had the aircraft repainted as *Ricky* but left the squadron insignia painted just below the canopy intact. The insignia was unique to the aircraft because Meyer, the squadron commander when he had received it, had forbidden it to be carried on any aircraft other than his own. Regardless, Wood was happy enough with the newly renamed aircraft and was awarded half an aerial victory while flying it. In the meantime, Carlo Ricci flew whatever aircraft were available and shared credit with Joseph Prichard for an Me-262 downed on April 10, 1945.

It was later that month when 44-15041 was assigned to Ricci. Ricci renamed the aircraft once more, this time as *Ron-Marie*, after a nephew and a girl he had met just before shipping overseas to Europe. It flew three more missions with Ricci at the controls before the end of the war. Following the cessation of hostilities this remarkable machine, like so many other famous aircraft, passed into obscurity.

As desperate for pilots as the Luftwaffe was during the last year of the war, it was often its own worst enemy in getting them into the field. The case of Helmut Rix is a good example. Rix finished his training as a multi-engine pilot in July 1944 and was subsequently designated for training in night fighters. Nevertheless, as frantic as the situation was over Germany, nothing was done with him through much of the summer. Finally, his orders were changed and he and many of the other pilots who had been waiting for night fighter training were sent to train as single-engine fighter pilots. He was eventually posted to JG 301, an operational unit, during December 1944. There, he was supposed to be brought up to standards—such as they were at that late point of the war—and introduced to combat.

Rix met ten pilots on the day he reported to his unit. By nightfall, eight of them had been shot down. Still, despite the need for more pilots, operational considerations and aircraft shortages conspired against Rix's introduction to combat. By the middle of February 1945 he still had not flown an operational mission. Late that month he was sent to sign for an FW-190D and return with it to the airdrome at Stendel. He recalled how completely dominant the Allied air forces were. "I traveled to Nieder-mendig and there I got stuck. Allied fighter-bombers, mostly Thunder-bolts and Lightnings, were masters of the air. The aircraft I was to ferry was damaged while taxiing and had to have a new propeller. In the meantime I watched the goings-on most of the time under cover of a one-man hole!"[7]

Rix got the new aircraft safely back to Stendel on February 28 and made his first combat sortie on March 2, more than eight months after graduating from training. On that day the leader of his four-ship flight climbed them toward a mass of eastward-bound B-17s flying at 27,000 feet approximately fifty miles north of Prague. As the tiny formation of FW-190s neared the big bombers the pilots set up for their attack. "We were in line-abreast formation," recalled Rix, "and ready for a frontal attack when my formation leader broke away to the left into a dive." Rix, unaware of what was happening, followed along with the rest of the flight. "Doing so, we got into a line astern formation with me as No. 4."

Rix never knew what, or who, hit him. In all likelihood it was Lee Kilgo and Earl Mundell of the 352nd's 486th Fighter Squadron. Still, those details were of little importance to the inexperienced German flier as he dove after the rest of his flight. "The lead aircraft was disappearing into the clouds when my plane shuddered and flames were licking around the front of my engine," he remembered. "In the panic that followed, I got rid of my cockpit hood, [canopy] but forgot to undo my straps first and so fed the flames with the aircraft out of control." Badly burned, Rix finally escaped his flaming aircraft and parachuted into several feet of snow. He was sub-sequently recovered by a farmer, delivered to the authorities and hospital-ized. He "released" himself from medical care several weeks later and returned to his unit just before the end of the war with only the one disas-trous mission under his belt. He never flew another.

The contrasts between the day-to-day activities of the USAAF and the Luftwaffe bordered on absurd during the last couple months of the war. While Rix and his comrades endured incessant Allied attacks together with continuous, near-hysterical haranguing by the German high command, their American counterparts were scolded for wearing dirty uniforms. While the 352nd was at Chièvres, the daily bulletin carried the following message on February 21, 1945: "Carelessness in the wearing of the uniform, which results in mixed uniform, untidy uniform, unauthorized use of flying clothing as outer garments, and improper uniform in civilian communities, is a discredit to the command and will not be tolerated. The provost marshal will cause all personnel whose appearance is below the required standard to be returned to their organizations and such violations will be reported to this headquarters."

Most of the men at the 352nd enjoyed their time at Chièvres. The group's intelligence section in particular was quite enamored with the arrangement. "Things were going well, very well. Our quarters were tres bon, the weather beautiful, the 'biere' very much like the brew back home (at least in taste), cognac and champagne available, almost everyone had learned to parley voo the basic phrases of the language and other conveniences were at hand in generous amounts."

But just as there were establishments near Bodney that were off limits to the 352nd's personnel for various reasons, there were similar places that the men were forbidden to visit in Chièvres. They were listed in the daily bulletin for February 18, 1945, and included Café de L'Union, Café du Cercle, Café Isabelle, and the residences of Alphonsin Labie, Jeanne Bassee, and Nelly and Suzanne Chevalier. Only two days later the daily bulletin carried a notice forbidding the men to be in any café or "similar places" during normal duty hours; violation risked apprehension by the provost marshal. Another notice in the same bulletin directed the men to cease driving or walking across residential lawns in Chièvres.

Some of the regulations and restrictions that were levied while the group was at Chièvres were certainly never considered when the group first left the United States for combat. An order in the 352nd's daily bulletin for February 24, 1945, makes this point: "ATTENTION ALL PERSONNEL (REPEAT). The German Bomb Dump Area South of the East-West runway of this airfield is herewith placed out of bounds to all persons except authorized demolition personnel. Subject area is posted with out of bounds signs." The same bulletin also warned against keeping explosives as mementos: "Under no circumstances will [explosive] shells of any kind be kept by personnel as souvenirs."

William Reese of the 486th recalled that while the group was at Chièvres, "that if we were not scheduled to fly the next day, we would meet in the bar for a little party time." He also remembered, "that after a night with champagne or wine, if one took a big drink of water the next day, you immediately were under the influence again without taking a drop of booze."[8]

Reese remembered the mission of March 21, 1945, when, after a night of drinking, he was asked to fill in for a flight leader who had come down with diarrhea. "Having never turned down a mission, I went to the briefing and came down with a terrible craving for a drink of water which I got afterward. I managed to arrive at my plane okay, but when I started to get in my crew chief asked me where my parachute was since it wasn't strapped to my back." Reese had forgotten it and his crew chief ran back to the squadron area and retrieved it but upon getting back to the aircraft found that Reese had also forgotten his maps and other mission data. Once more the crew chief took off at a run. "I realized something was amiss," recalled Reese, "and put on my oxygen mask, selected one hundred percent oxygen and went ahead and started the engine." The crew chief returned with Reese's missing material and he made the takeoff barely in time.

"The oxygen cleared my head and we had a normal escort mission with no problems but the mission wasn't over yet," he remembered. After following the bombers back across friendly lines, Reese detached with his flight to go look for trouble. "I took the flight down to about five hundred feet and flew back into enemy territory. For a while we didn't see anything to shoot at, but I noticed a railroad track going into a wooded area and decided to follow it and see if something was hiding in the woods." Something was indeed hiding in the woods; several boxcars sat on the tracks.

Reese set his flight up for a strafing run. "As I approached it from the rear, the walls of three cars flopped down and we were facing three carloads of four-barreled 20-millimeter antiaircraft cannons." Reese called for the flight to turn hard away to the left but the fourth man [Ervin Pryor] in his flight was hit. "He was still flying," Reese remembered, "but was trailing smoke, flying straight and level and trying to head home, all the while calling over the radio, 'Help me. Help me.'"

Reese got the rest of the flight together and chased his stricken comrade down. "I talked to him about how we had him in sight and that we were all going to get him home okay. All he would say is, 'I'm hurt. Help me,' so I knew he had been hit." Reese finally formed alongside the shot-up P-51. "As I pulled up on his wing, I saw his head slump forward. The plane went into a dive, crashed and burned." Helpless to do anything at all, Reese led his flight back to Chièvres.

It is a given that air combat over Europe during World War II was a confusing tumult. Descriptions of a particular event came in as many different versions as there were participants. Near the end of a lengthy encounter report, Henry White quite candidly declared he wasn't sure exactly what happened. "All this time there were so many enemy planes about and events were happening so fast I'm not sure that this sequence of events is in order."[9]

A more detailed example is illustrated by the encounter reports filed by three pilots with the 328th Fighter Squadron who downed an Me-109 on March 3, 1945. On that day, Earl Duncan was leading White Flight on a bomber escort mission near Dresden when an unidentified aircraft approached from the rear. The interloper dove away as Duncan swung his formation around to investigate. After dropping their external fuel tanks, the Mustang pilots closed the range as they passed through 20,000 feet.

"I identified it as an Me-109," recalled Duncan, "and took a couple of shots at him from approximately 350 yards getting a few hits around the wing roots."[10] Duncan's account differed from that of his element leader, William Sanford, who noted that he saw only "a strike" on the left wing. Duncan's wingman, Steve Price, recalled seeing "several strikes."[11]

All three accounts agree that Sanford opened fire next. Duncan recorded that Sanford flew in between him and the Me-109, fired, and scored several hits on the German's left wing. However, because he was pulling away from the fight, Duncan was unable to see what subsequently occurred. Sanford's account was more complete: "Crossing over the top of White Leader I fired a three-second burst at about 300 yards observing strikes walking along the port wing and fuselage near the wing roots. When the strikes reached the fuselage, the E/A snapped into a split-S and tumbled earthward out of control and crashed into the earth."

Sanford's description didn't quite square with Price's. Price did in fact observe that Sanford had scored "many strikes" on the Me-109, but noted that he followed the stricken aircraft through its split-S down to 17,000 feet where—rather than continuing down—it started back up into a climb.[12] Price "fired a one-second" burst as the Me-109 stalled, went into a spin and crashed. Neither Sanford nor Duncan noted Price's actions in their encounter reports.

The disparities in the different accounts were almost certainly due to two primary considerations. First were the physical constraints that kept every pilot from seeing every component of the event in its entirety. Aside from shooting down the enemy aircraft, the pilots also had to clear the sky around them to make sure that they weren't being bounced, while also making certain that they were not running into their comrades. Also, while maneuvering, it was sometimes impossible for the pilots to see in certain directions as parts of their own aircraft obstructed their views. The second important consideration was simply the fact that, in their excite-ment, the pilots simply didn't register or remember everything that they saw. Considering the life-and-death nature of air combat this is certainly understandable.

As the war drew down, the Allies had a tremendous number of Axis POWs on their hands. Housing and feeding them was a burden almost akin to keeping another army. In most instances the POWs posed no security threat, and in fact presented no escape risk; they had no realistic chance of fleeing from where they were held in the various Allied nations—as far away as the United States and Canada—and getting back to Germany. Consequently they were used for basic labor and farm work. In fact, some basic services were performed by German POWs at Bodney.

Jack Diamond remembered an incident that underscored how the dynamic between the adversaries had changed since the 352nd made its first tentative forays over Europe against a Nazi Germany that had seemed invincible: "Outside our 487th ready room there was an outhouse-type latrine with a trough on one wall with a small stream of water running through it, and a couple of toilets on the opposite wall. One day I walked in and a German POW was sitting on the toilet. Upon seeing me he imme-diately jumped to attention. I ignored him and just let him continue to stand at attention with his pants down around his ankles while I took a leak at the trough and left."[13]

Aside from the Me-262, the other German jet that saw significant service was the single-piloted, twin-engine Ar-234 jet bomber designed and manufactured by Arado. Although not produced in the same numbers as the Me-262, it became operational at about the same time during the autumn of 1944. Used primarily as a reconnaissance and bombing plat-form and weighing roughly the same as the Douglas A-20 Havoc, it was nevertheless fully aerobatic and fast, with a top speed that exceeded 450 miles per hour.

Don Bryan of the 328th Fighter Squadron had four separate encoun-ters with the Ar-234. His first came soon after it was introduced; he spot-ted it and mistakenly identified it as an A-26. "After we landed I fussed at my number four man for breaking radio silence. He pointed out that the aircraft I had identified as an A-26 had black crosses on it. We went to intelligence to review recognition photos and identified it as an Ar-234, and subsequently reported it up the chain to the Eighth Air Force. It must have been an early sighting because they called me out of bed and asked me to describe it in more detail. I ended that call by telling them that if they saw an A-26 without propellers going like hell, then it was an Ar-234. They never bothered me again."

The next time he saw the type was on December 12, 1944, in the vicinity of Verviers. He positioned himself to make a rear-quarter attack just as he would with any other aircraft. As it developed, he did not consider how fast the enemy ship was and never got close enough to fire his guns. The third time he saw one of the speedy bombers was on December 31, 1944, south of Verviers. Mindful of his previous encounter, he managed to get close enough to score a few strikes on the big jet but it still outpaced him and escaped.

Shooting down the Ar-234 while flying a slower, piston-engine fighter obviously required considerable skill and guile. Bryan exercised those attributes the fourth time he encountered the Ar-234 on March 14, 1945. Having just finished leading an escort of Ninth Air Force bombers near the Remagen bridgehead over the Rhine, he spotted an Ar-234 and dropped his external tanks to give chase. "He was traveling about 50 mph faster than we were," remembered Bryan, "and crossed the Rhine south of the bridge going west and then turned north making a very shallow dive run on the bridge, but did not drop his bombs."[14]

As the German jet came out of its dive, Bryan spotted a flight of P-47s to the northwest. Knowing that his aircraft wasn't fast enough to catch the jet bomber in a pure chase, Bryan anticipated that the Ar-234 pilot would also spot the P-47s and turn away to avoid them. With that in mind, Bryan banked toward the northeast hoping to cut him off. His intuition paid off. "When the E/A saw the P-47s he turned east and had to cross directly under me." Bryan barrel-rolled his P-51 down toward the enemy jet. "I wanted to keep an eye on him as it was still unknown whether or not the Ar-234 carried forward-firing armament."

Bryan opened fire on the enemy ship from approximately 250 yards and his marksmanship was good. "I hit him with the first burst and knocked his right jet out." The enemy pilot subsequently started a series of mild turns, climbs and dives as he tried to spoil Bryan's aim. It worked to some extent, but not well enough. "I fired almost all of my ammo at him," Bryan recalled, "and before I had finished I had knocked his left jet out and the E/A was emitting much white smoke." Despite the smoke, Bryan did not note any fire but in the end it didn't matter. "At about the time I had finished firing, he rolled over on his back and dived straight into the ground and exploded. Just before hitting the ground, the pilot of the E/A jettisoned his canopy but did not get out."

Although the Ar-234 had been in service for some months by the time Bryan scored his first victory against the type, details were still scarce. Bryan was pressed to compare his observations against the drawings that Allied intelligence was using:

> Wings okay. Nose more blunt with bulbous appearance at least 6 inches higher than the rest of fuselage. Top of fuselage appeared straighter than drawings. An antenna was rigged directly behind canopy with two objects resembling radar-stringers jutting from it. Another antenna on top of fuselage just to rear of wing. On under side [sic] of fuselage E/A appeared more square than drawings from mid-section back to tail.

Bryan's comments were fairly accurate and useful, but not nearly so useful as the actual Ar-234s which were captured even before the war ended less than two months later.

As the Allied armies penetrated deeper into Germany—both from the east and west—encounters between American and Soviet aircraft became more frequent. Those encounters didn't always go well, usually because of misidentification, and there were several instances that ended when one side or another accidentally shot down aircraft from the other side. Measures were put into place to help preclude such instances. A hand-scrawled note from the 352nd's mission archives delineated recognition signals that were to be used in the event that Soviet aircraft were encountered. It reads: "Russian recognition. Basic: Dip right wing 3-5 times. Secondary: Dip left wing."

Indications are that these signals produced only mixed results. An excerpt from the group's mission report summary for March 18, 1945 noted: 6 Yak a/c seen v/o Zielenzig, 1200 hours, 10,000 ft. Russian recognition signals successful." However, on that same day—indeed, at that same exact time—Albert Peterson went missing after encountering Soviet fliers. The mission summary report noted, "Lt. Peterson last seen over Oder N/O [north of] Frankfort [sic] at 12,000 ft [at] 1200 turning with 4 Yaks."

Peterson made it back to Bodney. Rather than getting shot down by the Yaks, he reported that he had been hit by German flak and forced down near the Oder River in a heavily forested area. He used his pocket compass and traveled eastward by night toward the Soviet lines. He was intercepted and nearly shot by Polish partisans who eventually delivered him to the Soviets. "When President Roosevelt died," he recalled, "all the Russians were genuinely saddened and at a large memorial service, they all tried to express their personal grief to me." He eventually returned to Bodney just before the war ended.

Joe Vickery also went missing the same day that Peterson went down—March 18, 1945. The mission summary report characteristically provided scant details as to what might have happened to him: "1 U/I Blue nose P-51, may have been Lt. Vickery, 487th Sqdn. vicinity Schwiebus on deck 1200, heading east." Regardless, he never returned. His loss was balanced to some degree by the 487th Fighter Squadron's claims for aerial victories over three Me-109s.

It is important to consider that whereas piston engines were fairly mature and reliable during the war, jet engines were not. It was axiomatic then that not only did the new engines experience high rates of failure compared to their piston-powered counterparts, but the pilots flying these advanced engines were also unfamiliar to some extent with how to best operate them. All these factors might have come into play when James Hurley of the 328th Fighter Squadron engaged an Me-262 north of Magdeburg, Germany on March 30, 1945.

On that day the 352nd was escorting bombers when an Me-262 was spotted in a Lufbery with three P-51s at 22,000 feet. Hurley shed his drop tanks and dove into the fray from 26,000 feet. At about the same time the Me-262 disengaged from the other Mustangs and fled to the northeast. Hurley still had an altitude advantage and was able to keep his speed up as he chased the German in a slight dive. "I chased him for about 15 minutes on a heading of 60 degrees at about 400 mph from 20,000 feet to about 15,000 feet when he leveled out," Hurley recorded in his encounter report. "I noticed I was closing on him, when he turned on both jets and started pulling away."[15]

Hurley's comment, recorded during the war when relatively little was known about the Me-262, indicates some ignorance about the new jet. It is impossible that the German pilot could have fled for fifteen minutes without his engines running. It is more likely that he had been operating the engines at a power setting that was less than the maximum and had only added more power when Hurley failed to give up the chase.

In fact, Hurley almost did stop his pursuit: "He was almost out of sight; I had been chasing him for twenty minutes and had decided to give up the chase when I noticed both jet units quit smoking and the E/A started a slight diving turn to the left." Hurley moved to cut off the German jet in its turn and closed the range slowly. When the Me-262 rolled out of its turn Hurley continued to gain at a quickening rate indicating that its pilot must have reduced power to the engines in order to save fuel or perhaps because he thought he had lost his pursuer. There is also the possibility that the engines were experiencing mechanical difficulties.

"I started firing at him as soon as I was in range," recalled Hurley. "I fired one long burst. I ceased firing, but noticed I was closing very fast so I started firing again. When I was about 150 feet behind the E/A I observed strikes in the lower part of the cockpit, left wing root, and left jet unit." Pieces came off the Me-262 as Hurley overflew the stricken aircraft. "The E/A then started into a climbing turn to the left; I saw the canopy come off and the ship nose over from about 5,000 feet and crash into the ground. There was a great explosion and much fire where the E/A hit. I saw no chute." Although there is no way to know how or why Hurley was able to chase down the faster German aircraft, his observation that the crash was accompanied by a significant fire indicates that the Me-262 had plenty of fuel when it went down.

Of course, the fact that the Allies vastly outnumbered the Germans in the air by that time of the war also worked against the Me-262 fliers. Like every aircraft of the day, the new jet had to take off and land from an airfield. That being the case, Allied fighter pilots often stationed themselves near Luftwaffe airfields and waited to ambush aircraft as they took off or landed; it was in these phases of flight that the Me-262 was most vulnerable.

Such an incident was described by Hermann Buchner, an Me-262 pilot with JG 7. He had fought much of the war on the Eastern Front as a ground attack pilot yet still was credited with fifty-eight aerial victories. Of those, twelve were scored against the USAAF and the RAF while flying Me-262s during the early months of 1945. The veteran flyer was caught by a P-51 as he landed, desperately low on fuel, on April 8, 1945. "With my last drops of fuel," Buchner recalled, "I lined up to land, convincing myself that there were no enemy fighters in the area, that the air was clear. Diminish speed, undercarriage and flaps out, and turn to land in from the west."

Although he didn't know it, Buchner was being pursued: "Actually, everything went like clockwork, then just before I set down something blazed from my right wing, and I could also make out hits on the ground in front of me. As I landed, the enemy fighter made further shots at the engine mounts. My machine began to burn." Buchner brought his flaming aircraft to a halt and only barely managed to escape. He sprinted a safe distance—parachute pack banging against his legs—and lost consciousness. He never flew another mission.[16]

It is true that the Me-262 was much faster than any of the Allied piston engine fighters. Nevertheless, the Me-262 was not exempt from the laws of physics. Under aggressive maneuvering the new German fighter generated drag and lost airspeed just as much as any other aircraft. But whereas piston engine types accelerated relatively quickly, the Me-262's rudimentary jet engines pushed it to maximum speed very slowly. Consequently, Me-262 pilots were at a disadvantage if they chose to get into a hard-turning dogfight. Hermann Buchner, a Luftwaffe pilot through the entire war—and a successful Me-262 pilot—confirmed this when writing of a sortie that occurred on March 19, 1945: "We met Mustangs, but we had no successes; you could not defeat Mustangs unless you surprised them."[17]

This fact is further illustrated by the encounter report filed by Earl Duncan of the 328th Fighter Squadron on April 10, 1945. On that day, the twenty-eight-aircraft P-51 formation that Duncan was leading in support of a bombing raid near Berlin was attacked by a flight of eight Me-262s. "After the initial pass," recalled Duncan, "some of the 262s tried to attack again, but their speed had dropped off and we could successfully attack them."[18]

Duncan and his wingman, Richard McAuliffe, dove on an enemy jet flying several thousand feet below them. The Me-262 pilot dropped down to low level to get away from the pursuing Mustangs. It did no good as both Duncan and McAuliffe had the German bracketed from the rear. "I closed to firing range from the left and rear," Duncan said, "and fired a two-second burst from almost astern at 250 yards. I did not see any strikes, however the enemy pilot jettisoned the canopy and pulled the ship straight up."

Duncan was unable to pull enough lead to get off another shot. Instead, he followed the German in his climb and actually overran him. "I could see the pilot trying to get out," Duncan remembered. "At the top of the climb, the Me-262 stalled to the right and Major McAuliffe came in and set the right engine on fire. The pilot got out but never opened his chute. The Me-262 went into a flat spin and crashed." McAuliffe recalled that he was firing as the German leapt from his aircraft and surmised that his gunfire might have hit him. On completing the mission Duncan and McAuliffe shared credit for destroying the enemy jet.

That day, April 10, 1945, was also noteworthy for the opposition offered by the Luftwaffe's jet forces. The Germans put up approximately thirty Me-262s operating as distinct, two-ship flights. They made a definite impression on the 352nd's fliers. The mission report stated, "All jet a/c very aggressive," and "Cooperation of individual jets in the pairs [was] excellent."

These observations validate the fact that many of the jets were operated by skilled, veteran pilots. And they were effective as noted by the report which additionally stated, "Jets destroyed bombers in one pass apiece." The earlier-noted aggressiveness of the German pilots was further emphasized by the notation that the "Jets attacked fighters in between passes at bombers." Nevertheless, the 352nd's blue-nosed Mustangs scored against the Me-262s and sustained no losses. The report notes that Cuthbert "Bill" Pattillo damaged one of the jets and shared a victory credit for another with an unidentified P-51 pilot from another group.

Carlo "Ric" Ricci also scored that day which marked his eleventh mission. "It was late in the war," he remembered, "and there was little activity, except that the German jets were still laying for the bombers."[19] From his position at the rear of the squadron Ricci watched as the squadron leader and another member of his flight dropped out of the formation with engine problems. At the same time, Ricci's flight leader rolled up on a wing and dove abruptly for the deck; Ricci tipped over in hot pursuit. "By the time we leveled off above the treetops I found myself left behind." Anxious not to get left alone, Ricci rammed his throttle into War Emergency Power. The engine surged and Ricci's anxiety eased as he pulled abreast, but well left of the rest of his flight.

Looking ahead, Ricci saw that they were chasing an Me-262. "When the German pilot faked a right turn and made a sweeping left turn, I cut across and ended up behind him. But when I flipped on my camera and gun switches, I could see he was way out of range as his wingtips were way inside the circle of diamonds on the K-14 gunsight." Notwithstanding the long range Ricci fired four long bursts at the enemy jet.

"At that final burst," he said, "the jet began to smoke, pulled up to about 300 feet and the pilot bailed out. He was so far ahead of my plane that he was on the ground with his chute collapsed and looking up at me as my plane roared over." Ricci remembered that the German flyer wore a black leather flying suit. As he pulled for altitude with the rest of his flight, Ricci caught sight of the airfield that the Me-262 pilot tried to reach before being shot down. "We saw smoke spires," he recalled, "and the sun shining on clusters of parachutes from bombers that had gone down in that area."

Ricci was flush with success as the flight made its way home to Chièvres. "But some of the fun disappeared," he remembered, "when we missed the base because of haze." My radio went out and I signaled I was down to thirty gallons of gas and was pointed to a British grass field in northern France." Once he was safely on the ground his British hosts treated the frustrated Ricci to a cup of tea while they fueled his aircraft. Topped off, he made his way back to Chièvres and filed his post-mission report. "I was told that another pilot [Joseph W. Pritchard] claimed he had strikes on the jet before I shot it down. Rather than create a fuss, I shared the jet. However, my film showed the red explosion and the white parachute going down."

The pair of silvery Mustangs arced hard in a descending turn before leveling off just above the ground. They were moving fast and the steady, silky howl of their engines rolled across the Czech countryside; heads snapped in their direction.

Ahead of them was the German airfield at Ceske Budejovice. The two pilots selected their targets and squeezed their triggers. Below them, the gunners defending the airfield did the same. The first Mustang exploded in mid-air. Captain Raymond Reuter, the commanding officer of the 339th Fighter Group's 305th Fighter Squadron was dead. The date was April 17, 1945. The end of the war was only three weeks away.

The second P-51 was also hit and it flew only a very short distance before crashing near the village of Zaluzi. A local man, Jan Smejkal, hauled the unconscious pilot from his broken aircraft and took him to an aid station in a horse cart. There the Germans gave him first aid but refused to move him to a hospital. Smejkal did it himself. He loaded the pilot back into the cart and drove him more than five miles to where the American flyer could get better care.

Smejkal's kindness was for nothing. Bill Preddy died without ever regaining consciousness. After losing a daughter during childbirth before the war, Earl and Clara Preddy lost both their sons—both fighter pilots— during the war.

By the spring of 1945, there was little real need to keep the 352nd in Belgium under the control of the Ninth Air Force. Accordingly, the unit started the move back to Bodney on April 5, 1945. The group's last mission out of Chièvres was flown on April 12, and operations resumed out of Bodney on April 16.

Although it was clear that the war was nearly over by mid-April 1945, it was only nearly over rather than entirely over. Accordingly, the 352nd still flew missions and men still died. James White remembered the morning of April 19: "I was in the ready hut reading newspapers and magazines. No one else was there. Not a soul."[20]

The 328th Fighter Squadron was taking off and blue-nosed Mustangs roared overhead four abreast. "They were low," White remembered. "I thought to myself that if they got much lower someone was going to hit the tree tops." He stepped outside to watch. "Before I got to the door I heard a boom."

White rushed toward a wood where an aircraft had gone down. On arriving he came upon the smoldering body of John Reiners. "Wisps of smoke rose from his parachute as I peered into his blackened face. It was John alright. No one else was around, just John and me. It was so peaceful. Shadows and splashes of sunshine lay on the ground. I ran back for help but in my state of mind I could not fully fathom the grief that would come over me later . . . he was such a good-looking boy. . . ."

Reiners was the 352nd's last casualty.

The 352nd's daily bulletin for April 19, 1945 included the following notice: "Any person on this Station having a claim against or who is indebted to 1st Lt JOHN F. REINERS, 0-832408, AC, contact 1st Lt JULIUS J. BEYER, 0-860681, AC, 328th Fighter Squadron, as soon as possible."

The daily bulletin never reported when pilots were lost, but throughout the war when a pilot was shot down or otherwise killed it printed notices like the one above. It was part of a process that was similar to putting an estate in order. Debts and claims, insurance matters and other financial affairs had to be settled. Additionally, next of kin had to be notified regardless of whether the pilot was listed as missing or killed. Moreover, his personal effects had to be collected, boxed and sent home or put in storage. Punchy Powell remembered, "It fell mostly on his best friends to pack up his foot locker after carefully checking to see there was nothing in his belongings which might be embarrassing to his widow or family. The S-2 guys [intelligence section] were also involved to make sure no security issues were involved. Quite often it took a while to get these things back to the family—it was a rather low priority."

The group didn't hold memorial services for its fallen pilots. Firstly, there was simply too much to do to stand everything and everyone down. Moreover, repeated memorial services would have dulled the intent, detracted from the task at hand and been a depressing and unneeded reminder of the dangers the pilots faced on every sortie. Don McKibben recalled the perspective that he shared in common with most of his comrades. "Everyone knew the risks and accepted the fact that some of us— but always someone else—would not make it. When a friend was lost there was grief, but it was contained, and private."

At 1105, on May 3, 1945, the 352nd's three squadrons—totaling forty-seven blue-nosed P-51s—got airborne out of Bodney. Of those, three aircraft aborted for mechanical reasons and a fourth escorted them back to base. The three squadrons split and patrolled assigned areas in general support of bombing operations over Germany. Not a single German fighter was sighted. Glen St. John of the 328th went missing, but otherwise nothing of note happened.

A few days later, St. John showed up back at Bodney. And on May 8, 1945, the war in Europe was over.

"Betty and I were home in Thorpe, West Virginia, when the war ended," Punchy Powell recalled. "I just remember being so happy knowing that my friends Pappy [Fred] Yochim and Jaime Laing would be out of the POW camps. We didn't have any special celebration, but everyone in town was elated. There were so many of my high school friends who never returned."

Don McKibben was in Norfolk, Virginia when the war in Europe ended. "VE Day found me back in P-47s, teaching fighter tactics and gunnery and such," he remembered. "When I left Bodney in late summer 1944, I severed the connection cleanly. Most of my contemporaries who survived were also back in the States, and I knew only a few of the guys who remained at Bodney. Instead of looking back, my new bride and I, along with most everyone else, focused on the war with Japan, without a clue to how it could be ended without paying a huge price in casualties."

At the end of April 1945, Don Bryan was among the very last of the original 352nd pilots remaining with the group. He had completed 138 missions. "I was replaced so that someone new could say they were part of the end of the war. When it was over, I was on a ship headed back to the States."

There was relief at Bodney when the war ended, but no great and raucous celebration. Too much had been spent in the winning. Too much lost youth, too much lost time, too much lost life. And the men were tired. Moreover, although the war against Germany was over, Japan had yet to be defeated.

EPILOGUE

The 352nd was still at Bodney making preparations to deploy to the Pacific when Japan surrendered and World War II ended. The group was sent back to the United States in November 1945 and subsequently decommissioned. Although its legacy was assigned to various units during the succeeding years, those organizations had different numeric designations and missions, and no real ties to the original group. Like the 352nd, they were also idled or underwent significant transformation during the following decades. In short, official assignments of lineage aside, the 352nd as a fighter group essentially disappeared shortly after the war ended.

There were very few fighter groups in the USAAF that failed to perform well, but only a small handful of them had a legitimate claim to true greatness. The 352nd was among those. The group flew on 420 missions and was credited with 519 aerial victories and more than 250 German aircraft destroyed on the ground. George Preddy and John C. Meyer were the third and fourth highest-scoring USAAF aces in Europe and were additionally the two highest-scoring P-51 pilots in history. In total, 29 pilots from the 352nd reached ace status. The Distinguished Service Cross—second only to the Medal of Honor—was awarded ten times to men from the 352nd.

Although the 352nd, like most units, did not have a postwar career, the men who comprised it carried its legacy in their hearts and minds through the rest of their lives. Many of them stayed in military service and seven of them reached the rank of general. One of them, John C. Meyer, was the only fighter pilot from World War II to earn four-star rank. However, the vast majority of them—their jobs complete—returned to civilian life where they created the wonderment that was postwar America. It was a nation like no other in history and one that continues as the world's military, industrial, scientific and industrial leader. Brief recaps of the postwar careers of a few of the 352nd's men follow:

Don McKibben carefully considered a military career but wasn't convinced that the politics and culture of postwar service were a good fit.

Ultimately he opted to return to the position he took with Kodak in 1941. He enjoyed a very successful career and retired as a corporate director in 1982. He currently resides in Maine.

Robert "Punchy" Powell stayed in the reserves for several years following the war and was recalled to active service during the Korean conflict. As a civilian he enjoyed a very successful career as an advertising manager in the publishing industry until retiring in 1987. His passion during the last several decades has been the preservation of the 352nd's legacy.

Ted Fahrenwald left the service almost immediately after returning to the States. At the same time, he wrote a manuscript that described his adventures after bailing out over Normandy on June 8, 1944. Almost seventy years later, it is being published at the same time as this book. Postwar, Fahrenwald managed a small steel mill in Chicago with his brother Frank. He passed away in 2002.

Command of the 352nd was the highlight of Colonel Joe Mason's career. During the 23 years following his departure from the group he was never promoted and served a long series of short stints in various capacities before retiring in 1967. He passed away in 1974.

John C. Meyer, predictably, had the most successful military career of the men who made up the 352nd. He commanded an F-86 fighter wing during the Korean War and scored two aerial victories against communist MiG-15s. He assumed posts of increasing responsibility and eventually reached four-star rank and command of the Strategic Air Command from 1972 to 1974. He retired in 1974 and died of a heart attack in 1975 at the age of 56.

William Whisner, who scored 15.5 aerial victories with the 352nd, went on to score five more in Korea, thus becoming one of only seven men from the United States to attain ace status in two different wars. Sadly, he died of complications from bee stings in 1989.

Ed Heller, aside from the five aerial victories he scored with the 352nd, scored three-and-a-half more during the Korean War. He was downed over China and spent more than two years as a prisoner of the Chinese before being repatriated in 1955. He retired from the Air Force in 1967 and passed away in 2004.

The 352nd's first ace, Virgil Meroney, survived the war as a POW. He stayed in the service and flew combat during both the Korean and Vietnam Wars. During the latter war, he flew two combat missions with his son who, sadly, was killed partway into his combat tour. Meroney retired from the service as a colonel in 1970 and passed away in 1980.

Ray Littge was credited with ten aerial victories while flying with the 352nd. He survived the war but was killed in 1949 in a flying accident while at the controls of an F-84D Thunderjet.

Jim Bleidner, John C. Meyer's armorer, returned to the States and his "barely used wife" during the summer of 1945. As an agriculture and rural development officer with USAID—together with his exceptional wife, Marjory Wylam—his life's work centered on improving lives in Central and South America through the design and management of projects that increased the production and marketing of food. He stayed active as a consultant into the 1990s and lives today in Florida.

Unlike most of his contemporaries, Don Bryan stayed in the service and served in a variety of capacities until retiring as a lieutenant colonel in 1964. He spent fifteen years on a second career with an engineering firm in upstate New York before moving to Georgia and running a sprinkler installation business. Sadly, Bryan passed away just as this book was going to press.

AUTHOR'S NOTE

As an aviation historian, a writer, and a combat-experienced fighter pilot, this project looked like it would be an easy one. It was to be my eighth book and outwardly seemed to involve little more than recounting the actions of a single unit during a relatively short wartime career. What could be easier?

But as the effort got underway, it threatened to overwhelm me. I found that the 352nd Fighter Group's history was almost too rich, too full of spirit, and too suffused with drama. I felt like a starving man at a grand feast: there was so much remarkable material that I was challenged to find a good starting place. Ultimately, I did find such a place but was often challenged to let go of one compelling person or topic and move to another.

I possessed the group's official records—more than 10,000 pages—to support my work. But at war's end, these documents weren't archived with an eye toward helping me write a book nearly seventy years later. Consequently, as important as they were, the records were great time suckers that yielded their treasures in haphazard fashion. There were instances when I made brilliant discoveries after five minutes of searching. There were also periods when several hours of casting about produced nothing worthwhile whatsoever.

Still, as important as the official documentation was, it didn't provide much depth or color about the men who made up the 352nd—and it was obviously the men who made the history. During its operational career, the unit numbered nearly 1,000 officer and enlisted personnel. As individuals, they were among the brightest young men America could produce. As a team—as a fighter group—they were the equal of any similar unit anywhere in the world. And as part of a greater team, the U.S. Army Air Forces, they helped make possible the greatest bombing campaign in history. It was an effort that was crucial to the defeat of Nazi Germany.

Ultimately, following my brief period of panic, I told the story of the 352nd as simply as I could, starting at the beginning and finishing at the end, and along the way, I provided as much historical context as I believed was necessary to put the group's actions in perspective, but not so much as to lose the reader. As I did so, I drew upon my own background as a fighter pilot to describe and evaluate the subtleties that were part of the great air war that raged over Europe from 1943 until the Germans surrendered in 1945.

Soon after the 352nd Fighter Group arrived in England during the summer of 1943, it was assigned to the 67th Fighter Wing, part of the Eighth Air Force's VIII Fighter command. In part, this story is the story of all the fighter groups of VIII Fighter Command. That makes sense because not only were the men who made up the individual groups largely from the same cultural and social milieu, but they operated the same equipment, flew the same missions, and practiced the same tactics. Consequently, the units tended to be rather homogenous. Indeed, a contemporaneous observer said as much during 1944: "The groups are uniformly good in spirit and ability, and if one closed one's eyes and walked at random into a pilots' ready room, it would be impossible from their conversation, their appearance, or the horseplay to identify one group from another."

That being said, each of VIII Fighter Command's groups differed from the others in nuanced ways that were manifested in their records. Some of them had strong and aggressive leaders who were superlative flyers; the 56th's Hubert Zemke comes to mind. Others benefitted from the experience that was won in blood and heartache by the groups that came before them; an example was the 357th, which didn't fly its first mission until February 1944 yet compiled an outstanding record. Others, for a variety of reasons, simply didn't get as much traction; the 356th was one of these and was known as a hard-luck unit.

Then there were those fighter groups that had a certain indefinable quality to them. There was something about their mix of leadership and talent, together with the luck they made and the luck that tapped them on the shoulders, that made them standouts. Chief among these fighter groups was the 352nd.

Flying P-47s initially, and later its famous blue-nosed P-51s, the group scored 519 aerial victories. That tally was the fourth highest among the VIII Fighter Command's fifteen fighter groups. Of the three groups that outscored it, one was in combat a year longer and the other, five months longer. Only one other fighter group had a better victory-to-loss ratio in aerial combat, and no other group had a better victory-to-loss ratio in total air and ground victories.

The 352nd produced twenty-nine aces—men who scored five or more aerial victories. One of its fliers was the Eighth Air Force's first ace-in-a-day. Moreover, the group counted a total of four aces-in-a-day on its rolls—more than any other group. Overall, it destroyed 779 enemy aircraft while losing 76 of its own men to all causes while deployed overseas.

It is impossible to dissect the composition and actions of the group and declare with certainty why it was so successful. But my hope is that by telling the story as clearly as I can—and as much as possible through the eyes of the 352nd's men—the reader will gain at least a sense of what made the unit special. Indeed, regardless of why, there is no doubt that it was indeed extraordinary.

Only a relatively small cadre of World War II veterans remains as this book is published. This fact presented obvious disadvantages, but also at least one upside. The chief problem was that there were fewer actual participants to interview—and because memories fade, the details the veterans provided were sometimes unclear or inconsistent. On the other hand, the survivors felt less constrained when discussing negative or controversial aspects of the war or of former comrades who have passed.

Although I understand and appreciate where these men came from and what they accomplished, I did not gold-plate them. Rather, I presented them as I found them either through official documents or via the recollections of their comrades. I confirmed what I knew already: the World War II generation was made up of the same personalities and attributes as their ancestors and their progeny. And although they were largely hard-working, intelligent, and likable, there were also a handful of men who were otherwise. Nevertheless, in doing the research, I found myself becoming friends with men who are long gone. Such a thing speaks volumes about the character of the 352nd Fighter Group.

It was impossible to cover even briefly the actions of every pilot who flew with the 352nd; there were more than 300 of them. Likewise, there were more than 1,000 enlisted support men. The constraints of space, and the rigor required to tell the story as tightly as possible, precluded covering even some of the group's most successful pilots. This is unfortunate. Nevertheless, the actions of the men described herein are outstanding representations of the 352nd's efforts as a whole; they cover a wide gamut of missions while underscoring specific and important perspectives of the air war over Europe. Sourced with material from the veterans, official documents, and other important material—and processed with the benefit of hindsight and the historical record—I hope this work will become the seminal book on American fighter group operations over Europe during World War II.

ENDNOTES

A foundational reference source for this book was the body of official documents generated by the 352nd Fighter Group during its wartime career. Virtually all of these documents are available from the Albert F. Simpson Historical Center archives at Maxwell Air Force Base, Alabama, as microfiche roll transfers to CD. The specific rolls are B0305A, B0306, B0307, B0308, and B0309. The reader is advised that these rolls are terribly organized and that the quality of reproduction ranges from unreadable to satisfactory. Moreover, information is missing; for instance, the author was unable to locate any encounter reports for the 486th Fighter Squadron. Nevertheless, the data on the rolls is undoubtedly the richest source of official information on the 352nd Fighter Group.

During the course of the book's development the author exchanged hundreds of e-mails and dozens of phone calls with Robert H. Powell Jr., Donald McKibben, and Donald Bryan. In order to avoid cluttering the narrative with references that add little value, these correspondences are not cited. Rather, all quotations and attributions related to these gentlemen were sourced from the aforementioned exchanges unless otherwise noted.

CHAPTER 1: THEY WERE BOYS FIRST
1. Eugenia Christensen, *Growing Up with Wyoming: The Life of Fremont Miller* (Lander, WY: Mortimore Publishing, 1998), 11–126.
2. E-mails between author and Ted Fahenwald's sister, Caroline Fahrenwald Price, 11–12 January 2012. All subsequent information on Fahrenwald's early life is derived from these exchanges.
3. Joe Noah and Samuel Sox Jr., *George Preddy: Top Mustang Ace* (Osceola, WI: Motorbook International Publishers & Wholesalers, 1991), 1-19.
4. Noah and Sox, *George Preddy*, 40.
5. Ibid., 48.

CHAPTER 2: BIRTH OF THE 352ND FIGHTER GROUP
1. Bernard Boylan, *Development of the Long-Range Escort Fighter*, Air Force Historical Study No. 136, (Maxwell AFB, AL: USAF Historical Division, Research Studies Institute, Air University, 1955), 25–35.
2. Noah and Sox, *George Preddy*, 5.
3. George Arnold, recorded interview, n.d.
4. Letter to Robert H. Powell, Jr. from Albert Marchese, 23 October 1985.
5. Collected Letters of Theodore P. Fahrenwald, 13 April 1943.
6. Ibid., 22 April 1943.

7. Ibid., 7 May 1943.
8. Ibid., 10 May 1943.
9. Ibid., 6 April 1943.
10. Telephone interview with William Hendrian, 2 April 2011.
11. Noah and Sox, *George Preddy*, 59–63.
12. Antony Mireles, *Fatal Army Air Forces Aviation Accidents in the United States* (Jefferson, NC: McFarland & Company, 2006), xi.
13. E-mail to Robert H. Powell Jr. from Donald McKibben, 18 November 2011.
14. Robert H. Powell Jr., *Above the Mountains*. Unless otherwise noted, references to or quotes by Powell about his P-47 training, deployment to England, and early days at Bodney are sourced from this unpublished memoir.
15. Collected Letters of Theodore P. Fahrenwald, 28 May 1943.
16. Ibid., 3 June 1943.
17. Ibid., 4 June 1943.
18. E-mail to Brent Wilson from Donald McKibben, 12 October 2011.

CHAPTER 3: TO ENGLAND
1. U.S. Air Force Historical Study No. 174, *Command and Leadership in the German Air Force* (USAF Historical Division, Aerospace Studies Institute, Air University, 1969), 17.
2. Noah and Sox, *George Preddy*, 65.
3. Robert H. Powell Jr., et al., *The Bluenosed Bastards of Bodney: A Commemorative History* (Dallas: Taylor Publishing Co., 1990), 26–27.
4. Richard Davis, *Bombing the European Axis Powers: A Historical Digest of the Combined Bomber Offensive, 1939–1945* (Maxwell AFB, AL: Air University Press, 2006), 132.
5. Ibid., 158.
6. Noah and Sox, *George Preddy*, 66.
7. Ibid., 68.

CHAPTER 4: COMBAT
1. *Narrative History, Intelligence Section*, 352nd Fighter Group.
2. Diary of Fred M. Allison, Jr., 487th Fighter Squadron, 352nd Fighter Group.
3. Collected Letters of Theodore P. Fahrenwald, 4 November 1943.
4. Boylan, *Development of the Long-Range Escort Fighter*, 121.
5. William Reese, unpublished, n.d. memoir, 68.
6. Karl K. Dittmer, *Old Tat: Memoirs of a Fighter Pilot* (Self-published, 1998), 45.
7. Boylan, *Development of the Long-Range Escort Fighter*, 128.
8. Ibid., 196.
9. Heinz Knoke, *I Flew for the Führer* (New York: Berkeley, 1959), 103–4.
10. Collected Letters of Theodore P. Fahrenwald, 15 November 1943.

CHAPTER 5: ON THE SCOREBOARD
1. Encounter Report, John C. Meyer, 487th Fighter Squadron, 352nd Fighter Group, 26 November 1943. Meyer's subsequent description of this fight is derived from this source.
2. Encounter Report, Donald K. Dilling, 487th Fighter Squadron, 352nd Fighter Group, 26 November 1943. Dilling's subsequent description of this fight is derived from this source.
3. Encounter Report, John R. Bennett, 487th Fighter Squadron, 352nd Fighter Group, 26 November 1943. Bennett's subsequent description of this fight is derived from this source.
4. Noah and Sox, *George Preddy*, 72.

5. Encounter Report, Virgil K. Meroney, 487th Fighter Squadron, 352nd Fighter Group, 1 December 1943. Meroney's subsequent description of this fight is derived from this source.
6. Encounter Report, John R. Bennett, 487th Fighter Squadron, 352nd Fighter Group, 22 December 1943. Bennett's subsequent description of this fight is derived from this source.
7. Encounter Report, George E. Preddy, 487th Fighter Squadron, 352nd Fighter Group, 1 December 1943. Preddy's subsequent description of this fight is derived from this source.
8. Collected Letters of Theodore P. Fahrenwald, 23 December 1943.
9. Encounter Report, David T. Zimms, 328th Fighter Squadron, 352nd Fighter Group, 22 December 1943.
10. Encounter Report, Quentin L. Quinn, 328th Fighter Squadron, 352nd Fighter Group, 22 December 1943.
11. Encounter Report, James L. Laing, 328th Fighter Squadron, 352nd Fighter Group, 22 December 1943.
12. Collected Letters of Theodore P. Fahrenwald, 23 December 1943.
13. E-mail to Robert H. Powell Jr. from Donald McKibben, 18 November 2011.
14. George Arnold, recorded interview, n.d.
15. Encounter Report, Winfield E. McIntyre, 487th Fighter Squadron, 352nd Fighter Group, 20 December 1943.
16. Encounter Report, Donald K. Dilling, 487th Fighter Squadron, 352nd Fighter Group, 20 December 1943.
17. Encounter Report, George E. Preddy, 487th Fighter Squadron, 352nd Fighter Group, 22 December 1943. Preddy's subsequent description of this fight is derived from this source.
18. *George & Lizzie*, www.preddy-foundation.org/memorials/george-lizzie/. Accessed 2 January 2012.
19. Diary of Fred M. Allison, Jr., 487th Fighter Squadron, 352nd Fighter Group.
20. Noah and Sox, *George Preddy*, 82.
21. News Release, 352nd Fighter Group, 2 March 1944.
22. Collected Letters of Theodore P. Fahrenwald, 23 April 1944.
23. Letter to Robert H. Powell Jr. from Jack Diamond, n.d.
24. Powell, et al., *Bluenosed Bastards of Bodney*, 35.
25. Lt. Col. Waldo H. Heinrichs, 66th Fighter Wing, USAAF, *A History of VIII USAAF Fighter Command* (England, 31 October 1944), 264.

CHAPTER 6: A NEW YEAR

1. Daily Bulletin, Headquarters, AAF Station A-84A, 23 February 1945.
2. Collected Letters of Theodore P. Fahrenwald, 8 November 1943.
3. Knoke, *I Flew for the Fuhrer*, 106.
4. Ibid., 112.
5. Collected Letters of Theodore P. Fahrenwald, 1 January 1944.
6. James H. Doolittle and Carrol V. Glines, *I Could Never Be So Lucky Again* (New York: Bantam Books, 1992), 352.
7. Heinrichs, *History of VIII USAAF Fighter Command*, 112.
8. Ibid., 242.
9. Knoke, *I Flew for the Fuhrer*, 113–14.
10. Collected Letters of Theodore P. Fahrenwald, 10 January 1944.
11. Noah and Sox, *George Preddy*, 84.
12. Haywood S. Hansell Jr., *The Air Plan That Defeated Hitler* (Atlanta: Higgins McArthur/Longino & Porter, Inc., 1972), 121.
13. Doolittle and Glines, *I Could Never Be So Lucky Again*, 355.

14. Encounter Report, Clayton E. Davis, 487th Fighter Squadron, 352nd Fighter Group, 29 January 1944. Davis's subsequent description of this fight is derived from this source.
15. Noah and Sox, *George Preddy*, 83–86.
16. News Release, 352nd Fighter Group, n.d.
17. Norman Franks, *Another Kind of Courage: Stories of the UK-based Walrus Air-Sea Rescue Squadrons* (Somerset, England: Patrick Stephens Ltd, 1994), 46–47; and Heinrichs, *History of VIII USAAF Fighter Command*, 146.
18. Noah and Sox, *George Preddy*, 83–87.
19. Frank E. Ransom, *Air-Sea Rescue 1941–1952*, U.S. Air Force Historical Study No. 95 (Maxwell AFB, AL: USAF Historical Division, Air University, 1954).

CHAPTER 7: THE MISSIONS

1. Roger A. Freeman, *The Mighty Eighth, Warpaint and Heraldry* (London: Arms & Armour Press, 1998), 45.
2. Marc Hamel, et al., *Bluenoser Tales: 352nd Fighter Group War Stories* (Decatur: Powell Publishing, 2010), 194.
3. Encounter Report, John C. Meyer, 487th Fighter Squadron, 352nd Fighter Group, 15 April 1944. Meyer's subsequent description of this incident is derived from this source.
4. George Arnold, recorded interview, n.d.
5. Ibid.
6. Hamel, et al., *Bluenoser Tales*, 179–80.
7. Ibid., 177.

CHAPTER 8: FUEL AND NERVES

1. Encounter Report, Fremont W. Miller, 328th Fighter Squadron, 352nd Fighter Group, 4 February 1944. Miller's subsequent description of this fight is derived from this source.
2. Collected Letters of Theodore P. Fahrenwald, 19 December 1943.
3. George Arnold, recorded interview, n.d.
4. Smith Cotton's World War II Memorial, "Joseph Sweeney," web.sedalia.k12 .mo.us/schs/WWII/sweeneyR.htm. Accessed January 14, 2012.
5. Encounter Report, Wendell F. Parlee, 328th Fighter Squadron, 352nd Fighter Group, 4 February 1944. Parlee's subsequent description of this fight is derived from this source.
6. Encounter Report, Wendell F. Parlee, 328th Fighter Squadron, 352nd Fighter Group, 16 March 1944. Parlee's subsequent description of this fight is derived from this source.
7. Mark K. Wells, *Aviators and Air Combat: A Study of the U.S. Eighth Air Force and R.A.F. Bomber Command* (London: University of London, 1992), 142.
8. Ibid., 156.
9. Ibid., 161.
10. Collected Letters of Theodore P. Fahrenwald, 10 April 1944.
11. Knoke, *I Flew for the Fuhrer*, 118.
12. Ibid., 122.
13. Howard Mingos, *The Aircraft Yearbook for 1946* (New York: Lanciar Publishers Inc., 1946), 465.
14. Encounter Report, George E. Preddy, 487th Fighter Squadron, 352nd Fighter Group, 13 February 1944.
15. Encounter Report, Raymond G. Phillips, 328thth Fighter Squadron, 352nd Fighter Group, 8 February 1944. Phillips's subsequent description of this fight is derived from this source.

CHAPTER 9: MORAL DILEMMA

1. Encounter report, Virgil K. Meroney, 487th Fighter Squadron, 352nd Fighter Group, 8 March 1944. Meroney's subsequent description of this fight is derived from this source.
2. "WWII Brutality, Richard 'Bud' Peterson P-51 Ace Interview," www.youtube.com/watch?v=Q8LVlYJ5eJU. Accessed, 26 May 2011.
3. Southern Oregon Warbirds, Personal Histories, B-17, Ralph Bates. www.southern oregonwarbirds.us/b17a.html. Accessed May 21, 2011
4. Encounter report, Edmond Zellner, 328th Fighter Squadron, 352nd Fighter Group, 19 May 1944. Zellner's subsequent description of this fight is derived from this source.
5. William Reese, unpublished memoir, n.d., 84-85.
6. William Stansbeary, *Close Encounters with Fighter Pilot Stanley Miles*, www .airportjournals.com/display.cfm/Centennial/0805030. Accessed July 7, 2012.
7. Encounter report, Robert G. O'Nan, 487th Fighter Squadron, 352nd Fighter Group, 10 April 1944.
8. Letter from Supreme Allied Commander General Dwight D. Eisenhower to Air Officer Commanding RAF Bomber Command, Air Chief Marshal Sir Arthur T. Harris and Commander United States Strategic Air Force, Lieutenant General Carl A. Spaatz, 2nd June 1944. Source—Public Record Office WO 219 325.
9. Richard G. Davis, *Bombing the European Axis Powers: A Historical Digest of the Combined Bomber Offensive, 1939–1945* (Maxwell AFB, AL: Air University Press, 2006), 336.

CHAPTER 10: MARCH MADNESS

1. Collected Letters of Theodore P. Fahrenwald, 11 March 1944.
2. Encounter report, John R. Bennett, 487th Fighter Squadron, 352nd Fighter Group, 11 March 1944.
3. Encounter report, Ralph W. Hamilton, 487th Fighter Squadron, 352nd Fighter Group, 11 March 1944.
4. Encounter report, Robert H. Powell, Jr., 328th Fighter Squadron, 352nd Fighter Group, 11 March 1944.
5. Encounter report, John F. Thornell, 328th Fighter Squadron, 352nd Fighter Group, 11 March 1944. Thornell's subsequent description of these events are derived from this source.
6. Encounter report, William T. Halton, 328th Fighter Squadron, 352nd Fighter Group, 11 March 1944. Halton's subsequent description of these events are derived from this source.
7. Encounter report, John B. Coleman, 328th Fighter Squadron, 352nd Fighter Group, 11 March 1944.
8. Encounter report, Raymond G. Phillips, 328th Fighter Squadron, 352nd Fighter Group, 11 March 1944.
9. Mission Summary Report for mission of 11 March 1944, 487th Fighter Squadron, 352nd Fighter Group, dated 14 March 1944.
10. Armament discussions and quotes from James Bleidner are sourced from a series of e-mail exchanges between the author and Bleidner during the period 10-20 February 2011.
11. Encounter report, Sanford K. Moats, 487th Fighter Squadron, 352nd Fighter Group, 29 July 1944. Moats's subsequent description of this fight is derived from this source.
12. E-mail to author from James Bleidner, 16 February 2011
13. Collected Letters of Theodore P. Fahrenwald, 26 August 1943.
14. Letter, Alton Wallace to Marc Hamel, 1 July 1995.

CHAPTER 11: MUSTANGS

1. Encounter report, John B. Coleman, 328th Fighter Squadron, 352nd Fighter Group, 13 May 1944. Coleman's subsequent description of this fight is derived from this source.
2. Encounter report, John W. Galliga, 328th Fighter Squadron, 352nd Fighter Group, 21 June 1944. Galliga's subsequent description of this fight is derived from this source.
3. Encounter report, William E. Montgomery, 328th Fighter Squadron, 352nd Fighter Group, 27 September 1944. Galliga's subsequent description of this fight is derived from this source.
4. Hamel, et al., *Bluenoser Tales*, 57–58.
5. Collected Letters of Theodore P. Fahrenwald, 16 April 1944.
6. Collected Letters of Theodore P. Fahrenwald, 30 April 1944.
7. Collected Letters of Theodore P. Fahrenwald, 29 September 1943.
8. Collected Letters of Theodore P. Fahrenwald, 2 October 1943.
9. Collected Letters of Theodore P. Fahrenwald, 4 June 1944.
10. Collected Letters of Theodore P. Fahrenwald, 8 March 1944.

CHAPTER 12: THE ENEMY FIGHTERS

1. Central Fighter Establishment, Report No. 3, A.F.D.S. Report No. 147, Tactical Trials—Me.109G-6/U-2.
2. Jay P. Spencer, *Focke-Wulf Fw 190: Workhorse of the Luftwaffe* (Washington, DC: Smithsonian, 1989), 39.
3. Encounter Report, John C. Meyer, 487th Fighter Squadron, 352nd Fighter Group, 10 April 1944.
4. Encounter Report, John C. Meyer, 487th Fighter Squadron, 352nd Fighter Group, 11 September 1944.
5. John Weal, *Focke-Wulf Fw 190 Aces of the Russian Front* (Oxford, England: Osprey, 1995), 36.
6. *Report of Comparative Combat Evaluation of Focke-Wulf 190-A/4 Airplane*, Bureau of Aeronautics, USN, 1944.
7. Spencer, *Focke-Wulf Fw 190*, 40.
8. Encounter Report, Virgil K. Meroney, 487th Fighter Squadron, 352nd Fighter Group, 29 January 1944.
9. Informational Intelligence Summary-No. 44-14, *P47 vs. FW-190 Trial Tests*, USAAF, 30 April 1944.
10. Hamel, et al., *Bluenoser Tales*, 176.

CHAPTER 13: THE GRAY ENEMY

1. Collected Letters of Theodore P. Fahrenwald, 10 January 1944.
2. McKibben's recollection of this incident is derived from e-mail exchanges with the author. The remainder is from Hamel, et al., *Bluenoser Tales*, 63–69.
3. Encounter Report, Virgil K. Meroney, 487th Fighter Squadron, 352nd Fighter Group, 8 March 1944.
4. Heinrichs, *History of VIII USAAF Fighter Command*, 167.
5. Ibid., 51–52.
6. Doolittle and Glines, *I Could Never Be So Lucky Again*, 365.
7. Encounter Report, Robert I. Ross, 487th Fighter Squadron, 352nd Fighter Group, 8 April 1944.
8. Thomas G. Ivie, *352nd Fighter Group* (Oxford, England: Osprey, 2002), 34.
9. Collected Letters of Theodore P. Fahrenwald, 9 April 1944.
10. Encounter Report, Frederick A. Yochim, 328th Fighter Squadron, 352nd Fighter Group, 9 April 1944, filed circa May 1945. Yochim's subsequent description of this fight is derived from this source.

CHAPTER 14: ACES

1. Radio Script. Captain Walter E. Starck, *Classroom of the Air*, n.d.—circa summer 1944.
2. Encounter report, Walter E. Starck, 487th Fighter Squadron, 352nd Fighter Group, 10 April 1944. Starck's subsequent description of this fight is derived from this source.
3. Encounter report, Robert H. Berkshire, 487th Fighter Squadron, 352nd Fighter Group, 27 May 1944.
4. Encounter report, William W. Furr, 328th Fighter Squadron, 352nd Fighter Group, 27 May 1944. Furr's subsequent description of this fight is derived from this source.
5. Encounter report, David T. Zimms, 328th Fighter Squadron, 352nd Fighter Group, 27 May 1944. Zimms's subsequent description of this fight is derived from this source.
6. Encounter report, Donald W. McKibben, 486th Fighter Squadron, 352nd Fighter Group, 19 April 1944. McKibben's subsequent description of this fight is derived from this source.
7. Wells, *Aviators and Air Combat*, 106.
8. Encounter report, Glennon T. Moran, 487th Fighter Squadron, 352nd Fighter Group, 29 May 1944. Moran's subsequent description of this fight is derived from this source.
9. News release, 352nd Fighter Group, 11 December 1943.
10. Encounter report, Glennon T. Moran, 487th Fighter Squadron, 352nd Fighter Group, 15 May 1944.

CHAPTER 15: VICTORY CLAIMS

1. Heinrichs, *History of VIII USAAF Fighter Command*, 207.
2. Encounter report, Richard C. Brookins, 328th Fighter Squadron, 352nd Fighter Group, 30 May 1944. Brookins's subsequent description of this fight is derived from this source.
3. Headquarters, Air P/W Interrogation Detachment, Military Intelligence Service, Ninth Air Force, 65/1945, 373.2, Enemy Intelligence Summaries, Hermann Goering, U.S. Army, June 1945, pgph. #50.
4. Ibid., #49.
5. Encounter report, Carl J. Luksic, 487th Fighter Squadron, 352nd Fighter Group, 20 April 1944.
6. Encounter report, Glennon T. Moran, 487th Fighter Squadron, 352nd Fighter Group, 27 May 1944.
7. Heinrichs, *History of VIII USAAF Fighter Command*, 157.
8. Hamel, et al., *Bluenoser Tales*, 197.
9. "Top Ace of the Mighty Eighth," *Air Classics*, vol. 22, no. 2 (1986): 70.
10. Hamel, et al., *Bluenoser Tales*, 179.
11. Ibid., 177.
12. Ibid., 193.

CHAPTER 16: THE DEADLIEST GAMBLE

1. Collected Letters of Theodore P. Fahrenwald, 14 April 1944.
2. News release, VIII Fighter Command ("Ajax"), n.d.—circa April 1944.
3. Collected Letters of Theodore P. Fahrenwald, 14 October 1943.
4. Encounter report, Robert K. Butler, 487th Fighter Squadron, 352nd Fighter Group, 13 April 1944.
5. Encounter report, John R. Bennett, 487th Fighter Squadron, 352nd Fighter Group, 22 December 1943.

6. Encounter report, Henry W. White, 328th Fighter Squadron, 352nd Fighter Group, 28 May 1944.

7. Encounter report, Samuel E. Dyke, 328th Fighter Squadron, 352nd Fighter Group, 21 June 1944.

8. Hamel, et al., *Bluenoser Tales*, 87–93. Much of Richmond's story is extracted from Hamel's excellent work.

9. Christensen, *Growing Up with Wyoming*, 135–48; and Hamel, et al., *Bluenoser Tales*, 79–86.

10. Encounter report, Donald S. Bryan, 328th Fighter Squadron, 352nd Fighter Group, 30 January 1944.

11. Collected Letters of Theodore P. Fahrenwald, 14 May 1944.

12. Encounter report, Clayton E. Davis, 487th Fighter Squadron, 352nd Fighter Group, 22 April 1944.

13. Jay A. Stout, *The Men Who Killed the Luftwaffe: The U.S. Army Air Forces against Germany in World War II* (Mechanicsburg, PA: Stackpole Books, 2010) 219.

14. Encounter report, Robert I Ross, 487th Fighter Squadron, 352nd Fighter Group, 13 April 1944. Ross's subsequent description of this fight is derived from this source.

15. Encounter report, Carl J. Luksic, 487th Fighter Squadron, 352nd Fighter Group, 19 May 1944.

16. Encounter report, Robert H. Sharp, 328th Fighter Squadron, 352nd Fighter Group, 19 May 1944.

17. Encounter report, Francis W. Horne, 328th Fighter Squadron, 352nd Fighter Group, 13 May 1944. Horne's subsequent description of this fight is derived from this source.

18. News release, 352nd Fighter Group, 17 May 1944.

19. Encounter report, Marion J. Nutter, 487th Fighter Squadron, 352nd Fighter Group, 13 May 1944.

20. Collected Letters of Theodore P. Fahrenwald, 15 November 1943.

CHAPTER 17: FAILED GUNS AND VARIED TACTICS

1. Noah and Sox, *George Preddy*, 107.

2. Encounter report, Eugene L. Clark, 487th Fighter Squadron, 352nd Fighter Group, 19 May 1944. Clark's subsequent description of this fight is derived from this source.

3. Encounter report, William T. Whisner, 487th Fighter Squadron, 352nd Fighter Group, 30 April 1944. Whisner's subsequent description of this fight is derived from this source.

4. Encounter report, Marion J. Nutter, 487th Fighter Squadron, 352nd Fighter Group, 30 April 1944.

5. Encounter report, Walter E. Starck, 487th Fighter Squadron, 352nd Fighter Group, 27 May 1944. Starck's subsequent description of this fight is derived from this source.

6. Encounter report, George E. Preddy, 487th Fighter Squadron, 352nd Fighter Group, 20 April 1944.

7. Encounter report, Ralph W. Hamilton, 487th Fighter Squadron, 352nd Fighter Group, 8 May 1944.

8. Hamel, et al., *Bluenoser Tales*, 178.

9. News release, 352nd Fighter Group, 9 May 1944.

10. Encounter report, David E. McEntire, 487th Fighter Squadron, 352nd Fighter Group, 12 May 1944.

11. Encounter report, William W. Furr, 328th Fighter Squadron, 352nd Fighter Group, 30 May 1944. Furr's subsequent description of this fight is derived from this source.

12. Adolf Galland, *The First and the Last: The Rise and Fall of the Luftwaffe: 1939–1945, by Germany's Commander of Fighter Forces* (New York: Ballantine Books, 1967), 261.

13. Headquarters, Air P/W Interrogation Detachment, Military Intelligence Service, Ninth Air Force, 65/1945, 373.2, *Enemy Intelligence Summaries, Hermann Goering*, U.S. Army, June 1945, pgph. #117.
14. Ibid., pgph. #118.
15. Galland, *First and the Last*, 262.
16. Heinrichs, *History of VIII USAAF Fighter Command*, 255.
17. News release, 352nd Fighter Group, n.d.—circa May 22, 1944.

CHAPTER 18: D-DAY
1. 352nd Fighter Group, *History of Headquarters*, June 1945.
2. Letter to Robert H. Powell, Jr. from Paul Klinger, 22 February 1992.
3. All material in this chapter related to Fahrenwald is derived from his book, *Bailout over Normandy: A Flyboy's Adventures with the French Resistance and Other Escapades in Occupied France*, currently scheduled for publication by Casemate in 2012. It is an extraordinary account.
4. Hamel, et al., *Bluenoser Tales*, 102–8.
5. George Arnold, recorded interview, n.d.
6. Telephone report, 487th Fighter Squadron, 7 June 1944.
7. Noah and Sox, *George Preddy*, 113.
8. Letter to Robert H. Powell Jr. from Harold Stanfield, n.d.
9. William Reese, unpublished memoir, n.d., 39–41.
10. Nelson Jesup letter home, 9 July 1944.

CHAPTER 19: TO THE OTHER SIDE
1. Don McKibben wrote of his experiences for the 486th Fighter Squadron's unofficial history, *Angus, 486th Fighter Squadron*. Quotes from McKibben are taken from that publication, pages 13-20.
2. News release, 352nd Fighter Group, July 15, 1944.
3. William Reese, unpublished memoir, n.d., 35.
4. News release, 352nd Fighter Group, n.d.
5. Ibid.

CHAPTER 20: LONGER LEGS AND LONGER MISSIONS
1. Hamel, et al., *Bluenoser Tales*, 99.
2. Nelson Jesup letter home, 9 July 1944.

CHAPTER 21: CLEARING THE TABLE, CLEARING THE SKY
1. Encounter Report, George E. Preddy, 487th Fighter Squadron, 352nd Fighter Group, 6 August 1944. Preddy's subsequent description of this fight is derived from this source.
2. Noah and Sox, *George Preddy*, 140.
3. Hamel, et al., *Bluenoser Tales*, 196.
4. Letter to Robert H. Powell, Jr. from Jack Diamond, n.d.
5. Dittmer, *Old Tat*, 51.
6. Letter to Robert H. Powell, Jr. from Jack Diamond, n.d.
7. Letter to Robert H. Powell, Jr. from Paul Klinger, 22 February 1992.
8. Encounter Report, Charles J. Cesky, 328th Fighter Squadron, 352nd Fighter Group, 6 August, 1944.
9. Encounter Report, Walter S. Smith, 487th Fighter Squadron, 352nd Fighter Group, 27 November 1944, filed circa May 1945. Smith's subsequent description of this fight is derived from this source.
10. Fahrenwald, *Bailout over Normandy*, 1–40.

CHAPTER 22: SUMMER WITH THE FRENCH

1. Reese's experiences described in this chapter are sourced from his unpublished memoirs, 41–62.

CHAPTER 23: TAKING CARE OF BUSINESS

1. Telephone interview with Clarence "Spike" Cameron, 3 April 2011.

CHAPTER 24: UNHERALDED HEROICS

1. Material on Joseph Broadwater and the 352nd's mission of 12 September 1944 is sourced from a report generated by Thomas Clarke: *The Lost Fighter Pilot: The Case of Joseph Broadwater*, September 11, 2000. Clarke mailed this report to Air Force officials, senators, and congressmen in an unsuccessful effort to see Broadwater posthumously awarded the Medal of Honor for his actions of 12 September 1944.

CHAPTER 25: TO THE SOUND OF THE GUNS

1. Encounter report, Richard C. Brookins, 328th Fighter Squadron, 352nd Fighter Group, 27 September 1944. Brookins's subsequent description of this fight is derived from this source.
2. U.S. Air Force Historical Study No. 78, *Morale in the AAF During World War II*, (Maxwell AFB, AL: USAF Historical Division, Air University, 1953), 23–26.
3. Wells, *Aviators and Air Combat*, 131.
4. Collected Letters of Theodore P. Fahrenwald, 18 September 1944.
5. Hermann Buchner, *Stormbird* (Manchester, England: Crécy Publishing Ltd., 2000), 216–17.
6. Ivie, *352nd Fighter Group*, 86–87.
7. News release, 352nd Fighter Group, 13 September 1944.
8. News release, 352nd Fighter Group, 11 September 1944.

CHAPTER 26: GRINDING THROUGH THE FALL

1. Noah and Sox, *George Preddy*, 146.
2. Ibid., 151.
3. Headquarters, Air P/W Interrogation Detachment, Military Intelligence Service, Ninth Air Force, 65/1945, 373.2, *Enemy Intelligence Summaries, Hermann Goering*, U.S. Army, June 1945, pgph. #25.
4. Ibid., pgph. #53.
5. E-mail to Robert H. Powell Jr. from Connie Ross Fowler, July 28, 2002.
6. Heinrichs, *History of VIII USAAF Fighter Command*, 114.
7. Telephone interview with Clarence "Spike" Cameron, 3 April 2011.
8. Noah and Sox, *George Preddy*, 149.
9. Ibid.
10. Encounter report, William J. Stangel, 328th Fighter Squadron, 352nd Fighter Group, 2 November 1944. Stangel's subsequent description of this fight is derived from this source.
11. Encounter report, Arthur E. Hudson, 328th Fighter Squadron, 352nd Fighter Group, 2 November 1944. Hudson's subsequent description of this fight is derived from this source.
12. Encounter report, Charles E. Rogers, 328th Fighter Squadron, 352nd Fighter Group, 2 November 1944.
13. Encounter report, Donald S. Bryan, 328th Fighter Squadron, 352nd Fighter Group, 2 November 1944. Bryan's subsequent description of this fight is derived from this source.
14. Letter to Robert H. Powell Jr. from Francis R. Hill, n.d.
15. Nelson Jesup letter home, n.d.

16. Dittmer, *Old Tat* (Self-published, 1998), 49–50.
17. Encounter report, William T. Halton, 487th Fighter Squadron, 352nd Fighter Group, 27 November 1944. Halton's subsequent description of this fight is derived from this source.
18. Encounter report, John C. Meyer, 487th Fighter Squadron, 352nd Fighter Group, 8 May 1944. Meyer's subsequent description of this fight is derived from this source.
19. Encounter report, Charles J. Cesky, 328th Fighter Squadron, 352nd Fighter Group, 27 November 1944. Cesky's subsequent description of this fight is derived from this source.
20. Encounter report, Charles J. Cesky, 328th Fighter Squadron, 352nd Fighter Group, 25 December 1944.
21. Heinrichs, *History of VIII USAAF Fighter Command*, 331.
22. Letter to Henry H. Arnold from Carl A. Spaatz, 3 September 1944, Library of Congress, Spaatz Collection, Box #143.

CHAPTER 27: MORE MISTAKEN IDENTITIES

1. Encounter report, William E. Fowler, 487th Fighter Squadron, 352nd Fighter Group, 8 May 1944.
2. Telephone Report, 487th Fighter Squadron, 352nd Fighter Group, 12 June 1944, Reel #B0307, Pg.1944.
3. Encounter Report, John R. Bennett, 487th Fighter Squadron, 352nd Fighter Group, 11 September 1944. Bennett's subsequent description of this fight is derived from this source.
4. Encounter report, John C. Meyer, 487th Fighter Squadron, 352nd Fighter Group, 13 April 1944. Meyer's subsequent description of this fight is derived from this source.
5. Davis, *Bombing the European Axis Powers*, 293.
6. Encounter report, Karl M. Waldron, 487th Fighter Squadron, 352nd Fighter Group, 21 November 1944. Waldron's subsequent description of this fight is derived from this source.
7. Hamel, et al., *Bluenoser Tales: 352nd Fighter Group War Stories*, 228–31.
8. Encounter report, Walter E. Starck, 487th Fighter Squadron, 352nd Fighter Group, 27 November 1944, filed circa May 1945. Starck's subsequent description of this fight is derived from this source.
9. Encounter report, William T. Halton, 487th Fighter Squadron, 352nd Fighter Group, 27 November 1944.

CHAPTER 28: TO THE CONTINENT AND TRAGEDY

1. Letter to Robert H. Powell Jr. from Albert Giesting, n.d.
2. Letter to Robert H. Powell Jr. from Richard Brock, n.d.
3. E-mail to author from Raymond Mitchell, 14 September 2011.
4. Cyrus Reap with unknown interviewer, 6 December 1991.
5. Legend of Y-29.
6. Noah and Sox, *George Preddy*, 166.
7. Hamel, et al., *Bluenoser Tales*, 266–67.
8. Encounter report, James Cartee, 328thth Fighter Squadron, 352nd Fighter Group, 25 December 1944. Cartee's subsequent description of this fight is derived from this source.
9. Noah and Sox, *George Preddy*, 161.
10. E-mail to author from Ray Mitchell, 29 April 2011.
11. Noah and Sox, *George Preddy: Top Mustang Ace*, 165.
12. Ibid.
13. Tafel material derived from collection of letters from Tafel to his family, via Robert H. Powell Jr.

CHAPTER 29: MAKING HISTORY

1. Encounter report, Raymond H. Littge, 487th Fighter Squadron, 352nd Fighter Group, 27 December 1944. Littge's subsequent description of this fight is derived from this source.
2. John Manrho and Ron Putz, *Bodenplatte: The Luftwaffe's Last Hope* (Mechanicsburg, PA: Stackpole Books, 2004), 227–76. Much of the subsequent material is extracted from this very rigorously researched book. It is recommended to readers with an interest in the overall operation.
3. Marc Hamel and Robert Powell, "New Year's Day Legend: Pilot and Crews Describe the Incredible Aerial Battle over Y-29 on 1 January 1945," *Air Classics* (November 2002): 24.
4. Two undated letters to Robert H. Powell Jr. from Albert Giesting.
5. *Narrative History*, 487th Fighter Squadron, 352nd Fighter Group.
6. Manrho and Putz, *Bodenplatte*, 238.
7. Letter to Robert H. Powell Jr. from Carl Galloway, n.d.
8. Letter to Robert H. Powell Jr. from Albert Giesting, n.d.
9. Encounter report, John C. Meyer, 487th Fighter Squadron, 352nd Fighter Group, 1 January 1945. Meyer's subsequent description of this fight is derived from this source.
10. Richard J. DeBruin, *352nd Fighter Group, 8th Air Force 'The Blue Nosed Bastards of Bodney, Second to None:' Y-29 Asch Belgium, 23 December 1944–27 January 1945* (Self-published), 15.
11. Encounter report, Alexander F. Sears, 487th Fighter Squadron, 352nd Fighter Group, 1 January 1945.
12. Encounter report, Raymond H. Littge, 487th Fighter Squadron, 352nd Fighter Group, 1 January 1945. Littge's subsequent description of this fight is derived from this source.
13. Letter to Robert H. Powell Jr. from Wayne Stock, n.d.
14. Letter to Robert H. Powell Jr. from Henry Cottrell, 1 February 1993.
15. Letter to Robert H. Powell Jr. from Richard Brock, n.d.
16. Letter to brother Robert Nutter from Marion Nutter, 7 January, 1945.
17. Letter to Robert H. Powell Jr. from Alden Rigby, 12 April 1991.
18. Encounter report, Alden P Rigby, 487th Fighter Squadron, 352nd Fighter Group, 1 January 1945. Rigby's subsequent description of this fight is derived from this source.
19. Encounter report, Dean M. Huston, 487th Fighter Squadron, 352nd Fighter Group, 1 January 1945. Huston's subsequent description of this fight is derived from this source.
20. Encounter report, Sanford K. Moats, 487th Fighter Squadron, 352nd Fighter Group, 1 January 1945. Moats's subsequent description of this fight is derived from this source.
21. DeBruin, *352nd Fighter Group, 8th Air Force*, 16.
22. Encounter report, Henry M. Stewart, 487th Fighter Squadron, 352nd Fighter Group, 1 January 1945. Stewart's subsequent description of this fight is derived from this source.
23. Encounter report, William H. Whisner, 487th Fighter Squadron, 352nd Fighter Group, 1 January 1945. Whisner's subsequent description of this fight is derived from this source.
24. Encounter report, Walter G. Diamond, 487th Fighter Squadron, 352nd Fighter Group, 1 January 1945. Diamond's subsequent description of this fight is derived from this source.
25. Letter to Robert H. Powell, Jr., from Thomas Colby, 11 January 1995.
26. Marc Hamel and Robert Powell. "New Year's Day Legend: Pilot and Crews Describe the Incredible Aerial Battle over Y-29 on 1 January 1945." Air Classics, November 2002, 24.

27. Encounter report, William T. Halton, 487th Fighter Squadron, 352nd Fighter Group, 1 January 1945.
28. Letter to brother Robert Nutter from Marion Nutter, January 7, 1945.
29. Legend of Y-29
30. Letter to Robert H. Powell, Jr. from Carl Galloway, n.d.
31. Letter to Alden Rigby, from Maria and Lambert NLM, n.d. circa 1994.
32. Manrho and Putz, *Bodenplatte*, 271.
33. Cyrus Reap with unknown interviewer, 6 December 1991.
34. DeBruin, *352nd Fighter Group, 8th Air Force*, 16.
35. Manrho and Putz, *Bodenplatte*, 274.
36. Letter to Robert H. Powell Jr. from Arthur Snyder, 6 September 1994.
37. Letter to Robert H. Powell Jr. from Walter Starck, 25 July 1991.
38. Letter to Robert H. Powell Jr. from Richard Gates, 13 June 1989.
39. Doolittle and Glines, *I Could Never Be So Lucky Again*, 391.
40. DeBruin, *352nd Fighter Group, 8th Air Force*, 16.
41. Letter to Robert H. Powell Jr. from Arthur Snyder, 6 September 1994.
42. Letter to Robert H. Powell Jr. from Albert Giesting, n.d.
43. Noah and Sox, *George Preddy*, 157.
44. Letter to Robert H. Powell Jr. from Richard Brock, n.d.

CHAPTER 30: FINISHING THE FIGHT
1. E-mail to Robert H. Powell Jr. from Thomas Lauderdale, 27 March 1998
2. www.preddy-foundation.org/preddy-bios/bill-preddy, accessed 2 January 2012.
3. Hamel, et al., *Bluenoser Tales*, 196.
4. William Reese, unpublished memoir, n.d., 99–100.
5. Telephone interview with Clarence "Spike" Cameron, 3 April 2011.
6. Telephone interview with Frederick Powell, 29 December 2011.
7. Hamel, et al., *Bluenoser Tales*, 325.
8. William Reese, unpublished memoir, n.d., 101–2.
9. Encounter report, Henry W. White, 328th Fighter Squadron, 352nd Fighter Group, 28 May 1944.
10. Encounter report, Earl D. Duncan, 328th Fighter Squadron, 352nd Fighter Group, 3 March 1945.
11. Encounter report, William H. Sanford, 328th Fighter Squadron, 352nd Fighter Group, 3 March 1945.
12. Encounter report, Steve R. Price, 328th Fighter Squadron, 352nd Fighter Group, 3 March 1945.
13. Letter to unknown from Jack Diamond, 7 January 2004.
14. Encounter report, Donald S. Bryan, 328th Fighter Squadron, 352nd Fighter Group, 14 March 1945.
15. Encounter report, James C. Hurley, 328th Fighter Squadron, 352nd Fighter Group, 30 March 1945. Hurley's subsequent description of this fight is derived from this source.
16. Buchner, *Stormbird*, 241.
17. Ibid., 233.
18. Encounter report, Earl D. Duncan, 328th Fighter Squadron, 352nd Fighter Group, 10 April 1945. Duncan's subsequent description of this fight is derived from this source.
19. Letter to Robert H. Powell, Jr. from Carlo Ricci dated 9 May 1989.
20. E-mail to Marc Hamel from James White, 8 November 2000.

BIBLIOGRAPHY

Air Ministry (A.C.A.S. [I]). *The Rise and Fall of the German Air Force (1933 to 1945)*. Richmond, England: The National Archives, 2008.

Buchner, Hermann. *Stormbird*. Manchester, England: Crécy Publishing, Ltd., 2000.

Busha, James P. *New Year's Resolutions: 352nd FG Pilots Surprise the Surprise Attackers*. Flight Journal (December 2010).

Boylan, Bernard. *Development of the Long-Range Escort Fighter*. U.S. Air Force Historical Study No. 136, USAF Historical Division, Research Studies Institute, Maxwell AFB, AL: Air University, 1955.

Christensen, Eugenia. *Growing Up with Wyoming: The Life of Fremont Miller*. Lander, WY: Mortimore Publishing, 1998.

Davis, Richard G. *Carl A. Spaatz and the Air War in Europe*. Washington, D.C.: Smithsonian Institute Press, 2006.

———. *Bombing the European Axis Powers: A Historical Digest of the Combined Bomber Offensive. 1939–1945*. Maxwell Air Force Base, AL: Air University Press, 2006.

DeBruin, Richard J. *352nd Fighter Group, 8th Air Force, 'The Blue Nosed Bastards of Bodney, Second to None:' Y-29 Asch Belgium, 23 December 1944-27 January 1945*. Self-published, 1994.

Dittmer, Karl K. *Old Tat: Memoirs of a Fighter Pilot*. Self-published, 1998.

Doolittle, James, H., and Carroll V. Glines. *I Could Never Be So Lucky Again*. New York, NY: Bantam Books, 1992.

Fahrenwald, Madelaine, and Donald W. McKibben, eds. *Collected Letters of Theodore P. Fahrenwald*. January 2011.

Fahrenwald, Theodore, P. *Bailout over Normandy: A Flyboy's Adventures with the French Resistance and Other Escapades in Occupied France*. Havertown, PA: Casemate Publishers, 2012.

Fischer, Wolfgang. *Luftwaffe Fighter Pilot: Defending the Reich Against the RAF and the USAAF*. Translated by John Weal. London, England: Grubb Street, 2010.

Forsyth, Robert. *Jagdgeschwader 7 'Nowotny.'* London, England: Osprey Publishing, 2008.

———. *Jagdverband 44: Squadron of Experten*. London, England: Osprey Publishing, 2008.

Franks, Norman. *Another Kind of Courage: Stories of the UK-based Walrus Air-Sea Rescue Squadrons*. Somerset, England: Patrick Stephens Ltd, 1994.

———. *Battle of the Airfields, Operation Bodenplatte, 1 January 1945*. London, England: Grub Street, 2009.

Freeman, Roger A. *The Mighty Eighth, Warpaint and Heraldry*. London, England: Arms & Armour Press, 1998.

Frisbee, John L. "Four Star Ace." *Air Force Magazine* 72 (May 1989).

Galland, Adolf. *The First and the Last: The Rise and Fall of the Luftwaffe: 1939–1945 by Germany's Commander of Fighter Forces*. New York: Ballantine Books, 1967.

Goldman, Martin R. R. *Morale in the AAF During World War II*. U.S. Air Force Historical Study No. 78. Maxwell AFB, AL: USAF Historical Division, Air University, 1953.

Hamel, Marc L., Robert H. "Punchy" Powell, and Samuel Sox Jr. *Bluenoser Tales: 352nd Fighter Group War Stories*. Decatur, GA: Powell Publishing, 2010.

Hamel, Marc L., and Robert Powell. "New Year's Day Legend: Pilot and Crews Describe the Incredible Aerial Battle over Y-29 on 1 January 1945." *Air Classics* 38, No. 9 (October 2002).

Hammel, Eric. *Air War Europa: America's Air War against Germany in Europe and North Africa, 1942–1945.* Pacifica, CA: Pacifica Press, 1994.

Hansell, Haywood S., Jr. *The Air Plan That Defeated Hitler.* Atlanta, GA: Higgins McArthur/Longino & Porter, Inc., 1972.

Heilmann, Willi. *Alert in the West.* Translated by Mervyn Savill. London, England: William Kimber, 1955.

Huston, John W., ed. *American Air Power Comes of Age: General H. "Hap" Arnold's World War II Diaries.* Maxwell AFB, AL: Air University Press, 2002.

Ivie, Thomas G. *352nd Fighter Group.* Oxford, England: Osprey Publishing Limited, 2002.

———. "Top Ace of the Mighty Eighth." *Air Classics* 21, No. 6 (1985).

———. "Top Ace of the Mighty Eighth." *Air Classics* 22, No. 2 (1986).

Knoke, Heinz. *I Flew for the Fuhrer.* Translated by John Ewing. New York: Berkeley, 1959.

Mahncke, Alfred. *For Kaiser and Hitler: The Memoirs of Luftwaffe General Alfred Mahncke, 1910–1945.* Translated by Jochen Mahncke. West Sussex, England: Tattered Flag Press, 2011.

Manrho, John, and Ron Putz. *Bodenplatte: The Luftwaffe's Last Hope.* Mechanicsburg, PA: Stackpole Books, 2004.

Mingos, Howard. *The Aircraft Yearbook for 1946.* New York: Lanciar Publishers Inc., 1946.

Mireles, Anthony. *Fatal Army Air Forces Aviation Accidents in the United States.* Jefferson, NC: McFarland & Company, 2006.

McNabb, Chris. *Order of Battle: German Luftwaffe in WW II.* London, England: Amber Books Ltd., 2009.

Noah, Joe and Samuel Sox Jr. *George Preddy: Top Mustang Ace.* Osceola, WI: Motorbook International, 1991.

O'Leary, Michael. *Building the P-51 Mustang: The Story of Manufacturing North American's Legendary World War II Fighter in Original Photos.* North Branch, MN: Specialty Press, 2010.

Powell, Robert H., Thomas Ivie, and Samuel Sox. *The Bluenosed Bastards of Bodney: A Commemorative History.* Dallas, TX: Taylor Publishing Co., 1990.

Parker, Danny S. *To Win the Winter Sky: Air War over the Ardennes, 1944–1945.* London, England: Greenhill Books/Lionel Leventhal, Ltd., 1994.

Ransom, Frank E. *Air-Sea Rescue 1941–1952.* U.S. Air Force Historical Study No. 95. Maxwell AFB, AL: USAF Historical Division, Air University, 1954.

Spencer, Jay P. *Focke-Wulf Fw 190: Workhorse of the Luftwaffe.* Washington, DC: Smithsonian, 1989.

Stout, Jay. *The Men Who Killed the Luftwaffe: The U.S. Army Air Forces against Germany in World War II.* Mechanicsburg, PA: Stackpole Books, 2010.

Suchenwirth, Richard. *Command and Leadership in the German Air Force.* U.S. Air Force Historical Study No. 174. Maxwell AFB, AL: USAF Historical Division, Aerospace Studies Institute, Air University, 1969.

Watry, Charles A. *Washout! The Aviation Cadet Story.* Carlsbad, CA: California Aero Press, 1983.

Weal, John. *Focke-Wulf Fw 190 Aces of the Western Front.* London, England: Osprey Publishing, 1996.

———. *Bf 109F/G/K Aces of the Western Front.* London, England: Osprey Publishing, 1999.

Wells, Mark, K. *Aviators and Air Combat: A Study of the U.S. Eighth Air Force and R.A.F. Bomber Command.* London, England: University of London, 1992.

INTERNET SOURCES

AirPort Journals.com. www.airportjournals.com/display.cfm/centennial/0805030. Accessed January 24, 2012.

Army Air Forces Material Command Flight Section, Wright Field, Dayton Ohio, May 18, 1943. www.spitfireperformance.com/mustang/mustangtest.html. Accessed April 7, 2011.

Diary of Fred M. Allison Jr., 487th Fighter Squadron, 352nd Fighter Group. www.flight-simulationforums.com/viewtopic.php?t=1640.

www.spitfireperformance.com/mustang/combat-reports/352-moats-1jan45.jpg. Accessed November 12, 2011.

www.spitfireperformance.com/mustang/combat-reports/352-stewart-1jan45.jpg. Accessed January 5, 2012.

George & Lizzie. www.preddy-foundation.org/memorials/george-lizzie. Accessed January 2, 2012.

High Iron Illustrations—Ist Lt. Frederick Powell—Pilot/POW 486th Fighter Squadron, 352nd Fighter Group. www.highironillustrations.com/rogues/frederick_powell.html. Accessed February 21, 2012.

Smith Cotton's World War II Memorial, "Joseph Sweeney." web.sedalia.k12.mo.us/schs/WWII/sweeneyR.htm. Accessed January 14, 2012.

Southern Oregon Warbirds, Personal Histories, B-17, Ralph Bates. www.southernoregonwarbirds.us/b17a.html. Accessed May 21, 2011.

Stansbeary, William. *Close Encounters with Fighter Pilot Stanley Miles*. www.airportjournals.com/display.cfm/Centennial/0805030. Accessed July 7, 2012.

"WWII Brutality, Richard 'Bud' Peterson P-51 Ace Interview". www.youtube.com/watch?v=Q8LVlYJ5eJU. Accessed, 26 May 2011.

MISCELLANEOUS SOURCES

Angus, 486th Fighter Squadron. Unofficial unit history, circa July 1945.

Arnold, George, recorded interview, undated.

Central Fighter Establishment, Report No. 3, A.F.D.S. Report No. 147, Tactical Trials—Me.109G-6/U-2.

Clarke, Thomas W. *The Lost Fighter Pilot: The Case of Joseph Broadwater*. Report, September 11, 2000.

Informational Intelligence Summary-No. 44-14. *P47 vs. FW-190 Trial Tests*. USAAF, 30 April 1944.

The Legend of Y-29. 487th Fighter Squadron, informal unit circular, undated.

Letter from Supreme Allied Commander General Dwight D. Eisenhower to Air Officer Commanding RAF Bomber Command, Air Chief Marshal Sir Arthur T. Harris and Commander United States Strategic Air Force, Lieutenant General Carl A. Spaatz, 2nd June 1944. Source—Public Record Office WO 219 325

Powell, Robert. *Above the Mountains*. Unpublished, undated memoir.

Reese, William, unpublished, undated memoir.

Radio Script. Captain Walter E. Stark. *Classroom of the Air*. Undated—circa Spring 1944.

Report of Comparative Combat Evaluation of Focke-Wulf 190-A/4 Airplane. Bureau of Aeronautics, USN, 1944.

ACKNOWLEDGMENTS

Icould have chosen to write about any number of fighter groups. After narrowing down the very best candidates, I chose the 352nd because of Bob "Punchy" Powell. He lived the story and for more than three decades has been an avid steward of the group's history. Before the advent of the personal computer, he chased down fellow comrades, officer and enlisted, by pawing through old personnel rosters and cross-referencing them to city telephone directories at his local library. From these efforts, he wrote more than 1,000 letters by hand in order to organize and form the 352nd Fighter Group Association. Those early exhausting efforts catalyzed the creation of a very active veteran organization that sponsored more than two dozen reunions and a body of members that is active to this day. As a result, much of the 352nd's history that would have been lost was instead recorded and catalogued.

And despite the fact that he coauthored and edited two different books about the group, Punchy eagerly sponsored me in my effort to preserve the group's history in my own style. During the writing of this book, I visited him at his home over a period of several days and was in contact with him at least twice a day for more than a year. He is mentally sharp and possesses an energy that would embarrass a man several decades his junior. Moreover, he is exceedingly modest and, I assure you, is blushing as he reads these words for the first time.

In short, this book is as good as it is because of Punchy. But it could have never happened without his wife, Betty. It is customary to throw a virtual garland at the wife of someone who has done great work. But to do only that would be a disservice to Betty. She fielded phone calls, hosted guests, addressed envelopes, licked stamps, organized reunions, and spent money—sometimes a lot—to support the preservation of the 352nd's legacy. She still does much of this today. Most of all, she has supported Punchy. For all these reasons, you'll note this book is dedicated to her. I'm sure she'll understand that it is also, in part, a nod to all the good wives who have supported their military men.

Ted Fahrenwald is dead. But he left behind a collection of letters and an unpublished manuscript that are an absolute treasure. His gift for storytelling was magnificent, and this work about the 352nd is more colorful because of it. I'm excited that his lost manuscript, *Bailout over Normandy*, is going to press at the same time as this work. Many thanks to his daughter, Madelaine Fahrenwald, for allowing me access to her father's letters and his unpublished manuscript. Additional thanks are due to Don McKibben, who helped to preserve them.

Marc Hamel is an outstanding writer. He is also a great friend of the 352nd. No one who was not part of the group knows more about its pilots than Marc. He became great friends with many of them, and during those years of association, he collected and archived a body of stories that would otherwise have disappeared into oblivion as the men passed. From these, he wrote a number of excellent articles which he shared for this book. Many thanks to him.

Don McKibben and Don Bryan flew with the 352nd from the beginning. James Bleidner was an armorer through the unit's entire career while Wayne Marks served just as long in the intelligence shop. Ray Mitchell joined the 352nd as a replacement pilot just before D-Day. They were all very gracious with their help and kept me from embarrassing myself more than once. Their recall of the smallest details helped to make this book different from most. Their help enabled me to write with a color and knowledge that I would have otherwise been without.

Sam Sox maintains the mother of all photograph repositories. He literally has thousands upon thousands of photographs of the 352nd's men and equipment. And he is expert on it all—able to distinguish a P-51K from a P-51D with his eyes closed simply by touching a photograph to his head. Seriously, his expert selection of photographs truly enhanced this story's text. Although most of the photos are credited to USAAF photographers, they were collected, archived, and forwarded to me by Sam Sox.

Joe Noah founded the Preddy Memorial Foundation, which preserves the history of Greensboro, North Carolina's famous brothers. His cousin, George Preddy, was a pilot with the 352nd and history's greatest P-51 ace. Joe was gracious with his help and allowed me to quote extensively from his book, *George Preddy: Top Mustang Ace.*

Wayne Mark provided valuable insight on the workings of the 352nd's intelligence and operations shops that was useful for its detail. And although I didn't cover their specific actions in detail, Jim Graves, George Middleton, and Charlie Price—all P-51 pilots—were gracious with their time and helped me to create an authentic picture of the group's later actions.

Others I must thank are author Tom Ivie; my agent, E. J. McCarthy; my friend Eric Hammel; and my friends at Stackpole Books, especially Chris Evans and David Reisch. My friends and fellow analysts and historians, Dr. John Stillion and Dr. James Perry, gave the manuscript a critical review and made excellent suggestions that contributed materially to the goodness of the book. Those who provided additional help are Doug Meroney, Betty Reese, Kurt Dittmer, Bill Espie, and Richard Gonzales. Finally, my clever and beautiful wife, Monica, let me take the time to write it. She is mostly nice, sometimes.

INDEX